PEACE BE WITH YOU

PEACE BE WITH YOU

Christ's Benediction
Amid Violent Empires

EDITED BY

SHARON L. BAKER & MICHAEL HARDIN

Foreword by
Willard M. Swartley

Cascadia

Publishing House
Telford, Pennsylvania

copublished with
Herald Press
Scottdale, Pennsylvania

Cascadia Publishing House orders, information, reprint permissions:
contact@CascadiaPublishingHouse.com
1-215-723-9125
126 Klingerman Road, Telford PA 18969
www.CascadiaPublishingHouse.com

Library of Congress Cataloguing-in-Publication Data
Peace be with you : Christ's benediction amid violent empires / edited by Sharon L.
Baker and Michael Hardin ; foreword by Willard M. Swartley.
   p. cm.
Chiefly rev. essays delivered at a conference held in Aug. 2007 at Messiah College.
Summary: "This book's 14 authors explore whether it is the Christian church's role to
sustain cultures and empires or to take a prophetic stand in relation to the human sit-
uation." [summary]"--Provided by publisher.
Includes index.
ISBN-13: 978-1-931038-73-7 (6 x 9" trade pbk. : alk. paper)
ISBN-10: 1-931038-73-2 (6 x 9" trade pbk. : alk. paper)
1. Nonviolence--Religious aspects--Christianity--Congresses. 2. Peace--Religious as-
pects--Christianity--Congresses. 3. Church and state--Congresses. 4. Nonviolence--
Religious aspects--Anabaptists--Congresses. 5. Peace--Religious aspects--Anabap-
tists--Congresses. 6. Church and state--Anabaptists--Congresses. 7. Anabaptists--
Doctrines--Congresses. I. Baker, Sharon L., 1956- II. Hardin, Michael. III. Title.

BT736.6.P43 2010
261.8'7--dc22

2010002813

17 16 15 14 13 12 11 10   10 9 8 7 6 5 4 3 2 1

To our students

CONTENTS

Foreword by Willard M. Swartley   9

Editors' Preface   12

1 Preemptive Peacemaking: Subverting Constantine
   Through a Better Story   •   17
   By Brian McLaren

2 Liberalism: The New Constantinianism   •   28
   By Craig A. Carter

3 Keynoting the Keys: Unlocking the
   Gates to the Kingdom of God   •   55
   By Sharon L. Baker

4 Just Policing: A New Face to an Old Challenge   •   80
   By Andy Alexis-Baker

5 After Whiteness: Tradition, Virtue,
   and Theopolitical Nonviolence in a (Post)colonial
   Constantinian Age   •   100
   By Derek Alan Woodard-Lehman

6 Against Empire: A Yoderian Reading of Romans   •   120
   By Ted Grimsrud

7 Why the World Needs Christian
   Leaders Committed to Peacemaking   •   138
   By Richard T. Hughes

8 *Depravatio Crucis*: The Non-Sovereignty of God in John
   Caputo's Poetics of the Kingdom • 148
   By B. Keith Putt

9 A View from the Porch: A Case Study in
   Liminality and Local Theology • 183
   By James F. S. Amstutz

10 Is Voluntary Baptism the Answer
    to the Constantinian Question? • 201
    By Anthony Siegrist

11 Using Girard to Address Factions
    in a Christian Community • 218
    By Jean F. Risley

12 God in the Hands of Angry Sinners:
    The Misdiagnosis of Wrath and Ephesians 2 • 234
    By David B. Miller

13 Matthew's Post-War Lament:
    "We Made the Wrong Choice" • 243
    By Reta Halteman Finger

14 Must There Be Shunning? Tradition,
    Mimesis, and Resacralization in Historic Peace
    Church Orthopraxy • 263
    By Jonathan Sauder

The Index   289
The Contributors   296

FOREWORD

This book's title and subtitle signal the direction, but readers will encounter surprises. In juxtaposing peace and empire in the full title, one expects Constantinian forms of church to come under fire. But who would guess that "voluntary baptism" would be a culprit (Siegrist)? The book throws curves, good ones at that.

McLaren contrasts Jesus' peacemaking to unjust war, just war, regulated war, and preemptive war. Jesus calls us to "preemptive peacemaking." His chapter is a good conclusion to my study, *Covenant of Peace* (Eerdmans, 2006). *Nonviolence* may open doors to peacemaking, but in itself fails the Jesus model. In similar vein, Baker's "keys to the kingdom" identify love, forgiveness, and reconciliation as keys that open the doors to the kingdom's justice and peacemaking. Abraham Heschel and Chris Marshall witness to biblical and restorative justice respectively.

Carter's critique of liberalism exposes its inconsistent view of freedom, which wilts before Jesus' freedom that flows from *truth* (John 8:32). Some things are wrong—and thus ouch to liberalism's tolerance that names everything good or okay, *except* truth-claims, exposing liberalism's fundamentalism. Jesus' freedom is not privatized. True peace accepts limits (given in Scripture) on desires, e.g. consumerism and capitalism.

Alexis-Baker blows the whistle on the drift among pacifists (e.g Cortwright and Schlabach) to think that "policing" is compatible with nonviolence. "Policing" did not exist in the world of the Bible (Yoder's distinction between war and policing is anachronistic). If one thinks policing sits well with a nonviolent ethic, read Alexis-Baker, and think again. "Just" policing leads to a new *just* Constantinianism that accommodates violence to achieve peace.

Woodard Lehman addresses the tacit Constantinianism of dominant white anglo churches, an operative of post-colonialism. Recovery from its "orthodox" sociological dominance happens only through "density" of relationships with non-anglos, leading to "orthopraxy" and openness to be under the tutelage of an African-American church. Amstutz's later chapter shows movement toward recovery, through a porch-building ministry of Akron Mennonite that leads to a cross-cultural liminality, but it also confesses: There's a long way to go. Whether Woodard Lehman thinks this is a step to recovery may open lively discussion.

Grimsrud focuses on Yoder's reading of Romans in *The Politics of Jesus*. Yoder's interpretation of Romans 13:1-7 does not passively reify the empire's violent rule but puts the powers, created and fallen, under judgment yet also with "redeemable" hope, in tension with the cross and the church's witness. Sum: No to empire; No to violent resistance; Yes to communities of resistance.

Hughs calls for church leadership that exposes the myth of a U.S. Christian nation. The dominant culture lies, and Christian leaders must point the church to Jesus' kingdom teaching and community. God's kingdom means care for the poor and oppressed, in contrast to serving the elite and privileged. Hugh's cites a catena of New Testatment texts, substantiating his theses on Jesus' kingdom vision. Finger's essay, focusing on Matthew's passion narrative perceived from a post-A.D. 70 war perspective, exposes both Pilate and the Jews as "making the wrong choice"—taking the "wide road" to destruction rather than the narrow road of Jesus' discipleship. Postwar perspective intensifies Jesus' love of enemy teaching.

Both Putt and Miller challenge our God-image: Putt, theologically; Miller, exegetically. Keith Putt "redeems" Caputo, despite his "devilish hermeneutics," by focusing on his "theoethic"—*God's weakness* in abandonment of Jesus on the cross. His "*theologia crucis* is genuinely a *depravatio crucis*, a 'perversion of the cross,'" in that the cross and all it symbolizes pervert the oppressive and violent powers of the world." Caputo opposes Constantinianism, embracing the "particularism" of the gospel. Putt connects Caputo to Girard, Yoder, and Hauerwas, ending with his own critique of Caputo.

Miller's exegetical foray into "by nature children of wrath" in Ephesians 2:3 teases us to rethink why we there connect God to *wrath*. Rather than attending to internal evidence, commentators resort to intertextual uses of "wrath of God" and read God into this text as the source of wrath—humans worthy of God's wrath. But Leslie Mitton sees the parallel, "sons of disobedience" in v. 2: "children of wrath means people in whose lives you can see the effect of wrath, that is the punishment that follows sin, the evil consequences of sin" (236).

Siegrist contends that voluntary baptism, now popular as an expected social rite of passage, has become a new Constantinianism that disconnects baptism from belief and ethics. Those voluntarily baptized continue to reflect the dominant culture about them. Baptism ought to lead to costly discipleship and *unity* in ethical belief and practice. It doesn't, forcing "rethinking" of the practice. Sauder, on "shunning," examines the gulf between what this meant to early Anabaptists and what it later came to mean. The latter, protecting the insular community, disconnects from radical discipleship. The "new wine" is now only water for *purification*, no longer gospel. Both Siegrist and Sauder show how culture betrays gospel.

Risley provides a good resource for congregational process of conflict, calling churches to reverse the conditions that empower scape-goating (Girard), namely, how to forestall:
- secrecy and lack of conscious awareness of the process;
- lack of empathy with potential victims;
- negative emotional reactions to those perceived to be different.

These essays provoke fresh thought, and intrigue at unexpected places, like the Samaritan woman who encounters a Jewish man at the well offering her "living water." These essays warn us not to allow the Constantinianisms of dominant culture to lose the new wine by reverting to the old wineskins of empire mentality. Otherwise we'll miss out on the joy of the wedding (John 2:1-11; 3:29; Rev 22:17).

—*Willard M. Swartley, Elkhart, Indiana, is Professor Emeritus of New Testament, Associated Mennonite Biblical Seminary. He is the author of* Covenant of Peace *(Eerdmans, 2006) and many other books.*

EDITORS' PREFACE

Imagine all the people living life in peace.
—John Lennon

The relationship between the church and the world has been an uneasy one. Much like our human relationships it has consisted of flirting, total commitment, outright hostility, manageable communication, and all manner of in-betweens. For over two thousand years Christian faith traditions in various cultures have had to ask about this relationship. The answers given have been simplistic, complex, variegated, honest and dishonest, political, social, philosophical, theological, and more. In short, there is no single answer that seems to suffice, and every generation must discern for itself how it will approach its understanding of church and world.

The renewed interest in Empire and the myriad of books published on the topic of _____ and Empire (fill in the blank) in the United States brings to the fore this discussion in our own time. For some, America is the New Empire, an incarnation of the empire of the Apocalypse, a resurgent version of ancient empire, the Babylon of biblical prophecy, the whore that deceives. Yet for others, America as Empire is salvation, bringer of enlightenment, democracy, freedom, and free markets. This clash of views within the churches only highlights that this problem is not yet solved, nor does a solution appear for the foreseeable future. It would seem that we bring our own hopes or disillusionments to the table when we discuss the relation of Christian faith to politics and that these presuppositions inform our conclusions; conclusions based not on evidence as much as an emotional commitment to a worldview each of us thinks is "God-given."

After 9-11 we moved into a new phase of conflict. Previously, wars were fought between nation-states; now we are in an ideological conflict of a war against terror. This war is fought both with words and with guns. It is a war that has no exit strategy. It is a utopian war fought by leaders who think that violence can overcome violence, that the problem is the solution. The stance of the United States on torture during the Bush administration (2000-2008) was a clear indication of this strategy; torture demands torture in return. The invocation of *lex talionis*, an eye for an eye, has not brought an end to our conflicts but taken us back to the archaic response of primitive religion. In regard to the problem of violence, we are not evolving but regressing. Our hope for world peace or peace within our time is grounded in the illusion that all we need is a great big blast of violence to stop the perpetrators of violence. My stick is bigger than your stick, so you watch out.

Thus Christianity finds itself mired in a situation in which it rejects violence in theory but justifies violence in reality, for the real world, so we are told, only understands the bigger stick concept. We have lived with the post-Constantinian synthesis of church and state for some 1,500 years and found it lacking. Christians of all stripes are less and less enamored with the power of the state, indeed with power in general. It is also the case that the rediscovery of Jesus has focused our awareness that his nonviolent "revolution" is distinctly different than all of the other revolutions we have experienced in this millennium and a half.

This collection of essays comes at this issue with the definite presupposition that peace as the world knows peace, in contrast to the peace that God gives, are two different realities. They do not have the same grounding although they have the same result—the cessation of violence. For our violence, controlling and containing our violence, is the key issue that faces us as a species today. We develop bigger and more effective weapons to deter our enemies from using their weapons while they in turn also develop more powerful weapons to deter us from using ours. And so worldly peace is usually a stalemate, with erstwhile war being the inevitable outcome when we don't see eye to eye and a perceived slight escalates into full conflict.

The peace generated by the Christian church differs drastically from the peace provoked by the world's domination systems. When Jesus told his disciples that "peace I leave with you; my peace I give to you; *not as the world gives*," he spoke of a peace not begotten of force and violence but a peace born of love and justice (John 14:27 emphasis added).

For centuries, the church's complicity with the "peace" the world gives has driven the peace that Christ gives into obscurity. Consequently, as in the past, the church needs prophetic voices. These voices cry out in the wilderness, beseeching us to repent of our sins, to turn from the false peace wrought by kingdoms of the world into the true peace intrinsic to the kingdom of God. Jesus Christ leaves us with a benediction of peace—the peace of God, the peace of God's kingdom, and the peace of God's people. And we, the people of God, who bear God's image, also bear the responsibility to make peace as ministers of reconciliation and as a sweet aroma of Christ in every place.

Although work refining them has continued into 2010, the core of these essays stems from a conference held at Messiah College in August 2007 sponsored by Preaching Peace (www.preachingpeace.org). Our goal was to find a synergy that dealt with what Christianity without violence would look like. These presentations span the spectrum of discourse—theological, philosophical, ethical, practical. Craig Carter, Sharon Baker, and Brian McLaren brought the keynote addresses. Each of these speakers represents a different theological tradition that is wrestling with the problem of violence and peacemaking within the churches.

To help discussion within the churches, Preaching Peace has created a DVD featuring Dr. Sharon Baker (Messiah College), Dr. B. Keith Putt (Samford University) and Michael Hardin that can be used in tandem with this book for group discussions. There are eight twenty-minute sessions oriented to a lay audience with a study guide. These DVD's can be found at the website, www.preachingpeace.org.

We would like to thank Messiah College for their gracious hospitality. Along with faculty members of the Department of Biblical and Religious Studies, our time together was stimulating and challenging in an atmosphere where real conversation could occur. Special thanks, of course, to our contributors and to all those who support them in their important work. As always, we thank Michael's wife Lorri Hardin for her administrative work and behind the scenes labor that makes Preaching Peace events flow so smoothly. Sometimes we are asked if we have ever seen an angel. Michael replies, "Yes, I married one."

—*Michael Hardin,*
  Executive Director, Preaching Peace
  Lancaster, Pennsylvania

—*Sharon L. Baker*
  Assistant Professor of Theology and Religion, Messiah College
  Grantham, Pennsylvania

PEACE BE WITH YOU

Chapter 1

Preemptive Peacemaking: Subverting Constantine Through a Better Story

Brian McLaren

In our day, as in Jesus' day, six stories form the identities of individuals, families, communities, parties, races, nations, religions, and civilizations. Together, they sustain, energize, and perpetuate the status quo. Jesus exposes these six stories as bad news. He provides a transforming alternative and creates a community dedicated to replacing status-quo empire with a new way of peace, justice, hope, and life. This chapter provides a theological framework for preaching, congregational development, and spiritual formation in this way of peace.

Some time ago, I was invited to speak on this subject of pre-emptive peacemaking in Rwanda. As you probably know, somewhere between 800 thousand and one million people were killed there in 1994, in 100 days. Now, some fifteen years later, the average churchgoer in Rwanda in many cases still has not heard any talk about a connection between the gospel and not killing each other. At our recent gathering, there was a group of Kenyans. They had thought they were in a relatively peaceful and stable country, far different from Rwanda, until in December 2007 and January 2008 it felt as if Kenya's own lid was ripped off—and suddenly churchgoing people started killing each another in post-election violence, just as Rwandans had in post-assassination violence.

During one of the breaks, I sat with this wonderful lady from Kenya. She's a co-pastor in the Pentecostal church. She's co-pastor with a man—not her husband (she's single)—but a man of another tribe. When the violence came to her city and started in January, all the members of the other tribe got together and came up with a list of all the homes in that village owned by members of her tribe. They organized themselves, went house to house, and burned down all those houses. Her co-pastor participated in the burning down of her own house—as did many of her church members of the other tribe. Five months later, she was still interned in a displaced persons' camp. So as we talked, she began to weep and said, "When I go back to my village I will have to work again with that man as my co-pastor and we will have to try to put our church back together—after all that's happened. It won't be easy."

IMPORTANCE

These same kinds of stories happen here in America and continue to happen elsewhere. I had the opportunity to be at Yale for a "Common Word" gathering—some of you will have heard about this dialogue between Muslims and Christians. There Prince Ghazi of Jordan gave a talk I will never forget—and I think anyone in that room will remember this. He was talking about hatred and fear between Christians and Muslims, and he asked, "Do any of you doubt that if there is another holocaust in Europe, this time it will be Muslims—Muslim lives going up in smoke?" Meanwhile, many of our churches are getting an awful lot of messages about how we should be afraid of Muslims.

But Muslims around the world are much more afraid of us. And remember: We've got many more weapons than they have, a lot more planes and aircraft carriers and other military resources. We are members of this incredibly powerful, well-armed nation and of the community of Jesus Christ in this nation. So we have to figure out not just how to understand Jesus' good news of the kingdom of God, which is his good news of PEACE, but alsho how to proclaim that good news, calling more and more people to repentance before too many more lives are destroyed in violence. What we're talking about today—for people of Rwanda and Kenya, and for people in the U.S. and the Muslim world—is literally a matter of life and death.

PREEMPTION PERSPECTIVES

Dorothy Day—until she passed in 1980—was a Catholic activist known for her social justice campaigns in defense of the poor, forsaken, hungry, and homeless, and who espoused nonviolence and hospitality for the impoverished and downtrodden. She said, "Why was so much done in remedying social evils instead of avoiding them in the first place? Oh! Where were the saints to try to change the social order, not just to minister to the slaves but to do away with slavery?"

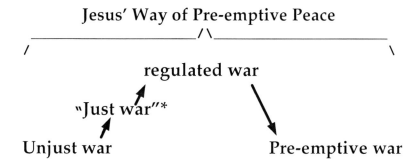

PROGRESS?

When you think about history, about dealing with issues of war—you know in one sense, in theory at least, that "just war" should be better than "unjust war," where anyone can do anything they want to anyone they want. But I like the way Walter Wink renames so-called "just war theory" as "preliminary violence reduction theory." Or as Keith Putt has reminded us, John "Jack" Caputo renames "just war theory" as the "lesser of two evils theory." In recent centuries, we have raised the bar even higher than the old versions of just war theory. Through the Geneva Conventions and other treaties we have moved above "just war" toward a kind of "regulated war."

Then of course in recent years we've seen a radically new theory of war be announced and instituted, with no justification, with neither dialogue nor debate, called "pre-emptive war." Meanwhile, we have continuing "progress" in the kill-power of our weapons, from fist, to stone, to knife, to spear, to arrow, to gun, to cannon, to automatic weapons, to grenades and bombs, to land mines, to missiles, to nuclear bombs, to biological chemical weapons. No wonder so many of us feel we are at a critical moment, asking, Where do we go from here?

JESUS' WAY OF PRE-EMPTIVE PEACE

As a follower of Jesus, I believe Jesus was right—about everything. And I think he was right about peacemaking. I think Jesus' way can be described as a way of "pre-emptive peace" rather than "pre-emptive war." So I believe that Jesus calls us to go beyond cleaning up the disasters of war once they happen and instead to invest our best energies in preventing war, genocide, and injustice from happening in the first place. Would we, recalling Dorothy Day's wise words, rather heal and keep healing from the traumas of war, genocide, and injustice . . . or help prevent them?

Of course that raises the question, how? How do we prevent them? As followers of Jesus, what resources do we bring to this question of how to make a difference?[1]

GOSPEL FULLNESS—NEWS!

The gospel of the kingdom of God is bigger and deeper and richer than many of us—any of us—realize. The word *gospel*—good news—means the announcement of something that's happened, the announcement of an event, an occurrence that has a bearing on our lives like an important news story.

The American Catholic novelist Walker Percy told a parable to illustrate the unique character of news as opposed to mere information or dogma. He described a group of scholars gathered together to hear a lecture on physics. They were all studiously taking notes and occasionally nodding their heads and maybe tapping feet on the ground.

The lecture goes on and on. People struggle to stay awake. Then a janitor walks up the aisle, leans over, and whispers something in the ear of the physics lecturer. The lecturer says, "Excuse me, ladies and gentlemen. I have just been told there is a fire in the foyer and we must evacuate the building immediately—but you need to leave by the side entrances up here, not by the main entrances in the foyer."

Now at that moment, Percy said, people did not continue taking notes and nodding their heads. Suddenly the category of information had changed . . . from information to news. In that split second, the speaker abducted the crowd and translated them into a new reality. He dislocated them from their abstracted state as objective, interested but disinterested observers and note-takers, and baptized them into a predicament. Percy realized that we only hear news when we understand ourselves to be in a predicament.

Today we are in a predicament of stories. We live by stories yet our current ones are not only failing but destroying us. Here are six dominant stories, along with Jesus' alternative story:

GOD'S INVITATION INTO PREEMPTIVE PEACEMAKING		
Story	*Focus*	*Call to repentance*
DOMINATION There would be peace *if only WE were in control, in charge!* (e.g. Romans, Herodians, Sadducees)	US over THEM (e.g. empire, ideology) US—no them (genocide)	Don't dominate; serve instead.
REVOLUTION There would be peace *if only THEY weren't in control!* (Zealots)	US versus THEM	Don't seek revenge; reconcile instead.
PURIFICATION There would be peace *if only THEY would change! (Or go away!)* (Pharisees)	Some of US versus others of US (scapegoating)	Don't scapegoat or exclude; embrace and welcome the other instead.
ISOLATION *It's hopeless! There will be no peace. We must withdraw–God will evacuate us!* (Essenes)	US—without them	Don't isolate; instead draw near and empathize.
ALIENATION/ VICTIMIZATION *We're mistreated and nobody cares. There will be peace when our suffering is acknowledged.* (prostitutes, tax collectors, the poor)	US—because of them	Don't be a victim; realize God is for you.
ACCUMULATION *Social peace is impossible, but personal peace is attainable through wealth.* (rich elite)	US competing with them	Don't hoard, but give and seek the common good.
KINGDOM OF GOD— *It's available now!* There can be peace through seeking God's kingdom and justice.	Some of US for ALL OF US Love ⇔ Forgive ⇔ Reconcile	Rethink everything! Rebuild! Heal! Liberate! Love God, neighbors, enemies. Follow Jesus to learn to be part of a new creation and kingdom.

Jesus' kingdom message says to those living by the domination narrative, "Listen, you are partly right—you want peace. That's a good thing. And you're also right to associate peace with the right use of power. But your way of using power—to dominate—is not God's way. It won't lead to peace. You need to use your power for the common good, in service, for justice and reconciliation. That will lead to peace."

I see this working out in the interaction between Jesus and the rich young ruler. When Jesus says, "Sell all you have, give to the poor, come, follow me," I think he's saying, "Look! You're obviously part of the domination narrative. You're young. And already you're rich. And you're a ruler, which means you're basically working with the Romans. So you're very successful in gaining and using power. What I want you to do is to divest your power within that system, and now join me in serving the poor. Join me in living by this different narrative."

Similarly, in each of the narratives, Jesus invites a kind of redemption and transformation. He's not saying to the victimized, "Don't worry about it. That's in the past. You've not been wrong. Forget about it. It's okay." He says instead, "No! You have been wronged by others. But if you aren't careful, you'll end up being defined by your victimization. So I'm calling you to the painful work of facing and feeling the wrongs done against you and eventually being able to confront and forgive those who have wronged you. This is going to require deeply spiritual transformation. This is going to require you becoming more like your father in heaven, whose behavior toward people isn't based on how they treat God. God's behavior toward people is based on God's goodness and love." So when Jesus says *be perfect as your father in heaven is perfect,* he's saying, "Come and join the kind of merciful and generous perfection that God has for you." It's a profound invitation to each group of people not to wipe their story out in a kind of forced amnesia but to bring their story into this bigger one, the redeeming story of the kingdom of God.

Now we must face the fact that any religion—including Christianity—can be used as camouflage for the first six destructive narratives. So we can have the religious domination narrative that says, *"We're in charge and its God's will for us to be in charge.* That's obviously why we've had the success we've had, because God is with us and has given us dominion over others." Then there are the religious militants. *"We're going to have our revolution in God's name,"* says the revolution narrative. "We're David fighting Goliath, and God will help us blow our oppressors away in the name of the Lord." In the religious purification narrative, we say, "God can't bless us because of those sinners over there. It's obvious that God wants those people to be cleansed from our society."

When we think in terms of stories, we don't have to shame or blame people; instead, we focus on the stories which people use—and which, in a sense, use them—in destructive ways. The flesh-and-blood people aren't the enemy; the enemy is the stories they have come to believe, trust, and live out. We need to practice a kind of exorcism in regard to these stories. Exorcism was a vital part of Jesus' work. Exorcism diagnoses evil not in the person's being or essence, but rather in something alien and evil, something that indwells and possesses the person, motivating and directing behavior toward conflict and violence.

So we need to "name our demons" and reject them. What are the hidden root problems? What are the unseen issues about which we fear to speak? What are the evil powers and systems that destroy life?

One of these key demons in all of these narratives is the demon of advantage. By advantage I mean self-interest sought at the expense of the common good—self-interest versus the common good. Advantage could be any of the three deadly "P's" of the false self: power, possessions, prestige. If you want to think of a legion of demons, you can think about the legion of demons called "-ism": egotism (advantage for me); tribalism (advantage for our tribe); classism (advantage for our social class); authoritarianism (advantage for dictators and cronies); ideology/partisanship (advantage for our party or philosophy); nationalism/colonialism/empire (advantage for our nation); religious supremacy (advantage for our religion); or consumerism (advantage for our species and generation).

Nationalism is one of our most popular demons; we in the U.S. have to figure out what it means for a nation so full of advantages to come to terms with Jesus' words—that from those to whom much is given, much is expected. Religious supremacy is another popular demon. As followers of Jesus, I think we have to be especially suspicious of religious supremacy—not as an act of relativism but as an act of fidelity to Jesus as opposed to a religion that we associate with Jesus. There is also a demonic form of liberalism, in which we turn freedom into a fetish; and in conservatism, through which we idolize an idealized past. In consumerism, we idolize advantage for our species—with carelessness toward all the other creatures that God made. Or we might also say that consumerism seeks advantage for our generation only, careless about the legacy we leave to future generations—environmentally, economically, socially.

By identifying the evil not in people but in demonic, suicidal stories, we won't judge others as stupid or idiots or infidels or whatever. Instead we will understand that a spirit has control of them, which makes them behave in ways they don't desire. We can thus join Jesus in a compassionate view of people who are "harassed and helpless— like sheep without a shepherd," people who, like the demoniac boy, keep behaving suicidally against their nature and will, throwing themselves into the fire.

When we live by the six destructive narratives, we create vicious cycles that work in predictable ways. First, there is offense—an injustice or insult. In response, the victims feel hurt, anger, and perhaps hatred. Then come threats of revenge, which lead to mutual fear. Driven apart by fear, people retreat into isolation, and in isolation communication decreases and ceases, enabling each side to vilify and dehumanize the other "behind their backs." In that context, there will be new offenses, new injustices. And the vicious cycle spins on toward escalating injustice and violence—increased domination, resentment and reaction, and so on.

In Rwanda I was with a group of visitors to a genocide memorial, Kigali Genocide Memorial Center. When word of the genocide spread through the countryside, 4,000 people—Tutsis and their friends—fled to this Catholic church compound to avoid being killed. But instead of finding safety, they were herded together and burned—so the church became a genocidal oven and mass grave.

I was there with a Native American brother, Richard, a wonderful committed Christian in his native tradition. Many Native Americans have a special cultural sensitivity toward human remains. As part of the memorial, the back of this church was filled with shelves full of the bleached bones of the victims. The skulls and femurs and tibias and fibulas and ribs were all laid out . . . shelf upon shelf full of bones, dry bones, an intentionally repulsive display. But I think for Richard, because of his background with its sense of the sacredness of human remains, it was almost pornographic. It was offensive in ways that I don't think I could ever fully understand, but I could see it as he began to weep . . . and then started singing a prayer in his Lakota language, asking God to have mercy on what we humans have done to one another.

As after his prayer we walked outside of the building, Richard and I looked up at a big hand-painted sign on the building, written in the Kinyarwandan language. We couldn't understand it, so I snapped a photograph of it. Later we showed someone the picture and asked what it meant: "If you knew me, you would not kill me."

The sign demonstrated what happens when cycles of injustice and fear create isolation, making it so much easier to vilify and dehumanize people whose names and humanity we don't know.[2]

Suddenly you realize why the Gospels include Jesus' individual encounters with Samaritans and lepers and Romans and Pharisees and prostitutes. You see how Jesus worked to make sure that these people were not kept at a distance, on the other side of the road, but rather that they were brought near to be known, then and now. Because if we know them, we will not kill them.

How different is the space created by the story of the kingdom of God from the spaces created by stories of domination, revolution, purification, isolation, victimization, and accumulation! No wonder we are sent into the world to cast out evil spirits—the spirits of domination, revenge/revolution, scapegoating, isolation, alienation/victimization, and accumulation! How beautiful and crucial is our calling to liberate people everywhere from the stories that possess them and drive them to suicidal and homicidal behavior!

We believe and proclaim a story about a gracious and glorious Creator who creates this world and in it creates human beings who—foolishly, selfishly, ignorantly—tear themselves out of that story of creation and start living by other stories, stories of destruction. Like Jesus, we look at the crowds who are harassed and helpless, like sheep without a shepherd. We say, "You're trying to make a domination narrative work. But it never will work. There's another way to do this. You're stuck in a revolution or victimization narrative. I understand. God cares about the injustice you suffer too, and God doesn't want you to be oppressed. Yes, God wants to liberate you, but not through violence. God has another way. God wants to make you an agent of a new creation, a new way, a new age, a new life, a new story." As pastors, we gather people to try to help them live by this different story, to teach them the practices and ways of this different story.

When I was a pastor, my favorite part of our weekly worship service was the benediction—not because I was glad for our gathering to be over, but because I loved the idea of sending people out to go live this different story and share it with others. To me, that was very motivating, very inspiring—to collaborate with the Holy Spirit leading, preemptively making peace. I saw ministry, and see it, as a life-and-death matter.

NOTES

1. I addressed this subject in an introductory way in my book *The Secret Message of Jesus: Uncovering the Truth that Could Change Everything* (Nashville, Tenn.: Thomas Nelson, Nashville, 2007), especially ch. 17, *The Peaceable Kingdom*. Here are a few excerpts from that chapter.

The secret message of Jesus, by dealing with the root causes of war [and violence], . . . does not promise the easiest, fastest, safest, and most convenient method of ending violent conflict—but it offers, I believe, the only sure one. Perhaps as few people today will be willing to believe and practice this message as when it was first proclaimed. There are plenty of popular escape hatches for those who don't want to go there. But perhaps nearly 2000 years of trying these alternatives should begin to make us ready to consider that Jesus may have been more right, more practical, and wiser then we realized, and his secret message may have meant what it said about loving—not killing—our enemies (p.156).

It is time, I believe, for people who have confidence in Jesus and his message to lead the way in imagining what could happen—say over ten or twenty or a hundred years—if increasing percentages of our budgets were diverted from peacekeeping through weaponry to peacemaking through actively addressing the underlying causes of conflict—causes of like injustice, lack of compassion, racism, corruption, and lack of free and ethical press, and poverty—and the fear, hatred, greed, ignorance, and lust that fuel them. Either way the cost will be high, it's just a question of which kind of cost we would prefer to pay (p.160).

In the meantime, the word of John of the Baptist should be heard by everyone who has power: "Repent and bring forth fruits of your repentance!" (see Luke 3:8) Soldiers, politicians, military strategists weapons manufacturers, and taxpayers who pay their salaries may ask, "What about us? What should we do?" Journalists, news directors, TV and radio anchors and reporters, and bloggers would join them: "What about us? What should we do"? (p.160).

John the Baptist would answer, I believe, and just as he did back in the months before Jesus emerged on the scene: "Don't abuse your power. And listen to the One whose way I was sent to prepare." (p.161).

Whether we're presently [anti-violence] pacifists or supporters of preliminary violence reduction theory, whenever we pray, "Your kingdom come; your will be done on earth as it is in heaven," we're praying that war and violence will end and God's shalom will come. That in itself is an act of [preemptive] peacemaking, because we're seeking to align our wills with God's will, our dreams with God's dream (p.161).

2. Meanwhile Emmanuel Katongole and Chris Rice, *Reconciling All Things:*

A Christian Vision for Justice, Peace and Healing (Downers Grover, Ill: InterVarsity Press, 2008) seek to provide as a compelling alternate viusion of reconciliation. They see Christian hope attracting people to heartfelt leadership based on "a God-ordained transformation of the consequences of the Fall into the new creation spoken about by the apostle Paul." Reporing on a gathering in Africa, ranging across Uganda, Rwanda, Sudan, Congo, and Burundi, they describe the Spirit at work, quoting (p.52ff):

> One of our biggest surprises was learning of the incredible courage it took for these leaders to gather. On our final evening together, Congolese united Methodist Bishop Ntambo Nkulu Ntanda spoke of the wars between the countries of the Christians gathered. He told of how the old stories about Uganda's former dictator Idi Amin haunted him, how Uganda's recent war with the Congo had taxed him, how he'd never come to Uganda before and was terrified when he arrived at the Airport.

> But the gathering changed that. "Here Emmanuel, a Ugandan embraced me when I walked in," Natanda said. "I had never worshiped with someone from Sudan, and here there is a Sudanese. Here there have been Anglicans, Methodists, Baptists, Catholics and Pentacostals, all worshiping." With a laugh he declared he was extending his stay in Uganda for two days. "If reconciliation happens, they will say it started here. I'm going back to the Congo with a new story to tell about Uganda."

> Ntanda's story points to our vocation as Christ's ambassadors of reconciliation—a transformation into a new story that resists narrow boundaries and loyalties. In the world turned upside down, we worship One who walked right side up. As we worship and followed Jesus, we are conformed to have his strange image. So we bear the strange marks of God's new creation amid a world still in the grip of the old.

Chapter 2

LIBERALISM: THE NEW CONSTANTINIANISM

Craig A. Carter

INTRODUCTION

At first glance, it would seem that the book's treatment of being a peace church in a Constantinian world is about fifty years out of date. According to Stanley Hauerwas and William Willimon, Constantinianism ended one Sunday evening in 1963. In their book *Resident Aliens* they write:

> That evening has come to represent a watershed in the history of Christendom, South Carolina style. On that night, Greenville, South Carolina—that last pocket of resistance to secularity in the Western world—served notice that it would no longer be a prop for the church. There would be no more free passes for the church, no more free rides. The Fox Theater went head to head with the church over who would provide the world view for the young. That night in 1963, the Fox Theater won the opening skirmish.[1]

In the fifty years since 1963, traditional Christianity has been steadily losing culture-shaping influence. In my book, *Rethinking Christ and Culture: A Post-Christendom Perspective*, I argue that Hauerwas and Willimon are correct and we now live in the "post-Christendom era" of the West. Christianity no longer holds a place of dominance in Western culture and is no longer able to impose its religious and ethical beliefs on society either by moral suasion or by coercion.

But this does not mean that we live in a "post-religion era," as many Western intellectuals have been anticipating for well over a century. The "secularization thesis," which held that secularization inevitably follows modernization and the rise of modern science, is now itself comatose.[2] The Iranian Revolution of 1979, the astonishing world-wide growth of Pentecostalism in the twentieth century, and the pervasiveness of New Age spirituality show that religion is not going to wither away any more than the state did under Soviet Marxism. The role of Christianity in such Western countries as the U.S. versus Europe, for example, varies enough to make blanket statements unwise. However, much of the West is not becoming non-religious; rather, it is becoming non-Christian.[3]

Christianity has now been privatized and relegated to the margins of life. Western culture is a melting pot of various religions and spiritualities in which old paganisms mix with Eastern religions and scraps of the scientific outlook to form something new. Oprah is the great guru of late modern religion—a bit of Hinduism here, a Celtic song there plus a Buddhist meditation practice, and a few sayings culled from the words of Jesus and rearranged so as to fit into the Gnostic heresy she advocates.

This is religion in the modern world. You like the beauty of the Catholic liturgy? Fine. But you like the laid back approach to sexuality in the Hindu tantric sex manuals? You can have that too. And you also want to worship the goddess as an expression of your raised environmental consciousness? No problem. It can all fit in because the most important thing is that you "own" your personal spirituality. We have designer clothes, designer babies, and designer religion. People like Oprah Winfrey get rich serving as religious consultants who aid individuals in sorting through the options and choosing what is "best for them" in the flea market of religion.

But there is one characteristic that all the spiritualities, traditions, and practices have in common. They are all essentially private and individualistic. In late modernity, there is also a public religion, but it is not a traditional one like Christianity or Islam. It has to pose as a non-religion because it relegated Christianity to the realm of the private by claiming that all religion must be expelled from the public square. Nevertheless, it functions as the established religion of Western culture. It presents itself as being absolutely true and binding as do all serious religions—even to the point of demanding blood sacrifice. This public religion is the Constantinian established religion of the late modern West. It is not Christianity but it *is* a derivative of Christianity, a heretical off-shoot of orthodox Christianity sometimes called "Liberalism." Liberalism is the new Constantinianism. But what do I mean by liberalism? To answer that question, we need to examine some history and define some terms.

THE RISE OF LIBERALISM

The early church emerged from its struggle with the persecuting Roman Empire by creating a Christian culture that endured for over a thousand years called Western Christendom. Its high point was the thirteenth century, and it began to decline from the fourteenth century on. Eventually, Christendom was replaced by modernity. Late medieval philosophical trends, the Renaissance, and the Reformation were all important, but the key moment in the creation of modernity was the Enlightenment.

The Enlightenment

The Enlightenment was a movement in European thought that began to flourish in the seventeenth century and continues to this day. After the devastating Protestant-Catholic Wars of Religion that began after the Reformation and ended with the Peace of Westphalia in 1648, most European intellectuals and politicians came to see traditional religion as a threat to public peace that must be banished from the public square.

As William Cavanaugh shows, this led to the invention of two things: the realm of the private, to which religion was banished, and the modern nation state, which gradually replaced the church in Western society and came to be seen as the source and guarantor of human rights, liberty, justice, and peace.[4] Religion was blamed for all the evils of society, especially for intolerance and violence, while the state was extolled as the rational approach to governing human affairs so as to maximize the happiness of the population. Out of the Enlightenment came the two great modern religions, capitalism and Marxism, both heretical offshoots of Christianity.

Capitalism claims that there are historical and economic laws of the market to which we must conform and that, if we respect freedom of trade and commerce, then prosperity is sure to follow. Capitalism presents itself as the scientific discovery of the laws by which economics works in much the same way as Newtonian physics is a discovery of the laws by which the physical world works. Capitalism claims to be the highest development of civilization to date because, for the first time, we have begun to manage our political economy according to reason.

Marxism builds on capitalism but sees capitalism as a partly true yet inadequate system; it represents a phase in historical development as if it was final when, in fact, it is not. Marxism claims that there are historical and economic laws which inevitably will assert themselves in history as capitalism destroys itself, the workers rise in revolution, and the utopia of the classless society follows this revolutionary class struggle. Marx also presented his view as a truly scientific system because it claimed to be the first system of political economy to be completely in accord with reason.

What these two ideologies have in common is much more important than their disagreements. First, both claim to be "scientific." They are rationalistic attempts to apply the method of empirical science to all areas of life and to bask in the reflected glow of the prestige of modern technology. Second, both promote "secularism." But what is secularism? It is crucially important to realize that it is not the same as "the secular." Before Christianity, there was no such thing as "the secular" because society as a whole was sacralized. The concept of "the secular" emerges in the thought of St. Augustine.[5]

For Augustine, "the secular" is a way of describing the world in the present time between the first and second comings of Christ in which the kingdom has come, but not yet in its fullness, and entities like the Roman Empire still exist even though they have no eschatological future in the New Heavens and New Earth. Augustine makes room for both a church which is on pilgrimage toward the City of God and also for a City of Man, being built now in this world. The City of God includes all men and angels who love God, while the City of Man consists of all whose loves are disordered by being curved inward or misplaced in idolatry.

The visible, institutional church contains both true and false Christians currently living upon the earth, so it is not identical with the City of God, which contains the true Christians of all ages, past, present, and future plus the holy angels. Some who are part of the earthly, institutional church are really part of the City of Man. The earthly state, on the other hand, is not reducible only to non-Christians and thus is not simply identical with the City of Man. The state contains both believers and unbelievers because Christians live in the church *and* the state during this age—the *saeculum*. The life which believers and unbelievers share on this earth is the realm of the secular.

For Augustine, the secular is neither the sacred (which is the realm of the church) nor is it the profane (the realm of false worship or idolatry). The secular is not automatically evil just by virtue of being the secular. In fact, Christians who live and work within secular institutions like the state, education, business, or other areas may humanize those areas as they work for justice and a partial peace. Of course, peace can never be perfect and human institutions, such as the state, can never be perfect in this age. Nevertheless, the secular is not for that reason to be abandoned by Christians.

The secular is a stage on which a great drama is being played out and on which good and evil are mixed together. Both the church and the state can reflect elements of both the City of God and the City of Man. The key to understanding Augustine's thought is to keep these four key terms separate and not to let any two of them become identified with each other. The role of the concept of "the secular" in Augustine's thought is to preserve the critical distinction between what is going on around us in history and the future kingdom of God. The concept of "the secular" creates an eschatological tension, which prevents us from seeing any human institution (not the church nor the state or any other human institution) as either completely good or completely evil.

This eschatological tension came close to collapse during the Middle Ages, and this led to the evils of Christendom, for which Augustine was unjustly blamed because he was inadequately understood. In those moments during which Christendom allowed the church practically to absorb the state and its legitimate powers into itself so that the state became virtually a department of the church, the eschatological tension between this age and the future age of the kingdom of God was slackened.

When this tension dissipates completely, the resulting all-powerful church/state becomes demonic. But this eschatological tension can be reduced in more than one way; in modernity the very opposite happens as the state absorbs the functions of the church by privatizing the church and making it irrelevant to political ethics and philosophy. The modern state threatens to become the all-powerful state/church, a mirror image of the Christendom mistake. When the modern state becomes totalitarian, as it has on numerous occasions in the twentieth century such as in the Soviet Union or Nazi Germany, it becomes demonic. It must be noted that, despite currently popular prejudices, the scale of evil produced by the modern state/shurch exceeds greatly the evil produced by the medieval church/state.

The word *secularism* (as opposed to "the secular") has only been in use in English since the nineteenth century.[6] Secularism is an ideol-

ogy that has come to denote the absence of religion and the cultivation of public affairs without reference to God. Whereas "the secular"
for Augustine simply denoted the world outside the church, which
could be Christian or pagan and was not necessarily profane, "secularism" is, ostensibly, the deliberate exclusion of religion from as
much of life as possible. But in reality, it is only a "metamorphosis of
the sacred"[7] into a new form of religion that pretends to be "that
which comes after the death of religion."

Both capitalism and Marxism are heretical deviations from
Christianity because they deny God, replace the church with the
state, deny the reality of original sin, replace divine providence with
human reason, and transform the kingdom of God into a utopian
myth. Modernity, in both its capitalist and its Marxism forms, celebrates secularism as freedom *from* religion in reaction to the dominance of the church in Christendom. Modernity is thus a reaction
against Christendom's collapsing of Augustine's eschatological tension in the all-powerful church/state.

But instead of restoring the eschatological tension, it inverts the
mistake of Christendom and makes the state dominant instead of the
church, thus launching yet another attack on the secular as a space in
which both Christians and non-Christians can mingle freely. The
state takes over the totalitarian role of the church and proves much
more murderous and arrogant. As Alexander Solzhenitsyn said, the
biggest problem with Soviet Marxism was that it tried to build a new
society while pretending that God did not exist;[8] Marxist atheism is
as much a religious position as is Christian belief in God. Christendom and modernity share the same core problem. Both collapse the
Augustinian eschatological tension by identifying either the church
(Christendom) or the state (modernity) with the kingdom of God.

Liberal Democracy

It is essential to grasp the point that contemporary Western, liberal democracy combines elements of capitalism and Marxism in a
synthesis. The division of politics into "left" and "right," which arose
during the French Revolution, means that in liberal democracy the
political spectrum consists of different kinds of liberals. Within liberal democracy, everyone is a liberal.

To become dominant, liberalism had to vanquish conservativism.
Conservatives wanted to maintain many aspects of the culture of
Christendom, such as monarchy, common law, and religion, but they
were defeated—earlier and more decisively in France and Germany
than in the Anglo-Saxon world—but finally everywhere in the West.[9]

To avoid confusion, it is important to remember that what we call "neoconservatism" today is just a conservative form of liberalism. It fully accepts liberalism in the areas of economics and politics while trying to remain conservative in matters relating to family, civil society and religion. But it is very difficult to straddle the divide between the Left and the Right in this way. Examples of neoconservatives would be Catholics Michael Novak and Richard John Neuhaus, and the evangelicals in the Religious Right. But in the end, they have to be understood as conservative liberals, not as a genuine alternative to liberalism. So, as far as political movements in the West are concerned, Liberalism now reigns supreme.

Left-wing liberals are often called "progressives" and are dominant in the Democratic Party in the United States and in the New Democratic Party in Canada. They tend to stress individual freedom in matters relating to sexual ethics but are conservative in economic matters insofar as they argue for rather more state control and not complete freedom for the market. Left-wing liberalism is comfortable with big government and top-down solutions to social problems designed by experts, and liberals often tend to draw on neo-Marxist theory to criticize unrestrained capitalism. But their use of Marxist theory is done in the name of personal freedom and they believe that the purpose of big government is to empower individuals. Left-wing liberals generally distrust the family and civil society, but they view big government as the ally of the individual who must overcome tradition and the "narrowness" of race, religion, nationality, ethnic background and so on to become a self-realized, autonomous individual, which is the highest goal of liberalism.

Right-wing liberalism (or neoconservativism) is dominant in the Republican Party in the United States and to a lesser extent in the Conservative Party in Canada. If Bill Clinton epitomizes left-wing liberalism, Ronald Reagan epitomizes right-wing liberalism. Right-wing Liberals stress individualism in economic matters (the unregulated market) but not in matters relating to sexual morality. Right-wing liberalism is comfortable with big government and top-down solutions when it comes to issues relating to national security and crime and tends to reject Marxist theory root and branch as being at odds with individual freedom. But in rejecting Marxism it also encourages the growth of" the national security state" through military spending and readiness to resort to violence to protect the economic interests of the state.

Politics in the Western world today revolves around the clashing ideologies of Right and Left. But in the Western democracies, the

Right does not stand for fascism (despite the attempts of left-wing partisans to claim that this is so) and the Left does not stand for Marxism (despite the attempts of right-wing partisans to claim that this is so). Both the Right and the Left share a basic commitment to the empowerment of the self-realizing, autonomous self as the highest good of politics and in this sense are both species of Enlightenment liberalism. The hard totalitarianism of fascism and communism is rejected, but liberalism leaves itself open to a soft totalitarianism of the Absolute State, unlimited by the claims of the family and civil society, seizing total control over the life of its citizens in the name of guaranteeing them their individual freedom.

The key point here is that aspects of Marxism and capitalism have merged together to form contemporary liberal democracy. While the free market has indeed triumphed, the idea of democracy as (relative) economic equality based on the redistribution of income has also triumphed as well.[10] Liberalism combines the ideas of economic freedom (private ownership of the means of production) with personal freedom (the empowerment of individuals for self-realization). Thus the free market and the welfare state come together in a harmonious synthesis in which the All-Powerful State becomes the guarantor of the right of the individual to self-realization. As Lesslie Newbigin put it,

> The nation-state replaces the holy church and the holy empire as the centerpiece in the post-Enlightenment ordering of society. Upon it devolves the duty of providing the means for life, liberty, and the pursuit of happiness. . . . If—for modern Western people—nature has taken the place of God as the ultimate reality with which we have to deal, the nation-state has taken the place of God as the source to which we look for happiness, health and welfare.[11]

As the deification of the state progresses, secularism becomes first thinkable, then normal, and finally mandatory. As Karl Barth put it, "Uninterruptedly absorbed in progress toward its own deification, the state feels less and less the need that God should be spoken about. The tasks of popular instruction and education seems to depend less and less on the theologians."[12] The enormous prestige of the state as the guarantor and source of the resources necessary for individual empowerment tends to raise the state to the level of divinity and eliminates the need for theology or any reference to divine revelation.

It should be noted that the self envisioned here is one conceived only as an object in the material world, and the realization sought is the full realization of the material, space-time self. The self with which modernity concerns itself is thus a soul-less self and the religion of modernity is a materialistic one. Thus freedom is the object of worship, liberalism is the religion, the state is the church, and the state/church takes the place of God in the culture of liberal modernity. As the successor religion to Christianity in post-Christendom Western culture, liberalism is more firmly established today in a Constantinian sense than Christianity ever was in the West and, therefore, teeters much closer to the brink of the demonic.

THE ESSENCE OF LIBERALISM

But what is the essence of liberalism? What makes liberalism itself and not something else? To understand liberalism, we must examine four central concepts in liberalism: freedom, desire, consumption, and progress.

Freedom

In liberalism, freedom is defined negatively as "freedom from constraint." Individuals must be free to do whatever they want. Whether I can do whatever I want is the ultimate test of whether or not I am free. This is very different from the Christian idea of freedom as the will being drawn toward the good. For Christians, being free means doing God's will and thus fulfilling our true nature as his creatures. As Pope John Paul II put it, in accordance with the mainstream of the Christian tradition, "Acting is morally good when the choices of freedom are *in conformity with man's true good* and thus express the voluntary ordering of the person toward his ultimate end: God himself, the supreme good in whom man finds his full and perfect happiness."[13]

To obey the Word of God is to do that for which we were created and to find joy. But to go against the Word of God is to become enslaved to our appetites and to lose our freedom. What I want to argue here is that the liberal notion of freedom is self-contradictory.

An article by philosopher Louis Groarke is the clearest explanation of why this is so and I will draw on it extensively in the following section. He writes:

> In this paper I argue that a pervasive "religion as tyranny" view has its roots in a philosophical misunderstanding about human freedom. The established liberal view . . . conceives of freedom primarily in negative terms as freedom of choice or amoral au-

tonomy. I argue that this approach . . . leads inevitably to a wide-ranging indifferentism and that indifferentism is incompatible with Christianity. [14]

Groarke notes that in the age of secularism, religion is portrayed as conservative and reactionary, whereas those who oppose religion in the name of individual autonomy are heroes. Since freedom is seen as "unfettered individual choice" (258), religion is bad because it *imposes limits on choice*. Noting that great thinkers like Aristotle and Aquinas recognize the importance of "first principles," without which we would have to argue backward forever to justify anything, he says that modernity proposes negative liberty or amoral autonomy as its first principle.

But as soon as you accept a negative concept of freedom as your first principle, religion (as well as all systems of morality) inevitably and necessarily appears tyrannical. So the best way to counter the "religion as tyranny" view is not through "one more attempt to water down the dogmatic or moral content of religion to satisfy the liberal craving for ever more freedom of choice" (259). This is the strategy that liberal Protestantism has been using for two hundred years now, and it has not worked. All that has happened is that the so-called "new atheists," such as Richard Dawkins and Christopher Hitchens, are calling for the final step of eradicating the idea of God from modern society altogether. Like the Russians retreating in World War II, liberals have tried to fight a war of attrition and prevent total collapse of Christian theology, but the problem is that liberal theology is running out of territory to defend. [15]

Groarke defines liberalism as the belief that "freedom understood as the right to decide for oneself without outside interference is the ultimate political or moral value." [16] He argues that, as time goes on, liberalism must grant more and more autonomy to individuals or else it risks making itself appear incoherent. This is why those who claim to reject theoretical liberalism, but think that practical liberalism is better than all the alternatives, are deluded. They mistake what can only be a temporary rear-guard action for a permanent solution.

John Rawls, for example, famously attempted to forge a non-contradictory account of liberalism by balancing two competing ideals: the liberal ideal of freedom of choice (which he calls the "right") and the utilitarian ideal of universal human welfare (which he calls the "good"). [17] His rule is that the right is before the good. But Rawl's compromise collapses because his definition of freedom does not permit him to assert this rule. Groarke demonstrates this rather easily in the following manner:

Suppose we believe in assertion X. Assertion X might be the Christian view; the Marxist view, the positivist view, the homosexual view, whatever. Suppose that assertion X leads to the conclusion that "y is the good." Call the claim "y is the good" A, and the claim "y is not the good" B. According to liberalism, we are allowed to assert A, but not if this requires us to assert that A is better than B. But asserting "A" is equivalent to asserting "not B." A and B are contradictories; A = not B, and B = not A. So how can we assert A without simultaneously proclaiming that A is better than B?

If we feel strongly positive about A, we must by the very nature of the case feel strongly negative toward B. Groarke asks, "How can I powerfully feel, for example, that prayer is part of the good life, without feeling with equal intensity that the view that prayer is trivial is seriously flawed?" So the upshot of this is, How is liberalism necessarily more of an open conversation than any other form of ethics or politics? Actually, liberalism tends to suppress vigorous conversation. The tendency is away from strong convictions of any kind. Groarke shows that there is no place in liberalism for those who have strong convictions about what is true, because those who have strong convictions about what is true also have strong convictions about what is false.[18] Liberalism is self-contradictory because it undermines its own first principles, since it has no way to assert that anything actually is true including itself.

Groarke asserts that liberalism is not a true pluralism; it is rather Indifferentism. Indifferentism is the belief that all metaphysical, epistemological, moral, and religious views are more or less equally valid. This means that liberalism is committed to defending the belief that one religion is as good as another, which is very different from (actually incompatible with) saying that minority religions should be tolerated. One can't tolerate what one approves; one simply affirms what one approves and therefore does not need to tolerate it. Thus liberalism is not really tolerant of anything with which it disagrees.

As popularly stated, liberalism has two components: 1) the idea that freedom is non-interference; and 2) the no-harm rule. The crucial problem is that there is no way to deduce #2 from #1. The no-harm rule must be derived from some substantive understanding of human nature and objective values. But this is just what liberalism cannot do. And, to make matters worse, not everyone agrees with the no-harm rule. Nietzscheans, for example, oppose such a restriction of individual freedom and the will to power. If I am superior and can get away with it, why should I not harm another person? Groarke summarizes the dilemma:

> Theoretical liberalism champions freedom understood as non-interference as the ultimate value. If we do not impose order on society, however, some people will likely prey on others. Liberalism obliges us to intervene to curtail this natural chain of events. This seems paradoxical, however. If *non-interference* is the supreme value, we apparently can only preserve non-interference by *interfering*. It turns out, then, that liberal authors are not arguing for *unlimited* interference, but on the contrary for *limited* interference. But then non-interference cannot be the first principle of justice after all.[19]

Non-interference cannot be the first principle because if we have to decide when to interfere and when not to interfere, we must either do so arbitrarily (i.e. when the mob howls) or on the basis of some sort of principle that would be logically before a negative view of freedom and, therefore, would be our real first principle. This means that liberalism is dependent on some other set of religious and/or philosophical convictions that citizens of a liberal democracy happen to hold and is dependent in two ways: first, to convince people that the strong should be restrained from preying on the weak, and second, to determine when to interfere and when not to do so. Liberalism, we must therefore conclude, is inadequate as a public religion.

On the other hand, Christianity posits a very different account of freedom: "Autonomy is freedom of choice *exercised in the direction of an objective good*."[20] Liberal authors believe that freedom exists apart from morality, so they can conceive of free agents acting immorally. But Christians cannot. For Christianity, freedom can never clash with morality because "Only moral human beings are truly free" (267). But, since liberalism excludes all accounts of human nature and human flourishing, preferring to define freedom as freedom from constraint, it cannot distinguish between choices that liberate and those that enslave. Therefore, vice must be protected equally with virtue. Groarke summarizes: "On the liberal account, immoral agents actually are freer than moral agents, for they have more choices" (268). The more immoral you are, the freer you are. This outright absurdity demonstrates the moral bankruptcy of liberalism. By way of contrast, this is what Jesus teaches about freedom:

> "If you hold to my teaching, you are really my disciples. Then you will know the truth and the truth will set you free." (John 8:31b-32, NIV)

Jesus replied, "I tell you the truth, everyone who sins is a slave to sin. Now a slave has no permanent place in the family, but a son belongs to it forever. So if the Son sets you free, you will be free indeed." (8:34-36)

Jesus is clear that real freedom is based on truth and is the opposite of sinning. The truth is Jesus' teaching, so knowing and doing the truth is true freedom. Sin is slavery, not freedom.

By making individual choice absolute, liberalism falls into idolatry, which leads to slavery. Liberals claim that religious believers are still free to believe what they want and that liberal society does not oppress them. But liberals misunderstand Christianity at this point. From a Christian point of view, the individual should *not* believe whatever she or he wants but actually has a duty to believe *the truth*. To believe anything but the truth is to make oneself susceptible to idolatry. So when liberals argue that Christians are free in a liberal society because they are free to believe whatever they want, they fail to see that Christians do not wish to be free to believe "whatever they want." Christians do not understand faith to be an arbitrary or unconstrained act of the human will, which is the only kind of belief allowed in liberal society. From a Christian perspective, liberal freedom privileges idolatry, while disallowing Christianity.

Now we are in a position to see the real essence of liberalism. By divorcing itself from any substantive account of the truth, liberalism has nothing left to substitute for truth but will. As David C. Schindler notes: "If freedom is choice, then the affirmation of things as *intrinsically* good, as having a value independent of any will and therefore as making a claim on the will, is a threat to freedom because it establishes a limit to power."[21] Liberalism denies that things can be intrinsically good because it is committed to the primacy of the will. This means that liberalism is helpless to prevent the triumph of the will. Its own inner logic leads directly to Nietzsche's position that since there are no objective values, the will of the "Superman" must become the source of new values. This also explains why liberalism is so threatened by Christianity. Christianity affirms some things as intrinsically good. With its false view of freedom as freedom from constraint, liberalism sees this as a limitation of the freedom of the individual to choose for himself.

So, in its zeal to protect individuals from religion, liberalism exposes them to the will to power of the strong. To imagine that we are all safe just because we are protected from religion is a stunningly naïve view of the world for people who have lived through the twentieth century. Liberalism is simultaneously too trusting of political power and too suspicious of religious doctrine. Liberalism is a Christian heresy which is incoherent and thus inadequate as a basis for democracy, human rights, peace, and justice.

Desire

Another crucial concept in liberalism is the concept of desire. We all have desires of various kinds—for food, for drink, for security, for sex, for power, for meaning, and for many other things. Liberalism says that our desires are good and should be satisfied.

Christianity, on the other hand, says that it is a bit more complicated than that. This issue was clarified in the Pelagian disputes between Augustine and followers of Pelagius.[22] Augustine says that our desires are good but fallen and so need to be disciplined—not destroyed but disciplined. We were created by God with a desire for God and while it is appropriate to indulge our natural, physical desires we need to do so within the boundaries created by God's law, because if we seek satisfaction of our desires outside those boundaries, they take over our lives and prevent us from finding our ultimate fulfillment in God. In that case, our desires lead us to death. Our true desire—for God—is hidden in our many desires for good things and the challenge is to let desire direct us upward to God, rather than trapping us in this world only. As David C. Schindler puts it in his description of Augustine's understanding of the nature of evil: "At the root of any choice of evil there is thus a half-hearted willing."[23]

The exaltation of choice as good in and of itself is what makes liberalism inimical to the cultivation of the moral life. Both right-wing and left-wing liberalism are at fault here. As Christopher Lasch puts it: "Ritual deference to 'traditional values' cannot hide the right's commitment to progress, unlimited economic growth and acquisitive individualism."[24] During the Enlightenment, the private vices (envy, pride, and ambition) became public virtues because they stimulated invention and production. Human desire came to be seen as historical, rather than natural, and therefore insatiable. In other words, we do not simply have a finite number of needs rooted in our created nature; we have innumerable desires limited only by our imagination. Rather than seeing excessive desire as sinful, liberalism sees it as the generator of economic growth and progress. Adam Smith and his followers thus undermined the Christian understanding of desire and completed the Pelagian rejection of original sin.[25] Unlimited desire leads to unlimited demand and unlimited economic growth and is therefore seen as good.

Christianity sees fallen human desire as being in need of discipline, so that our desires can be directed ultimately toward God.[26] This is the purpose of morality. Our desires must be disciplined or they will lead us to slavery and death. Christianity sees our sexual desires, for example, as perverted by sin and in need of disciplining by chastity and marriage. Modernity, however, sees no reason why sexual desire should be restrained; in fact Sigmund Freud and much of twentieth-century liberal thought views such restraint as unhealthy repression. Liberals see the restraint of sexual desire as the product of social control; thus a hermeneutic of suspicion is applied to any movement or church that dares question the idea that sexual gratification is good in and of itself and should never be limited by anything other than the freedom of others.

Unlimited sexual desire should be understood as one with the desire for unlimited material goods; the sexual revolution is a form of consumerism. Consumerism is the right word because in sexual activity that has been detached from procreation and marriage, sex becomes persons consuming other persons as if they were things.[27] Actually, this makes the sexual revolution the very worst form of consumerism, since it is persons, rather than impersonal objects, that are consumed. Persons become objects that give us pleasure and are valued for the pleasure they give, not for themselves. We see this most clearly in pornography and prostitution, but we can also see it in the culture of casual sex that dominates college life today.

The problem with neoconservatism is not that it wants to protect the most intimate and personal relationships of human beings from being degraded into consumerism or mere contracts. Defending the family, after all, is a way of fighting for humanism as over against capitalist individualism and consumerism. The problem with neoconservativism is that it concedes too much to capitalism by surrendering the whole of economic life to "market forces" and in so doing makes us slaves of those forces that undermine the family.

Ronald Reagan portrayed himself as the champion of "family values," but according to Christopher Lasch, there is no reason to think that he really cared about their restoration. As Lasch observes, "What he really cared about was the revival of the unregulated capitalism of the twenties: the repeal of the New Deal."[28] So the neoconservatives are misguided at best and hypocritical at worst in attempting to defend family values while at the same time defending unrestrained capitalism and the consumerist culture it spawns.

It is important to see, however, that the reason Reagan could not defend the family is not merely that he was hypocritical but also that his political ideology made it *impossible* for him to do so because capitalism is based on the self-realization of autonomous individuals and on the goodness of unlimited desire. Consumerism wars unceasingly against all limits on desire. And because it encourages unchecked and undirected desire, it is incompatible with the discipline of marriage and genuine community. Theoretical liberalism thus is anti-family, anti-child, and anti-marriage.

Christianity teaches that there is congruence between God's command and our created nature. Yet we fear that if we obey God, we will be stunted, unfulfilled, and miserable. (This was the Serpent's lie to Eve in the Garden.) It takes faith to believe that obedience leads to joy because especially in our fallen condition obedience often leads to self-denial and pain at first. Yet, to disobey causes us to miss out on the joy of total obedience. This is why we are instructed to count it all joy when trials and tribulations enter our lives (James 1:2). Jesus referred to this paradox when he called his disciples to deny themselves, take up their cross, and follow him because whoever wants to save his life will lose it, but whoever loses his life for the sake of following Christ will find it (Mark 8:34ff).

Of course, in modernity, from Descartes and Kant on, nature is conceived very differently from Christianity. In modernity, freedom is power to choose arbitrarily; the will of the value-creating human person is fundamental. So, rather than seeing nature as something with which we as creatures must come to terms in some way, liberalism sees nature (including human nature) as just so much raw material that we can conquer, manipulate, and shape according to our will.

Consumption/Work

A third important concept in understanding liberalism is that of consumption, which replaces work in the lives of modern people. The conservative and Christian view of life sees work as a task set by God for human life, a task that is supposed to be rewarding and enriching, though difficult and taxing. In such a world view, work is intrinsically valuable. Christianity's understanding of work derives from the Bible. God placed Adam in the Garden before the Fall and told him to "work it and take care of it" (Gen. 2:15 NIV).

For modern liberals, however, work is a necessary evil. In industrial society, it is often boring, fragmented, and repetitive. Workers often are cut off from the joy and satisfaction of making something useful by the extreme division of labor. For Christians, since the Fall work has become more difficult and more work is required to make a living, yet work is still good and essential to a fulfilling life. For Christians, struggle is part of life in this world. But for liberals, the goal is to reduce the need to work as much as possible and ideally to eliminate it altogether one day. Here we have a disagreement over what is really most conducive to true humanism: work and struggle or leisure and consumption.

Through work we make material things and these things are useful and helpful. The value of things partly derives from the work of making them, in the Christian worldview. But for liberals, only the consumption of material goods and services has value, so if consumption can happen without human labor by means of machines, that is all the better.

For Christians, leisure is a blessing and the Sabbath is a day of rest for refreshment and preparation for more work. But for liberals, leisure is an end in itself; ideally every day could be Sabbath, in which case, of course, it would no longer have the character of a sabbath. For Christians, work has inherent value and is one of the chief ways by which persons express their personhood. For liberals, work is degrading and meaningless; the meaning of life is consuming things.

Progress

Next we must consider the notion of progress. At the heart of liberalism is the belief in progress. Liberals view Modernity as progress insofar as it leaves Christendom behind. Technological science is the means by which progress happens and is at the heart of modern liberalism. To understand what liberalism means by progress, we must compare four views of history.

First, there is the *cyclical view*. This is the default view of most of the world and the most common view before the rise of Israel and Christianity. Eastern civilization views history as an endlessly repeating circle on the model of the agricultural seasons. The universe is seen as eternal and souls are reincarnated according to how people live during their lifetimes. There is no progress in this view except for individual souls in the cycle of birth and rebirth.

Second, there is the *biblical-Augustinian view*. This view builds on the self-revelation of God to Israel, which culminated in Jesus Christ. The period of history we now live in is the period between the first and second comings of Christ. It is the time for the preaching of the gospel of Jesus Christ to the entire world. We bear witness to the kingdom, but we do not bring it into being for that is the work of Christ. This period of history will come to an end with the second coming of Jesus Christ, who will judge the living and the dead and bring into being the union of Heaven and Earth and the renewal of all things.

Third, there is the *utopian view*. This view can be either secular or religious. It believes that we can build a perfect City of Man, here upon this earth (the Marxist classless society) or a perfect City of God here upon this earth (the kingdom of God). Postmillennialism, the social gospel, liberation theology, and various theocratic experiments from all periods of church history are examples. This view has led to innumerable disasters, bloodshed, and sorrows.

Fourth, there is the *modern idea of progress*. This view sees a continuous and ongoing improvement in the material conditions of life and the increasing self-realization of autonomous individuals. The vision of gradual improvement is modeled on the gradual development of modern science, which is the basis for the technology that gives us material comforts. There is no divine intervention in history, just a continuous development of society by means of immanent forces that will guide us gradually to a greater and greater degree of perfection. As Eugene McCarraher puts it, "Modern political thought rests on the suppression of its redemptive hopes."[29] Just as Augustine perceived the Roman Empire as "a dim archetype" of the church, William Cavanaugh views the modern nation-state as a false copy of the body of Christ that offers an alternative soteriology in the form of the progressive self-realization of autonomous individuals.[30]

By way of summary, we can say that the essence of liberalism is the freedom of the individual to do whatever he or she wants. Freedom becomes a first principle—an idol. But this concept of freedom is not the same as the Christian understanding of freedom. It is actually a heretical distortion of it, which views freedom as choice itself—freedom without constraint, rather than freedom for the good. Liberalism views human desires as good and the indulging of them as the highest goal of life. Therefore, consumption, not work, is the highest good for a human being. Progress is defined as having more and more individuals empowered to realize themselves through consumption of material goods and services. Progress is guaranteed by the market, which produces wealth, and the state, which redistributes it. Progress goes on forever according to liberalism, and we should not expect, nor do we need, a divine intervention in history.

A BIBLICAL-AUGUSTINIAN
CRITIQUE OF LIBERALISM

How do we as Christians respond to modernity and the liberalism which animates it? How can we live in modern, secular, liberal culture as Christians? How do we bear witness to the gospel of Jesus

Christ in a world that views freedom, desire, consumption, and progress this way? Here are five briefly stated suggestions.

Face Up to Idolatry

First, we must refuse to worship the idol called "the modern state," which has been invented in modernity specifically as a replacement for the public role of the church. The church of Jesus Christ is a public institution that claims the highest loyalty of her members, who are free to live as citizens of any city, state, or empire they happen to be born into insofar, and as long as, that citizenship does not usurp, replace, or take precedence over a Christian's ecclesial identity. To the extent that being a citizen of a nation state involves false worship or disobedience to church law, the Christian is placed in a situation in which persecution and martyrdom may be expected, since disloyalty to Jesus Christ is not a legitimate option for a Christian.

George W. Bush did not invade Iraq in the name of Christianity—he invaded Iraq in the name of freedom and democracy, which is to say, in the name of liberalism. What we need to realize is that liberalism is not tolerant. It is at bottom a matter of will and it is a totalizing discourse just as much as any religion ever was or will be. It is a matter of rational argument and, if that fails, cruise missiles. Liberalism is a religion in plain speech—and it demands blood sacrifice. The blood of young Americans killed in battle is shed for the goddess Liberty and she requires regular sacrifice. The blood of Iraqis killed in the invasion of their country is a sacrifice offered to the goddess Liberty to prove our devotion to spreading her message of "freedom."

As Christians in a post-Christian, Constantinian world, we must worship the God of the Scriptures who does not require blood sacrifice from us. He calls us to put our faith in him and in his Son Jesus Christ, whose death on the cross is the end of sacrifice. The doctrine of creation is an ontology of peace, but it only makes sense in an eschatological framework. The world was created good and only disobedience and self-will brought sin into it and cut human beings off from their creator. The gospel teaches us that, one day, history will culminate in a marvelous divine intervention in which the kingdoms of this world will be transformed into the kingdom of God. Both creation and new creation are historical and we should not expect time and space to end with the second coming. But we should expect the second coming to occur before the kingdom of God can come in its fullness.

Resist the Culture of Death

Even though we know that we cannot (and should not) create a Christian society or imagine that we can bring in the kingdom of God by political efforts, we should recognize the value of trying to prevent people from exercising the will to power in destructive ways. We must boldly proclaim the truth of the gospel of Jesus Christ to our culture and call everyone to repentance, faith, and conversion. But our most important calling is to resist the powers and live our lives without reliance upon violence and death as ways of solving our problems. Insofar as the church buys into the false religion of individual freedom as freedom from constraint, the church will fail in her mission of proclaiming the gospel. We must preach that freedom is found in Jesus Christ alone at all times using words whenever necessary.

We know that, to the world, the Christian message can often seem to be condemning, constricting, and insulting to a "world come of age," which has been "liberated" by modern technology. But we must not be intimidated by the gods of this age who are not real gods; nor can we allow the fear of rejection or mockery to make us trim our message to fit the prejudices of the times, as liberal Protestants constantly tend to do.

We must confront the culture of death at many points, not just on the important issue of unjust war. We must also affirm the sanctity of life from conception to natural death and the right to life as the basic right on which all other human rights depend. We as a culture have a strong tendency to attempt to solve all sorts of social problems with an act of violence. We must say to ourselves, to each other, and to all who will listen that violence is not the solution to our problems—it is the problem! It is no more the solution to the problem of unplanned pregnancy than it is to the problem of how to deal with criminals or with disputes between neighbors. Jesus Christ is the Way, the Truth, and the Life, and he calls us to renounce violence, take up our cross, and follow him.

We must not shy away from the strange paradox of the gospel, that we only find eternal life when we are prepared to lose it for the sake of Christ. We must proclaim that freedom lies on the far side of obedience and that all attempts to pretend that humans are not answerable to God ends in slavery and despair.

Cultivate Desire For God

In a world full of unfocused and out-of-control desires, we must not fall into the trap of appearing to be preaching a Buddhist-like message that extinguishing all desire is the ideal. Apologists for modernity love to portray Christians as cranky old kill-joys who hate pleasure and just want to make everyone else as miserable as they are, but this tired old caricature has outlived its usefulness.

We need to ensure that we are heard to say two crucially important things about desire. First, we need to stress that we were created by God as erotic beings whose desires ultimately lead us to God—unless something goes wrong. Second, we need to say that something *has* gone drastically wrong with human desiring, with the result that the goodness of desire has been perverted by human sinfulness. We need to preach that people need not less but more desire.

As C. S. Lewis put it, we fool around with minor things like food and sex when we have been created for eternity and for God. The true liberation of desire is not the autonomous self indulging its appetites but participating in goodness through revelation and learning to discipline desire by turning it toward God. When our greatest desire is for God, all other desires fall naturally into their subordinate and proper places. And when that happens, we find ourselves able to exclaim with the Psalmist: "O Lord how I love your law!" (Ps. 119:97 NIV)

Make Peace With Nature

Liberalism's destructive tendencies can be seen in many areas of modern life as human beings try to conquer, master, manipulate, and overcome both human and non-human nature. We can see it in air and water pollution, the destruction of biodiversity, global warming, industrial agriculture and the decline of the family farm, the sexual revolution, reproductive technologies, abortion, euthanasia, eugenics, the dissolution of family ties, population decline, and the inability of parts of the Western world even to reproduce themselves, the breakdown of community, loneliness and suicide, the degradation of work into meaningless repetitive activity, the increasing bureaucratization of life, degrading music and entertainment fixated on sex and violence, the total commercialization of life and the ubiquity of advertising. The list could go on and on, but the point is that modern, Western society is at war with nature and that liberalism is at the root of the conflict.

We must humbly confess that this is *our* society that is at war with nature and that we are part of that society. Let judgment begin at the house of God! Let us *show* the way to a future in which limits are accepted and desires disciplined so that we can live in harmony with our environment and in a sustainable manner.

Let us also demonstrate how it is possible to live at peace with our own bodies and to control them with the self-restraint that is the foundation of marriage and family life. Let us reunite what modernity has put asunder, namely procreation and sexual union. Let us turn away from the trend to make human reproduction a matter of technology in such a way that it is torn from the embrace of lovers and put into a sterile laboratory and treated as an impersonal, technical act of making, rather than a personal act of procreation.

This means struggling to extricate ourselves from the consumerism that is destroying us. The church is in such dramatic trouble in the West because we are so enslaved not by capitalism, defined as the private ownership of the means of production, but by the lust within us for luxury, pleasure, and ease of life that fuels the capitalist machine. All forms of Marxist critique mislead us at this point because they all train us to identify external structures as the source of evil and oppression and to ignore our own perverted desires. Liberal theology that brushes aside what the Christian tradition has called "original sin" in favor of seeing sin as originating from unjust social structures has fallen into the Pelagian heresy that the church has battled since Augustine and that has become dominant in modernity. If we ask why the church is growing and healthy in Africa today and shrinking and anemic in the West, we are asking the right question. Do we have the courage to give the answer Stanley Hauerwas gives in his commentary on Matthew? He writes:

> The parable of the sower is not often considered by those concerned with the loss of the church's status and membership in Europe and America, but it is hard to imagine any text more relevant to the situation of churches in the West. Why we are dying seems very simple. It is hard to be a disciple and be rich.[31]

Is it not because of our wealth, our luxury, and our resulting sense of superiority and self-satisfaction that we see no need for God? Are we not blinded by wealth, as were so many of the individuals Jesus encountered in the Gospels?

Our problem is, How can we preach what we do not practice? I believe that God will raise up among us witnesses to evangelical poverty—individuals and communities who accept voluntary poverty for the sake of preaching the gospel to the rich—and that it will be these individuals and communities who will preach the gospel with power. Only by forsaking wealth and power can we preach the converting power of the gospel today in North America to the rich (which in this context is nearly everyone). We need to be saved from the corrupting power of greed, the addiction to shopping, and the need for the constant stimulation of new things.

Again Marxism cannot help you, because Marxism lives by the same covetousness as does consumer capitalism. Marxism uses the demon of envy to fuel class warfare and promises the same endless abundance as capitalism even as it accepts the inherent goodness of insatiable desire for material things. But Christianity makes social justice rest, not on envy, but on solidarity of rich and poor within the church. Christianity can preach that the rich should give their money away because riches are only a snare anyway. Christianity says that if we have food and clothes, we should be content (1 Tim. 6:6-8). In Christianity, things are a means to ends, not ends in themselves.

Redefine Progress

When it comes to the doctrine of progress, some serious de-mythologizing is in order. Progress sounds good, but there is just one little problem. Progress does not happen. Human nature remains pretty much the same today as it was in the Middle Ages or the Roman Empire or the Old Testament. Human beings are fallen creatures, and to imagine that becoming technologically clever necessarily makes us any more just or self-controlled or obedient to the natural law and to the law of God is just wishful thinking.

Surely, one would think, the myth of progress could not have survived the Holocaust. Surely, there would not be even one reflective person left in the world who would affirm the myth of progress after watching the most scientifically advanced country in Europe, the cradle of the Reformation, the world leader in philosophy, art, and culture, descend into savagery and demonic evil. Yet politicians are eager to be known as progressives, the American Dream lives on, and the masses are willing to believe that the heirs of Bach and Dostoevesky are progressing to greater and greater levels through rock music and "reality" television. How can this be?

People today believe in progress for one simple reason—because they have accepted an overly narrow definition of progress. Progress occurs whenever the gross national product expands, real income goes up, and the standard of living rises. It does not matter if the greatest contribution to the rise in the gross national product comes from increased food production or from increased military spending. It does not matter if suicide rates are up as long as people have more spending power. It does not matter if churches are empty as long as shopping malls are full. Progress is material progress—period. If you narrow it down to nothing but material progress, it is true that we as a civilization have more rich people, and richer rich people, than any other civilization that preceded us.

But it that sufficient reason to call us more advanced than any other civilization? We have used nuclear weapons. We are pushing the ecological limits of the planet in our narrow-minded drive for profit and pleasure, and there are increasing signs that our so-called "progress" is soon going to come to a crashing halt. Yet, the truth is that many of us simply don't care. We want to enjoy the party while it lasts—eat, drink, and be merry, we say, for tomorrow we die. "As it was in the days of Noah, so shall it be in the days of the Son of man" (Matt. 24:38-39 NIV).

There will be no heaven on earth built by science, technology, and human wisdom. This is the dream that always turns into a nightmare. The new heavens and the new earth will come into being only when the Lord Jesus Christ returns in glory to set up his glorious and ever-lasting kingdom and between us and that kingdom lies the day of judgment. There is no kingdom without the king and there is no jus-tice without judgment. There is no shortcut to utopia, and this con-sumer society in which human desire is running out of control is threatening to destroy the good earth upon which we live. Progress is a myth invented by marketers and spin doctors who want to con-vince us that we can satisfy the insatiable with the finite.

CONCLUSION

I want to summarize what I have said as concisely as possible. If our goal is to become a true peace church, then all that I have tried to say can be boiled down to this maxim: *If we want peace, we must accept limits.* To acknowledge ourselves as creatures is to acknowledge that we have natural limits—limits to our knowledge, limits to our power, limits to our lifespans, and limits on our ability to change na-ture. To acknowledge limits is to embrace freedom as obedience, a hierarchy of desires with desire for God at the peak, the responsibil-ity to work and care for the earth, and the hope of the return of Christ.

The essence of modernity is the refusal of limits. Modernity pro-claims that humans are god-like beings who can change themselves and the environment at will. It sees all nature as merely raw material to be shaped according to our will. This is why the theology of modernity is the heretical doctrine that freedom means freedom from constraint of any kind. This is what binds together the sexual revolu-tion, eugenics, reproductive technologies, environmental degrada-tion, the exploitation of the poor by global capitalism, and Western consumerism—all are forms of human activity that disregard all limits, whether natural or revealed. They exhibit what Augustine called the *libido dominandi* (the lust for domination).

   To reject the modern notion of freedom is to embrace limits in the form of God's Word. So I conclude that, if there is to be any real hope for Western culture—any future for our civilization—it can only come from a return to, and embrace of, law. It is, perhaps, somewhat ironic that, for a liberal culture, it turns out that the good news is the message of God's law embedded in creation and written in Scripture. For an age like ours, law is gospel.

NOTES

   1. Stanley Hauerwas and William Willimon, *Resident Aliens* (Nashville: Abingdon Press, 1989), 16.

   2. See the essays in Peter L. Berger, ed., *The Desecularization of the World: Resurgent Religion and World Politics* (Grand Rapids: Wm. B. Eerdmans Publishing Co., 1999).

   3. For a helpful argument against the myth of the disenchantment of the modern world and for the sacral nature of modern liberalism, see Eugene McCarraher, "The Enchanted City of Man: The State and the Market in Augustinian Perspective" in *Augustine and Politics*, ed. J. Doody, K. L. Hughes, and K. Paffenroth (Lanham, Md.: Lexington Books, 2005), 261-96.

   4. See William Cavanaugh, "A Fire Strong Enough to Consume the House: The Wars of Religion and the Rise of the State," *Modern Theology* 11:4 (October 1995): 397-420.

   5. For an excellent description of the secular in St. Augustine's thought, see R. A. Markus *Saeculum: History and Theology in the Theology of St. Augustine* (New York: Cambridge University Press, 1970). For an updating and defense of his original thesis in the light of recent trends, see *Christianity and the Secular* (Notre Dame, Ind.: University of Notre Dame Press, 2006).

   6. Emmet Kennedy, *Secularism and Its Opponents from Augustine to Solzhenitsyn* (New York: Palgrave Macmillian, 2006), 1-2.

   7. Norman O. Brown, as quoted by Eugene McCarraher, "The Enchanted City of Man," in *Augustine and Politics*, 286.

   8. Solzhenitsyn discussed this theme in his Templeton Address, London Guildhall, May 10, 1983, "Godlessness, the First Step to the Gulag." For the text of the speech, see *The Solzhenitsyn Reader: New and Essential Writings 1947-2005*, ed. Edward E. Ericson and Daniel J. Mahoney (Wilmington, Del.: Intercollegiate Studies Institute, 2009). For a good discussion of this speech in the context of Solzhenitsyn's thought in this period, see Joseph Pearce, *Solzhenitsyn: A Soul in Exile* (Grand Rapids, Mich.: Baker Book House, 2001), 247-8.

   9. There are, of course, various kinds of conservatism, even if one does not regard Neoconservatism as a legitimate expression of conservatism. Unfortunately, space does not permit us to differentiate between them and consider which kind is most compatible with Christianity. Although it is true that conservatism is in eclipse today, it is also true that Western liberalism is now in serious trouble due to its internal contradictions. This essay as a whole may

be understood to be a modest attempt to clear the ground for the development of a new form of post-secular Augustinian conservatism, which can serve as an alternative to liberalism during the long sad denouement of the modern West and beyond. Given the internal contradictions of liberalism, which this essay attempts to expose, the future of the West, in my view, depends on a recovery and updating of a viable form of Augustinian Conservatism. Contributors to such a project include: G. K. Chesterton, C. S. Lewis, J. R. R. Tolkein, Alexander Solzhenitsyn, Alasdair MacIntyre, Hans Urs von Balthasar, Pope John Paul II, and Pope Benedict XVI.

10. This is one of the weaknesses of Francis Fukuyama's thesis about the "End of History." See *The End of History and the Last Man* (New York: Avon Books, 1992). Fukuyama portrays 1989 as the triumph of liberal democracy over Marxism without giving sufficient attention to the ways in which late twentieth-century liberal democracy itself has been influenced by Marxism. It was only by taking up the egalitarian impulses of Marxism into itself in the New Deal that capitalism was able to survive and triumph. Liberal democracy is an attempt to synthesize the equality principle of Rousseau with the Anglo-Saxon principle of individual freedom. Of course, the most important failing of Fukuyama's thesis was the hubris that Western culture is permanent and final, rather than ephemeral and destined to crumble in time like all the other empires of history. It is worth noting that his mistake has been made by apologists for every major empire in the past as well. An essential trait of every major world empire is to believe the lie of its own finality, which is why the sack of Rome, "the eternal city," in 410 AD was such a traumatic event for those who lived at that time.

11. Lesslie Newbigin, *Foolishness to the Greeks: The Gospel and Western Culture* (Grand Rapids: Wm. B. Eerdmans, 1986), 27.

12. Karl Barth, *Church Dogmatics I/2,* trans. Geoffrey W. Bromiley et. al., ed. Geoffrey W. Bromiley and Thomas F. Torrance (Edinburgh: T. and T. Clark, 1057-77), 759.

13. Pope John Paul II, *Veritatis Splendor* [The Splendor of Truth], first issued in 1993 (Boston: Pauline Books and Media, 2003), section 72. The italics are in the original.

14. Louis Groarke, "What is Freedom? Why Christianity and Theoretical Liberalism Cannot Be Reconciled," *Heythrop Journal* 47 (2006), 257-74. See also his book: *The Good Rebel: Understanding Freedom and Morality* (Madison, N.J.: Fairleigh Dickinson University Press, 2002).

15. Interestingly, although Dawkins promotes science as the alternative to religion, his real objections to Christianity actually are liberal and political in nature. In his hands, science becomes a political/religious ideology useful for fighting against Christianity.

16. Groarke, "What is Freedom?, 259-60.

17. John Rawls, *A Theory of Justice* (Cambridge, Mass.: Harvard University Press, 1971).

18. Groarke, "What is Freedom?, 263.

19. Groarke, "What is Freedom?, 266. The italics are mine.

20. Groarke, "What is Freedom?, 267. Italics are mine. See David C. Schindler's excellent treatment of how this point is made in Augustine's writings in: "Freedom Beyond Our Choosing: Augustine on the Will and Its Ob-

jects" in *Augustine and Politics*, 67-96.

21. David C. Schindler, "Freedom Beyond Choosing: Augustine on the Will and Its Objects," in *Augustine and Politics*, 91.

22. For an illuminating discussion of how modernity has been influenced by some of the same Stoic and Pelagian ideas that were vigorously opposed by Augustine, see Michael Hanby, *Augustine and Modernity* (New York: Routledge, 2003).

23. David C. Schindler, "Freedom Beyond Our Choosing: Augustine on the Will and Its Objects," in *Augustine and Politics*, 85.

24. Christopher Lasch, *The True and Only Heaven: Progress and Its Critics*, (New York: W. W. Norton and Co., 1991), 22.

25. Lasch, *The True and Only Heaven*, 52ff.

26. For an account of desire from an Augustinian perspective, see chapter one of William Cavanaugh, *Being Consumed: Economics and Christian Desire* (Grand Rapids: Wm. B. Eerdmans, 2007).

27. For a profound and sophisticated alternative to this position, see the writings of John Paul II, especially his early book, *Love and Responsibility*, trans. H. T. Willetts (San Francisco: Ignatius Press, 1981), and his later Wednesday Catecheses delivered as pope and collected in *Man and Woman He Created Them: A Theology of the Body*, trans. and ed. Michael Waldstein (Boston: Pauline Books and Media, 2006).

28. Christopher Lasch, *The True and Only Heaven*, 515.

29. Eugene McCarraher, "The Enchanted City of Man," 271.

30. William T. Cavanaugh, "The City: Beyond Secular Parodies" in *Radical Orthodoxies*, ed. J. Millbank, C. Pickstock, and Graham Ward (New York: Routledge, 1999), 182ff.

31. Stanley Hauerwas, *Brazos Theological Commentary on the Bible: Matthew* (Grand Rapids: Brazos Press, 2006), 129.

Chapter 3

KEYNOTING THE KEYS: UNLOCKING THE GATES TO THE KINGDOM OF GOD

Sharon L. Baker

THE KEYNOTE

As a keynote speaker at a Preaching Peace conference held at Messiah College in August 2008, I felt responsible to note some topic of key relevance, to note the keys of the conference, so to speak, for those listening to the keynote address, and now for those of you reading it. Consequently, I am going to note some very specific keys that I hope will prove relevant to those working toward peace in a world constantly at war, largely with the support of the church. These keys are the keys to the kingdom of God.

In reflecting upon these keys, however, I became aware of the need to note the idea of the key itself. If I am to keynote the keys, what are they? What is a key? Am I talking about keys in regard to music, where I would then need to sing on key, or to play in the key of, say, C? Am I talking about keys in the sense of enclosure, of locking something up, barring access to it, keeping it hidden from prying eyes? Or am I speaking about a key that decodes a secret encryption, that reveals or unlocks a previously undeciphered message? If I am keynoting the keys to the kingdom of God, maybe I am talking about the church—a church key.

I don't feel comfortable using that nomenclature, though, since a church key is used to open a can of beer, and we all know that Anabaptists don't drink beer in front of each other! Consequently, I will switch to the Greek and use the Greek key *ecclesia* or the "ecclesiastical keys" instead. Please take note, then, that in this second of three keynote addresses, I am keynoting the keys to the kingdom of God—ecclesiastical keys that crack the code to "being a peace church in a world at war."

One crucial difficulty confronts us, however. As Jesus praises Peter for disclosing him as the Messiah, he hands Peter the keys to the kingdom but does not disclose the manner of their use, the map they decode, the locks they unlock, or the music they play. The very keys that are to decrypt, reveal, unlock, and open up for us the secrets of the kingdom of God remain encrypted, concealed, veiled in secrecy. Rather than congratulating himself for a correct answer that guarantees him the position of progenitor of the papacy, Peter might have served the church more advantageously by asking a few key questions concerning the nature of the keys that Jesus gave to him. He did not. As a result, the keys that disclose to us the kingdom of God have themselves not been disclosed to us. We are left behind to speculate on what they are, to find the key to the keys. Sometimes the attempt at deciphering what something *is* begins more productively by attempting to decipher what it is *not*—what the keys are *not*—a negative key-ology, if you will.

Contemplating what the keys are *not* reminds me of a painting by Mark Tansey, "The Key." It portrays our first parents' expulsion from the Garden of Eden. The towering gate and its enormous stone pillars replicate those crafted by Lorenzo Ghiberti for the baptistery of the cathedral in Florence, Italy. Michelangelo supposedly called them the Gates of Paradise. At the top of the pillar on the left a stone angel stands guard with a sword, barring entry into the garden. Crowning the right pillar a serpent coils its way around a tree branch.

The gates are locked tight. A frustrated man, we'll call him Adam, with head bent in dismay, leans with one hand on the gate, holding in the other hand a large keychain. It appears that three keys dangle from it, useless. Behind him, the woman, we'll call her Eve, in a slinky evening gown, waits with hand-on-hip-foot-tapping-impatience. You can't see her face, but even a scant knowledge of female body language tells you that she is not keeping her exasperation to herself. The keys do not fit the lock; they do not unlock the gates. Without a divine locksmith to re-key the bolt, the hapless couple is locked out of the Garden and cannot get back in. They stand east of Eden, looking from the outside world into the paradise that God had prepared for them.

The keys Adam holds in his hand will never open *those* gates—they are *not* the keys to paradise. Yet he holds the keys, and keys are meant to unlock something locked, to open up something that had previously remained closed and undisclosed to us.

Is it possible that God never meant for the man and the woman to return to paradise but instead prepared something new, something surprising, something now at hand, possibly something unlocked and opened up by the keys that the first the man and woman, then Peter, and now we, hold in our hand? Might those three keys unlock the gates not back into Eden but into the kingdom of God? Do they disclose to us the way of salvation, the way leading toward ultimate restoration with God—which is the key message of the Bible? If so, we can assume that the keys Jesus gave to Peter were not meant for recapitulation into a previous state of innocence, but were meant instead to unlock, to open up, to disclose the way for a new creation, a nation of those living in tune with the keys of the kingdom of God.[1]

THE THREE KEYS OF THE KINGDOM

Although we might assume that the keys to do not fit the locks that would gain us entry back into paradise, no indisputable code exists to help us decrypt the keys of the kingdom. The conundrum of the keys continues to intrigue us. There's nothing I like more than the intrigue of a mystery other than the satisfaction of solving one. I suggest, therefore, that we allow this alluring enigma to elude us no longer and, as a thought experiment, make a speculative attempt to decode the keys.

Since three keys appear to hang on "Adam's" keychain in the Tanzey painting, I want to propose three keys that may possibly correspond to the keys of the kingdom that the church has in her possession. Our speculative thought experiment prompts the imagery of three keys functioning like those of a bank vault that requires three separate keys used in consecutive order to unbolt three locks on a heavy stainless steel door guarding the bank's most precious commodity. Analogously, the three keys of the kingdom turn consecutively in combination with three locks to unbar the way into the kingdom of God, releasing its immeasurable treasures for all those who enter in.

To unlock the mystery of the first key, a quick search of Scripture reveals a crucial component for life in God's kingdom. In a conversation with an attorney bent on catching him in a legal loophole (quoting Deut. 6:5), Jesus clues us in to two key commandments that sum up the entire law and the prophets. The lawyer asks him,

> "Teacher, which is the greatest commandment in the Law?" And [Jesus] said to him, "'You shall love the Lord your God with all your heart, and with all your soul, and with all your mind.' This is the great and foremost commandment. The second is like it, 'You shall love your neighbor as yourself.' On these two commandments depend the whole Law and the Prophets."

Love, therefore, sums up the entire law and forms the foundation for the gospel message.

The apostle Paul also emphasizes the significance of love to the law, writing that "love does no wrong to a neighbor, therefore, love is the fulfilling of the law" (Rom. 13:10). When, out of love, Hosea seeks to redeem his adulterous wife and when Joseph refuses to condemn his pregnant betrothed, they are not breaking the Law but fulfilling the law of love.[2] The ancient Jewish philosopher Philo singles out these two commandments as the ones that, like a keystone in an arch, bear the entire burden of all the other commandments. He says: "God asks nothing . . . difficult, but only . . . just to love him," and the law "stands preeminent in enjoining fellowship and humanity."[3]

In Mark 12:34, Jesus implies that when we love God and others, we enter very close to the kingdom of God. The love of God for us, and the love of God in us, draws us near not only to the kingdom but to God and to each other. John 3:16 and 1 John 4:7-12, for example, affirm that the divine love for us aroused in God the desire to open the way for our salvation through Jesus Christ.

Consequently, the love of God breathes and kindles within us a love for others. In fact, Jesus gives us the key to revealing God's love to the world, exhorting the disciples, and therefore us, to love one another as he has loved them. By such love, all people will know we are followers of Jesus as we reflect the alluring beauty of God's love for all to see. That love invites people from every race, nation, society, and economic position to become members of God's kingdom of love and justice.[4] Jesus exhorts us not only to love each other but also to love our enemies. Paul tells us that without love we are bankrupt, obnoxious noise-makers, zeros. Love—authentic, unselfish, long-suffering, abiding love—endures forever. When all is said and done, when all is dead, decayed, gone up in smoke, love remains—only love.[5] Jesus gives us the key that unlocks the gates to unlimited love.[6]

Jesus confronts evil with no weapon other than love and exhorts us to do the same, to overcome evil with love.

In our decryption of the keys of the kingdom, therefore, it appears that the first key dangling from our keychain is love—love of God, love of neighbor, love of self, and even love of enemies. With the *key of love* in hand, and the love of God in heart, we can unlock the first bolted latch into the kingdom and release upon the world the uncoercive force of unlimited love that Jesus promises even the gates of hell cannot overpower (Matt. 16:18).[7]

We insert the key of love into the first lock securing the gates into the kingdom of God. The first bolt opens. The next key linked onto the kingdom key ring springs from love and is empowered by love. According to the well-known theologian Miroslav Volf, the key to the good news that unlocks and, combined with the other two keys, opens the gates into the presence of God is forgiveness—*forgiveness* kindled by God's love, I submit, solves the mystery of the second key.[8]

John the evangelist and Paul the apostle corroborate our conjecture. John asserts that God first loved then forgave (1 John 4:9-10; John 3:16). According to Paul, love motivated God to forgive even while we were still enemies—quite a deconstruction of retributive justice (Rom. 5:8, 10). Love unleashed fosters forgiveness, and forgiveness looses us from slavery to sin, and sets us free to enter into relationship with God.

The biblical message pinpoints forgiveness of sin as the way to enter into the kingdom of heaven. For instance, in the Old Testament, deeply influenced by their conception of a God impassioned with lovingkindness, who is always ready and willing to forgive, and who delights in mercy, the Hebrew people testified to the extravagance of divine forgiveness. The pages of the book of Psalms practically drip with the tears of those who freely beseech God for forgiveness—and receive it. Isaiah, Jeremiah, Amos, and Hosea sing the praises of a God who is slow to anger and abounding in lovingkindness, whose mercies are new every morning, who generously forgives transgressions and redeems the undeserving.[9]

The New Testament as well testifies to the centrality of forgiveness, giving us a glimpse into the lives of Zacchaeus, the woman at the well, the paralytic lowered through the roof, the woman caught in adultery—freely given forgiveness, all in opposition to the legalistic interpretation of the Law that freely rendered retribution.[10] Throughout his ministry, and even as he hangs on the cross, Jesus looses human beings from the bondage of sin and opens up to all peoples and nations the gates to heaven with the key of forgiveness.

The words of Jesus from the cross provide a clue to the importance of forgiveness.[11] Struggling in the throes of death he utters a brief prayer to God, "Father forgive them, for they do not know what they do" (Luke 23:34), and then to the thief on cross next to him, he scandalizes righteous eavesdroppers by saying, "truly I say to you, today you shall be with me in paradise" (23:43).[12] The thief experiences the closing of the door on earthly existence while at the same time, through love and forgiveness, Jesus opens the door leading to life with God.

In these instances and others, Jesus breaks into human history and brings from heaven to earth the kingdom of God with the key of forgiveness. This key of the kingdom unlocks and opens, it unbinds and loosens. Forgiveness liberates us from the prison of an otherwise irreversible past and transforms the future from one of condemnation and retribution to an open future of redemption and reconciliation.[13] Unlimited, repetitive forgiveness is the second of three keys that open the triple locking mechanism into the kingdom of God.

Forgiveness alone, however, does not completely unlock the gates leading into the kingdom of God. One more key remains that unlocks the last bolt, that deciphers the last remaining code into the kingdom—*the key of reconciliation*. This third key is the culmination of forgiveness. In fact, without forgiveness, reconciliation would not be possible; and without reconciliation no one could enter into a restored relationship with God.[14] I suggest, therefore, that reconciliation opens the last lock into the kingdom and makes possible the redemption of our past and the restoration of our future as we enter forever into the loving presence of God.

"To reconcile" means "to make peace between enemies." Romans 5:10 confirms this definition, stating that "while we were still enemies we were reconciled to God through the death of Jesus." I believe we may safely say that reconciliation is the purpose of God in salvation history.[15] The repetitive appeal in the Gospels to repent of our sin and to forgive others theirs emphasizes the importance of reconciliation. We repent and forgive to reconcile with God and others. Our worship of God takes second place to reconciling with a brother or sister.[16]

Paul reiterates the vital importance of reconciliation, declaring that the ministry of Jesus and now our ministry as ambassadors of Christ is reconciliation. It epitomizes the crux of the entire gospel message, the goal of the life, death, and resurrection of Jesus, and the purpose of our participation in the kingdom of God. Through Jesus and now through his body the church, the voice of the Spirit calls all persons to be reconciled to God, to work as ambassadors of Christ, ministers of reconciliation, entreating others to be reconciled to God as well.[17] With a turn of this key the final bolt slides open, releasing us from death to life, from revenge to restoration. We who were once bound by death are now loosed by the keys of love, forgiveness, and reconciliation, the keys of the kingdom, into a future of restored relationship with God.[18]

The three keys in combination trigger a chain reaction of unlocked bolts. Love opens the lock to forgiveness. Forgiveness unlocks the way to reconciliation. Reconciliation releases us from Hades and Death, gains us entry into the kingdom, resulting in complete restoration to God. These three keys of the kingdom dangle not uselessly but purposefully, held together in perfect harmony by a key ring that resounds in tune with a paean of praise that never ends.

THE JUSTICE OF THE KEYS

Now that we have theoretically solved the mystery of the keys, only the enigma of the key ring remains encrypted. Allow me one more exercise in speculation as I suggest that divine justice serves as the keychain that holds intact the three keys of the kingdom of God. Some may argue that to link these three keys to divine justice casts God as a susceptible softy who lets the guilty get away with murder. At first glance, it appears so; but a more intent gaze into the heart of divine justice discloses something more profound and, I claim, more in tune with God's character as revealed through Jesus Christ.

According to Howard Zehr, whether or not biblical justice focuses on retribution or restoration remains an important issue, one that lies at the heart of our understanding about God's nature, character, and actions in redemptive history.[19] Biblical interpretation always arises from our own presuppositions, history, and social context. The way we view justice often stems from our own interpretations of God—if we interpret Scripture as mainly focusing on God's wrath and punishment of sin, we will likely interpret justice as more retributive. If our biblical interpretation of God places greater focus on divine love and grace, our views of justice will likely be reconciling and restorative.

The Old Testament often repudiates retributive notions of justice and, instead, sanctions restorative justice. God rejects retributive justice when Cain, who deserved the death penalty for killing his brother, is shown mercy; Hosea rejects retribution when his wife, who commits adultery, is spared death by stoning. The prophet

Amos "points his prophetic finger" at justice and declares that God does not desire our festivals and sacrifices, our loud songs and solemn assemblies, but rather, God longs for justice to flow like water over the land (Amos 5:24).

The imagery of flowing streams of fresh water to describe justice is noteworthy. Water is a rare and precious commodity in the communities of the Middle East. Particularly rare, almost non-existent, are streams that continually flow through the arid land. Water provides and ensures that life in the desert will continue—no water, no life. Justice, like water, is pro-life. Water, especially that in the imagery of Amos as a perennial, ever-flowing stream, restores the dry ground and parched throats to life, satisfying the longing of the land and of the thirsty inhabitants. In other words, the imagery of justice as a continual flowing stream over the land imposes upon us a beautiful picture of something redemptive, restorative, and life giving that satisfies the longing of those in need. God's justice, therefore, acts like a stream that flows continually, repeating over and over again redemptive life-giving activity, a repetition of justice flowing along like life-sustaining water over the land.[20]

Interpreting divine justice through the lens of Jesus, of his life, teachings, death, and resurrection, challenges retribution and paints a picture of justice that reconciles and restores people to God and to others. For instance, Jesus specifically rejects retributive justice in Matthew 5 when he instructs us to turn the other cheek, to go the extra mile, and to love our enemies. Jesus always seems to "err" on the side of grace, serving justice not by exacting retributive, tit for tat, or *quid pro quo* exchanges, but by sacrificing the exchange, the payment in kind, to reveal a different kind of justice, a justice that gives freely out of love.[21]

The God of Jesus does not demand the proverbial eye-for-an-eye form of justice. Jesus deconstructs traditional forms of economy driven justice by paying the workers in the vineyard the same wages even though some worked longer than others.[22] In proclaiming the kingdom of God, Jesus preached justice. He "showed [a] distrust of long robes and religious power,"[23] exerting all of his energies, his entire life, death, and resurrection, into remedying social injustice, into standing on the side of justice by standing on the side of the marginalized, the widow, the orphan, the diseased, and the social outcast. Instead of strengthening the bars that hold us captive to violence and the cycle of retributive justice, God opens the way for peace and restoration through unlimited, boundless divine love, forgiveness, and reconciliation.[24]

That being the case, the key of unlimited love has a place on the keychain of divine justice. Despite common conceptions, justice and love do not hang in tension as opposites. When viewed from the perspective of divine love, the standards of justice are driven by a desire for restoration, relationship, and harmony with God and others.[25] In other words, divine reconciling justice is love in action that seeks to make things right, to reconcile with God and others. N. T. Wright rightly professes that "God's love is the driving force of [God's] justice."[26] John Dominic Crossan sings in the same key when he uses the analogy of the body to explain the relationship of love to justice. He writes that "[j]ustice is the body of love, love the soul of justice. Justice is the flesh and love, love is the spirit of justice. When they are separated, we have a moral corpse. Justice without love is brutality."[27]

The biblical witness supports the connection of love to justice when in Leviticus 19:17-18 it exhorts the faithful to love their neighbors by foregoing vengeance and grudge bearing, forgiving them instead.[28] In Deuteronomy 10:18, God serves justice by loving the alien, or in postmodern theological terms, the wholly other. In a profoundly beautiful passage (Isa. 30:18), God waits on high, longingly, lovingly, and like a spurned lover, aches to shower graciousness upon us—*because God is a God of justice*. The justice of God takes place as an event of hospitality shown to the stranger, as love offered freely without expectation of return, as forgiveness shown even to those who do not deserve it, as the transformation of lives that experience the healing touch of God.

Medieval theologian Peter Abelard too speaks of justice in harmony with mercy and with love. He says that "justified [forgiven] for free means that you are justified not because of your outstanding achievements or gains but thanks to God's mercy who was the first to love us" and observes that "in the time of mercy it is God's justice that he gives us and through which we are justified and the name for it is love.[29] For Abelard the justice of God, through love and in mercy, results in the forgiveness of sin without condition or compensation.

That being the case, the key of unlimited forgiveness hangs on the keychain of justice as well. If biblical justice seeks to make things right, to reconcile and then to restore relationships, forgiveness of sin is complicit with justice in that it moves us toward that goal. The Jewish notion of sin portrays a picture of shackles, something that binds us, that paralyzes us, that demands punishment through payback, and that locks us up in bondage to a debt. Forgiveness of sin, therefore, is the opposite of retribution. It means "to release," "to break the shackles of sin," much like a crippled person is healed and released from illness.

When Jesus told the crippled man lowered through the roof that his sins were forgiven, he meant that he was healthy again, not crippled, not held down or impaired with the shackles that locked him up in his handicap. When Jesus said, "your sins are forgiven," the gates to his paralytic prison were unlocked. He was released from the bondage of sin and the burden of suffering retribution. He could walk in God's forgiving justice.[30]

In the same way, God releases us through forgiveness from the endless rhythm of operating on the basis of a tit for a tat . In English, the word *forgive* means "to give away," "to release" something we have on someone else. If retributive justice were served, the offense would be held and brought to account. There would be nothing to give away, nothing to forgive, the debt incurred by the offense would have been paid. Instead, we give away the debt by forgiving it; we release someone from the debt that we have every right to collect.[31] Jesus was just such a forgiver and healer of bodies and souls. By his potent form of forgiving, by giving away the debt of sin, by not collecting the payment, he shocked and scandalized those intent on payback and who did not want then or now to "let sinners take a walk."[32]

In the teaching of Jesus, we are exhorted through forgiveness to break the cycle of retribution, an eye for an eye, of getting even,. We are to dismiss our debtors by forgiving those who offend us, by releasing them from any requirement to right the wrong, or from the threat of punishment. Catholic philosopher and theologian Jean-Luc Marion contends that we all have in us a spirit of revenge. Rather than forgive without condition, we desire to repay evil with a counter-evil (which makes the need for repayment itself a counter-evil). In revenge or retributive justice, we do not repair the offense. The innocent victim becomes a culprit in return for an unstable balance of "justice." Marion suggests that to quit the cycle of evil, we suffer the initial offense, we absorb the cost. As our example, Jesus absorbs the cost of evil by forgiving it, by refusing to transmit it, by blocking it.

The demand for revenge deprives those who are bound up and imprisoned in the violent cycle of retribution of future reconciliation and of love. Marion writes that "revenge does not reestablish the prior state, but condemns the future to an irremediable impossibility of living; it does not restore the present to its past plentitude, but wrecks the possibility by insulting the future."[33] As soon as a person executes an act of revenge or retribution, the possibility for a restored relationship is lessened. Because God's intent is to restore relationships, Jesus privileged forgiveness rather than retribution and by doing so "threw all human accounting in confusion."[34] These notions of forgiveness resonate also with Hannah Arendt, who argues that forgiveness is the opposite of retribution, which binds us and constrains us, locking us up into a vicious cycle of violence. Forgiveness enables us to unlock and break loose from the cycle of retribution, which is what Jesus modeled and taught through his life, death, and resurrection.[35]

Jesus does not ask us to forgive unconditionally only one time. In following his example, he multiplies forgiveness in an unending cycle, asking us repeatedly to forgive seventy times seven times, which literally means over and over again without calculation or limit.[36] As we continually ask God to forgive us, we enter the kingdom of repetition, of reciprocal forgiving, and we imitate God's re-creative, transforming activity, forgiving what goes amiss in life.[37]

In case we are quick to make an accusation against a cheap form of forgiveness both on our part and God's, I believe that confession remains a positive aspect of forgiveness that keeps the offense in the memory of the offender. We must never forget the offense we commit against the other so that it does not occur again. We can also know, however, that through forgiveness our past is reinterpreted, the offense is matched with God's unconditional forgiveness. B. Keith Putt compares the psychological stance of the forgiven victimizer to Derrida's conception of giving death . . . almost. He claims that as the victimizer feels pain, suffers pain again (repentance) for his sin and no longer desires to be that old self, he gives death to himself, almost, not completely. By "almost" giving death to his old self, "the old self maintains a continuity with the new [self] and, in doing so, retains responsibility for the previous victimizing act."[38] In like manner, Jesus urges the *victim* to give death . . . almost . . . to the self that deserves retribution so that the forgiveness comes from a new self, a self whose heart has changed and is not bound up in the relentless circle of *quid pro quo.* In this manner the gift of death gives the gift of life to the one forgiven.[39]

As a key turns a lock, forgiveness turns us around and opens us to up to *metanoia,* a thinking back, a change of mind, often translated "repentance." Forgiveness requires that we change our minds about demanding retributive justice and that we give up the offense and its restitution. The unlocking of metanoia transforms offense into healing. We relinquish the power of retribution with the power of forgiveness. Consequently, to forgive, we must contemplate the past with a desire to transform it, change our minds, unlock the door keeping guard over our grudge and let the offense go, release the offender from the prison of retained injury, forgive him, in the same way we also want to be released from debt and forgiven.[40]

Forgiveness does not annul the past or condone a sin. Instead, it transforms and heals the past. If God were merely to annul the sin of the past, then the offender would be innocent. God would also annul the need for forgiveness, for there would not be anything left to forgive. Consequently, the sin must be left standing, not forgotten completely, not dismissed or wiped away, but placed under erasure, becoming an "offense without offense."[41] Forgiveness does not revise history so that the sin never occurred, but it "strikes a blow against the *past itself*, releases us, unlocks the gates of the prison of the past so that the weight of the past is lifted. By forgiving, we repair the past by giving it a new meaning and by giving the offender a new beginning.[42]

As a result, the sinner who receives forgiveness, whose past has been repaired and who has received new life, is open to the possibility of metanoia himself, of changing his mind, of receiving a new heart.[43] As forgiven sinners, our pasts are given a new interpretation, one that includes love and reconciliation within its realm. So we see that the past and the event of the sin are not forgotten. In remembering the sin, however, we remember its cleansing through forgiveness so that both the sin and its forgiveness are remembered simultaneously.[44] Just as in great works of art one may detect the artist's errors and subsequent corrections by the faint traces of lines that have been "erased" (interestingly named *pentimenti* or "repentances"), forgiveness of the sin "erases" the errors and covers them with new color, giving vibrancy and new life.

As in the case of Zacchaeus, genuine forgiveness often leads to repentance.[45] Non-retaliatory forgiveness may have profound consequences for the one released from sin with such sacrificial abandon. In fact, the expenditure of forgiveness often results in a response of repentance that proves just as costly. Thomas Aquinas comments that "an equal gift of grace means more to the penitent who deserves punishment than to the innocent who has never incurred it."[46] When a person is brought face to face with his or her sins and experiences the unexpected grace of forgiveness rather than the expected retributive punishment, real repentance may occur. As articulated by Gil Bailie, "Jesus seems to have understood that the only real and lasting contrition occurs, not when one is confronted with one's sin, but when one experiences the gust of grace that makes a loving and forgiving God plausible."[47]As Abelard asserts in his moral exemplary theory of atonement, forgiveness wins a person over through the love inherent in the act and by eliciting the good that resides in one who expects (and deserves) retribution but receives redemption instead. Forgiveness calls to the offender with love, summoning him or her to take responsibility for the offense, to give up the self-involvement, and to repent.[48]

The emphasis of forgiveness is not only on repairing the past but on preparing a better way into the future.[49] Forgiveness redeems the past and makes possible a hopeful future. As Desmond Tutu expresses it, "without forgiveness, there is no future."[50] Forgiveness acts as a catalyst for reconciliation and renewal of a relationship with God and others that generates hope for a new future. Through forgiveness the Spirit of God seeks to transform sinners into saints and saints into service for the furtherance of the kingdom so that unconditional love and forgiveness effectively operate outside the vicious economic circles of retributive "justice." Favoring a pro-forgiveness stance rather than adhering to a pro-payment dogmatics of just deserts is what John Caputo calls a "mad economy" of the kingdom of God, an economy that is no economy but is instead good news, the good news of forgiveness without return, with no conditions attached, of reconciliation, renewal, transformation, and loving service in the name of Jesus.[51]

Such is the gift of God, the kingdom of God, of the mad economy of forgiveness, of justice, and of love that seek to reconcile all creation to God.[52] Paul attests to the madness of God's forgiveness when he writes that in Christ "we have redemption, the forgiveness of sins" (Col. 1:14), and "that God was in Christ reconciling the world to himself, not counting their trespasses against them" (2 Cor. 5:19). How did God reconcile the world to God's self? By not counting our sins against us; in a display of divine reconciling justice God forgives us. Justice holds the keys of love and forgiveness that unlock the first two deadbolts into the freedom of God's kingdom and the restoration of wounded relationships.[53]

The third key of unlimited reconciliation attached to the keychain of divine justice draws upon forgiveness and grows out of the notion that God is reconciling the world to God's self. The very character of the Christian faith is reconciliation leading to restoration. Accordingly, the character of divine justice must also be reconciling and restorative—a notion supported by the biblical witness.[54] For instance, the Law seems more concerned with reconciliation than with retribution. Old Testament scholar Abraham Heschel asserts that biblical justice is "a power that will strike and change, heal and restore, like the mighty stream bringing life to the parched land. . . ."[55]

Moreover, the meaning of justice in the Old Testament is conceived by contemplating God's repeated deliverance of the people from oppression, reconciling and restoring the covenant relationship. Over and over again God seeks to reconcile with offenders with undeserved love, forgiveness, and mercy, despite their actions.[56] In fact, we may even say that the most important ingredient of God's justice is in rescuing, reconciling, and restoring—that reconciling justice forms the keystone of God's hopes and intentions for the world.[57] The prophet Isaiah speaks of divine reconciling justice and the peace it fosters, proclaiming that "justice will dwell in the wilderness, and righteousness abide in the fruitful field. The effect of righteousness will be peace, and the result of righteousness, quietness and trust forever" (Isa. 32:16-20). The prophet Amos reveals God's ultimately redemptive purpose and points out that the people and their nations benefit by living according to God's reconciling justice, because such justice brings peace.[58]

Reconciling rather than retributive justice is also a key theme in the New Testament.[59] New Testament writers do not focus on retributive justice but on a justice that redeems. Whereas in Western terms justice is closely tied to the civil arena of law making and penalties for law breaking, New Testament justice goes beyond the legal sphere into the realm of reconciliation. We see a movement away from the pursuit of retributive justice toward the pursuit of reconciliation that leads to restoration.[60] Jesus implies this movement during his visit to the synagogue in Luke 4:16-20. He reads from Isaiah 61:1-2 saying, "The Spirit of the Lord is upon me because he anointed me to preach the gospel to the poor. He has sent me to proclaim release to the captives, and recovery of sight to the blind, to set free those who are downtrodden, to proclaim the favorable year of the Lord." And he closes the book without finishing the rest of the passage, which reads, "and the day of vengeance of our God." What Jesus leaves out of this reading is revealing. His omission of vengeance acts as a rejection of retributive justice and an acceptance of his commission to bring about the justice of reconciliation and restoration.[61]

Romans 5:8 describes reconciling justice by stating, "God shows divine love for us in that while we were yet sinners Christ died for us," and "while we were enemies we are reconciled to God" (Rom. 5:10). Notice that these verses in Romans reveal the nature of divine justice and take us through our triple-keyed unlocking mechanism. God's love triggers God's forgiveness through the sacrificial death of Jesus, which then paves the way for God's reconciliation.

In addition, the book of Colossians discloses the spirit of divine justice as well. Beginning in the first chapter, God works through Jesus to deliver people from evil and to reconcile them to God and to each other. The life, death, and resurrection of Jesus result in radical reconciliation between normally estranged or segregated groups of people—between God and humanity and then between Jews and Gentiles, slaves and free persons, male and female (Col. 3:11). Divine justice as it appears in Colossians reconciles and restores. It delivers us from the domain of darkness (Col. 1:13); it forgives us and redeems us from sin (Col. 1:14). God's reconciling justice unifies us in the perfect bond of peace (Col. 3:14), and it "knits hearts together in love" (Col. 2:2)—good news to be sure![62]

In contemporary thought, Charles Moule, who works in the field of criminal and civil justice, contends that divine justice—the deepest level of justice—is reconciling rather than retributive. Whereas retributive justice seeks to fit the sentence to the crime and attempts to control wrongdoing through punishment, reconciling justice forgives the crime and seeks to redeem wrongdoing through the repair of the relationship. He states that "the first great step toward justice at the deepest level is, paradoxically, when the victim [could be God] abandons quantitative justice, waives the demand for 'just' retribution, and begins to become ready to forgive—that is, to meet the damage by repair," through reconciliation.[63]

Reconciling justice is also transformational justice. It pierces the darkness of retributive violence with the grace of God and the message of peace through love, forgiveness, and reconciliation. Thus justice serves as the keychain from which dangle the three keys to the kingdom of God. To do justice is to love; to do justice is to forgive; to do justice is to reconcile—a chain reaction in which love forgives, forgiveness reconciles, and reconciliation restores—all characteristics of divine justice, God's reconciling justice. God calls us to serve this form of justice.

In a violent, vengeful culture God appears consistently to move the people of the kingdom, the possessors of the keys, away from the violence of retributive justice. God calls them—us—instead to new heights of justice from the nonviolent creation of the world, via the prophets, through Jesus, and to Paul. God calls us to justice that fulfills the law of love, offers the grace of forgiveness, and promotes the peace of reconciliation.[64]

In the first centuries of the nascent church, believers heard God's call and followed Jesus' teachings on nonviolence and love for the enemy almost literally. They used the keys of the kingdom productively to open the way to God. But how has the contemporary church fared? Has Christendom risen to the call? We test our success by its fruits, and it appears that most of our trees are barren. We, meaning Christendom, hate our enemies. We seek retribution and excommunicate or kill those who do not live and think like we do.

THE MISSING KEYS, THE CHANGED LOCKS

How did the early church's pattern of nonviolence change so drastically? Many Anabaptist scholars believe the change occurred as Christianity found tolerance and gained favored status in the political realm. The church assimilated into the Roman Empire that embraced it, renouncing the mission of peace and nonviolence taught by Jesus in favor of defending itself and the empire against its enemies, not by loving them, but by killing them.[65] The Roman Empire, along with all the rising and falling empires preceding and succeeding it, functioned personally, politically, judicially, and militaristically in a society philosophically and pragmatically steeped in and seized by retributive theories of justice.[66]

Throughout both Testaments of the Christian Scriptures, God works to re-interpret justice from retributive to restorative, sacrifice from external blood shedding to internal life giving, and love of self to love of the stranger. However, the message was lost in the streams of civilization that permeated and engulfed the people.[67] Consequently, the teachings of Jesus on enemy love, nonviolence, and reconciliation with others naturally kicked against the goads not only of the imperial Roman philosophical and existential infrastructure but also against human nature historically conceived and empirically known. Love for the enemy was a scandalous thought, and reconciliation rather than retribution entirely impractical. According to Walter Wink, "the removal of nonviolence from the gospel blasted the keystone from the arch," as Christianity fell more and more into patterns of abuse, intolerance, and violence.[68] The church now plays off-key, out of tune with the teachings of Jesus, and there are some of us who are quite keyed-up over it. Why might that be the case?

Granted, Jesus does not give Peter the keys to paradise; he gives him the keys to the kingdom of God. But when Jesus gives Peter the ecclesiastical keys to the kingdom, he is talking about binding and loosing, locking and unlocking, entering into something previously barred to us, undisclosed, something that has us on the outside, face pressed between the wrought iron gate slats begging entrance, knuckles bruised from knocking for someone to open the door. We have not been expelled from God's kingdom like our first parents were barred from the garden. In our complicity with the world's power structures, however, we have unwittingly locked ourselves out of the kingdom and switched the keys from those Jesus gave us to those held by the powers of the world. The keys Christendom has in its hands do not fit the lock. We shake and rattle the massive gate but we who have conformed to the kingdom of the world cannot overcome it—the bolted latch remains secure. When the church grasped hold of the Constantinian keys, it lost its grip on the keys to the kingdom given to it by Jesus.

Instead of the key of love, Christendom holds the key of judgment, unlocking hatred that leads to injustice and violence. Instead of wielding the key of forgiveness, we use the key of retributive justice that unleashes the cycle of violence and cuts off the hope of reconciliation and a peaceful future. Instead of sliding the key of reconciliation into the lock that frees the prisoners from retribution, we judge and condemn, seek punishment and death, keeping sinners eternally locked up in our hellish dogma without hope of redemption. With our self-righteous doctrines of divine wrath, punishment, and eternal suffering, we shut the door on love, forgiveness, and reconciliation in the faces of those we feel don't deserve such grace. We have changed the locks and traded the keys of the kingdom for the keys of the world.

In thinking about switched keys and changed locks, Revelation 3:20 comes to mind. In another metaphorical image Jesus stands outside the door knocking, desiring to gain entrance, seeking the fellowship—followship—of those he loves. The door he knocks on is the door of the church. He cannot get in. His keys don't fit—the locks have been changed. We huddle together inside the church peeking out to see who has the nerve to interrupt our important church service with his rude knocking. We don't recognize him; with his scruffy clothes and long hair he doesn't look like one of us. We are too busy to take time for a stranger; if we open the door we might have to invite him to stay for our potluck dinner. We scoff with officious dignity, ignoring the knock behind the safety of locked doors. But Jesus is a persistent stranger; he keeps knocking. As we peer more closely through the keyhole it dawns on us that the steadfast stranger, Jesus, can unlock for us the secrets of "being church" in a world locked into the power structure and political system of the Roman Empire.

RETRIEVING THE KEYS,
UNLOCKING THE GATES

Regardless of the church's adulterous liaison with the empires of the world, the teachings of Jesus remain crucially significant to the Christian way of life. The scope of Christ's love and the boundlessness of his forgiveness provide not only reconciliation to God but also serve as an example to others who desire to live their lives following in his steps. Christ provides and enables a new kind of life, loving the unlovable and forgiving the unforgivable, promoting peace and justice rather than violence and abuse, standing in solidarity with those less fortunate, with the lepers of today's society, with those suffering from AIDS, with gays, lesbians, blacks, Jews, Arabs—in short, all those abused by the powers that be. The kingdom of God is made up of such as these. Through Christ's words and actions he called forth the kingdom and set it in motion on earth. By announcing that the kingdom is at hand, Jesus proclaimed that it is here, now, right at this minute, a kingdom made up of all those who hear and obey God's call to justice, to love, and to peace.

If the time of the kingdom is now, the time of justice is always now as well. The urgent demand for justice comes to us from every back alley, from the beggars and the poor and the ill and the stranger. Every time we respond to the call of justice with an open hand and an open heart, justice comes in that moment, interrupting the status quo.[69] As those responding to the call of the kingdom of God, we too imitate Christ's justice, seeking out the one, one by one, as ambassadors of reconciliation effecting restorative justice in the land. When justice calls, God is calling. As participants in the kingdom of God and as a messianic people, our responsibility is to do justice; we are to be "bent into the service of justice." In service to justice, we respond to the cries of a child who calls out to us. Our response to the divine call that says "here I am for you in reconciling love" to the other is justice.[70] Justice calls us; justice is love and reconciliation in action, love calling for action. When we do justice, we do the truth in love, which is more than just speaking. "The name of God is the name of justice, and justice is not a thought but a deed, and its truth is attained only in doing the truth, in making justice happen in truth. Justice is not had by talking the talk in solemn assemblies, but by walking the walk in the inner cities. The justice of God, the God of justice—that is a deed," the answer to how we remedy the situation of the misplaced keys.[71]

In this manner, by doing justice, we bring about the kingdom, the epoche of the Messiah—the kingdom in which God's love rules. The kingdom of God enlists all who do justice, all who follow the way of Christ, which is the way of reconciling justice. The kingdom of God or of justice "does not turn on formal invitation lists and formal memberships, but includes anyone who does justice in spirit and in truth. Anyone who loves God is born of God. The kingdom of God is a how, not a what."[72] As a result, the kingdom of God hinges upon love, acceptance, and hospitality toward all peoples whether or not they obtain the correct papers, carry an official ID badge, or recite the right creed. The kingdom of God, in being a kingdom of justice, is also a kingdom of love.

The current age may be marked by violence, injustice, hatred, and death; the world's domination systems may be formidable and resilient, but they are not eternal fixtures forever embedded in God's future for creation. Jesus "unmasks the mechanisms of domination" and "invites his people to challenge and create alternatives" alternatives that will break the spiral of violence and retribution.[73] The key role of the church, as a kingdom community, is not to serve itself but to serve justice, promoting peace and nonviolence as ministers of reconciliation and ambassadors of Christ. God makes an appeal through us to a world infected with hatred to be a sweet-smelling aroma of Christ wherever we live, wherever we go, to whomever we meet by loving, forgiving, and reconciling the world to God. In doing justice we respond to oppression and hatred with nonviolent love. Through the teachings of Jesus and the power of the Spirit we unmask, disarm, and gain victory over the rebellious world structures that threaten to destroy us. The keys to success are justice served through love, forgiveness, and reconciliation. Jesus has handed those keys to us.

NOTES

1. Perry Yoder, *Shalom: The Bible's Word for Salvation, Justice, and Peace* (Nappanee, Ind.: Evangelical Publishing House, 1998), 39. Yoder believes that salvation or reconciliation with God is the central message of the Bible, and that salvation is based upon divine justice predicated upon the Hebrew concept of shalom.

2. Arthur Paul Boers, *Justice that Heals: A Biblical Vision for Victims and Offenders* (Eugene, Ore.: Wipf and Stock Publishers, 2008), 59-60.

3. David Noel Freedman, ed. *The Anchor Bible Dictionary*, vol. 4 (New York: Doubleday, 1992), 264.

4. John 13:34-35.

5. 1 John 4:7-12; Matt. 5:44; 1 Cor. 13.

6. Howard Zehr, *Changing Lenses: A New Focus for Crime and Justice* (Scottsdale, Pa.: Herald Press, 1990), 149-150; Boers, *Justice that Heals*, 34, 43-45. See Perry B. Yoder, *Shalom*, 128. For Yoder, love forms the core of kingdom ethics.

In other words, love is key.

7. Placher, *Jesus the Savior: The Meaning of Jesus Christ for Christian Life* (Louisville, Ky.: Westminster John Knox Press, 2001), 149.

8. Miroslav Volf, "Forgiveness, Reconciliation, and Justice" in *Forgiveness and Reconciliation: Religion, Public Policy, and Conflict Transformation*, ed. Raymond G. Helmick, S.J. and Rodney L. Petersen (Philadelphia: Templeton Foundation Press, 2001), 41; Rodney L. Petersen, "A Theology of Forgiveness: Terminology, Rhetoric, and the Dialectic of Interfaith Relationships" in *Forgiveness and Reconciliation*, 15. Forgiveness means the remission of sin which frees us and opens up for us the gates of the kingdom of God. See Acts 2:38, 5:32, 8:22, 10:43, 26:18; Eph. 1:7; Col. 1:14; Heb. 9:22, 10:18; Rom. 4:7; James 5:15; 1 John 1:9, 2:12; Matt. 2:7; Mark 4:12, 1:4, 4:12; Luke 1:77; 24:47.

9. Ps. 103, 130; Is.43:25, 55:7; Jer. 18:23, 31:34; Mic. 7:18; Hos. 14:4. Also Neh. 9:17; Ps. 51:1-2, 86:5; Exod. 32:32, 34:6-9, 1 Kings 8:27-30, 46-50. See Petersen, "A Theology of Forgiveness," 20-21; Robert L. Browning and Roy A. Reed, *Forgiveness, Reconciliation, and Moral Courage: Motives and Designs for Ministry in a Troubled World* (Grand Rapids, Mich.: Wm B. Eerdmans, 2004), 76.

10. Luke 19:1-10; John 4:1-26; Luke 5:20; John 8-11. See also Boers, *Justice that Heals*, 45; Christian Duquoc, *Forgiveness* (Minneapolis, Minn.: Fortress Press, 1986), 38.

11. Jn. 20:21-22. See Geiko Muller-Fahrenholz, *The Art of Forgiveness: Theological Reflections on Healing and Reconciliation* (Geneva, Switzerland: World Council of Churches, 1997), 7. Yoder asserts that the word most frequently used in the Bible in relation to sin, is forgiveness. Sin hinders the relationship between God and humanity. It needs to be forgiven. That God forgives sin is very good news. Yoder, *Shalom*, 50.

12. All humanity lacks total control of its life, context, and history that make up who each person is. The sin that put Jesus on the cross represents the sin of all humanity, therefore, all humanity is included in the forgiveness Jesus prayed for from the cross. See Richard Holloway, *Doubts and Loves: What is Left of Christianity* (Edinburgh: Canongate Books Ltd., 2001), 223.

13. Raymond Studzinski, "Remember and Forgive: Psychological Dimensions of Forgiveness" in *Forgiveness*, 12-13. Duquoc, *Forgiveness*, 38. Lee C. Camp, *Mere Discipleship: Radical Christianity in a Rebellious World* (Grand Rapids, Mich.: Brazos Press, 2008), 70.

14. Studzinski, *Forgiveness*, 19. Petersen, "A Theology of Forgiveness," 19.

15. Rom. 5:10.

16. Duquoc, *Forgiveness*, 58-59.

17. 2 Cor. 5:18-20. Zehr, *Changing Lenses*, 132.

18. My speculative keyology of the kingdom makes a significant distinction between reconciliation and restoration. While love motivates forgiveness, forgiveness leads to reconciliation so that restoration can then take place. In other words, we are not restored to a full relationship unless we first acknowledge and receive forgiveness and reconcile with God. Restoration is a result of reconciliation. For example, Joseph forgave his brothers their betrayal but his forgiveness did not bear the fruit of restoration until he spoke words of forgiveness, and both he and his brothers "kissed and made up," or reconciled (Gen. 47-50).

19. Howard Zehr, *Changing Lenses*, 46. I am aware that the entire Bible is

filled with notions of both retributive justice and restorative justice. The focus, however, has long been on the retributive aspects of justice as is obvious from our criminal justice system, atonement theories, and constructions of an eternal hell. Much of the violence inflicted upon innocent people throughout our history may be due in large part to our concepts of divine justice as retributive. I suggest that it is time to focus on divine justice as restorative and reconciling so that our behavior toward others may be based upon love instead of violence and hatred. See also Browning, *Forgiveness, Reconciliation, and Moral Courage*, 78.

20. See also Ps. 65:9-14; Ps. 1:3.

21. John D. Caputo, *The Prayers and Tears of Jacques Derrida: Religion without Religion* (Bloomington, Ind.: Indiana University Press, 1997), 338-339; Amos 5:24. Along with Derrida, Caputo likens deconstruction to justice. Deconstruction is not out to level the law or destroy meaning. It is out to open up the law for reinterpretation, difference, to take frozen interpretations and loosen them up so that other voices can be heard, other previously hidden and squelched (valid) interpretations can come to the fore. It brings texts (and institutions such as the church) into question, knocks them off their idolatrous pedestals so that they are level with all the other voices trapped inside. If, for example, historical texts (which are someone's interpretation of what occurred), or even scriptural interpretations, are not revisable, amendable, open to deconstruction, then they are in danger of fostering hatred, abuse, and violence. In this manner, deconstruction is justice. For further discussion see Caputo, *Weakness of God: A Theology of the Event* (Bloomington, Ind.: Indiana University Press, 2006), 27, 140; Caputo, *Prayers and Tears*, 2-6.

22. Zehr, *Changing Lenses*, 138, 151-153. Zehr asserts that the primary function of biblical justice is to make things right in order to produce shalom—well-being for the community. Violence and retribution rarely, if ever, makes things right or brings about shalom. Mt. 20:1-16.

23. Caputo, *Weakness of God*, 27-28, 52.

24. Raymund Schwager, S.J., *Must There be Scapegoats?*, trans. Maria L. Assad (San Francisco: Harper & Row, Publishers, 1987), 207.

25. Yoder, *Shalom*, 45; Zehr, *Changing Lenses*, 139.

26. N.T. Wright, *What Saint Paul Really Said: Was Saint Paul of Tarsus the Real Founder of Christianity?* (Grand Rapids, Mich.: Wm. B. Eerdmans, 1997), 110-111. See also Boers, *Justice that Heals*, 35; Christopher D. Marshall, *Beyond Retribution: A New Testament Vision for Justice, Crime, and Punishment* (Grand Rapids, Mich.: Wm. B. Eerdmans, 2001), 50-51; Isa. 30:18 according to which, "God will rise up and show mercy to us, for God is a God of justice." Mercy is often equated with love in Hebrew.

27. John Dominic Crossan, *God and Empire: Jesus Against Rome, Then and Now* (New York: HarperOne, 2008), 190.

28. Zehr, *Changing Lenses*, 149. See Soren Kierkegaard, *For Self Examination; Judge for Yourself!* ed. By Howard V. Hong and Edna H. Hong (Princeton, N.J.: Princeton University Press, 1990), 9-12. Kierkegaard professes that love's justice forgives us of our sin.

29. Abelard, *Epistle to the Romans 3:22, 24* in *A Scholastic Miscellany: Anselm to Ockham*, ed. Eugene R. Fairweather (Philadelphia: The Westminster Press, 1954), 275-277. Abelard equates divine justice with divine love. Divine love

forgives human sin. See Richard E. Weingart, *The Logic of Divine Love: A Critical Analysis of the Soteriology of Peter Abelaird* (London: Clarendon, 1970), 121.

30. Mark 2:1-12.

31. Carroll, *Constantine's Sword: The Church and the Jews—A History* (Boston: Mariner Books, 2002), 394.

32. John D. Caputo, *More Radical Hermeneutics: On Not Knowing Who We Are* (Bloomington, Ind.: University of Indiana Press, 2000), 189; Caputo, *Weakness of God*, 129-130. Cf. Bruce Chilton, *Rabbi Jesus: An Intimate Biography* (New York: Random House, Doubleday, 2000), 110.

33. Jean-Luc Marion, *Prolegomena to Charity*, trans. Stephen Lewis (New York: Fordham University Press, 2002), 2-15; John D. Caputo, *On Religion* (New York: Routledge, 2001), 35; Caputo, *Weakness of God*, 170; Hannah Arendt, *The Human Condition* (Chicago: University of Chicago Press, 1958), 236-240; Luke 6:29-30; Girard, *The Scapegoat Scapegoat*, trans. by Yvonne Freccero (Baltimore: John Hopkins University Press, 1986), 212.

34. Caputo, *Against Ethics* (Bloomington, Ind.: University of Indiana Press, 1993), 112.

35. Arendt, *The Human Condition*, 240.

36. Matthew 18:22.

37. Caputo, *Weakness of God*, 151-142, 155, 212-213; Caputo, *Prayers and Tears*, 227-229; B. Keith Putt, "Prayers of Confession and Tears of Contrition: John Caputo and a Radically 'Baptist' Hermeneutic of Repentance" in *Religion With/Out Religion: The Prayers and Tears of John D. Caputo*, ed. James H. Olthius (New York: Routledge, 2002), 64-66. Anthony Bartlett, *Cross Purposes: The Violent Grammar of Christian Atonement* (Harrisburg, Pa.: Trinity Press International, 2001), 219-220, 207-208, compares repeated forgiveness to the spirit of non-retaliation carried to term in the death of Christ, a spirit we now imitate in the forgiving of sins. We now take part in the repetition of human forgiveness: "Father forgive us as we forgive other" (244-245).

38. Putt, "Prayers of Confession and Tears of Contrition," 74-75. Bartlett reverses the conception of the gift of death with his own theory of the gift of life. He claims that the death of Christ, as he yielded up, let go, released his Spirit, reverberates with the spirit of forgiveness throughout all of time. This spirit of forgiveness "is proactive, not merely responsive; it is an affirmation of life in death, not death in life, "good news" rather than "the gift of death" (Bartlett, *Cross Purposes*, 246). A blend of Putt and Bartlett enables us to claim that forgiveness gifts us with life in the giving of ourselves over to the death of our desire for retribution. For further study on the cost of forgiveness see Miroslav Volf, *Forgiveness, Reconciliation, and Justice*, 46. He believes that forgiveness doesn't stand outside of justice but is possible only as justice; it presupposes justice (p. 45).

39. Putt, "Prayers of Confession and Tears of Contrition," 75-76. For a full treatment of the gift of death see Derrida, *The Gift of Death*, trans. David Wills (Chicago: University of Chicago Press, 1995).

40. Caputo, *Against Ethics*, 111-112; Caputo, *Weakness of God*, 148-149; Caputo, "Holding on by Our Teeth: A Response to Putt," in *A Passion for the Impossible: John D. Caputo in Focus*, ed. Mark Dooley (New York: SUNY Press, 2003), 254. Cf. Arendt, *The Human Condition*, 240, n. 78.

41. Caputo, *Weakness of God*, 186, 222.

42. Caputo, *Weakness of God,* 223-224, 228. Caputo clearly believes that the old adage, "forgive the sinner, but not the sin," takes away from forgiveness. He asserts that "[i]f I forgive the doer but not the deed, the offender but not the offense, then I am inserting an important condition into my forgiveness." In a conditional forgiveness of this sort, we imply: "I do not forgive you in those moments of your life where you were or are still sinning or are planning to sin some more. So once again, I am not forgiving sinning, which needs forgiveness, but non-sinning, which does not" (*Weakness of God*), 224.

43. Caputo, *Weakness of God,* 230. Cf. Emmanuel Levinas, *Totality and Infinity*, trans. by Alphonso Lingis (Pittsburg: Duquesne University Press, 1969), 282-283. Levinas claims that pardon, or forgiveness, is retroactive and represents the reversibility of time. Pardon acts upon the past by repeating the event and purifying it. Pardon "conserves the past pardoned in the purified present" (283). It does not make the pardoned person innocent but allows for a happiness of reconciliation. See also the concept of being made a new creature in Christ in 2 Corinthians 5:17.

44. Caputo, *Weakness of God,* 209, 228, 230. Bartlett, in *Cross Purposes,* 243, describes the absolute gift of the cross as a gift that breaks apart the chronology of time. In other words, forgiveness (first realized in the cross) reaches back across chronological time and changes/heals the past. In forgiveness we surrender to loss, transforming the past moment as contingent in a free act of unbounded for-giving. In so doing, we imitate Christ in forgiving again and again in a manner completely undetermined by chronological time (Bartlett, 251, 254).

45. Duquoc, *Forgiveness, 64.*

46. St. Thomas Aquinas, *Summa Theologiae*. Blackfriars edition. New York: McGraw-Hill Book Company, 1964-1966), IIaIIae, q. 106, a. 2, ad 3; Ia, q. 20, a. 4, ad 4 (Hereafter cited at *ST*).

47. Gil Bailie, *Violence Unveiled: Humanity at the Crossroads* (New York: Crossroads Publishing Company, 1997), 208-209.

48. C. F. D. Moule, *Forgiveness and Reconciliation* (London: SPCK, 1998), 23, 26, 31-32. Moule states that in such a case, "forgiveness is ruthless in the severity of its judgment, although judgment in its deepest sense is never a destructive condemnation, but is essentially restorative."Cf., Bailie, *Violence Unveiled,* 209.

49. Muller-Fahrenholz, *The Art of Forgiveness,* 29.

50. DesmondTutu, "Introduction" in *Exploring Forgiveness*, ed. Robert D. Enright and Joanna North (Madison, Wis.: University of Wisconsin Press, 1998), xiii.

51. Caputo, *Weakness of God,* 17-18. Here Caputo likens the madness of the Kingdom of God to the story of the Madhatter in *Alice in Wonderland,* writing that "[t]he Kingdom is a (sic) as any hatter's party, but it is divinely mad."

52. Caputo, *Weakness of God,* 208, 235.

53. Petersen, "Theology of Forgiveness," 11-13.

54. Volf, *Forgiveness and Reconciliation,* 36; Zehr, *Changing Lenses,* 154-155, 190.

55. Abraham Heschel, *The Prophets* (Peabody, Mass.: Hendrickson Publishers, 2007), 213; Marshall, 4, 53. Marshall believes that God's justice is not primarily retributive or distributive but reconciling, restorative, and recon-

structure.

56. Marshall, *Beyond Retribution*, 5; Boers, *Justice that Heals*, 35-36. (Micah 6:3-4, 7:18-19; Ps. 103:8-10).

57. Boers, *Justice that Heals*, 35.

58. Millard Lind, Ted Grimsrud, Loren L. Johns, *Peace and Justice Shall Embrace: Power and Theopolitics in the Bible: Essays in Honor of Millard Lind* (Telford, Pa.: Pandora Press U.S., 2000), 73. Grimsrud connects redemption with divine justice.

59. Luke 1:68-79, 2:29-32.

60. Moule, *Forgiveness and Reconciliation*, 45.

61. John Yoder, *The Politics of Jesus* (Grand Rapids, Mich.: Wm. B. Eerdmans, 1994), 34-35. Yoder believes that Jesus' omission of "the year of the Lord's vengeance" would have struck his listeners as a significant statement. Jesus was, in effect, revealing a kingdom of non-violence.

62. Yoder, *Shalom*, 67-68.

63. Moule, *Forgiveness and Reconciliation*, 41-42 (bracketed additions mine).

64. Boers, *Justice that Heals*, 31-34.

65. Jane Elyse Russell, "Love Your Enemies: The Church as Community of Nonviolence," in *The Wisdom of the Cross* (Grand Rapids, Mich.: Wm. B. Eerdmans Publishing Company, 1999), 379; Gerald W. Schlabach, "Deuteronomic or Constantinian: What is the Most Basic Problem for Christian Social Ethics? In *The Wisdom of the Cross*, 450. Schlabach does not place the blame for the violent turn of the church entirely on Constantine or Constantinianism. He uses it as a heuristic device so that the contemporary Church can see how far we have strayed from the teachings of Jesus. If anything, Constantinianism points to a specific time when the Church itself bought into anti-Christ teachings for its own political, social, and ecclesial benefit.

66. See John Dominic Crossan, *God and Empire*, 88-95.

67. See Marshall, *Beyond Retribution*, 4-5, 35-41, 50-53. Marshall builds a case for the Old Testament concept of justice as non-retributive, peace-making, and reconciling as opposed to the traditional retributive theories of justice modeled in most personal ethical behaviors, penal systems, nation/states, and military organizations. See also Crossan, 88-94.

68. Walter Wink, *Engaging the Powers: Discernment and Resistance in a World of Domination* (Minneapolis, Minn.: Fortress Press, 1992), 217.

69. Caputo, *Prayers and Tears*, 150, 80-81, 98, 114; Caputo, *On Religion*, 28. Caputo's notions of justice, the messianic, and hospitality coincide with those of Jacques Derrida, whose views of justice and the Messianic are ethico-political and have to do with justice and democracy to come. For further discussion on Derrida's theories of justice and democracy, see Jacques Derrida, *Rogues*, trans. Pascale-Anne Brault and Michael Naas (Stanford, Calif.: Stanford University Press, 2005); Caputo, *Prayers and Tears*, 142.

70. Caputo, *Against Ethics*, 38-39; Caputo, *More Radical Hermeneutics*, 181. Cf. Jeff Dudiak, "Bienvenue—Just a Moment" in *Religion Without Religion: The Prayers and Tears of John D. Caputo*, ed. James H. Olthuis (New York: Routledge, 2002), 16-18.

71. Caputo, *On Religion*, 138, 124, 130-131, 140; Caputo, *More Radical Hermeneutics*, 180. The conception of God as an event that disturbs and sur-

prises the status quo as described in *Weakness of God*, corresponds to justice and God as the name for justice, as an event that disturbs and interrupts the social structures in place. In responding in doing justice we take part in God's justice and we *do* justice to/for/with Jesus himself (Matt. 25:40).

72. Caputo, *On Religion*, 138.

73. Camp, *Mere Discipleship*, 69, 97; Timothy Gorringe, *God's Just Vengeance: Crime, Violence, and the Rhetoric of Salvation* (Cambridge: Cambridge University Press, 1996), 58; Jack Nelson-Pallmeyer, *Jesus Against Christianity: Reclaiming the Mission of Jesus* (Harrisburg, Pa.: Trinity Press International, 2001), 276.

Chapter 4

JUST POLICING: A NEW FACE TO AN OLD CHALLENGE

Andy Alexis-Baker

In the 1990s, the media and government officials heralded NATO's bombing of Kosovo as "a landmark in international relations." This landmark would replace the old politics of self-interest and usher in a new world order in which universal human rights were protected and groups that violated those rights were held accountable.[1] British Prime Minister Tony Blair declared "a new millennium" in which the enlightened Western nations would fight "not for territory but for values. For a new internationalism where the brutal repression of whole ethnic groups will no longer be tolerated. For a world where those responsible for such crimes have nowhere to hide."[2] German philosopher Jürgen Habermas said the NATO bombings in Kosovo should be understood as an "armed peacekeeping mission" carried out by "conscientious pacifists."[3] Another prominent German scholar, Ulrich Beck, described this event as a "new military human-ism" and "military pacifism" that brings about "a revolution in the classical understanding between war and peace . . . attack and defense, just and unjust."[4] Said succinctly in Orwellian terms, this stance signals a new era in which "war is peace."[5]

Subsequent years and new conflicts have stripped the luster off of this "new military humanism." As it turns out, the West has intervened or not intervened in others' violent disputes with the same old self-interested motives.[6] Nevertheless, military humanitarian intervention remains a hot topic and Christian pacifist ethicists have added to the political and cultural reflections. In his book, *Peace: A History of Movements*, peace advocate David Cortright supports the above analysis that "the nature of war has changed dramatically in recent decades."[7] The hallmark of these "new wars" is their deliberate and systematic abuse of human rights in intrastate conflict between ethnic or religious groups. Cortright argues that "absolute pacifism," which rejects defensive war and humanitarian military interventions, is not a proper response to this shift in the nature of war. Instead, he argues for "pragmatic pacifism," which combines "the pacifist and just war traditions allow[ing] for a broader and richer examination of the peace tradition, one that more accurately reflects the thinking of those who consider themselves part of the peace movement" (16). Rather than warfare, this type of pacifism is open to "police actions" as long as they are "constrained, narrowly targeted, and conducted by proper authority within the rule of law" (15). Pragmatic pacifism is part of a "cosmopolitan politics" that places priority upon protecting civilians from human rights abuses more than on state sovereignty (5).

In this same line of thought, Gerald Schlabach has developed a theory he calls "just policing."[8] He argues that just war proponents and pacifists could converge if just war proponents reconceived war as policing and if pacifists would "support, participate, or at least not object to operations with recourse to limited but potentially lethal force" that enforce international law.[9] Rather than justify war according to abstract criteria, just policing would draw on international law to pursue suspected criminals. War calls upon people to accept far more civilian casualties than does policing (4). Moreover, although just war proponents advocate exhausting all reasonable avenues before unleashing war, in practice the theory gives a blank check to those who wish to wage war and less violent avenues are swept aside. By contrast, policing does not lend itself to such misinterpretation; in popular imagination the police are restrained in their lethality (71). Only when just war theorists have made violence exceptional under the circumstances of policing will pacifists and just war theorists finally have the conditions for reconciliation.[10]

Schlabach and Cortwright are not alone in their stance. Indeed, Glenn Stassen and other notable Christian ethicists have also promoted a "third way" between pacifism and just war theory that allows room for military intervention "in cases where human rights are egregiously violated."[11] Yet in this essay I question the assumption that Western policing models represent an inherently less violent approach to conflict. On the contrary, policing can be just as or more violent than warfare for several reasons. First, police departments, particularly ones in urban areas, are more militarized than Schlabach and others have admitted. Second, community policing, a central model in these theories, is even more problematic than militarized policing because of the ease with which it scapegoats "outsiders." Finally, even nonviolence in the hands of the police is simply a technique for domination that Christians should shun. All of this taken together throws serious doubt on the ability of Christian ethicists to significantly bridge the gap between just war and pacifism. Indeed, it is more likely to make Christian pacifists into just war theorists under a different name.

POLICE/WAR DISTINCTIONS
AND HISTORICAL CONTIGENCY

Schlabach's and others' inability to see the threat of violence that is inherent in the just policing theory may be attributed to the superficial distinctions these thinkers make between war and policing and to their assumptions about the conditions for conflict.[12] Appealing to John Howard Yoder, they argue that there are *structural* differences between policing and war[13] and assume that these differences have existed since ancient times. Yet the distinction between war and policing only became possible when police institutions came into existence. As a result, even Yoder made a fundamental mistake of anachronism when he stated that "the function of bearing the sword to which Christians are called to be subject [in Romans 13] is the judicial and police function; it does not refer to the death penalty or to war" (203). Similarly, just policing advocates make the same error when they suggest that the distinction between policing and war is natural and has always existed.

A simple historical review reveals an alternative and more accurate viewpoint. Police forces have not always existed. For example, neither the typical Greek or Roman *polis* had a police force nor a standing army available to quiet disturbances, enforce contracts, or apprehend criminals; citizens themselves performed these tasks.[14] One catches a glimpse of this arrangement in Acts 21. In this chapter, Paul's presence in the temple caused some people to cry out, "Men of Israel, help. . . ." This was the common cry made by anyone who had been victimized. When someone called for help in this way, everyone nearby was expected to aid the person. Thus a crowd aided the men and dragged Paul out of the temple and began to beat him. Responding to what sounded and looked like a riot, the military commander gathered some soldiers to quell a potentially unsettling disturbance (Acts 21:31).[15] The authorities' response exhibits the fact that throughout the empire the military's function was to suppress riots and rebellions, not to arrest people for crime. In *Public Order in Ancient Rome*, Wilfried Nippel goes so far as to state that "we do not even know to what degree (if at all) the Roman authorities undertook prosecution of murder."[16]

This system of crying out for help from one's neighbors in the event of a problem carried on through the Middle Ages. In England, this way of dealing with crime became more organized under the Normans, who established sheriffs in every local district (shire reeve) to ensure locals paid their taxes. In 1285 the Statute of Winchester codified a volunteer night watch system to supplement the sheriff. Volunteers' responsibilities included firefighting, maintaining street-lamps, and managing stray animals as well as various hygienic and administrative tasks.[17]

Centuries later, English colonists imported the sheriff and watch system to the Americas. In 1636 Boston established the earliest watch.[18] Paul Revere's famous ride in which he shouted, "The British are coming!" is an example of night watchmen alerting a town to danger. As in England, watch volunteers and conscripts did not wear uniforms, were unarmed, and though involved in many community-based activities, were not primarily responsible for crime prevention.

The Rise of Nation-States and Policing

Far from being a longstanding institution, policing as we know it emerged with the advent of nation-states. According to historian and sociologist Charles Tilly, the early modern state-makers gained legitimacy through a process of 1) destroying their external enemies; 2) destroying their internal enemies, 3) providing protection to their clients; and 4) taxing the population to recruit an army and police force to do the first three.[19] He argues that, in the early European states "there is a close relationship between policing and the other processes of control and extraction . . . European states used their legal apparatus not merely to hold off threats to public order, but to define 'disorder,' create 'disorder,' and press their right to suppress the same disorder."[20] State-making created a social space in which the state could be a primary actor via its police. They defined disorder as all kinds of activities that mostly poor and peasant people engaged in, stirred up fear of impending disasters and violence, and then promised to protect people from it.

To grasp Tilly's argument, it is important to understand that he is *not* arguing that the state concocted imaginary threats, like setting off a bomb and blaming someone else nor is he suggesting murder and rape are fictions invented by the state.[21] Instead, he claims that the state redefined previously accepted activities and groups into crimes and criminals respectively. Therefore, when the term *police* began to spread across Europe in the late fifteenth century, it signified an administrative science that regulated nearly every aspect of life. Thousands of books on police from this period identified their primary concerns as "religion, morals, health and subsistence, public peace, the care of buildings, squares, and highways, the sciences and the liberal arts, commerce, manufacture and the mechanical arts, servants and laborers, the theater and games, and finally the care and discipline of the poor."[22]

In this new paradigm, idleness was a threat to the new political-economic order and was therefore criminalized. In contrast to medieval law, which simply codified existing norms, these police ordinances helped create a society in which the state executed the same moral power the church had previously assumed.[23] New bureaucratic institutions had to be created to enforce this new order and to reshape both society and individuals so that they could become efficient members of the new order.

Policing, Slave Patrols, and Class Conflict

In the United States, preventative policing developed out of emerging race and class conflict. In the South, police forces evolved from slave patrols designed to catch runaway slaves, monitor their social behavior, restrict their movement, and thwart revolt.[24] Armed with guns, ropes, and whips, patrolmen guarded countryside roads to verify that traveling slaves had a valid pass; they raped women; and they generally harassed, threatened, and abused black people, especially those without passes.[25] Often, these groups refrained from killing the slaves because of the slaves' economic value.

In 1785 the first modern police force arose out of slave patrols in Charleston, South Carolina, called the Charleston Guard and Watch. This department had a distinct chain of command, uniforms, sole responsibility for policing, salary, authorized use of force, and a focus on preventing "crime." According to one member, the unit's main responsibility was "keeping down the niggers,"[26] which it did with terrifying precision. The Atlanta police department that arose in 1874 also exhibits the typical southern police force. The leading causes of arrest, including disorderly conduct, public intoxication, loitering, arrest "on suspicion," "on warrant," larceny and prostitution,[27] served to target and control the newly freed black population.

In one shocking example, the Atlanta police arrested a black man on suspicion because he sold a mule for what the police considered too cheap a price.[28] In another, an Atlanta newspaper, in 1903, called for stricter enforcement of vagrancy laws, which were aimed at "idle shiftless negros—for the majority of the crimes punished in the city court are committed by this class."[29] These police actions reflected white opinion that black people had left farms to avoid work, and to engage in crime against white people, and represented a white response to the emancipation of black slaves. This fact was not lost on many southern black intellectuals, one of whom offered this indictment: "We have lived in Atlanta twenty-seven years, and we have heard the lash sounding from the cabins of slaves, poured on by their masters, but we have never seen a meaner set of low-down cut throats, scrapes, and murderers than the city of Atlanta has to protect the peace."[30]

Like their southern counterparts, northern police departments were designed to curb the "dangerous class,"[31] not dangerous crime. Boston's 1834 City Marshal's report enumerated police department functions, such as enforcing traffic and building regulations, but did not refer to "crime."[32] Instead, "vices" such as drinking and vagrancy occupy the document.[33] After instituting a police force, St. Louis' arrest records for 1874 registered a total of 42 arrests for felonious violent crime (murder, robbery and rape) and 16 arrests for burglary in a city of 300,000 people. Yet there were over 2,500 arrests for vagrancy, nearly 8,000 for drunkenness, 1,600 for profane language and 3,300 for disturbing the peace. Unsurprisingly, most of those arrested were immigrants or black.[34] In city after city, fledgling police forces combated vices of the poor, not violent crime. Thus the thin blue line between order and chaos divided the rich (order) from the poor (chaos).[35]

Northern police departments also helped to consolidate political power. In the nineteenth century, New York's Tammany Hall tightly controlled police posts. In most cities, the police learned to back the politicians in power because new regimes customarily fired existing police, replacing them with loyal pawns. Following the Los Angeles election in 1889, the Kansas City election in 1895, the Chicago and Baltimore elections in 1897, almost the entire police forces were fired and replaced with supporters of the new regime.[36] Thus the police promoted voter turnout, monitored voting stations, ignored ballot stuffing, and beat citizens who voted against the current administration.[37]

Lessons of History: Policing does not Serve the Common Good

Christian ethicists who claim that the police represent the common good and protect the weak do so without attending to the history of the institution. Contra the ahistorical arguments of Schlabach and Duane Friesen, police are a recent invention that have neither represented the common good nor benefited the poor and marginalized.[38] Instead, police have promoted particular interests and established a particular order, siding with those who paid them and the dominant racial and economic groups from their inception. The police did not result from inevitable forces of history but from calculated moves to maintain social stratification. Christians should be cautious because history does not vanish but materializes in the present. As police historian Eric Monkkonen wrote, "The historian must preserve a radical doubt as to the need for police, thus insuring that the proper energy goes into accounting for their existence."[39]

COMMUNITY POLICING

In addition to making a distinction between war and policing and purporting an ahistorical reading of police history, just policing advocates have also embraced community policing as an international paradigm because it seems to provide an alternative to police militarization. Gerald Schlabach, for example, claims that community policing is "a new name for an old strategy" that places police on foot patrols, into community meetings, and integrates them "into the neighborhoods."[40] In his view, community policing provides an opportunity to "make policing less violent overall" through community partnerships and nonviolent methods (44). This, Schlabach maintains, can be a model for international relations because it allows

> the sort of work on root causes of violence and conflict that pacifists advocate as basic for achieving real peace with justice, (2) a continued but modified role for apprehending criminals, and (3) ample room for developing less violent and nonviolent tactics for even that apprehension. (43-44).

In agreement, Tobias Winright claims that beyond crime fighting, the police work with community members "to prevent and solve their problems."[41] Citing the "broken windows theory," Winright claims that the police can revitalize communities by confronting neighborhood nuisances that increase residents' fears.[42] What is striking, however, is that Schlabach and Winright have so little to write on such an important theory that they tout as a model for international policing. A more careful examination of community policing reveals its troubling aspects.

Community Policing and Militarization

In their arguments for policing on an international scale, just policing advocates routinely look to large, well-trained urban police forces as a model for their project. Yet in most urban police departments, community policing is inextricably intertwined with militarization and violence. For example, the New York Police Department (NYPD) uses Special Weapons and Tactics (SWAT) teams for routine patrols. One officer described their approach:

> We conduct a lot of saturation patrols. . . . We focus on "quality of life" issues like illegal parking, loud music, bums, neighbor troubles. We have the freedom to stay in a hot area and clean it up—particularly gangs. Our tactical enforcement team works nicely with our department's emphasis on community policing.[43]

While flaunting a massive display of force, these units "target suspicious vehicles and people" and "stop anything that moves." Consequently, even a Midwestern officer boasts: "We usually don't have any problems with crack-heads cooperating" (470). Criminologists Peter Kraska and Victor Kappeler report that sixty-three percent of police officers responding to a survey agreed that paramilitary units "play an important role in community policing strategies" (472). Thus Schlabach and Winright's attempt to separate militarization from community policing contradicts the testimony of officers themselves, making theirs a false distinction.

Scapegoating and Community Policing

Militarization is only one of the problems with community policing. In fact, a deeper and perhaps more troubling part of this practice is its tendency to scapegoat members of the community. As many theologians and ethicists know, René Girard has posited that people desire what other people desire, which leads to conflict that can eventually engulf a community into hostilities. To resolve this conflict, communities often seize upon vulnerable people to blame for the rising tide of violence. This mechanism unifies the group, channeling their imitative desires upon punishing the scapegoat rather than upon harming each other. Although this scapegoating process is inherent in community policing, it is ignored by just policing advocates.

Community policing programs were developed in response to the "broken windows" theory, which was advanced by criminologists James Q. Wilson and George Kelling. According to Wilson and Kelling, unaddressed problems in a community—problems like neglected broken windows—signal that nobody cares about a neighborhood, leading troublesome outsiders to view the areas as a potential haven. This in turn causes residents to fear "disorderly people. Not violent people, nor, necessarily, criminals, but disreputable or obstreperous or unpredictable people: panhandlers, drunks, addicts, rowdy teenagers, prostitutes, loiterers, the mentally disturbed."[44] Because failing to maintain orderly appearances leads to a downward spiral of neglect, fear, and crime, police must ward off nuisances to protect or restore the community's order and vitality. In the community policing paradigm, allowing even law-abiding homeless people or panhandlers to go unchecked is like allowing a broken window to remain unfixed: such "negligence" invites outsiders with a penchant for criminal activity to think that the community does not care and to invade the premises.[45]

Girard claims that community members must not view scapegoats as an integral part of the community; scapegoats must have no advocates for the process to work well.[46] Similarly, community policing must strip undesirable people of their support and rights in order for it to function. For example, the New York Transit Authority targeted almsgivers, hoping to convince them that giving to panhandlers harms rather than helps them. Before New York began a campaign to change people's views, refusing to give to a beggar signaled that a person was "coldhearted, or cheap, or uncaring."[47] The poster campaign sought to reverse this sentiment by changing a social stigma into a virtue: "The [Transit] Authority told the public that it was wrong to give to panhandlers—that panhandlers were people who needed help, but that by giving to panhandlers, one made it less likely they would get help. To help the panhandlers . . . one must not give to them" (1040).

To reinforce the view that withholding charity is virtuous, city councils across the U.S. have passed laws that prohibit feeding the homeless. Activist groups like Food Not Bombs and Christians from the Simple Way intentional community in Philadelphia have suddenly found themselves in jail as a result.[48] For example, after

Philadelphia passed such a law, Christians gathered in a park to celebrate the Eucharist with homeless people. The action eventually led
to mass arrests.[49] These laws changed the social meaning of feeding
the homeless from almsgiving and charity to a crime that stigmatizes
givers with an arrest record and inconveniences them with time
spent in jail and in court.

More importantly, these laws also criminalize the homeless and
strip them of their allies, making the scapegoating process easier.
This is not an "abuse"[50] of policing but an integral part of a theory
that feeds upon an "us versus them" dichotomy.[51] Thus even if the
police involved operated without weapons, the division and intolerance inherent in this community makes it suspect from a Christian
perspective.

Whose Community? Which Order?

This scapegoating process in community policing exposes a significant problem for political theorists, police administrators, and
theological ethicists who advocate community policing: none of
these groups have adequately defined what they mean by community. Since divergent political groups conceive of community in potentially contradictory ways, the term often functions ideologically.
"Community can be the warmly persuasive word to describe an existing set of relationships, or . . . an alternative set of relationships. . . .
[I]t never seems to be used unfavorably, and never to be given any
opposing or distinguishing terms."[52]

Thus, combining the term *community* with *policing* creates positive connotations aimed at silencing prospective opponents. For who
in their right mind could be against community? And if the community is served by policing, who can be against the police?

Indeed community policing deploys the word *community* against
some people. Community policing deflects awareness of the *contested*
nature of community and emphasizes *defending* the community from
outsiders. This move creates an illusion of consensus that masks conflict. For example, community policing theorists claim African-
American skepticism of the police results from crime and the breakdown of community. Contradicting this view is a *New York Times* report that found widespread suspicion of the police amongst black
people in Camden, New Jersey. Indeed residents' distrust for the police runs so deep that they hesitate to talk to the police even after violent crimes have been committed because they do not trust the police.
As a Harvard professor noted:

A lot of white Americans from suburban communities can't understand why people wouldn't talk to law enforcement . . . But in a lot of inner-city communities, there is so much hostility to the police that many people of color can't fathom why someone would even seriously consider helping them.[53]

In addition to mistrust between police and black residents, the article reveals an even wider chasm. As a women whose son's murderers are still at large indicated, "Snitching, telling on people, isn't something that I personally would involve myself with. . . . People don't want to talk to you if they think you're a snitch. If they were your friends, they're not your friends anymore. You're left totally all alone." According to the deputy attorney general for Camden, residents are often asked to surrender their children, friends, or someone with whom they are meaningfully connected people. For reason, "the number of witnesses who remain silent because they fear for their safety is probably less than one-tenth the number who refuse to talk because they fear the social repercussions."[54]

The problem for the police is that a socially complex community has created an obstacle for the simplified, bifurcated "community" of community policing. Community is not absent in Camden and similar neighborhoods; rather it operates on another economic and social level that thwarts the police function. Community policing, for these people, is actually a threat to their well-established familial and neighborly social networks.[55]

INTERNATIONAL
IMPLICATIONS OF COMMUNITY POLICING

This analysis of community policing raises important questions about the desirability of using community policing as an international paradigm. What does a broken window look like on the international scene? Who are the panhandlers, drunks, addicts, rowdy teenagers, prostitutes, loiterers, the mentally disturbed that are the human embodiments of broken when one's community is the globe? If international broken windows must be addressed so that they do not invite a spiral of unrest and violence, who is to notice and fix these windows? In community policing theory, it is an outside police force that aggressively drives out undesirable elements, often violating their rights in the name of community. Even on a local level, this has often increased violence rather than lessening it. On an international level, how can a sovereign nation not see this as an act of aggression?

How does this community policing doctrine not support a doctrine of pre-emptive strikes to stem possible threats?

Some might argue that on an international level a broken window would have to be a more serious occurrence that requires humanitarian intervention. But if this is the case—if policies of ethnic cleansing or actual acts of genocide become "broken windows"—then community policing is no longer a useful model. These extreme situations signal that the community has already lost its way to bandits and other criminals. Therefore in these horrific cases, the more fitting domestic analogy is one of intense and sustained rioting and the appropriate action by police would be to regain order through martial law and perhaps a shoot-to-kill policy. If community policing is about addressing the minor disorders that lead up these issues, then just policing advocates must first identify what the equivalent of a panhandler or broken window is on the international stage and provide concrete ideas for how an *international police force* would handle these disorders without devolving into what we know as war.

The history of policing also shows that people are not necessarily treated better when viewed as criminals rather than as enemies of war. In fact, when a group is criminalized and stripped of its status as a political group which might challenge the prevailing order, that group's claims are completely dismissed. For example, the label *terrorist* often functions to mark off one's own righteousness from the enemy's savagery. Since the prisoners in Guantanamo are not legal combatants in warfare, the label *terrorist* criminalizes and removes them from the protections of any law whatsoever. Legal combatants are immune from torture under international treaties. Yet these people, stripped of that status and made into a type of criminal and imprisoned, are subject to different rules that even allow torture. So in this case criminality is used to avoid all sorts of rules and conditions that just policing advocates would call for. Thus we have to ask if it is *necessarily* the case that treating people as criminals would reduce violence and promote peace on an international level.

PEACE CHURCH IDENTITY
IN A CONSTANTINIAN WORLD

The just policing agenda raises fundamental questions about peace churches. In attempting to reconcile pacifists and just war theorists, just policing seeks a common denominator in a practice that seeks to limit violence, but not necessarily to eliminate it altogether. At the heart of this project is an optimism about changing the world's institutions. The MCC Peace Theology Project team, which worked on developing a theology of security that embraced the just policing agenda, wrote that for people to "flourish," they "depend upon ordered systems." These ordered systems are the "societal institutions such as legal systems, political organizations, and economic structures" that serve the "common good." In this regard Friesen and Schlabach urge peace churches to "call the powers to their life-giving purpose."[56] Ted Koontz has suggested that this optimism about transforming the world would lead to advocating for peaceable policies while not refusing participation in violence, and that the increased focus on changing government would diminish Mennonite participation in *direct* service and intervention.[57]

Koontz's prediction seems verified by subsequent work on this issue. For example, Schlabach concludes his thought experiment on just policing by imagining "some kind of SWAT team with recourse to lethal violence." For him it is imaginable, albeit as an exception, for a Christian to be part of that SWAT team and to kill.[58] Likewise, James Reimer has endorsed the distinction between war and "policing." Unlike war, he argues, policing is best understood as "protecting the good and restraining evil with a minimum amount of force."[59]

Subseqently, Mennonites can love their enemies while serving in police occupations because policing is a form of peacemaking.[60] Several years later Reimer updated his thought, stating that we should not condemn "other Christians and the international community in their compassionate police-keeping, including military intervention in places like Sudan. *In fact, we ought to encourage and support such acts of 'love for the neighbor,' even within our own ranks.*"[61] Echoing Reimer and others, Pamela Leach asks "Can those who have difficulty with the notion of Anabaptist police officers nonetheless affirm the person who chooses this path, resourcing and supporting that officer to discern his or her role and attend to the work of the Spirit in a violent institution?"[62] In a recent consultation I participated in with Canadian Mennonite police officers, one of the officers adamantly asserted that policing was her "calling" and that she was trained to kill and would do so if she had to on the job. None of the participants in that consultation challenged her on this point.

We might further ask whether policing will open the doors of peace churches to military occupations. After all, if just policing advocates can credibly separate individual police officers who do not commit violence on the job from the larger system of violence which they participate in, why not make the same argument for the military? There are people who go their entire careers without using a weapon: air traffic controllers, doctors, psychiatrists, and other military employees. Yet they are part of a killing machine, every aspect of which is bent on making sure the military is as efficient and deadly as possible. Isn't it the same with police forces? Individuals may be good people who do not want to harm others, but they are part of a system, and to ignore that system does them and the church a disservice.

The problem here is not just that peace church members might advocate for peaceable policies while simultaneously participating in violence. Rather, the problem is that members of the peace church tradition have missed that even nonviolent solutions can be oppressive and damaging when wielded by police and other institutions that presume to create order. For example, while in the Birmingham city jail, Martin Luther King Jr. lamented the white church's support for the police but acknowledged that the police had "been rather disciplined in their public handling of the demonstrators. In this sense they have been rather publicly nonviolent."[63] In this instance, nonviolence was used as a tool, "to preserve the evil system of segregation." Though King consistently argued that means must be commensurate with the end sought, he lamented the use of moral means to preserve an evil end and claimed that "there is no greater treason than to do the right deed for the wrong reason" (301). Since a nonviolent society can still be oppressive and unjust, the absence of lethal force or use of peaceful tactics is not enough to justify Christian support of or participation in such a force.

That nonviolent action can be a tool of oppression leads us into the issue of Constantinianism. John Howard Yoder argued that the church should not fall into the trap of Constantinianism—of trying to control the structure of non-Christian society. Instead the church's primary responsibility is to build up the internal life of the church as a model for the world. Constantinianism shifts Christians from such an ecclesial focus to a wider level of civilization because it asserts that, "the true meaning of history, the true locus of salvation, is in the cosmos and not in the church. What God is really doing is being done primarily through the framework of society as a whole and not in the Christian community."[64] Koontz has argued that the project to systematically provide a theology and practice of security assumes that

> Mennonite Christians are already in positions of power, they need our advice, we are failing to love our neighbors if we don't give good, practical advice to the emperor, we have opportunities to promote peace through the exercise of power that we have not had previously, we need to defend our good neighbors

against bad neighbors, there is not a stark contrast between Christians and "the world," etc.[65]

Clearly such a worldview is operating in the just policing theory.

Yet Koontz's analysis on the Constantinianism of just policing, while accurate, does not fully explain why these ethicists have taken up *policing* as a paradigm. Although he demonstrates how Constantinian Christians assume they can save society by taking control of its reins, he does not expose the belief that supports this thinking, namely that the "civilized" world has the best models for responsible social action. The history of policing recounted in this essay makes it clear that we cannot naively assume that the institutions of the nation-state and the civilized world have any "life-giving purpose."

Indeed, when we look to "legal systems, political organizations, and economic structures" as our primary example for engaging the world—as is the case with just policing—we unwittingly legitimize systems of domination and oppression. By focusing on merely minimizing the violence of these systems of domination and control, just policing fails to ask the simple question of what a world that does not need to be controlled might look like.

CONCLUSION

Since the 1990s various ethicists have argued that the world has changed and that the line between war and peace is now substantially blurred. In light of what appears to be a new reality, several Christian ethicists have crafted and advocated a just policing theory to change the face of war and minimize the threat its violence poses. Yet these thinkers have developed this paradigm based on ahistorical arguments that distort the police's function in modern society and a model of community policing whose tactics include scapegoating undesirable people, stripping them of their rights, and in many cases using violence against them all in the name of protecting the "community."

Unlike just policing theory, my sustained analysis suggests that policing of any stripe is not a panacea for the ills of war. Problems inherent in community policing would only be magnified on the international scene, where "community" is more contested and complex and dominant players exert their will even more forcefully. While just policing's propositions are flawed from a practical standpoint, it is its challenge to peace churches that poses even more concern. Just policing may coax congregations that have confessed nonviolence as their *modus operandi* to accept violence and to see nonviolence as a technique.

   Christian ethicists who support just policing have too often failed to critique the deeper systems of domination and oppression that characterizes the structures to which they look toward. Without this analysis, just policing leads toward the Constantinian option, that perennial temptation that perpetually dangles before the church. The only question is whether they still have enough resistance to refuse the temptation.

NOTES

   1. Vaclav Havel, "Kosovo and the End of the Nation-State," *New York Review of Books*, June 10, 1999.

   2. Tony Blair, "A New Generation Draws the Line," *Newsweek* 133, no. 16, March 1, 1999, 40.

   3. Jürgen Habermas, "Bestialität und Humanität: Ein Krieg an der Grenze zwischen Recht und Moral," *Die Zeit*, April 29, 1999. Translation is mine.

   4. Ulrich Beck, "Der Militärische Pazifismus: Über den postnationalen Krieg," *Süddeutsche Zeitung*, April 19, 1999. Any translations from this article are mine.

   5. Ibid. See also Ulrich Beck, "War is Peace: On Post-National War," *Security Dialogue* 36, no. 5 (2005): 5–26.

   6. Even Kosovo was largely motivated by the same old politics. See Noam Chomsky, *The New Military Humanism: Lessons from Kosovo* (Monroe, Me.: Common Courage Press, 1999).

   7. David Cortright, *Peace: A History of Movements* (New York: Cambridge University Press, 2008), 4.

   8. See Gerald Schlabach, "Just Policing: How War Could Cease to be a Church-Dividing Issue," in *Just Policing: Mennonite-Catholic Theological Colloquium, 2002*, ed. Ivan J. Kauffman (Kitchener, Ontario: Pandora Press, 2004); Gerald Schlabach, "Just Policing and the Christian Call to Nonviolence," in *At Peace and Unafraid: Public Order, Security, and the Wisdom of the Cross*, ed. Duane K. Friesen and Gerald Schlabach (Scottdale, Pa.: Herald Press, 2005), 405-21; and *Just Policing, Not War*. ed. Gerald Schlabach (Collegeville, Minn.: Liturgical Press, 2007), 3–22; 69–108.

   9. Schlabach, ed., *Just Policing, Not War*, 3

   10. I should note that Schlabach drew from a growing body of Christians who have called for policing instead of war. For example, an MCC statement released after the attacks urged national leaders in the U.S. "to exercise restraint and respect for the process of international law and diplomacy." Likewise, Duane Friesen urged Mennonites to view the attacks as a crime rather than an act of war and claimed that the U.S. should "mobilize the international community in a 'police' action." In October 2001, John Paul Lederach called for "international policing and legal proceedings" to deal with the master-minds behind the attacks. As will become clear later in this book, calls

for international police forces have had a long history. The post 9-11 focus on policing has simply renewed debates that began in the medieval period.

11. Michael Joseph Smith, "Strengthen the United Nations and International Efforts for Cooperation and Human Rights," in *Just Peacemaking: Ten Practices for Abolishing War*, ed. Glen Stassen (Cleveland, Oh.: The Pilgrim Press, 2008), 154. In the introduction, Stassen, Friesen and Langan note that not all of the contributors to the working conference that produced the book agreed with Smith's chapter. See *Just Peacemaking*, 26. Furthermore, the authors claimed that they mean just peacemaking theory to supplement rather than replace the just war theory (or pacifism). Ibid., 2.

12. In an essay with Herald Press, I have examined how just policing theorists such as Schlabach and Jim Wallis have misused Yoder to further their agenda. I do not think Yoder would endorse the just policing agenda, and did not use the distinction to set up a systematic theology of security as these thinkers who invoke him have. See "Unbinding Yoder from Just Policing," in *Power and Practices: Engaging the Work of John Howard Yoder*, ed. Jeremy Bergen and Anthony Siegrist (Scottdale, Pa.: Herald Press, 2009), 147-165.

13. John Howard Yoder, *The Politics of Jesus*, 2nd ed. (Grand Rapids, Mich.: Wm. B. Eerdmans, 1994), 204.

14. M. I. Finley, *Politics in the Ancient World* (New York: Cambridge University Press, 1983), 18; David Cohen, *Law, Violence, and Community in Classical Athens* (New York: Cambridge University Press, 1995), 4.

15. The architecture of the fortress which housed the soldiers included a tower. A sentry in the tower would have been able to see the commotion and alert the tribune. See Brian Rapske, *The Book of Acts and Paul in Roman Custody* (Grand Rapids, Mich.: Wm. B. Eerdmans, 1994), 138.

16. Wilfried Nippel, *Public Order in Ancient Rome* (New York: Cambridge University Press, 1995), 2.

17. The Statute of Winchester was the only piece of English legislation dealing with policing for 600 years until the Metropolitan Police Act of 1826 established the London police.

18. Raymond Fosdick, *American Police Systems* (New York: The Century Company, 1920), 59, provides early sources for the Boston and Philadelphia watches. On Boston see Roger Lane, *Policing the City: Boston 1822-1885* (Cambridge, Mass.: Harvard University Press, 1967), 6; Eric H. Monkkonen, *Police in Urban America, 1860-1920* (New York: Cambridge University Press, 1981), 46.

19. Charles Tilly, "War Making and State Making as Organized Crime," in *Bringing the State Back In*, ed. Peter Evans, Dietrich Rueschemeyer, and Theda Skocpol (Cambridge, U.K.: Cambridge University Press, 1985), 181.

20. Charles Tilly, "Reflections on the History of European State-making," in *The Formation of National States in Western Europe*, ed. Charles Tilly and Gabriel Ardant (Princeton, N.J.: Princeton University Press, 1975), 49.

21. Tilly also argues that "to the extent that the threats against which a given government protects its citizens are imaginary or are the consequences of its own activities, the government has organized a protection racket." Thus, in Tilly's view, sometimes the state does fabricate threats. But more importantly, the state defines order and disorder which marks out the boundaries of policital conflict. See Tilly, "War Making and State Making as Orga-

nized Crime," 171.

22. Michel Foucault, *Security, Territory, Population: Lectures at the Collège de France, 1977-1978*, trans. Graham Burchell and ed. Arnold Davidson (New York: Palgrave, 2007), 334. Foucault cites Magdalene Humpert, *Bibliographie der Kamerlwissenschaften* (Cologne: K. Schroeder, 1937) who compiled a bibliography reaching back to the sixteenth century that included over four thousand titles dealing with police science.

23. Marc Raeff, *The Well-Ordered Police State: Social and Institutional Change through Law in the Germanies and Russia, 1600-1800* (New Haven: Yale University Press, 1983), 52–53.

24. Sally Hadden, *Slave Patrols: Law and Violence in Virginia and the Carolinas* (Cambridge, Mass.: Harvard University Press, 2001); Neil Websdale, *Policing the Poor: From Slave Plantation to Public Housing* (Boston: Northeastern University Press, 2001); and Kristin Williams, *Our Enemies in Blue: Police and Power in America* (Brooklyn, N.Y.: Soft Skull Press, 2004). These patrols were the result of trial and error, mixing the constable and watch systems with Caribbean slave patrols.

25. Williams, *Our Enemies in Blue*, 44.

26. Websdale, *Policing the Poor*, 50.

27. Eugene J. Watts, "The Police in Atlanta, 1890-1905," *The Journal of Southern History* 39, no. 2 (1973): 171.

28. *Atlanta Constitution*, July 29, 1885.

29. Quoted in Watts, "The Police in Atlanta, 1890-1905," *The Journal of Southern History* 39, no. 2 (1973): 171.

30. Ibid. Quoted also in Brendan Maguire, "The Historical Police in the United States: A Four City Analysis," in *The Past, Present, and Future of American Criminal Justice*, ed. Brendan Maguire and Polly Radosh (Dix Hills, N.Y.: General Hall, 1996), 42.

31. As one commentator, Charles Brace, described the dangerous classes in New York in 1872: "There are thousands upon thousands in New York who have no assignable home, and 'flit' from attic to attic, and cellar to cellar; there are other thousands more or less connected with criminal enterprises; and still other tens of thousands, poor, hard-pressed. . . . Let but Law lift its hand from them for a season, or let the civilizing influences of American life fail to reach them, and, if the opportunity afforded, we should see and explosion from this class which might leave the city in ashes and blood." Charles Brace, *The Dangerous Classes of New York and Twenty Years' Work among Them* (New York: Wynkoop & Hallenbeck, 1872), 29. See also Randall G. Shelden, *Controlling the Dangerous Classes: A Critical Introduction to the History of Criminal Justice* (Boston: Allyn and Bacon, 2001). For a nineteenth-century discussion of the unemployable "dangerous class" see Christopher G. Tiedman, "Police Control of the Dangerous Classes, Other than by Criminal Prosecution," *American Law Review* July-Aug. (1885).

32. Lane, *Policing the City: Boston 1822-1885* 19-20. See also his statistics for the rise in crimes "against public order" and a decrease in violent crimes from 1835 to 1900 in Roger Lane, "Crime and Criminal Statistics in Nineteenth-Century Massachusetts," *Journal of Social History* 2, no. 2 (1968): 159.

33. Monkkonen, *Police in Urban America*, 190, n. 13: "drunkenness became the single most important offense in Boston."

34. See also Lane, "Crime and Criminal Statistics in Nineteenth-Century Massachusetts," and Maguire, "The Historical Police in the United States: A Four City Analysis," 45.

35. Canadian police have been analyzed in a similar manner. See Helen Boritch and John Hagan, "Crime and the Changing Forms of Class Control: Policing Public Order in 'Toronto the Good' 1859-1955," *Social Forces* 66, no. 2 (1987).

36. Williams, *Our Enemies in Blue*, 62.

37. Marilynn Johnson, *Street Justice: A History of Police Violence in New York City* (Boston: Beacon Press, 2003), 14.

38. Schlabach, "Just Policing," 23; and Duane Friesen, "In Search of Security: A Theology and Ethic of Peace," in *At Peace and Unafraid*, ed. Duane K. Friesen and Gerald Schlabach (Scottdale, Pa.: Herald Press, 2005), 68–69.

39. Monkkonen, *Police in Urban America*, 24.

40. Schlabach, "Just Policing," 30.

41. Tobias Winright, "Community Policing as a Paradigm for International Relations," in *Just Policing, Not War*, ed. Gerald Schlabach, 142.

42. Ibid. Schlabach's references all use the broken windows theory as a basis for their studies. See Schlabach, "Just Policing," 71 n. 60.

43. Quoted in Peter B. Kraska and Victor E. Kappeler, "Militarizing American Police: The Rise and Normalization of Paramilitary Units," in *The Police and Society*, ed. Victor E. Kappeler (Prospect Heights, Ill.: Waveland Press, 1997), 472.

44. James Q. Wilson and George L. Kelling, "Broken Windows," *Atlantic Monthly* 249, no. 3 (1982): 30.

45. A homeless person is "in effect, the first broken window." Ibid.: 34.

46. René Girard, *Violence and the Sacred*, trans. Patrick Gregory (Baltimore: Johns Hopkins University Press, 1977), 13.

47. Lawrence Lessig, "The Regulation of Social Meaning," *University of Chicago Law Review* 62, no. 3 (1995): 1040.

48. For example, see "Orlando: 'Don't feed homeless'," *St. Petersburg Times*, July 26, 2006, and Michael Janofsky, "Many Cities In Crackdown On Homeless," *New York Times*, December 16, 1994.

49. Shane Claiborne, *The Irresistible Revolution: Living as an Ordinary Radical* (Grand Rapids: Zondervan, 2006), 233–34.

50. See Schlabach, "Just Policing," 43.

51. See Ibid., 45, and Winright, "Community Policing as a Paradigm for International Relations," 139, 41, who claim that this "us versus them" mentality is not present in community policing but only in the militarized version of policing.

52. Raymond Williams, *Key Words: A Vocabulary of Culture and Society* (Glasgow: Fontana, 1976), 76.

53. David Kocieniewski, "So Many Crimes, and Reasons to Not Cooperate," *New York Times*, December 30, 2007.

54. Ibid.

55. Black mistrust of police is much broader than just in Camden, New Jersey. For example, a relatively small city outside of Philadelphia called Coaxeville, where the sheriff and a dozen men once lynched a black man with impunity, has implemented a community policing program. Yet a local newspa-

per reported that one officer laments, "'[Black people] have their own little society, their own little culture,' Audette says, saying many blacks won't step forward when they witness crimes, even murders. 'I don't understand it.'" See Mark Fazlollah and Keith Herbert, "Old Town Tries New Approach," *Philadephia Inquirer*, December 18, 2007.

56. Duane K. Friesen and Gerald Schlabach, eds., *At Peace and Unafraid: Public Order, Security, and the Wisdom of the Cross* (Scottdale, Pa.: Herald Press, 2005), 160-61.

57. See Ted Koontz, "Grace to You and Peace: Towards a Gospel of Peace for the 21st Century" (paper presented at the Seeking the Welfare of the City: Public Peace, Justice and Order, Akron, Ohio, August 2004). Cited with Koontz's permission.

58. See "Just Policing: How War Could Cease to be a Church-Dividing Issue," 59.

59. James Reimer, "Christians and the Use of Force," *Canadian Mennonite*, August 30, 1999, 7. In another essay, Reimer defines policing broadly as "A metaphor for all forms of institutional life in civil society in which the exercise of power is necessary for maintaining discipline and order on domestic, municipal, provincial and international levels." James Reimer, "Policing and the Civil Order," in *Mennonites and Classical Theology: Dogmatic Foundations for Christian Ethics* (Kitchener, Ontario: Pandora Press, 2001), 494. In this essay Reimer argues that Conrad Grebel University should accept money from the Canadian Department of National Defense to research "human security."

60. In fact, some Mennonites had already begun. Eight police officers who attend Mennonite or Brethren in Christ congregations met at Conrad Grebel University College to confer with one another. See "Police Officers Focus on Peace Role," *Canadian Mennonite*, December 22, 2003 and "Police officers consider peace role, beliefs," *The Mennonite*, January 20, 2004.

61. James Reimer, "Is Force Sometimes Justified? *Gibt Es 'Legitime Gewalt?'*" (paper presented at the Seeking the Welfare of the City: Public Peace, Justice and Order, Akron, Ohio, August 2004), 6. Quoted with Reimer's permission; italics are mine.

62. Pamela Leach, "Gadfly Citizenship: Faithful Public Practices Beyond the National Security Model," in *At Peace and Unafraid*, 110.

63. Martin Luther King, "Letter from Birmingham City Jail," in *A Testament of Hope: The Essential Writings and Speeches of Martin Luther King Jr*, ed. James Melvin Washington (San Francisco: HarperSanFrancisco, 1991), 301.

64. John Howard Yoder, "Christ, the Hope of the World," in *The Royal Priesthood*, ed. Michael Cartwright (Grand Rapids, Mich.: Wm. B. Eerdmans, 1994), 198.

65. See Koontz, "Grace to Your and Peace."

Chapter 5

AFTER WHITENESS: TRADITION, VIRTUE, AND THEOPOLITICAL NONVIO-LENCE IN A (POST)COLONIAL CONSTANTINIAN AGE

Derek Alan Woodard-Lehman

POST-CONSTANTINIAN MELANCHOLIA[1]

Something has gone horribly wrong, or so we are told. The moorings and mores of our culture have been eroded, if not eviscerated. Ours is an historical moment of unprecedented crisis in which the very future of our culture, nation, and civilization itself are at stake. Those who would not so easily surrender to the relativistic multiculture of globalization are presently embroiled in "culture wars" and "a clash of civilizations."[2] Likewise those who would not acquiesce to the solipsistic hedonism of postmodernity are confronted by the prospect of doing "ethics after Babel" and affirming religious belief against an "heretical imperative."[3]

The present is an era after empire, after civilization, after virtue.[4] The hour is late, and the vandals are already at the gate. We teeter on the brink of "cultural devastation," and a "New Dark Ages" may already have settled in upon us.[5] Beleaguered by such challenges, how can the church go on? Can the gospel make sense? Is Christian ethics possible? As the psalmist asks, "If the foundations are destroyed, what can the righteous do?" (Ps. 11:3).

Paul Gilroy describes the desperation evident in this rhetoric of catastrophe as "(post)colonial melancholia."[6] The malaise afflicting the late modern West "is driven by the need to get back to the place or moment before the country lost its moral and cultural bearings. . . . (and the) turning back in this direction is also a turning away from the perceived dangers of pluralism and from the irreversible fact of multiculture."[7] This nostalgic yearning is a labor of reparative reasoning attempting to recover a lost past by which to effect the repair of a damaged present.[8] Facing the loss of both geopolitical power and cultural-ethical coherence, such discourses of cultural devastation, moral dissipation, and political dissolution valorize certain configurations of cultural-national identity and correlatively demonize those unwilling or unable to conform thereto. They thus constitute a problematic offering a particular account of political foreigners, ethical outsiders, and cultural strangers by which race and nation are coarticulated *vis a vis* citizenship, and the (ir)rationality, (im)morality, and (in)humanity of the Other are narrated as the cause of societal collapse.[9] Inasmuch as the culture(s), nation(s), and civilization(s) under threat are those of the West, this problematic of cultural devastation is a crisis of whiteness.

The revival of virtue ethics by Alasdair MacIntyre represents a theologically inflected iteration of this problematic. He convincingly argues that ethical judgments have lost their normative force. Moral language only makes sense within the coherent context of a common form of life provided by a tradition. Absent a shared conception of the good relative to which authoritative judgments of virtue and vice can be rendered, moral language is little better than emotivist opining. MacIntyre thus asserts that the only viable tradition surviving the dissolution wrought by the acids of modernity is that of the Aristotelian virtues. Inasmuch as the Aristotelian tradition retains premodern structures of authority and normative excellence, particularly as instantiated within the Roman Catholic Church, it thus can resist and reverse the fragmentation inherent in autonomous moral judgment and restore normative force to ethical speech.[10] Thus, MacIntyre's reparative gesture takes on a particular posture, adversarially positing tradition over and against modernity and postmodernity.

Stanley Hauerwas finds MacIntyre's traditionalism and its with-
ering critique of modernity and liberalism consonant with the radical
ecclesiology of John Howard Yoder. Its teleological, authoritative,
and habitual structure and correlative refusal of ethical autonomy respectively correspond to the "body politics" and "radical catholicity"
of Yoder.[11] MacIntyre further provides radical ecclesiology with a rigorous formal account of the interrelationship of means and ends
(practices and virtues relative to the good) within a shared form of
life extended across time and space (tradition).[12] This is open to
Hauerwas's own ethically reparative project curative of the theological maladies of Constantinianism and liberalism.[13] It resists the
sacralization of the state (Constantinianism) and responds to the secularization of public speech (liberalism) by demonstrating that ethics
requires a vision of the good determinative of a shared form of life
that is not simply reducible to rational self-interest—personal, national, or otherwise.

But, Hauerwas's adoption of MacIntyrian traditionalism is not as
straightforward as it might first appear. Though an admirer of the
Roman Catholic Church and Thomistic moral theology, Hauerwas
locates the substance for which the MacIntyre's formal account of the
virtues calls in Yoder, rather than Aristotle. More importantly, he
does not share MacIntyre's wider investment in Western civilization.
While MacIntyre is in search of a new Benedict who will establish alternative forms of community capable of sustaining the moral life in
these New Dark Ages, it is to be remembered that the ultimate outcome of the original Benedictine monasticism was the High Middle
Ages that produced Thomas Aquinas. For MacIntyre, both Benedictine monasticism and Thomistic Christendom are traditions equally
capable of sustaining the moral life.[14] For Hauerwas, Christendom itself is a threat to the (Christian) moral life; the devastation in view is
ecclesial, not civilizational.[15] Therefore, it is perhaps not wholly accurate to label Hauerwas a "MacIntyrian."

Though this observation is not synonymous with Jeffrey Stout's
critique of "the new traditionalism," I am indebted to him for signal-
ing the dissonance between the Yoderian and MacIntyrian strands of
Hauerwas's theopolitical ethics of nonviolence.[16] But, I submit that
Stout mischaracterizes Hauerwas's adoption of MacIntyre as a globally constructive project, rather than as a discrete critical move. That
is, Stout fails to recognize that Hauerwas applies MacIntyre to a specific theological problem—modernity and liberalism, rather than in-
tegrating him into a comprehensive system. I make this suggestion
based on Brad Kallenberg's Wittgensteinian reading of Hauerwas as

a practitioner of self-consuming, therapeutic, aporetic pedagogy.[17] Like Wittgenstein's philosophy, Hauerwas's theopolitics of nonviolence ought not to be approached as a system. Rather, it is a series of specific interventions intended to change the subject (both the topic and the self); "they aim at changing the sensibilities and skills of the reader," thus enabling her to go on.[18] Thus, the dissonance between the Yoderian and MacIntyrian elements is not an inconsistency or deficiency but instead is an aporetic opening by which Hauerwas draws his readers deeper into mystery of faith, the life of Christ, and the witness of the church.

Though this is the case, Hauerwas is not absolved of all complicity with the problematic of cultural devastation and its attendant (post)colonial Constantinianism. Inasmuch as "civilization, commerce, and Christianity ever go hand in hand" in generating and maintaining modernity, antimodern traditionalism is not enough to effect disavowal.[19] The MacIntyrian impulse, limited and altered though it may be, relies on "highly coherent and 'well-integrated' traditions" tending toward insularity.[20] Thus Hauerwas's particular iteration of traditionalism tends to leave untouched the ecclesial segregation mirroring that of the broader society. Stated with an Aristotelian inflection, homogeneously white congregations partake in the ambient white habitus characteristic of American society in general. In so doing, such congregations serve as a passive civil religion implicitly providing theological justification for the racialized social antagonisms and political violences constitutive of (post)colonial Constantinianism.[21]

Thus the problematic of cultural devastation and the (post)colonial condition implicit in the new traditionalism complicate matters. But, this is not finally devastating to Hauerwas's theopolitics. His adoption and adaptation of MacIntyrian traditionalism surmount one theological problem—the ethical and political autonomy of liberalism, while opening up yet another—ecclesial complicity in racialized segregation.[22] But this itself can be overcome by extending an underdeveloped component of Kallenberg's account of Hauerwas's aporetic pedagogy; namely, "that we ought always to attend to *differences*."[23] By so-extending this pedagogy in a direction I describe as kenotic, Hauerwas's theopolitics of nonviolence can overcome, at least provisionally, its tacit participation in what I have been calling here "(post)colonial Constantinianism."

With respect to present ecclesial conditions in the United States, this extensional recovery consists in the repudiation of whiteness and its ostensible crisis as manifest in the problematic of cultural devastation. This is, of course, a performative task and not merely descriptive. The sort of descriptions and practices necessary for disavowal are only possible within a community that "confound(s) the conventional distinctions between nationalism (i.e. the localized operations of whiteness) and cosmopolitanism (i.e. the globalized operations of whiteness)."[24] In short, the recovery of the intelligibility compromised by (post)colonial Constantinianism requires white Christians to place themselves under the tutelage of nonwhite ecclesial communities whose *aversive* modernity is resistant to the white supremacy of *European* modernity, thereby transgressing the identity constitutive of the American nation-state and nonviolently transcending the exclusions of whiteness.[25]

THE VICE OF VIRTUE: CULTURAL DEVASTATION AS CRISIS OF WHITENESS

Before undertaking the extensional recovery described above, fuller explication of the crisis of whiteness manifest in the problematic of cultural devastation is in order, especially as it is articulated by MacIntyrian traditionalism. Though not expressly theological, the analysis of David Theo Goldberg provides a compelling account of the operations of whiteness in, and as, the form of (post)colonial Constantinianism.[26] He identifies the mutual reinforcement of rationality, morality, and humanity *vis a vis* citizenship—capacity for self-rule; how the "citizen" becomes the normative subject, and thus determinative of the rational, the moral, and the human.[27] Like Hauerwas, Goldberg thus highlights the indissoluble unity of ethics and politics; and moreover, how ethics philosophically and culturally legitimize political violence.

Though especially true of modernity, Goldberg insists this has been the case throughout history and precedes the advent of European exploration and colonization. While the philosophical mode of morality and the governmental form of sovereignty vary across time, their underlying logic remains constant.[28] "Citizens" are moral, rational, human beings existing inside history and civilization; "barbarians" are immoral, irrational, inhuman beings existing outside history and civilization. Thus, ethics is fundamentally political anthropology. Beginning with Aristotle,

> A barbarian was one of emphatically different, even strange, language, conduct, and culture lacking the cardinal virtues of

wisdom, courage, temperance, and justice. The principle distinction was political. Hellenic democracy was contrasted with
barbarian despotism and tyranny. The democratic state alone
was deemed a free one, the state where political relationships—
and so distinctly human virtues—could flourish.[29]

That this originates in the Greek city-state, and the ethics and politics
of Aristotle, thoroughly implicates MacIntyrian tradition and virtue
in the operations of the citizen-barbarian distinction by which political violence is legitimated.[30]

Colonial modernity subsequently racializes this distinction as a
difference between Enlightened Europe and Darkest Africa. First it-
erated as a contrast between the European and the non-European, the
distinction later transposes into the difference between white and
non-white—paradigmatically between white and black. Moreover,
by linking this to soteriological status in the kingdom of darkness or
the kingdom of light, these distinctions were given explicitly theological rationales.[31] James Perkinson describes this as the illicit combination of the ethical, the political, and the theological into a "soteriologic" of whiteness.[32] Thus over time,

> The question "Are you savable within the spiritual economy of
> a redeemed Christian humanity?" becomes in enlightenment
> form, "Are you orderable within the scientific taxonomy of a
> civilized European humanity?"[33]

Race becomes a medium of political and theological exchange—
a (post)colonial Constantinian theopolitics; skin is *literally* a semi-
permeable membrane through which persons are, or are not, admitted into the coextensive body politic and body of Christ conceived as
the *corpus Christianum*.[34] Put directly, "The first modern supremacy
was Christian. White supremacy became its simplest shorthand."[35]

Thus, the catastrophic rhetoric melancholically invoking civilizational collapse and cultural devastation can be seen to be both the
most recent episode in the cyclical crisis of whiteness and as the present (post)colonial form of Constantinianism. While advancing the
critique of liberalism, Hauerwas's deployment of MacIntyre simultaneously reinscribes the very Constantinianism he seeks to disavow.
Even if Yoderian virtue substitutes for Aristotelian, MacIntyrian traditionalism partakes in the melancholic turning away from difference and the perceived dangers of multiculture identified by Gilroy.
Thus, as a theological iteration of (post)colonial Constantinianism, it
is untenable as a component of any theopolitics of nonviolence,

Hauerwasian or otherwise. But this is not to suggest, as Stout does, that the Yoderian and MacIntyrian components of Hauerwas's own theopolitics are strictly contradictory; only that they are incomplete, and that an additional therapeutic intervention is needed.

This is to say that the dissonance between MacIntyre and Yoder is a damning contradiction only if Hauerwas intends to construct a coherent systematic whole. But following Kallenberg, I suggest no such intention exists. Hauerwas never claims to bring MacIntyre and Yoder into systemic harmony, and it is not at all clear to me that he is obligated to do so. Instead, stated in a Wittgensteinian trope, "(We) must so to speak throw away the (MacIntyrian) ladder, after (we have) climbed up on it."[36]

Hauerwas's use of MacIntyrian traditionalism nonetheless implicates him in the problematic of cultural devastation. While MacIntyre aids in the extrication of the church from the ethical autonomy of modern liberalism, it does nothing to purge it of (post)colonial Constantinianism. Moreover Hauerwas's trading in the MacIntyrian rhetoric of catastrophe impedes the necessary disavowal by inadvertently reinforcing the soteriologic of whiteness.

What is required now is an additional intervention capable of moving beyond the new traditionalist impasse; what is needed is a means of surmounting the aporia posed by the explicit renunciation of liberalism and the implicit reassertion of its constitutive racialized social antagonisms and violences by segregated congregations. What is demanded, in short, are practices by which to overcome the white *habitus* dominating most American congregations.[37] But before attempting to do so, further discussion of white habitus is required.

SEGREGATION, SEEING, AND SAYING: WHITE HABITUS

Eduardo Bonilla-Silva describes a new "color-blind racism . . . (that) explains contemporary racial inequality as the outcome of nonracial dynamics."[38] He identifies "a white habitus, a racialized, uninterrupted socialization process that *conditions* and *creates* whites' racial taste, perceptions, feelings, and emotions and their views on racial matters."[39] Though drawn from the sociology of Pierre Bordieu rather than the philosophy of Aristotle or Wittgenstein, Bonilla-Silva uses many of the same categories and concepts as Hauerwas. At the heart of his analysis are the interrelating and reinforcing practices of story-shaped communities governing their normative descriptions of the world: a self-authenticating account of how things really are.

These take on an ideological function as certain descriptions become racial commonsense: the "'of course' way of understanding what is happening in the world."[40] Taken together, this "loosely organized set of ideas, phrases, and stories (serve as) . . . *collective representations* whites have developed to explain, and ultimately justify, contemporary racial inequality."[41]

This is to say, the chief feature of white habitus is its enclosure and insulation from other forms of life and their competing narrations. Such enclosure and insulation enables its particular description to remain uninterrupted and unchallenged and thus to become universal explanation—an explanation implicitly justifying the antagonisms and violences of (post)colonial Constantinianism.

Michael Emerson and Christian Smith develop a similar account of the ways in which the white church expressly produces, and is produced by, white habitus.[42] Like Bonilla-Silva, they identify the contrast between white explanations of social disparity as the outcome of nonracial dynamics and those of blacks who identify explicitly racialized and racist dynamics. Specifically they interrogate these phenomena relative to competing explanations of the ongoing segregation of the church.[43] Emerson and Smith identify three specific "religio-cultural tools" of whites echoing Bonilla-Silva's frames: "Accountable freewill individualism," "Relationalism," and "Antistructuralism."[44] Thus white explanations of ecclesial segregation and social inequality more generally tend to blame individuals for their disadvantage and to suggest social change is best effected through aggregated personal change; to identify (personal) relational causes and correlative solutions; and to insist that individual preferences are unassailable (e.g. for a neighborhood, and especially for a congregation or denomination), even if these foreseeably, and inevitably, lead to segregation and inequality.[45]

Even when concerned and committed to "racial reconciliation"—a particular kind of peacemaking—whites were largely unwilling to accept explanations that posited societal or structural causes to segregation and inequality. Thus, Emerson and Smith conclude, something is "lost in translation" between whites and blacks—even when together engaged in a shared struggle for reconciliation and peace.[46]

But perhaps more interesting to present discussion are the findings of Emerson and Smith relative to whites who are able to see and speak outside their dominant habitus. The *sine qua non* of whites transcending and transgressing their own racial habitus is "the density of (their) interracial experiences."[47] Density here denotes two things:

first, having a broad range of interracial contacts—not just one black friend; and second, that there is depth and longevity to these relationships—not just shallow, transient acquaintance. This stands in contrast to most respondents whose lives were "at least ninety percent white in their daily experience."[48] Only by having their native racial habitus constantly challenged and corrected by exposure and engagement with others could they accept the limits of their own descriptions as well as the validity of other descriptions by which such non-isolated persons came to recognize segregation and racially correlated social inequality as both real and morally significant.[49]

While echoing Bonilla-Silva in identifying racial isolation and insularity as the chief feature of white habitus, Emerson and Smith also highlight the additional danger of having this insularity *theologically* justified and *ecclesially* routinized. This returns us to the extension of Hauerwasian theopolitics by which the problematic of cultural devastation may be surmounted. As Hauerwas rightly insists, "Morally you can only act in a world that you can see, and you can only see *by learning to say*."[50] For Christians, ethical pedagogy comes primarily through the liturgy and the life of the congregation. This pedagogy of sight and speech, what Yoder calls body politics, determines "which conversations are worth having and which are not . . . what connections are worth making."[51]

What Bonilla-Silva and Emerson and Smith reveal is that white Christians literally cannot see, cannot say, and therefore cannot act ethically in ways that resist the world of (post)colonial Constantinianism. By learning to speak "the second first language of the faith" in predominantly homogenous congregations, a liturgical pedagogy of whiteness occludes these conversations and obscures these connections from being worthwhile and meaningful to white American Christians.[52]

In other words the insularity and isolation of homogeneous congregations means white Christians are familiar with only one set of descriptions and meanings. And "when we are fluent in only one set of concepts, we assume that this set is the only possible set, that our way of seeing the world *must* be correct."[53] This leaves the white church susceptible to the kind of ethical self-deception about which both Wittgenstein and Hauerwas are troubled. It allows white Christians, white congregations, white theology, and white ethics to "persistently avoid spelling out some feature of (their) engagement in the world"—namely its racialized character.[54]

In this case the refusal is in some measure an inability, a color-blindness preventing white Christians from seeing and saying what color means within conditions of (post)colonial Constantinianism. But inasmuch as this is something of a cultivated ignorance, it is ethically blameworthy; white Christians could, and should, know better.

If indeed, as Hauerwas rightly insists, "My body is *constituted* by the body called the church . . . (and) the church *is* the body from which we learn to understand our particular bodies," then white Christians cannot but know themselves as white, and cannot do otherwise than to understand themselves as raceless in the sense that Bonilla-Silva identifies as color-blind.[55] In homogenous white congregations, the body politics of the church thus reinforces the racialized politics of bodies constitutive of the modern nation-state and its violences. As James Perkinson puts it, "Space we might say, shapes habit."[56] White space produces white habitus.

So what is required is a different ecclesial spatialization than a MacIntyrian conception of the church as a highly coherent and well-integrated moral tradition. In short, we must recognize that "the very character of the (white) ecclesial community is the problematic rather than the resource for constructive retrieval, *hence inter-communal conversation* . . . is vital to expurgate hidden (racialized) power discrepancies."[57] Or to put it in a Hauerwasian idiom, the exilic and marginal stance taken by the church in relation to the world now must be reprised by white Christians within the church. Having achieved political disestablishment, white Christians must undertake an ecclesial and cultural disestablishment.

LITURGY AS KENOTIC PEDAGOGY: MULTICULTURAL CONGREGATION AS NEW POLITICAL IMAGINARY[58]

This second disestablishment is the marginal and exilic ethical labor of "disinvest(ing) in what we habitually feel and do, and turn(ing) ourselves into a project of becoming"—a Wittgenstinian (re)working of the self.[59] Such labor is not easy and cannot be accomplished by discursive means alone; the labor in view is a performative self-emptying, a kenotic repudiation of whiteness. As Hauerwas reminds, "Christian convictions are self-referential, but the reference is not to propositions but to lives."[60]

If white Christians are to learn the faith anew to be able to see and to speak an ethical world other than that of the raceless colorblindness of (post)colonial Constantinianism, they must inhabit a new ecclesial-liturgical space in which such an alternative political imaginary is possible.[61] This space and imaginary are to be sought in congregations that do not merely reinscribe and reinforce the operations of whiteness; that is in nonwhite and multicultural congregations.[62]

Although ecclesial relocation is the condition of possibility for the kenotic repudiation of whiteness, it is not enough in and of itself. In describing the Wittgenstinian therapeutic philosophy of Hauerwas, Kallenberg observes that one "(cannot) rightly be shaped by any dosage of *self*-administered medication."[63] This underscores the kenotic dimension I am suggesting here. Both the ends and the means in view are self-emptying. With respect to the latter, white Christians must rely on the tutelage of nonwhite Christians to (re)learn the second first language of discipleship.[64] Furthermore, the density of interracial experiences constitutive of a kenotic pedagogy must be sustained across time; the requisite understanding cannot be dispensed with as an intermediary step along the way. "Rather, understanding would require immersion into the life and language of the (other) culture deeply enough to have one's primitive reactions trained to run along the same rails as those of natural speakers."[65]

Thus the "attention to differences" I suggested at the outset must be an ongoing recognition of whiteness as a destructive differentiating violence, rather than the demonization of nonwhite others suggested by the problematic of cultural devastation.[66] The kenotic performance sufficient to the task of fostering a new political imaginary is one in which "blackness is the first mirror of white self-recovery—not its savior, not its surrogate or solace—but its pedagogue."[67] Speaking as a (post)colonial subject, Gilroy echoes this observation:

> At this point colonial and (post)colonial persons can acquire a distinctive mission. Our modern history as disenchanted descendants of people who were themselves commodified for sale on an international market or deemed expendable within the larger racial logic of Europe-centered historical processes, gives us ready access to a fund of knowledge that is useful in a number of areas. These insights are not ours alone but will belong to anybody who is prepared to use them.[68]

But even this is not enough. There are ways in which the kenotic move proposed here can have a docetic character; that is, having the appearance of self-emptying but lacking the substance thereof.[69]

To move beyond this, intercultural engagement must transcend mere self-knowledge. As Gilroy enjoins, "The self-knowledge that can be acquired through the proximity of strangers is certainly precious but is no longer the primary issue . . . it must take second place behind *principled and methodological cultivation of a degree of estrange-*

ment from one's own culture and history."[70] Put directly, "Imagining oneself as a stranger in a limited and creative sense (must) instructively be linked *to actually becoming estranged from the cultural habits one is born to.*"[71] This is consonant with the fundamental Hauerwasian insistence that a theopolitics is validated only by the kind of people it produces. *Vis a vis* the experiences and interests of diasporic Africans in the Americas, Osayande Obery Hendricks pointedly says,

> Call yourself whatever you will, mouth whatever rhetorics of revolution, wear whatever footwear, whatever headwear, however you wear your hair (dreadlocks chillin', braided styles of untold permutations, or a close svelte 'fro), whatever *bubas*, whatever *dashikis*, whatever jewelry beads earrings noserings. However often you might sing "Kemet on my Mind" trying to sound like Ray Charles, however often you might quote Asante, quote Diop, quote ben Jochannan, quote anybody who says anything somebody might someday claim to be "African." *If your project doesn't serve the liberative interests of people of African descent in the teeth of white supremacy, it is not Afrocentric.*[72]

That is, the self-knowledge and imagination cultivated by kenotic pedagogy can only be validated by the actual existence of reconciled congregations whose speech and action have integrity. Slavoj Zizek, himself a relentless critic of liberalism and multiculturalism, describes this as "the uncoupling of Christ (that) is *not* an inner contemplative stance, but the active *work* of love which necessarily leads to the creation of an *alternative* community."[73] To conclude, echoing Aristotle, James Perkinson adds, "Only a lifetime of unrelenting struggle against the ideology of white superiority and the materiality of white control could qualify one as an ally."[74] We might add, that only such relentless lifelong struggle could be considered to be a theopolitics of nonviolence, could qualify one as a Christian pacifist, or could count as a peace church.

NOTES

1. I begin by noting that this essay, perhaps like some others in this anthology, is not focused precisely on "the world at war," at least not with respect to the so-called war on terror. Instead it focuses on what I take to be a more fundamental ambient antagonism seething beneath the surface of our presumably post-racial, multicultural, cosmopolitical global village. That said, it goes without saying that this antagonism funds and manifests itself in the present global war whose ostensible enemy is Islamic fundamentalism.

2. See Samuel Huntington, *The Clash of Civilizations and the Remaking of the World Order* (New York: Simon & Schuster, 1997); Samuel Huntington, *Who Are We Now? The Challenges to America's National Identity* (New York: Simon & Schuster, 2004); and James Davidson Hunter, *The Culture Wars: The Struggle to Define America* (New York: Basic Books, 1991).

3. See Jeffrey Stout, *Ethics After Babel: The Languages of Morals and Their Discontents* (Princeton, N.J.: Princeton University Press, 1998); Peter Berger, *The Heretical Imperative: Contemporary Possibilities of Religious Affirmation* (Garden City, N.Y.: Anchor Press, 1979).

4. Most of those employing the rhetoric of catastrophe tend toward neo-conservative nationalism. Samuel Huntington does so, as do less erudite public figures such as Jerry Falwell and Pat Robertson who blame the 9-11 attacks on American cultural-moral laxity as evidenced by feminists and homosexuals among others. But, not all the participants in this discourse share this agenda. Some trade in these tropes descriptively or responsively, as does James Davidson Hunter who is something of a reluctant culture warrior. Peter Berger and Jeffrey Stout do so polemically, arguing the alarm is overwrought, its rhetorical excess absurd, the premise of devastation untenable.

5. See Jonathan Lear, *Radical Hope: Ethics in the Face of Cultural Devastation* (Cambridge, Mass.: Harvard University Press, 2006); Alasdair MacIntyre, *After Virtue*, 2nd. ed. (Notre Dame, Ind.: University of Notre Dame Press, 1984).

6. Paul Gilroy, *Postcolonial Melancholia* (New York: Columbia University Press, 2005). Though his reflections specifically concern the United Kingdom, they were originally given as lectures at University of California Irvine, and are applicable to similar (post)colonial conditions, such as those of the United States.

7. Paul Gilroy, *Postcolonial Melancholia*, 89-90.

8. Reparative reasoning is a practice of immanent critique, undertaking a correction to an inherited tradition made by another part of that same tradition for the community constituting and constituted by that tradition. That is to say, it is those belonging to a tradition, using their tradition's resources, to extend that tradition's practices. I am indebted to Jacob Lynn Goodson for this understanding, and to Stanley Hauerwas for providing me with Goodson's unpublished essay, "The Performance of Pragmatism in the Baptist Theology of Martin Luther King Jr: The Baptist Vision, the Logic of Scripture, and Reparative Reasoning." See also Peter Ochs, "Philosophic Warrants for Scriptural Reasoning," *Modern Theology* 22, no. 3 (2006): 465-82.

9. Though certainly not monolithic or univocal, I take it that there is an identifiable descriptive, discursive, and diagnostic center of gravity, here designated as the problematic of cultural devastation, the rhetoric of catastrophe, and (post)colonial/postimperial melancholia.

10. At the outset MacIntyre did not expressly link the Aristotelian tradition of the virtues to the Roman Catholic Church, although he has done so subsequently. But even in its earliest articulation, his argument relies on, and refers to the Aristotelian tradition of Thomistic moral theology.

11. See John Howard Yoder, "Introduction," in *For the Nations: Essays Public & Evangelical* (Grand Rapids, Mich.: Eerdman's, 1997), 8 n19; John Howard Yoder, *Body Politics: Five Practices of the Christian Community Before the Watch-*

ing World (Scottdale, Pa.: Herald Press, 1992), respectively. By "radically catholic," Yoder indicates that Christological nonviolence has purchase on the whole church, and is not just the "sectarian vocation" of the historic peace churches. Moreover, it is this nonviolence itself which constitutes (radical) catholicity; i.e. that Christian identity is more determinative than racial-ethnic and/or national-political identity, and therefore Christians don't kill one another—the "modest proposal for peace" persistently proffered by the Mennonite Central Committee.

12. Beyond the critical and formal elements mentioned here, it is not at all clear to me what "work" MacIntyre and Aristotle do in Hauerwas's project. Negatively, MacIntyre forcefully shows why the ethical autonomy of liberalism (Kantian and/or Rawlsian) cannot ground normative moral judgments. And formally, Aristotle describes how practices and virtues function within a tradition. That Hauerwas qualifies and corrects Aristotle at every turn in order to bring him into line with the Christian moral excellences of Yoder suggests that there may not be much, or any, positive work being done by MacIntyre and/or Aristotle. Chief among these corrections is that the normative exemplar of Christian courage is the martyr, whereas the exemplar of Aristotelian courage is the soldier. For a complete account of these qualifications and corrections, see Stanley Hauerwas and Charles Pinches, *Christians Among the Virtues: Theological Conversations With Ancient and Modern Ethics* (Notre Dame, Ind.: University of Notre Dame Press, 1997).

13. I pause to note here that for both Yoder and Hauerwas there is no meaningful distinction between theology, ethics, and politics. I follow their synonymous usage and will use "theopolitical ethics" and "theopolitics" to emphasize their unity.

14. Indeed it seems that, in some sense, the virtue of monasticism is its ability to incubate culture and the moral life. In this case, Benedictine monasticism does so between the destruction of Roman Christendom and the birth of medieval Christendom. And this would seem consistent with MacIntyre's overall Augustinian theology. Put another way, Macintyre's monastic impulse is tactical, or contingent. Hauerwas's is strategic, or necessary.

H. R. Niebuhr offers a similar account of monastic-sectarian Christianity with specific reference to Benedict. While he does so most notoriously in *Christ and Culture*, he advances an argument remarkably similar to MacIntyre's *After Virtue* in a little-known essay entitled "Back to Benedict?" *The Christian Century* 42 (July 2, 1925): 860-61. Like MacIntyre, on Niebuhr's account the monastic is merely a periodic corrective. For a full discussion of Niebuhr's treatment of monasticism and so-called sectarian ethics, see my essay "On the Christological Transfiguration of Culture: Toward a Mendicant Ethic" in *Studies in Christian Ethics* 21.3 (2008): 403-424.

15. The MacIntyrian project attempts to repair the damage done to ethical intelligibility by the *secularization* of culture. The Hauerwasian project attempts to restore ethical intelligibility lost in the *sacralization* of the state. For Hauerwas, the virtue after which we now live is expressly that of Christian discipleship, the ethical intelligibility compromised by Christendom. For MacIntyre, the virtue after which we live is more generally conceived, an ethical intelligibility compromised by the loss of Christendom.

To be clear these are not unrelated. But, sacralization is the abiding theological problem inherited from the juridical-political establishment of Christianity as a formal state religion. Secularization is a temporary pragmatic problem resulting from the cultural-conventional establishment of Christianity as an informal civil religion. Hauerwas is not concerned with secular declension per se, only with the enfeebling of the church's politics and speech that have come about as a result of its reliance on cultural-conventional establishment.

16. See Jeffrey Stout, *Deomcracy and Tradition* (Princeton, N.J.: Princeton University Press, 2004).

17. Brad J. Kallenberg, *Ethics as Grammar: Changing the Postmodern Subject* (Notre Dame, Ind.: University of Notre Dame Press, 2001).

18. Brad J. Kallenberg, *Ethics as Grammar*, xii.

19. The proclamation of this unholy trinity is attributed to churchman and explorer David Livingstone.

20. Jeffrey Stout, *Deomcracy and Tradition*, 138.

21. That is the routinization and universalization of whiteness as normative humanity. This is Constantinian in that it underwrites the racialized violences of the United States and denies the particular Jewish and nonviolent humanity of Jesus Christ.

22. This helps the church to go on in two senses. First, it surmounts the ethical autonomy plaguing the church. Second, it heuristically suggests the next steps by which the Church might likewise overcome the present iteration of Constantinianism. This diagnostic function in itself moves things forward.

23. Brad J. Kallenberg, *Ethics as Grammar*, 194. Such attention stands in stark contrast to the concern with sameness inherent in (post)colonial melancholia and MacIntyre's iteration thereof.

24. Paul Gilroy, *Postcolonial Melancholia*, 57.

25. This is a decidedly different reparative move than MacIntyre's suggested reversion to premodernity. For discussion of the concept of aversive modernity, see Paul Gilroy, *The Black Atlantic: Modernity and Double-Consciousness* (Cambridge, Mass.: Harvard University Press, 1993); Jon Cruz, *Culture on the Margins: The Black Spiritual and the Rise of American Cultural Interpretation* (Princeton, N.J.: Princeton University Press, 1999); and Molefi Kete Asante, *Race, Rhetoric, and Identity: The Architecton of Soul* (Amherst, N.Y.: Humanity Books, 2005).

26. See David Theo Goldberg, *Racist Culture: Philosophy and the Politics of Meaning* (Oxford: Blackwell Publishers, 1993), 14-40. Though we have used this parenthetical locution throughout, we have not yet commented thereupon. The parentheses within (post)colonial denote three things: 1) The continuity/legacy of the operations of whiteness from colonial to postcolonial conditions; 2) The uneven and variegated instantiation of such conditions—both locally and globally; and 3) The resurgence of neocolonialism via cultural and economic means.

In terms of Yoder's historiography of Constantinianism, the (post)colonial variety presently under discussion is a particular form of neo-neo-Constantinianism. While originating in political establishment (neo-Constantinianism), its vestiges now rest on cultural-conventional establishment (neo-neo-Constantinianism). With respect to its paradigmatic exemplification in the United States, the juridical segregation of whites and non-whites under Jim Crow ended nearly fifty years ago, but comparable levels of volitional segregation persist. Though the redlines have been erased from the electoral districting maps, they have been reinscribed on the heart (cf. Jer. 31:33, Rom. 2:29, and Deut. 30:6).

27. Given a Hauerwasian inflection, Goldberg describes the heresy by which the church has come to accept the replacement of the disciple by the citizen as the normative agent for Christian ethical reflection. This makes Christian ethics indistinguishable from imperial ethics and thus unintelligible. Put in terms of the usual anti-pacifist cavil, this is to shift from the question "What would have happened if *all Christians* had nonviolently resisted Hitler?" to the question "What would have happened if no one (i.e. *no citizens*) had violently resisted Hitler?"

28. Though we won't belabor the details here, Goldberg's account begins with Aristotle and proceeds to MacIntyre. En route he describes the ethical paradigms of virtue, sin and divine law, autonomy and obligation, utility and rights. He treats figures such as Aristotle, Augustine, Aquinas, Locke, Hume, Rousseau, Mill, Bentham, Kant, and Rawls.

29. David Theo Goldberg, *Racist Culture*, 21—emphasis added. For a thorough treatment of the linguistic and philosophical origins of the citizen-barbarian distinction, see Paul Cartledge, "Alien Wisdom: Greeks vs. Barbarians," in *The Greeks: A Portrait of Self and Others* (New York: Oxford University Press, 2002).

30. MacIntyre is not unaware of this problem. He admits "a moral philosophy . . . characteristically presupposes an anthropology" (Alasdair MacIntyre, *After Virtue*, 23). He notes, "The first of these (questions which unless they can be answered satisfactorily, endanger the whole Aristotelian structure) concerns the way in which Aristotle's teleology presupposes his metaphysical biology" (*After Virtue*, 162). With respect to this, he later concludes, "Although this account of the virtues (i.e. MacIntyre's Aristotelian account) is teleological, it does not *require* any allegiance to Aristotle's metaphysical biology" (*After Virtue*, 196).

Goldberg finds this inadequate and wholly unsatisfactory. As "MacIntyre admits exclusion is central to every one of his five accounts (of the tradition of the virtues) . . . it follows that MacIntyre can find no principled barrier, theoretical or institutional to racialized exclusions" (David Theo Goldberg, *Racist Culture*, 38.). Some of the force of this criticism can be deflected by appeal to the genetic fallacy. That is, just because the tradition of the virtues MacIntyre describes originates in a racialized, or racializable, metaphysical biology does not mean that it must persist in upholding such a biology. But, that an exclusionary logic persists throughout each of these varied iterations of the tradition suggests it is at least readily available to racialized exclusions. And further, MacIntyre's continued reliance on tropes of civilization and barbarity suggests this logic inheres more deeply in the tradition of the virtues than he cares to admit.

31. Note the obvious lexical, luminal, and liturgical parallels between the territorial, the individual, and the ecclesial by which subjectivity and solidarity are articulated reciprocally. Personal moral, rational, and ecclesial status directly correspond to political status; the last of these is the foundational

Constantinian move. This precipitates the concern of Southern slaveholders about the conversion of slaves. To recognize a slave as "saved" entailed that she was also moral, rational, and therefore human. Though rigorously denying the point, their unrelenting anxiety concedes it. So great was this anxiety that laws were enacted throughout the South denying the intuitive conclusion.

Note also the parallel to Macintyre's use of the trope "a new Dark Ages." The time and space periodized and demarcated by the rhetoric of catastrophe are determinatively European. The reference is to an embattled European epoch and empire. The demise lamented is that of *European* culture—i.e. whiteness. Such tropes have no effect outside this time-space, because that outside and those there dwelling are considered to exist beyond history and civilization. They are still in the Dark, having not (yet) been Enlightened. Thus, they cannot lose, or suffer the devastation of, that which they are taken to have not (yet) achieved.

32. James W. Perkinson, *White Theology: Outing Supremacy in Modernity* (New York: Palgrave Macmillan, 2004). By soteriologic he means "any (political) logic that discursively legitimizes a choice to risk the 'human absolute'— the suffering (or causing) of death—for the sake of preservation or accomplishment of a pure or whole identity (e.g. the territorial, political, and/or cultural integrity of a nation-state)" (James W. Perkinson, *White Theology*, 65).

With Goldberg, Perkinson insists that white supremacy and racialization are not accidental features of modernity; they are fundamental and foundational. This is likewise the case with their attendant theological justifications. Possession of the gospel was the surest sign of the rationality, morality, and humanity of Europeans. Lack thereof reciprocally confirms the irrationality, immorality, and inhumanity of non-Europeans. This precipitated the "white man's burden" compelling their going into all the world. That this gospel was aligned with the power of the state meant that they went forth pillaging as well as preaching. The theological underwriting of the colonial enterprise is not an *a posteriori* blessing, but an *a priori* condition of its possibility. Civilization and salvation are seen as synonymous. Thus to be propagated coextensively, and if need be, by force and violence.

Thus, Perkinson's soteriologic is another way of naming Constantinianism. Both he and Goldberg identify the deep micrologic governing the philosophical, ethical, political, and theological justification of colonization and the slave trade as that of just war. Following Aristotle's argument for natural slavery in the *Politics* and Locke's argument in the *Second Treatise*, it was asserted that Africans and Native Americans were justly conquered prisoners of war and could thus be exploited via forced labor. But even this logic was tenuous, engendering the notorious "Indian Doubt" with respect to indigenous peoples in South America.

33. James W. Perkinson, *White Theology*, 68. Thus, as a result of the processes of secularization, "Christian superiority climaxed in European supremacy" (*White Theology*, 157).

34. We might call this "the color of Constantinianism." I am indebted to J. Kameron Carter for this phrasing; see his recent *Race: A Theological Account*. (Oxford: Oxford University Press, 2008), 230.

35. James W. Perkinson, *White Theology*, 193. For an extended discussion of

the political operations of whiteness within the modern nation-state, see David Theo Goldberg, *The Racial State* (Oxford: Blackwell Publishing, 2001) and Michael Omi and Howard Winant, *Racial Formation in the United States: From the 1960'S to the 1990'S* (New York: Routledge, 1994). For an historical and sociological discussion of the diachronic morphology and variable social permeability of whiteness, see Matthew Frye Jacobsen, *Whiteness of a Different Color: European Immigrants and the Alchemy of Race* (Cambridge, Mass.: Harvard University Press, 1998).

36. *Tractatus* 6.54 quoted in Brad J. Kallenberg, *Ethics as Grammar*, 21.

37. White congregations, that is.

38. Eduardo Bonilla-Silva, *Racism Without Racists: Color-Blind Racism and the Persistence of Inequality in the United States*, 2nd. ed. (New York: Rowman & Littlefield Publishers, 2006), 2.

39. Ibid., 104.

40. Ibid., 75. Bonilla-Silva identifies a number of stock frames, narratives, and descriptors indicative of the universalization of white non-racial explanation. These include the frames of naturalization, minimization, and enculturation whereby racism is explained away as incidental, peripheral, or cultural—meaning a lack of certain values, rather than bias, explains why non-whites experience decreased social opportunities. Also common are etiological stories such as "I didn't get that job because of a black man," "My ancestors were immigrants and they made it," and "I have (a) black friend(s)."

41. Ibid., 208.

42. Michael O. Emerson and Christian Smith, *Divided By Faith: Evangelical Religion and the Problem of Race in America* (New York: Oxford University Press, 2000). Though their study focuses on evangelical Christianity, their underlying insights are more broadly generalizable to other forms of Protestantism in the United States.

43. With respect to ecclesial segregation, the basic contestation is whether or not ecclesial segregation existed. That is, whether or not the demographic distribution was itself meaningful at all. Whereas almost all blacks identified the distribution as segregation, many whites failed to do so, or disputed the identification. Description of this distribution as segregation either didn't occur to them or was rejected by them.

44. Emerson and Smith, *Divided By Faith*, 76.

45. Because the inequality and segregation in view are caused inadvertently by "innocent" preferences rather than intentional bigotry and malice, white habitus renders them amoral. Note the overwhelming commitment to theologically justifying choice and freedom, two classically Liberal values.

46. Emerson and Smith, *Divided By Faith*, 66. Namely that for whites the explanation is personal and spiritual, rather than temporal and social. Thus in the same way that Hauerwas insists that "Doire Columcille resides in a different narrative tradition than Londonderry," we might also say that the "America" named by whites and the "AmeriKKKa" named by some black radicals nominate different places in different conceptual worlds.

47. Ibid., 62.

48. Ibid., 80.

49. They could both say and see that racialized social inequality and the social antagonisms of cultural devastation were both theologically and ethi-

cally problematic.

50. Brad J. Kallenberg, quoted in *Ethics as Grammar*, 220.

51. Ibid., quoted in *Ethics as Grammar*, 126.

52. Thus, "From (Gloria) Albrecht's perspective . . . 'the establishment of a community grounded in a unified moral tradition' is simply the Enlightenment song in a different key" (Brad J. Kallenberg, *Ethics as Grammar*, 129).

53. Kallenberg, *Ethics as Grammar*, 208.

54. Stanley Hauerwas, "Self-Deception & Autobiography," in *The Hauerwas Reader*, ed. Michael Cartwright (Durham, N.C.: Duke University Press, 2001), 204.

55. Brad J. Kallenberg, quoted in *Ethics as Grammar*, 149.

56. James W. Perkinson, *White Theology*, 170.

57. John Thomson, *The Ecclesiology of Stanley Hauerwas: A Christian Theology of Liberation* (London: Ashgate Press, 2003), 174—emphasis added. Yoder himself suggests this, saying, "We must converse at every border" (John Howard Yoder, "The Hermeneutics of Peoplehood," in *The Priestly Kingdom: Social Ethics as Gospel*. Notre Dame, Ind.: University of Notre Dame Press, 1984, 41).

58. This suggestion is also made in the follow-up volume to *Divided By Faith*—Curtis Paul DeYoung et al., *United By Faith: The Multicultural Congregation as Answer to the Problem of Race* (New York: Oxford University Press, 2003). Cf, Emmanuel Katongole, "Greeting: Beyond Racial Reconciliation," in *The Blackwell Companion to Christian Ethics*, ed. Stanley Hauerwas, and Samuel Wells (Malden, Mass.: Blackwell Publishers, 2004).

59. J.K. Gibson-Graham, *A Postcapitalist Politics* (Minneapolis: University of Minnesota Press, 2006), 7.

60. Stanley Hauerwas, *Christian Existence Today: Essays on Church, World, and Living in Between* (Grand Rapids, Mich.: Brazos Press, 2001), 10.

61. I take "political imaginary" to be consonant with what Shaud Magid describes as the "fantasy" of liturgy. See Shaud Magid, "The Ritual is Not the Hunt: The Seven Wedding Blessings, Redemption, and Jewish Ritual as Fantasy," in *Liturgy, Time, and the Politics of Redemption*, ed. Randi Rashkover and C. C. Pecknold (Grand Rapids, Mich.: Eerdman's, 2006).

62. In *United By Faith*, the designation "multicultural" is taken to refer to those congregations in which no single ethnic group compromises more than 80 percent of the membership.

63. Kallenberg, *Ethics as Grammar*, 124.

64. On such relearning, see my essay "Through A Prism Darkly: Reading With Musa Dube" in *Cultural Encounters* 4.2 (Summer, 2008).

65. Kallenberg, *Ethics as Grammar*, 211. Note the obvious baptismal overtones in the language of immersion.

66. One reason I suspect Hauerwas thus far has been reticent to foreground attention to the Other as an integral part of his project is that the usual arguments for multiculturalism, pluralism, and cosmopolitanism trade in the language of rights. The Other is to be regarded and respected because she is a bearer of rights and a citizen. Hauerwas is right to resist such discourse. The theological grounds for so doing are manifest in present discussion. Moreover, Hannah Arendt, John Searle, and Giorgio Agamben reveal the problematic impotence of rights talk when it comes to actually guaranteeing the re-

gard and security of the Other absent the protection of the state.

But Hauerwas need not appeal to the theologically problematic and politically impractical discourse of rights. What is to be accorded to the Other can be established on the theological grounds that she is *imago dei*. Moreover, the prophets and the Gospels provide endless admonitions to welcome the alien and the stranger, care for the widow and the orphan, and to love the enemy—particularly vulnerable Others.

With respect to kenotic pedagogy, there is an additional dimension that escapes the usual rights-talk of liberalism. The kenotic move is to identify oneself as the Other. And more specifically to name oneself as the enemy and stranger in need of forgiveness and hospitality. This, I think, embodies Hauerwas's insistence that contrary to the political anthropology of Liberalism which identifies the subject as the citizen who bears rights, a Christian anthropology fundamentally identifies the subject, and especially oneself, as the beggar.

67. Perkinson, *White Theology*, 103.

68. Paul Gilroy, *Postcolonial Melancholia*, 56.

69. I take this to be true of many short-term cross-cultural immersions. When taken as complete in themselves rather than merely the first part of a longer sustained engagement, the intercultural element is vampiric and voyeuristic. It is merely an "ethnic" augmentation, the theological-ecclesial equivalent of "my one black friend." Though sustained engagement over time mitigates against this, it is no guarantee. See Jon Cruz, *Culture on the Margins*.

70. Paul Gilroy, *Postcolonial Melancholia*, 67 (emphasis added).

71. Ibid., 70 (emphasis added).

72. Osayande Obery Hendricks, "Guerrilla Exegesis: "Struggle" as a Scholarly Vocation," *Semeia* 72.1:85—first two emphases original, third added.

73. Slavoj Zizek, *The Fragile Absolute—Or Why is the Christian Legacy Worth Fighting for?* (London: Verso, 2000), 129-30.

74. James W. Perkinson, *White Theology*, 19.

Chapter 6

AGAINST EMPIRE:
A YODERIAN READING
OF ROMANS

Ted Grimsrud

John Howard Yoder, the Mennonite theologian and advocate for Christian pacifism, as much as anybody in the last half of the twentieth century, popularized the Christian critique of Constantinianism.[1] "Constantinianism" refers to a way of looking at power in social life. The term evokes the Roman emperor Constantine who, in the fourth century, initiated major changes in the official policies of Rome vis-à-vis Christians, changes by and large embraced by the Christians. Indicative of the changes, at the beginning of the fourth century, few Christians performed military service due to a sense of mutual antipathy between Christians and the military. By the end of the fourth century, the empire had instituted rules that made it illegal for anyone who was not a Christian to be in the military.

Yoder has been criticized for being overly simplistic in his use of Constantine as such a central metaphor.[2] I think the criticisms are largely unfair, but for this essay I want to concern myself with Yoder's application of this symbolic label more than whether it is fully historically appropriate or not. That is, what Yoder means by Constantinianism is simply this: believing that the exercise of power is necessarily violent, that the state appropriately holds a monopoly on the legitimate use of violence, that God's will is in some sense funneled through the actions of the heads of state, that Christians should work within the structures of their legitimately violent nation-states taking up arms when called upon to do so, and that history is best read through the eyes of people in power.

Most people who have read the Gospels agree that Jesus stands in tension with Constantinianism. For most Christians in the past 2,000 years, the apostle Paul has been seen as a key bridge who prepared the way for the Constantinian shift in the early fourth century CE. Thus it is no accident that, after Constantine, Paul's writings become central for Christian theology (much more so than the Gospels)—we see this already in the great "Father of the church," Augustine, in the late fourth and early fifth centuries. Augustine is still considered Christianity's greatest interpreter of Paul (along with the Augustinian monk, Martin Luther).

For John Howard Yoder, though, the Constantinian shift was not inevitable and certainly not a good thing, and Augustine and Luther are not definitive interpreters of Paul. In fact, for Yoder, Augustine's and Luther's interpretations of Paul have led to great mischief—not least in how these interpretations have leant themselves to presenting Paul (or at least Paul's theology) as a servant of empire.

My interest here is to look at Yoder's non-Constantinian reading of Paul and to suggest that indeed Paul's theology provides us powerful resources that might help us walk faithfully with Jesus today as peace churches in a world still all too Constantinian. Yoder devotes his book *The Politics of Jesus*[3] to explaining *what* Jesus' life and teaching have to say to empire.

A central part of his argument has to do with a way of reading the entire New Testament (and, implicitly, the entire Bible) in light of Jesus' life and teaching. This way of reading includes paying close attention to Paul's writings. One of Yoder's many challenges to the standard account of Christian faith is to make the case (in some detail) for reading Paul as in full *continuity* with Jesus.

THE MESSIANIC ETHIC

So, what is the "messianic ethic" that Yoder sees embodied by Jesus? Yoder develops his portrayal of Jesus' ethical message from a reading of the gospel of Luke.[4] We start with the words of Mary in Luke one that present the significance of the life she carries in her womb in terms of *social* transformation, lifting up the vulnerable and throwing down the powerful.

Luke makes it clear that the hopes among the people with whom Jesus related centered on the social and political renewal of Israel.

They expected the Messiah they hoped for to implement a transformation *in* history. Yoder believes that the key to understanding Jesus' ethical stance lay in recognizing that he embraced these hopes and presented himself as fulfilling them—but in ways very *different* than anticipated. Political? Yes, but a new kind of politics.

Jesus works to embody God's kingdom on earth, to serve as a *political* leader who will indeed liberate Israel and thereby provide "a light to the nations" (Luke 2:32). Jesus announces the "good news" of God, the presence of God's kingdom. These terms *gospel* and *kingdom* are both *political* terms. Jesus' work will have direct social and political significance.

When Jesus begins his public ministry (Luke 4:14-30), he affirms two central parts of many people's hopes—the time is *now* for a new work of the Spirit of God through God's anointed Servant ("today this Scripture is fulfilled," 4:21), the promised Messiah, and this new work will result in *social* transformation (this is now "the year of the Lord's favor," 4:19, that is, the time of Jubilee in line with the promises of Torah) (31).

What Jesus had in mind with these opening words is clear, Yoder insists. He announces "a visible, socio-political, economic restructuring of relations among the people of God" (32). As seen in Jesus' hometown, and as would be expected based on the experiences of earlier prophets in Israel, Jesus faced sharp opposition from the start. Since he proposed concrete changes, the forces that benefited from the status quo resisted ferociously.

In face of the opposition, Jesus formally created a counter-culture, a new social entity. Simply to proclaim a subversive message, while upsetting to people in power, would not threaten their status. However, to combine that verbal message with a social group actually embodying the messianic ethics and thereby effecting genuine change—now this would definitely gain the attention of the guardians of the present order. Jesus presented "an alternative to the structures that were there before, challeng[ing] the system as no mere words ever could" (33).

With his initial program stated and his new community established, Jesus goes on (in Luke's story) to spell out in some detail the general social philosophy of this new transformative community he establishes. The messianic ethic he articulates has as its core two key elements: imitating God's love even for God's enemies (Luke 6:35-36) and practicing a style of life utterly different from the "natural law" behavior of people in the world (6:32-34)—going beyond simply loving those who love you and doing good to those who do good to you.

This ethic, Yoder points out, only makes sense if the kingdom truly is present and if the kingdom indeed has to do with real, present, social and political life (34).

Jesus' ministry of social transformation led directly to his death. His "public career had been such as to make it quite thinkable that he would pose to the Roman Empire an apparent threat serious enough to justify his execution" (50). Evidence for this assertion may be seen in the comment that one of the disciples made to the "unknown man" he and his friends walked with on the road to Emmaus after Jesus' crucifixion. "We had hope that he was the one who would redeem Israel" (Luke 24:21). This comment reflects the perception that Jesus' ministry indeed had the impact of exciting hopes of direct political intervention. His was a call to social transformation where servanthood replaces domination, restorative justice replaces retribution, and inclusion of vulnerable people replaces class warfare.

Yoder makes two central arguments in *The Politics of Jesus*. The first, which we have just summarized, is to show that it is possible to read the story of Jesus (in fact, it is the best reading of this story) and understand that he is "of direct significance for social ethics" (11). The second argument is that what Jesus actually said and did in relation to social ethics remains truthful and applicable for our present day. In making this second argument, Yoder turns to the writings of the apostle Paul since they have so often been interpreted in ways that marginalize Jesus' own message.

Rather than seeing Jesus and Paul as representing two more or less mutually exclusive approaches to ethical life, Yoder suggests that we should see Paul as a faithful and accurate interpreter of Jesus' message. Jesus and Paul are not stage one and stage two of the development of Christian ethics that lead inevitably to Constantinianism. Rather, whatever we understand to be central to Jesus' message remains central for Paul.

Yoder details his affirmation of the close link between Jesus and Paul—and the latter's central relevance for our appropriation of the messianic ethic—in a series of chapters on four key elements of Paul's thought. These include discussions of the social character of justification, the challenge to the hegemony of the Powers, the call to revolutionary subordinations, and the true meaning of Romans 13.

JUSTIFICATION'S SOCIAL CHARACTER

One central way that the Christian tradition has placed a tension between Jesus' life and Paul's theology is in its understanding of

Paul's concept of "justification" (212). In this theological emphasis, the words and deeds of Jesus end up on the margins of theological development as a result of Paul's narrowing down the core of the gospel to justification by faith alone.

Paul, in this reading, opposed approaches to the work of God that could be focused in piety, religious practices, or ethical behavior so as to turn the believer's attention toward human good works rather than God's free gift. However, Yoder asks, "Does not the insistence that justification is by faith alone and through grace alone, apart from any correlation with works of any kind, undercut any radical ethical and social concern?" (213).

Even if Jesus himself taught and practiced a countercultural social ethics, according to the mainstream theological tradition, this part of his message has no long-term relevance. Paul understood that well and zeroed in on what matters most—justification by faith alone apart from "works righteousness."

Is this an accurate reading of the story told in the New Testament of Paul's actual teaching? Yoder says it is not, asserting that in fact for Paul "justification" has at its heart *social* concerns (215). According to Yoder, the heart of Paul's interests had to do with the social character of the messianic community. Would it be one community miraculously including as equals both Jews and Gentiles? Or would it be a loose association of distinct Jewish and Gentile sects? Or would it be made up only of those who "have first to become Jews according to the conditions of pre-messianic proselytism?" (216).

In Galatians, Paul challenged the movement within the Galatian community to limit access to the community for Gentile Christians based on what was to him a sinfully exclusionary reading of the gospel. Paul himself had *violently* persecuted followers of Jesus in the name of strict and exclusionary boundary markers that would keep Gentile Christians out (Gal. 2:13-14). Paul's theology of justification by faith in Galatians and Romans emerges directly from his own experience as the perpetrator of social injustice—and speaks to the importance he now saw in the churches embodying the new social reality Jesus inaugurated.

Paul's proclamation of the "righteousness" (or justice) of God—the message of justification—emphasized that the message goes forth "to both Jew and Gentile." That is, the message is proclaimed to *both* together so they join in one new community devoted to embodying the way of Jesus. This reconciliation of these former human enemies reflects the reconciliation that is most central for Paul. He was not nearly so much concerned with the end of "hostility" between

God and human beings (as a good Jew, he understood God to be merciful) as the end of the hostility between Jew and Gentile.

Paul argued in Galatians (see especially 2:14-21) that Jews and Gentiles must be joined together in *one* fellowship. "To be 'justified' is to be set right in and for that [new social] relationship." The term *justification* in Galatians hence links with the later language in Ephesians about "making peace" and "breaking down the wall" that previously alienated Jews and Gentiles (220).

Paul's most detailed theological statement, his letter to the Romans, also picks up this sense of the social nature of justification. Yoder points out,

> The issue of the polarity of Jew and Gentile is present at major turning points throughout the argument of the book, as well as in the introduction and conclusion. The foreground meaning of the issue of the place of the law was not systematic theological speculation about how human beings are to be made acceptable to God, but rather the very concrete Roman situation in which Jew and Greek, legalistic Christian and pagan Christian, needed to accept one another. (223-24)

Paul envisions in Romans a faith community that embodies Torah but without the exclusionary emphasis on defending boundary markers that had led Paul himself to become violent. Torah would be embodied most of all, according to 13:8-10, by the Romans loving their neighbors. The place of "justification" here is bringing together Jewish and Gentile Christians in one "just" (whole) community, established "apart from the law" by God's mercy shown in Jesus Christ (Rom. 3:21-26).

PAUL'S SOCIAL ANALYSIS: THE POWERS THAT BE

Another important way that Jesus' messianic ethic has been marginalized in the history of Christianity is the assumption that he did not give us a social philosophy but spoke rather primarily to the personal realm. "One of the strands in the argument against the normative claims made by or for Jesus has always been that his radical personalism is not relevant to problems of power and structure" (134). Even less has Paul been understood as providing a way of applying Jesus' ethical directives to our social lives (135-36).

Yoder suggests, however, that we have in Paul's writings insights to speak directly to social ethics. And these insights help us make sense of Jesus' message and strengthen both the link between Jesus' social ethics and Paul's and between theirs and ours.

Yoder, borrowing from insights gained especially from Hendrikus Berkhof,[5] teases out Paul's social thought under the rubric of "the Powers." The language of "the Powers" provides a way to speak of the structures of human life, realities beyond simply our individual persons or even beyond simply the sum of separate individuals— our institutions, traditions, social practices, belief systems, organizations, languages, and so on. The Powers language speaks metaphorically about the discrete "personalities" and even "wills" that these structures have.

(1) *The Powers are part of the good creation.* They were brought into being by God as a "divine gift" (140) that makes human social life possible. When God created human beings, necessarily elements of human life such as language, traditions, and ways of ordering community life all came into existence alongside the individual human beings. And like the original human beings, the Powers were also good.

This aspect of created reality is linked with Jesus Christ himself in Colossians 1:

> He is the image of the invisible God, the firstborn of all creation; for in him all things in heaven and on earth were created, things visible and invisible, whether thrones or dominions or rulers or powers—all things have been created through him and for him. He himself is before all things, and in him all things hold together. (Col 1:15-17).

Today we may want to say that this "Powers" language (not only "Powers," but also in Colossian 1 "thrones, dominions, rulers" and in Galatians, "the elemental spirits") metaphorically describes the necessary "regularity, system, and order" that human beings require to function socially. The Bible teaches that God has provided for these needs. The provision is part of the goodness of creation (141).

(2) *The Powers are fallen.* They are so closely linked with humanity that when human beings turned from God—spoken of traditionally as "the Fall" and described in the story of Adam and Eve—so, too, did the Powers. It is as if the Powers, as part of created reality, turn against human beings when humans are alienated from God. The fallen Powers then seek to take God's place as the center of human devotion, often becoming idols.

Yoder writes,

The Powers are no longer active only as mediators of the saving creative purpose of God; now we find them seeking to separate us from the love of God (Rom 8:38); we find them ruling over the lives of those who live far from the love of God (Eph 2:2); we find them holding us in servitude to their rules (Col 2:20); we find them holding us under their tutelage (Gal 4:3). These structures which were supposed to be our servants have become our masters and our guardians. (141).

(3) *The Powers remain necessary.* Despite their fallenness, the Powers retain their original function. Human beings still require the "regularity, system, and order" that only the Powers provide. Human life still requires ordering; the Powers are still used by God in the sustenance of human social life.

Consequently, the Powers are *both* a huge part of the problem human beings face in living in our fallen world *and* a necessary part of whatever solutions might be found. The human dilemma in relation to the Powers is that they simultaneously are a necessary part of our God-ordered existence and an inevitable force that seeks to corrupt this existence and separate us from God.

(4) *The Powers must be redeemed.* What is required for a potential resolution of the "Powers dilemma" is that the Powers be transformed (they cannot be abolished or ignored). The first step in such a transformation comes when people have their own awareness of and attitude toward the Powers transformed. Ultimately, the Powers have only the power that we give them by our allegiance and acceptance of their distorted portrayal of reality.

We must continue to understand ourselves as subject to the Powers.

> Subordination to these powers is what makes us human, for if they did not exist there would be no history nor society nor humanity. If then God is going to save his creatures *in their humanity*, the Powers cannot simply be destroyed or set-aside or ignored. Their sovereignty must be broken. (144).

That is, the Powers must be "put in their place." We need them but they should be our servants (on behalf of life) not our masters (idols that make us become like them). Such a putting the Powers in their place can only happen when we see them as what they are—*creatures*, not God substitutes.

(5) *Jesus does redeem the Powers.* Paul asserts that Jesus in fact has done precisely what was needed. He lived, Yoder writes,

a genuinely free and human existence. This life brought him, as
any genuinely human existence will bring anyone, to the cross.
In his death the Powers—in this case the most worthy, weighty
representatives of Jewish religion and Roman politics—act in
collusion. (144-5).

In responding to Jesus in this way, though, the Powers actually
helped their own defeat. Jesus' cross was actually a victory. He remained free from their allure, even in face of the deadly violence. In
doing so, he brings to light their true character. "By the cross [which
must always be seen as a unit with the resurrection] Christ abolished
the slavery which, as a result of sin, lay over our existence as a menace
and an accusation." As Colossians 2:15 tells us, on the cross he "disarmed" the Powers, "making a public example of them and thereby
triumphing over them" (146).

The Powers all too often are accepted as "the gods of the world."
Jesus' faithfulness to the death shows that such an exaltation of the
Powers is based on deception. God's presence in *Jesus* reveals that the
Powers that kill Jesus are rebels *against* God, not God's servants. The
religious and political leaders serve death, not the God of life. "Obviously, 'none of the rulers of this age,' who let themselves be wor-
shiped as divinities, understood God's wisdom, 'for had they known,
they would not have crucified the Lord of glory' (1 Cor. 2:8). Now
they are unmasked as false gods by their very encounter with Very
God; they are made a public spectacle" (146).

Christ's victory over the Powers, already present in the cross, becomes even clearer when God raises Jesus from the dead. In the resurrection, it becomes clear that Jesus' challenge to the Powers was *endorsed* and *vindicated* by God. In Jesus, God has ventured into the
Powers' territory, remained true to God's loving character, and defeated them (that is, allowed them to defeat themselves by crucifying
Jesus).

The Powers' main weapon—deluding people to give the Powers
loyalty—was taken from them. They were disarmed by Jesus' faithfulness. Such a disillusioning revelation frees all who walk with Jesus
to embrace life and wholeness (146-47). No Powers can separate us
from God's love unless we let them.

(6) *The Christian vocation is to live in freedom from Powers idolatry.*
Jesus' followers are called and empowered to embody his victory. We
do so for the sake of witnessing to the entire world of the truthfulness
of God's message of mercy and wholeness. This witness is for the
sake of the nations (see Rev. 21:24), indeed for all of creation (Rom.
8:19).

A crucial part of the witness to the Powers, the nations, and all of creation is the formation of communities of liberated people whose life together manifests their freedom from idolatry to the powers. For Paul, that messianic communities include reconciled Jewish and Gentile followers of Jesus stands at the heart of the gospel—reflecting his own transformation from violent zealot to nonviolent servant of Jesus. This social reconciliation, as we saw above, reflects what Paul considered justification to be about.

"The very existence of the church," Yoder states, "in which Gentiles and Jews, who heretofore walked according to the *stoicheia* ('elemental spirits') of the world, live together in Christ's fellowship, is itself a proclamation, a sign, a token to the Powers that their unbroken dominion has come to an end" (147-48).

Romans, when read in light of Paul's theology of the Powers, becomes a powerful witness against bondage to the values of empire and the values of Torah legalism. Both of these idolatries are challenged in Romans, reflecting the dynamics of both sides of the violence and alienation in Paul's own life. Romans proclaims a salvation from empire-idolatry and from Torah-idolatry. This salvation, accomplished "apart from the law" (that is, apart from legalistic adherence to sharp boundary markers that reflected Torah idolatry) and also apart from Empire, must be practiced and thereby displayed to the Powers, to the nations, to all of creation.

REVOLUTIONARY SUBORDINATION: NEITHER FIGHT NOR FLIGHT

Paul knew, all too well, that freedom in Christ must be lived in a broken world. So, he reflects, profoundly, on how Christian freedom may be lived most faithfully in an *unfree* world. Yoder draws on Pauline writings concerning subordination in interpersonal relationships to deepen his analysis of how Paul reinforces and applies Jesus' ethic. The German term *Haustafeln* has commonly been used by scholars in their discussions of these themes. Haustafeln means a set of "household rules," expectations for interpersonal relationships.

Yoder sees in these rules, when read in the broader context of the New Testament, a message of what he calls "*revolutionary* subordination." These household rules call upon Christians to walk with Jesus in our responses to our social situations. They are not regulations that simply endorse status quo power arrangements and require those in the "lower" positions to give all their power to their "superiors."

Paul's Haustafeln, addressed to the one without power, treat his addressees as responsible moral agents who have full (and equal) worth as human beings with those with higher social status. These addressees, according to Paul, have indeed been liberated in Christ and welcomed into full membership in Christ's assembly. However, quite likely these addressees are not in positions to claim that liberation fully while at the same time remaining (as they must) wholly committed to Jesus' path of loving their neighbors.

Paul echoes Jesus in holding up two equally crucial convictions. We are free in Christ *and* we are called to love even our enemies. In this love we refrain from smashing existing social arrangements. Paul's Haustafeln are best seen as part of his thinking on the processes of negotiating this liberation/path of love tension.

Contrary to the expectations in the broader culture, where submission is a one-way street, the newness of the messianic community Paul speaks to may be seen in part in how Paul challenges husbands, masters, and parents also to practice mutuality, in some sense subordinating themselves to those "below" them (178).

The main term that Paul uses, *hyptoassesthai*, could best be translated something like "subordinate yourself," more than flatly "submit to." It is not connoting slavish obedience. It is best defined by Jesus, who according to Paul in Philippians 2, being free, subordinated himself for our sake and gave himself for us. *And*, Paul emphasizes in Philippians 2:5, believers should "let this same mind be in you that was in Christ Jesus" (180).

This is how Yoder states it: "It is natural to feel Christ's liberation reaching into every kind of bondage, and to want to act in obedience with that radical shift. But precisely because of Christ we shall not impose that shift violently upon the social order beyond the confines of the church" (185). Of course, within the church, Christians have every right to challenge fellow Christian husbands, parents, and slave-holders to relinquish their dominance (as we see in Paul's letter to Philemon).

In Romans, Paul does not directly discuss the Haustafeln. However, taking seriously what he has in mind when he does discuss them might help us better understand his concerns in Romans. Romans has at its heart a strong concern for mutual subordination among the Christians in Rome. Paul develops his powerful theology of justification to emphasize, by the time we get to the end of the book, the crucial importance to the Roman Christians of loving one another (13:8-10), refraining from judging each other (14:1-12), avoiding making one another stumble (14:13-23), pleasing others and not oneself (15:1-6), and recognizing that the gospel is for Jews and Gentiles together (15:7-13).

Paul advocates a genuine revolution against Rome's hegemony. However, the revolutionary means he advocates are consistent with the healing mercy of God extended to the entire world. The certainty Paul has—and all followers of Jesus should have—in the world-transforming efficacy of God's healing mercy undergirds lives of patient love, extended even (as with God's own self) toward enemies.[6]

TURNING "ROMANS 13" ON ITS HEAD

All that has gone before in this paper prepares us now to turn to Romans 13. This passage (specifically 13:1-7) often serves as a counter-testimony in the Christian tradition to the belief that Paul taught nonviolent resistance to the Roman Empire and, more importantly for Yoder, Romans 13 is seen to go against the idea that Paul understood Jesus' messianic ethic as normative for Christian social ethics.

Our interpretation of Romans 13:1-7 should begin with reading these verses in light of their biblical context. From Egypt in Genesis and Exodus, then Assyria, Babylon, Persia, and down to Rome in the book of Revelation, the empires rebel against God and hinder the healing vocation of the covenant people. The entire Bible could appropriately be read as a manual on how people who follow Torah in seeking to love God and neighbor negotiate the dynamics of hostility, domination, idolatry, and violence that almost without exception characterize the world's empires.

Romans 13:1-7 stands in this general biblical context of *antipathy* toward the empires. If we take this context seriously, we will turn to these Romans verses assuming that their concern is something like this: *given* the fallenness of Rome, how might we live within this empire as people committed uncompromisingly to love of neighbor? Paul has no illusions about Rome's being, in a positive sense, a servant of God. However, we know from biblical stories that God nonetheless can and does use the corrupt nations for God's purposes. Yet these nations also remain under God's judgment.

In Romans, Paul discusses two major strains of idolatry: (1) the empire and its injustices that demand the highest loyalty and (religious) devotion and (2) a legalistic approach to Torah that leads to its own kind of violence (witness Paul's own death-dealing zealotry).

However, Paul understands these universal problems as a basis to affirm the universality of God's healing response. Indeed, *all* have

sinned and fallen short of the glory of God. *And all* may find salvation
in Jesus. The sovereignty of hostility to God ultimately bows to the
sovereignty of God's healing love.

In Romans 4–8, Paul develops further this message of the mercies
of God—reflected in Abraham's pre-circumcision trust in God that
serves as our model (ch. 4), in God's transforming love even of God's
enemies (ch. 5), in Paul's own liberation from his idolatrous "sacred
violence" (ch. 7), and in the promise that creation itself will be healed
as God's children come to themselves (ch. 8).

Chapters 9–11 involve Paul's deeper wrestling with his own experience as a Jew who had failed to recognize God's mercy revealed
in Jesus. However, Paul's failure (and the failure of many of his fel-
lows) ultimately did not stop the revelation of God's mercy. God's
electing mercy will have its merciful conclusion even with the un-
faithfulness of so many of the elect people.

For the rest of the letter, in response to this certainty about God's
mercy, Paul sketches the practical outworking of living in light of this
mercy—all for the sake of spreading the gospel to the ends of the
earth (i.e., "Spain," 15:28).

Chapters12–13 make up a single section in the structure of the
book. Yoder observes that

> Chapter 12 begins with a call to nonconformity, motivated by
> the memory of the mercies of God, and finds the expression of
> this transformed life first in a new quality of relationships
> within the Christian community and, with regard to enemies, in
> suffering. The concept of love then recurs in 13:8-10. Therefore,
> any interpretation of 13:1-7 which is not also an expression of
> suffering and serving love must be a misunderstanding of the
> text in its context. (196)

Yoder helps us look more closely at the actual passage, 13:1-7, itself.

(1) *Paul calls for a kind of revolutionary subordination in relation to
government.* These verses begin with a call to subordination, not literally to obedience. The term here reflects Paul's notion of "the *ordering*
of the Powers of God. Subordination is significantly different from
unconditional obedience. For example, the Christian who refuses to
worship Caesar but still permits Caesar to put him or her to death, is
being subordinate even though not obeying" (209).

(2) *Paul intends to* reject *any notion of violent revolution.*

> The immediate concrete meaning of this text for the Christian
> Jews in Rome, in the face of official anti-Semitism and the rising

arbitrariness of the Imperial regime, is to call them away from any notion of revolution or insubordination. The call is to a non-violent attitude toward a tyrannical government. (202-3)

(3) *Paul also intends to relativize the affirmation of any* particular *government.* While opposing revolution, these verses also do nothing to imply active moral support for Rome (or any other particular government). Paul here *echoes* Revelation 13, a text often contrasted with Romans 13. However, *both* passages advocate subordination in relation to whatever powers that be (201)—even along with the implication (more clear in Revelation) that this particular government is quite idolatrous and blasphemous.

(4) *God orders the Powers—a different notion than* ordaining *the Powers.* God is not said to *create* or *institute* or *ordain* any particular governments, but only to *order* them. "What the text says is that God orders them, brings them into line, that by God's permissive government God lines them up with God's purpose" (201-2). This sense of "ordering" implies that God's participation in human life is much more *indirect* than often understood. *All* states are "ordered" by God and thus in some sense serve God's purposes. However, no states are directly blessed by God as God's direct representatives—least of all the Roman Empire that executed Jesus.

(5) *Nothing here speaks to Christians as* participants *in the state's work.* "The functions described in 13:3-4 do not include any service that the Christian is asked to render. The 'things due to the authority' listed in 13:6-7 do not include any kind of participation or service" (203). Whatever it is that the state does, Paul is not endorsing Christians themselves having a responsibility to perform those tasks—especially if the tasks violate the call to neighbor love.

(6) *Paul calls for discrimination.* "Pay to all what is due them" echoes Jesus' call for discernment: "give to Caesar what is Caesar's and to God what is God's" tells us to be sure not to give Caesar the loyalty that belongs only to God; 13:7 says "render to all what is due them"; 13:8 says "nothing is *due* to anyone except love." Is what Caesar claims is due to him part of the obligation of love? (208).

(7) *Romans 13 is consistent with the Sermon on the Mount.* The logic that uses Romans 13:1-7 as a basis for participation in coercive practices relies on a disjunction between Romans 13:1-7 and the Sermon on the Mount. However, *both* Romans 12–13 as a unit and Matthew 5–7 instruct Christians to be nonviolent in all their relationships, including the social. Both call on the disciples of Jesus to renounce participation in vengeance. Both call Christians "to respect and be sub-

ject to the historical process in which the sword continues to be wielded and to bring about a kind of order under fire, but not to perceive in the wielding of the sword their own reconciling ministry" (210).

Romans 13:1-7, when read in light of Paul's overall theology, may be understood as a statement of how the revolutionary subordination of Christians contributes to Christ's victory over the Powers. Christians do so by holding *together* their rejection of Empire-idolatry with their commitment to active pacifism. Their most radical task (and most subversive) is to live *visibly* as communities where the enmity that had driven Paul himself to murderous violence is overcome— Jew and Gentile joined together in one fellowship, a witness to genuine peace in a violent world.

Such communities empower a freedom from the Powers idolatry. These are some of the imperatives from Romans 12–13 for living out such freedom:

- Nonconformity to the Roman world fueled by minds that are transformed, being shaped by God's mercy shown in Jesus rather than by the culture's "elemental spirits";
- humility and shared respect in the ministry of the faith community that recognizes and affirms all the gifts of those in the community;
- active love for one another leading to a renunciation of vengeance and a quest to overcome evil with good rather than heightening the spiral of violence with violent responses;
- respect for God's ordering work in human government that—fallen and rebellious as it may be—still serves God's purposes;
- a commitment to doing good (following Jesus' model that implicitly recognizes that genuinely doing good as defined by the gospel could lead to a cross)—and repudiation of temptations to seek to overcome evil with evil through violent resistance;
- work at discerning what belongs to God and what is allowable to be given to Caesar;
- an overarching commitment to authentic practice of Torah, summarized (following Jesus) as *love* of neighbor (here as in Jesus' Good Samaritan story, including the enemy).

ON BEING A PEACE CHURCH
IN A CONSTANTINIAN WORLD

I want to close with a few brief reflections on how this analysis of Paul might be applied to our present.

(1) *No to Empire.* Yoder's *Politics of Jesus* challenges us to apply Jesus' messianic ethic to our political life. With the awareness of Jesus message as *political*, we are sensitized to see the entire Bible from the creation story to the New Jerusalem as a critique of Empire and guide to faithful resistance to Empire.

Yoder seeks to hold together two uncompromisable convictions: resistance to Empire and commitment to pacifism. Resistance without pacifism ends up only heightening the spiral of violence and serving the domination of the Fallen Powers. Pacifism without resistance validates the stereotypes of the cultured despisers of pacifism— parasitic, withdrawal focused on purity, irresponsible.

One key lesson to learn from Paul, Jesus, John of Patmos, and the other prophets is how to discern, how to recognize the self-serving propaganda of rulers, how to recognize the dynamics of "lording it over," and to insist on the norm of servanthood as our key criterion for political discernment. Such a criterion should foster a sense of profound suspicion not only toward the more obvious imperial moves of U.S. neoconservatives but also of the "soft imperialists" and their "humanitarian interventions."

(2) *No to violent resistance.* We must not let Empire set our agenda or determine our means of resistance. We must not, in seeking to overcome evil, become evil ourselves.[7] We learn from our Yoderian reading of Paul that for those who would walk with Jesus, what should determine our agenda in relation to Empire should not be anger and hostility. Nor should it be a desire to wrest the steering wheel from, say, right-wingers through force and get the U.S. empire back on track as a benevolent superpower.

As Yoder points out, the true problem with Empire is not that some empires are not benevolent enough in their domination. It is the practice of domination itself. So, ultimately whatever resistance to Empire that hopes genuinely to operate in harmony with God's intentions for human social life must repudiate domination itself. Resistance that leads to more domination but with different figureheads on top ultimately is not nearly radical enough.

(3) *Yes to communities of resistance.* According to Paul, what God brings forth in response to human brokenness and the oppressions of the nations and their empires are communities of people who know God's peace and share that peace with all the families of the earth.

The formation and witness of these communities leads ultimately, in the biblical story, to the healing of the nations. Paul especially emphasizes the significance of these communities being made
up of reconciled enemies. In his response to Rome's hegemony, Paul
works tirelessly to create an alternative social reality, the *ekklesia*, that
practices the politics of Jesus within the *Pax Romana*. These new communities, made up of Jesus and Gentile alike, provide a context for
human flourishing.

This kind of politics remains the call for we believers today who
live within the *Pax Americana*. The most politically responsible work
followers of Jesus can engage in is the work of sustaining communities of healing. Places where enemies are reconciled, where prisoners
are set free, where Jesus' triumph over the Powers is truly embodied.

NOTES

1. See, for example, John Howard Yoder, "The Constantinian Sources of
Western Social Ethics," in *The Priestly Kingdom: Social Ethics as Gospel* (Notre
Dame, Ind.: University of Notre Dame Press, 1984), 135-51.

2. See essays by Gerald Schlabach, "Deuteronomic or Constantinian: What
Is the Most Basic Problem of Social Ethics?" in *The Wisdom of the Cross: Essays
in Honor of John Howard Yoder,* ed. Stanley Hauerwas, Chris Huebner, Harry
Huebner, and Mark Thiessen Nation (Grand Rapids, Mich.: Wm. B. Eerd-
mans, 1999), 449-71; and J. Alexander Sider, "Constantinianism Before and
After Nicea? Issues in Restitutionist Historiography" in *A Mind Patient and
Untamed: Assessing John Howard Yoder's Contribution to Theology, Ethics, and
Peacemaking,* ed. Ben C. Ollenberger and Gayle Gerber Koontz (Telford, Pa.:
Cascadia Publishing House, 2004), 126-44.

3. John Howard Yoder, *The Politics of Jesus,* 2nd. ed. (Grand Rapids, Mich.:
Wm. B. Eerdmans, 1994).

4. "The Kingdom Coming," *Politics,* 21-59. References to *Politics* in the
paragraphs to follow will be in parentheses in the text.

5. See especially Hendrikus Berkhof, *Christ and the Powers,* rev. ed.
(Scottdale, Pa., 1977). In the years since *The Politics of Jesus* was first published
in 1972, the authoritative work that has broadened and deepened Yoder's insights has been Walter Wink's three books: *Naming the Powers: The Language of
Power in the New Testament* (Philadelphia: Fortress Press, 1984); *Unmasking the
Powers* (Philadelphia: Fortress Press, 1986); and *Engaging the Powers* (Minneapolis: Fortress Press, 1992).

6. In light of the seventy-fifth anniversary of Dorothy Day's launch of the
Catholic Worker newspaper, May Day 2008, it is useful to consider Day's life
and work as an extraordinary expression of revolutionary subordination—
both in relation to the Catholic church and to the wider American society. In
her resistance to domination, Day nonetheless (usually) willingly subordinated herself to church authority and (by accepting her arrests) to state authority. But she (and her community) remained unbowed and undeterred in

their witness, with significant long-term transformative effect.

One example of the influence of the Catholic Worker movement may be seen in the increase of the number of Catholic conscientious objectors in the United States. During World War I, we know of only one person who was identified as a Catholic who was a legally recognized CO. By the time of the Vietnam War, more Catholics gained CO status than members of any other denomination.

7. See Nicholson Baker, *Human Smoke: The Beginnings of World War II, the End of Civilization* (New York: Simon and Schuster, 2008). Baker raises powerful questions about the moral impact of the prosecution of the war on American and British societies.

Chapter 7

WHY THE WORLD NEEDS CHRISTIAN LEADERS COMMITTED TO PEACEMAKING

Richard T. Hughes

One way to address the question, Why does the world need Christian leaders committed to peace making? is to ask it in light of Samuel P. Huntington's magisterial volume, *The Clash of Civilizations and the Remaking of World Order*. By now, the two fundamental premises that drive this volume are familiar ones—that "clashes of civilization are the greatest threat to world peace," and that "religion is a central defining characteristic of civilizations."[1] This means, quite simply, that religious leaders of the future will play an enormous role in preserving—or threatening—the peace of the world.

Albert Einstein explained what is really at stake in the question of war and peace when he offered this sobering assessment: "I do not know with what weapons World War III will be fought, but World War IV will be fought with sticks and stones."

But how can religious leaders, of all people, help to lead the world in ways of peace? In his book-length response to Samuel Huntington—*The Dignity of Difference: How to Avoid the Clash of* Civilizations—Jonathan Sacks offers an important first step. Each religion, Sacks argues, must abandon the illusion that it and it alone embodies universal truth. Instead, he writes that we "need to search—each faith in its own way—for a way of living with, and acknowledging the integrity of, those who are not of our faith. Can we," he wonders, "make space for difference? Can we hear the voice of God in a language, a sensibility, a culture not our own? Can we see the presence of God in the face of a stranger?"[2] In other words, he asks, can we make room for "the dignity of difference?"

That is a first step, but there is a second step as well. And as I outline this second step—which is the substance of this essay—I want to speak clearly and explicitly as a Christian whose chief concern is for Christian leaders of the future.

It's common knowledge that from the fourth century forward, Christian leaders have often been fervent advocates of violence and war. That fact is no less true today than it was during the twelfth and thirteenth centuries when Christian leaders advocated crusades against what they called the "Muslim infidels," or during the seventeenth century when Protestant and Catholic leaders alike summoned the faithful to slaughter their religious competitors.

More recently, at the outset of the war in Iraq, the pastor of the First Baptist Church in Atlanta told his congregation that "we should offer to serve the war effort in any way possible. . . . God battles with people who oppose him, and fight against him and his followers." Others, including Franklin Graham, son of Billy Graham, and Marvin Olasky, editor of the *World* magazine, suggested that the war would open up a whole new field for converting Muslims to the Christian faith. Still others, like Tim LaHaye, co-author of the best-selling *Left Behind* series of end-times books, suggested that by virtue of the war, Iraq would become "a focal point of end-times events" (5).

With preaching like that, it's hardly surprising to learn that when the war was still being planned, "some 69 percent of conservative Christians favor[ed] military action against Baghdad, 10 percentage points more than the U.S. adult population as a whole." And by April 2003, a month after the United States launched its preemptive strike against Iraq, the decision to invade that nation drew support from an astounding 87 percent of all white evangelical Christians.[3]

At the root of the militarism that has dominated so much Christian teaching and Christian leadership is the easy and facile confusion of the purposes of the Christian faith with the purposes of the American state, leading many to assume that the United States is, in fact, a Christian nation. A single example of this sort of confusion will suffice: Julia Ward Howe's "The Battle Hymn of the Republic," published in the *Atlantic Monthly* in 1862.

The first stanza of that majestic hymn equated "the glory of the coming of the Lord" with the cause of the Republic in America's Civil War. It then suggested that in the guns of the Union Army, God himself "hath loosed the fateful lightning of His terrible swift sword." Indeed, Howe concluded, amid that war, "His truth is marching on."

The third stanza spoke of a "fiery gospel writ in burnished rows of steel," thereby suggesting some connection between the gospel of Christ and the nation's military agenda.

But the fifth stanza did the most to confuse America's civic faith with the Christian religion, for it directly linked the work of Christ with the work of the Union Army, and the cross of Christ with the cause of temporal freedom.

> In the beauty of the lilies Christ was born across the sea;
> With a glory in His bosom that transfigures you and me;
> As He died to make men holy, let us die to make men free,
> While God is marching on.[4]

Over the years, millions of Christians have sung that song, fully convinced that they were singing a Christian hymn, or at least a hymn in keeping with the central themes of the Christian gospel. They could make that assumption because they firmly believed that the United States was, indeed, a Christian nation.

The notion of Christian America remains firmly entrenched in the American psyche. Indeed, the sociologist Christian Smith reports that "not only conservative Protestants but the majority of Americans believe that America was founded as a Christian nation."[5]

Obviously, there is a sense—and, in fact, a profound sense—in which America is a Christian nation. After all, some eighty percent of the American people claim to be Christian in one form or another. But the Christian character of the United States is comparable to the Christian character of the Roman Empire following Constantine, or the Christian character of the Holy Roman Empire in the sixteenth century. Christian trappings abound, but if one compares, for example, the Christian dimensions of the Holy Roman Empire with the teachings of Jesus, the differences are stunning.

Jesus counseled peace, but the empire practiced violence. Jesus counseled humility, but the empire engaged in a ruthless pursuit of power. Jesus counseled concern for the poor, but the empire practiced exaltation of the rich. Jesus counseled modesty, but the empire practiced extravagance. Jesus counseled simple living, but the empire encouraged luxurious living for those with the means to embrace that way of life. And while Jesus counseled forgiveness and love for one's enemies, the empire practiced vengeance.

Like that ancient empire, the United States abounds in Christian trappings. Still, the United States is an empire that embraces virtually all the values that have been common to empires for centuries on end. It seeks peace through violence; exalts the rich over the poor; prefers power to humility; places vengeance above forgiveness, extravagance above modesty, and luxury above simplicity. In a word, it rejects the values of Jesus, though many Americans wish to claim that the United States is a Christian nation.

The surest way to get a handle on all of this is to compare the notion of "Christian America" with the only phrase in the New Testament that even comes close to suggesting the idea of a Christian nation. That phrase is "the kingdom of God." And when we make that comparison, we quickly discover that the notion of Christian America, on the one hand, and the notion of the kingdom of God, on the other, are polar opposites.

There is no theme about which Jesus spoke with greater regularity than the notion of the kingdom of God. That phrase, or its equivalent, appears in the New Testament well over a hundred times, and it is impossible to understand the message of Jesus without grasping the meaning of that idea.

In almost every instance where that phrase appears, it is closely linked to two important themes. The first of the themes is compassionate concern for the poor, the dispossessed, those in prison, the maimed, the lame, the blind, and all those who suffer at the hands of the world's elites. In other words, the kingdom of God is where the powerless are empowered, where the hungry are fed, where the sick are healed, where the poor are sustained, and where those who find themselves marginalized by the rulers of this world are finally exalted.

The second of those themes consistently condemns those nations that amass their wealth and power on the backs of the poor and the dispossessed. Sharing in that condemnation are all the empires of the earth, including the politicians, businesspeople, religious leaders, and others who serve the imperial cause.

In other words, when Jesus uses the phrase *the kingdom of God*, the context is almost always a struggle between the reign or rule of God on behalf of the poor and the dispossessed, on the one hand, and the empires of this world that serve powerful and privileged elites, on the other. The New Testament, in fact, consistently views the empire as the arch-villain in the biblical drama. At the same time, there is no more important—nor a more pervasive—theme in the New Testament text than its message regarding God's concern for the powerless and the poor.

These are precisely the conclusions of some of the best and most recent New Testament scholarship—the work, for example, of John Dominic Crossan, Warren Carter, Richard Horsley, Barbara Rossing, and others.[6] And Walter Brueggemann, noted scholar of the Hebrew Bible, has suggested that the struggle between the people of God and the empire is an equally pervasive theme in that text as well. The people of God, Brueggemann notes, are called to acts of mercy, while the empire inevitably devotes itself to an infinite expansion of land, wealth, and power.[7]

I want to suggest that if there is any hope that Christian leaders of the future might become agents of peace instead of agents of war, they must abandon both the idea and the rhetoric of Christian America. They must embrace instead both the idea and the rhetoric of the kingdom of God.

Jesus spells out the relation of the kingdom of God to peace and nonviolence especially in the fifth through ninth Beatitudes, found in Matthew 5. All five of those Beatitudes counsel mercy, peacemaking, and nonviolence. "Blessed are the merciful," Jesus says in the fifth of these statements, "for they shall obtain mercy." And then in the sixth, "Blessed are the peacemakers, for they shall be called the sons of God."

The sixth, eighth, and ninth Beatitudes continue the themes of peacemaking and nonviolence since they pronounce blessings both on the pure in heart and on those who suffer persecution for righteousness' sake. Here is the way those Beatitudes read.

> Blessed are the pure in heart, for they shall see God.
> Blessed are those who are persecuted for righteousness' sake, for theirs is the kingdom of heaven.
> Blessed are you when men revile you and persecute you and utter all kinds of evil against you falsely on my account. Rejoice and be glad for your reward is great in heaven, for so men persecuted the prophets who were before you. (ASV)

Why do I suggest that these Beatitudes go together? Because those who are pure in heart are those who reject the impulse to hate when faced with oppression and persecution. And in the context of the Roman Empire, the poor were faced with oppression every day.

The fact is, later in the Sermon on the Mount, in his most explicit and radical teaching on peacemaking and nonviolence, Jesus enlarges on the Beatitudes that focus on these themes when he counsels love for one's enemies. Here are his words as reported in the gospel of Matthew.

> You have heard that it was said, "An eye for an eye and a tooth for a tooth." But I say to you, Do not resist one who is evil. But if any one strikes you on the right cheek, turn to him the other also; and if any one would sue you and take your coat, let him have your cloak as well; and if any one forces you to go one mile, go with him two miles. Give to him who begs from you, and do not refuse him who would borrow from you.
>
> You have heard that it was said, "You shall love your neighbor and hate your enemy." But I say to you, Love your enemies and pray for those who persecute you, so that you may be sons of your Father who is in heaven. (5:38-45 ASV)

It is difficult for Americans, so accustomed to violence and retribution, to imagine that Jesus could possibly have meant these teachings in any literal sense. Yet this theme of peacemaking and nonviolence is constant throughout the Christians' New Testament. In fact, there is no theme more central to what Christians call their "gospel" (good news), since the gospel focuses on the Christian claim that Jesus refused to resist those who sought to kill him but instead gave his life for the sake of others.'

According to Matthew, just hours before Jesus was crucified one of his disciples, in an obvious attempt to defend Jesus, drew a sword and "struck the slave of the high priest, and cut off his ear." But Matthew reports that Jesus said to his disciples,

> Put your sword back into its place; for all who take the sword will perish by the sword. Do you think that I cannot appeal to my Father, and he will at once send me more than twelve legions of angels? (26:51-54 ASV)

John's gospel reports that during the course of his trial, Jesus said to Pilate, "My kingship is not of this world; if my kingship were of this world, my servants would fight . . . ; but my kingship is not of this world." Indeed, it was not, for Jesus consistently claimed that he represented not the kingdoms of this world, but an altogether different kingdom that he called "the kingdom of God." And this kingdom was one of peacemaking and nonviolence.

After Jesus' death, his followers kept this very same vision alive. Here, for example, is the apostle Paul, in the epistle to the Romans.

Bless those who persecute you; bless and do not curse them.
. . . Repay no one evil for evil, but take thought for what is
noble in the sight of all. If possible, so far as it depends upon
you, live peaceably with all. Beloved, never avenge yourselves, but leave it to the wrath of God; for it is written,
"Vengeance is mine, I will repay, says the Lord." No, "if your
enemy is hungry, feed him; if he is thirsty, give him drink; for
by so doing you will heap burning coals upon his head." Do
not be overcome by evil, but overcome evil with good. (12:14-
21 ASV)

The truth is that for the most part, the early Christians conformed their lives to Jesus' teachings regarding peacemaking and
nonviolence for the first three hundred years of the Christian movement. The testimony from two Christian leaders during that period
makes this point clear. Tertullian (ca 155-230), for example, claimed
that Jesus' command to love one's enemies is the "principal precept"
of the Christian religion. In that light, he asked, "If we are enjoined to
love our enemies, whom have we to hate? If injured we are forbidden to retaliate. Who then can suffer injury at our hands?"

Again, Cyprian (c. 200-258) summarized the heart of the Christian faith like this:

That you should not curse; that you should not seek again your
goods when taken from you; when buffeted you should turn
the other cheek; and forgive not seven times but seventy times
seven. . . . That you should love your enemies and pray for your
adversaries and persecutors."

If the rejection of vengeance and the commitment to peacemaking and nonviolence was such a central part of the Christian religion
for its first three hundred years, it's fair to ask, what happened? Why
do most American Christians—and most Christians around the
world, for that matter—view Jesus' teachings on nonviolence as
noble ideals but finally unrealistic and unworkable?

There are doubtless many answers, but any response would
have to begin with the radical changes that transformed the Christian religion in the fourth century—first under the Roman Emperor
Constantine (272-337) and then under the Emperor Theodosius the
Great (347-395). Before Constantine, Rome had officially outlawed
the Christian religion, and for one to convert to the Christian faith
might well cost one's life. In 313, however, Constantine legalized
Christianity for the first time in its history. Then, in 391, Theodosius
made Christianity the only legal religion in the Roman Empire.

These decisions were far-reaching, for they created for the first time in Christian history the marriage of church and state, a marriage in which the state agreed to protect and honor the church, while the church would honor the state and its rulers by encouraging the faithful to conform to the rulers' decrees. Inevitably, those decrees included the command to participate in the empire's wars.

Under the circumstances, it's hardly surprising that Christian theologians now found ways for Christians to serve the empire by taking up the empire's sword. The first Christian theologian to work out a systematic justification for this radical change was Augustine (354-430) whose just war theory stated that Christians *could* participate in warfare—and Christian emperors *could* declare and wage war—but only with certain safeguards and constraints. A just war, for example, would be a defensive war, would be fought for a just cause, would be fought with good intentions, and would avoid the killing of non-combatants.

Standing at the heart of just war theory are the assumptions that war is inevitable and that the biblical vision of peacemaking and non-violence is finally illusory and impractical in this violent world.

Ironically, no one has made that case any more strongly than Samuel Huntington, who cites approvingly the Venetian nationalist demagogue in Michael Didbin's novel, *Dead Lagoon*. "There can be no true friends without true enemies," the Venetian says. "Unless we hate what we are not, we cannot love what we are. These are the old truths we are painfully rediscovering after a century and more of sentimental cant." In response to this affirmation, Samuel Huntington comments, "The unfortunate truth in these old truths cannot be ignored by statesmen and scholars. For people seeking identity and reinventing ethnicity, enemies are essential."[8]

Maybe so, but if there is any chance that Christian leaders might lead us toward peace and not toward war and conflict, those are precisely the assumptions they must challenge. Put another way, so long as Christian leaders assume that the imperial vision is both normative and true to life, and so long as they assume that the biblical vision of the kingdom of God is finally unworkable and irrelevant, there is no chance that they will offer leadership any different from the standard imperial leadership that has driven the world for centuries.

The truth is, Christian leaders of tomorrow must embrace a new paradigm for thinking about war and peace—a paradigm that is at the very same time an ancient paradigm, embraced both by Jesus and the early church.

Let me offer just one example of what that paradigm might mean. David Lipscomb was a religious leader in the American South from the Civil War through the early twentieth century. After the Civil War, he reflected on his own role during that conflict. "In the beginning of the late strife that so fearfully desolated our country," he recalled, "much was said about 'our enemies.' I protested constantly that I had not a single enemy, and was not an enemy to a single man North of the Ohio River."[9]

Lipscomb's statement stands in stark contrast with Samuel P. Huntington's assumption that "there can be no true friends without true enemies" and that, when all is said and done, "enemies are essential."

And when, in 1896, the United States employed the Monroe Doctrine to threaten war against Great Britain, Lipscomb offered leadership on other grounds. He wrote, "When the leading lights among politicians begin to advocate war in defense of the Monroe doctrine, it is high time . . . to commence preaching peace on earth and good will among men in defense of the doctrine of the Sermon on the Mount."[10]

Some will no doubt object that what I am saying is far too visionary to be workable. But religious leaders are not called to embrace and sanction imperial assumptions. They are called, instead, to offer a vision grounded in their religious traditions. And deep in the Christian tradition there lies a powerful vision for peace on earth and good will among all humankind.

Tragically, this vision has rarely been tried, even by those who wear the mantle of the Christian religion and claim to represent the Prince of Peace. But the hour has now grown late, and wars and the threat of wars now threaten the very existence of the planet. We have no more time to waste.

So now is the time for Christian leaders to claim a vision that, for the most part, they have been too timid to claim for the past 1,700 years. Now is the time for Christian leaders to proclaim the heart of the Christian gospel. Now is the time for Christian leaders to reject the values of an imperial culture and to embrace instead the values of the kingdom of God.

These are momentous tasks, but these are the tasks to which all Christian leaders are finally called. And these are the tasks they must embrace if we hope to avoid catastrophe in these extraordinarily perilous times.

NOTES

1. Samuel P. Huntington, *The Clash of Civilizations and the Remaking of World Order* (New York: Simon and Schuster, 1996), 42, 47.

2. Jonathan Sacks, *The Dignity of Difference: How to Avoid the Clash of Civilizations* (London/New York: Continuum, 2003), 5.

3. Jim Lobe, "Conservative Christians Biggest Backers against Iraq, Poll Shows," *Common Dreams News Center*, www.commondreams.org, October 10, 2002; and Charles Marsh, "Wayward Christian Soldiers," *New York Times*, January 20, 2006.

4. For the text of "The Battle Hymn of the Republic," along with an analysis, see David Hackett Fischer, *Liberty and Freedom: A Visual History of America's Founding Ideas* (Oxford: Oxford University Press, 2005), 331-32.

5. Christian Smith, *Christian America: What Evangelicals Really Want* (Berkeley: University of California Press, 2000), 199.

6. See, for example, Warren Carter, *Matthew and Empire: Initial Explorations* (Harrisburg: Trinity Press International, 2001), and *What Are They Saying About Matthew's Sermon on the Mount?* (New York: Paulist Press, 1994). See also Richard A. Horsley, *Jesus and Empire: The Kingdom of God and the New World Disorder* (Minneapolis: Fortress Press, 2003); Horsley, *Religion and Empire: People, Power, and the Life of the Spirit* (Minneapolis: Fortress Press, 2003); and Richard A. Horsley and Neil Asher Silberman, *The Message and the Kingdom: How Jesus and Paul Ignited a Revolution and Transformed the Ancient World* (Minneapolis: Fortress Press, 1997). See also Barbara R. Rossing, *The Rapture Exposed: The Message of Hope in the Book of Revelation* (New York: Basic Books, 2004).

7. Walter Brueggemann, "Alien Witnesses: How God's People Challenge Empire," *Christian Century* 124 (March 6, 2007): 28-32.

8. Huntington, *The Clash of Civilizations*, p. 20.

9. David Lipscomb, "Babylon," *Gospel Advocate* 23 (2 June 1881): 340.

10. Lipscomb, "From the Papers," *Gospel Advocate* 38 (9 January 1896): 17.

Chapter 8

DEPRAVATIO CRUCIS: THE NON-SOVEREIGNTY OF GOD IN JOHN CAPUTO'S POETICS OF THE KINGDOM

B. Keith Putt

//The time is fulfilled, and the kingdom of God is at hand; repent and believe in the gospel." Such is the *evangelium in nuce*, the good news of Christ in a nutshell, preserved in the gospel according to Mark 1:15. That beautifully concise expression of Jesus' proclamation of divine redemption takes on unique contemporary significance when one realizes how appropriately it correlates with various post-modern and postsecular theologies of the kingdom of God. Indeed, one might offer the following postsecular paraphrase of this verse: "The time is (the) 'to-come,' and the ironic, anarchic kingdom of the non-sovereign God is constantly an event at hand; open your heart and mind to the transforming call of the divine promise and live out the passion for the impossible through the undecidability of faith."

This particular paraphrase depends significantly upon the radically biblical postmodern hermeneutics of the gospel according to John—as in John D. Caputo, who is, himself, quite an accomplished connoisseur of nutshells.[1] On the one hand, it encapsulates many of the provocative themes that Caputo engages as he develops what he calls his "theopoetics of the kingdom." On the other hand, it telegraphs certain hermeneutical positions suggesting a postmodern, prophetic "biblicism" that casts suspicion on how traditional orthodoxies have (mis)interpreted Jesus' revelation of God. Furthermore, and perhaps surprisingly, it actually discloses theopolitical perspectives on the kingdom of God that connect Caputo with certain specific "peace church" traditions, positioning him as a new postsecular Kierkegaard directing a deconstructive attack upon Christendom.[2]

I acknowledge that translating divinely inspired Scripture into Caputo's deconstructive vocabulary might strike some as trafficking in heresy at best or the epitome of blasphemy at worst. After all, he associates himself directly with Jacques Derrida, who confesses that he rightly passes for an atheist, and with his philosophy of deconstruction, a philosophy that ostensibly embraces relativism, antirealism, and linguistic meaninglessness.[3] How could Caputo's Derridean "cold hermeneutics" with all its doom and gloom of rejecting truth, value, and knowledge possibly have anything salutary to contribute to an understanding of God's Word?[4]

Those with a shallow and/or secondhand knowledge of Caputo's work would answer definitively, "It cannot!" To be sure, any theology proposed by Caputo could only be a rejection of the certain truth of God's revelation and a denunciation of the blessed assurance that Jesus is the way, the truth, and the life. Of course, Caputo is aware of the "axiomatics of indignation" that dismiss his radical hermeneutics as nothing more than another species of skepticism and subjectivism.[5] He recounts that after delivering a lecture at a conservative Christian institution, a young coed approached and informed him that she knew precisely why he had been sent to her campus: The devil had sent him to test her faith![6]

Caputo celebrates such indictments. He acknowledges that he plays the devil's advocate with alacrity, going so far as to label his thought a "devilish hermeneutics."[7] Yet he is no emissary of the devil; on the contrary, he considers himself to be someone obsessed with loving God and someone who has always had a weakness for theology. He claims that modesty prevented him from heretofore accepting the label "theologian," since he always recognized how audacious it was for someone to claim to speak about God; however, he affirms that he cannot avoid speaking about God, specifically about the name of God, and now will accept that he is, indeed, a theologian.[8] Moreover, he insists that he is a *Christian* theologian, that he seeks to reinscribe a certain Christianity, one "focused on the image of weakness in the New Testament and the death of Jesus on the cross."[9]

Although Caputo rejects religious and ideological exclusivism regarding truth, revelation, and divine favor—considering such to be the grounds for some quite unholy, unloving, and unethical behavior—he, nevertheless, does not shy away from developing his theopoetics of the name of God within the functionally "exclusive" singularity of the life and teachings of Jesus of Nazareth.[10] He insists that Jesus reveals a God unlike the omnipotent and impassible deity of traditional metaphysics, a God who is either distant from the world as some Aristotelian "thought thinking itself" or involved in the world as a manipulating and coercive cosmic power. Instead, Jesus speaks of a God of love and mercy, one sensitive to the widow and orphan, a God who suffers with and for those who are oppressed, victimized, or ignored by the world. Such a God, however, disrupts the world's criteria for power and prestige and threatens the dominating hierarchy of the powers-that-be. Consequently, the world rejects that God and all who proclaim him, a rejection that leads inevitably to Jesus' being crucified as a religious and political threat to the *status quo*.[11]

In his recent quasi-systematic theology entitled *The Weakness of God*, Caputo acknowledges that Slavoj Zizek is "half right" to insist that the perverse core of Christianity centers on the divine abandonment of Jesus on the cross. Caputo gives Zizek half credit for having correctly identified the cross as the locus of Christianity's perversive dynamic, but he gives him *only fifty-percent* credit for failing to articulate the true focus of that perversity. He insists that Zizek fails to recognize that the cross performatively manifests precisely what Jesus discursively reveals in his kerygmatics of the kingdom of God.[12]

Caputo considers the crucifixion of Jesus to be so crucial to understanding the deconstructive and subversive implications of Jesus' kerygma of the kingdom of God that he allies himself with the apostle Paul in proclaiming a *theologia crucis*, a theology of the prophetic word (*logos*) of the cross (*stauros*) that reinterprets the relationship between God and humanity and scandalizes those who have established their position and prestige on violent protocols of control.[13] Caputo joins Luther in warning against allowing the *theologia crucis*, the theology of the cross, to be adulterated by a *theologia gloriae*, the theology of glory, that is, for the logic of the cross to be dismissed by those who prefer an ecclesiastical triumphalism, those willing to compromise Jesus' gospel and develop strong theologies more open to secular structures of domination, greed, and prestige—in other words, certain traditions of the Constantinian church triumphant.

If one considers Caputo's emphases on the prophetic, subversive, and critical dynamics of Jesus' kerygma of the kingdom of a suffering God as a response to the cruciform violence of the world, along with St. Paul's hermeneutic of the scandalizing word of the cross, then one could claim, using Zizek's nomenclature, that Caputo's *theologia crucis* is genuinely a *depravatio crucis*, a "perversion of the cross," in that the cross and all it symbolizes pervert the oppressive and violent powers of the world. The cross discloses God's "no" to suffering and violence and God's "yes" to the "least of these," to those excised, excommunicated, and executed by the principalities and powers of the world.

Referring to Caputo's "staurological" poetics of the kingdom as a *depravatio crucis* also allows one to recognize his "attack upon Christendom," his negative response to the Constantinian church, which has in various ways capitulated to the very demonic forces that rejected Jesus. Caputo believes that the church has a poor record over the centuries in remaining faithful to the kingdom of God, allowing itself to be seduced by the world and the promise of social and political influence. Consequently, one can read *depravatio crucis* in both senses of the genitive. There is the *perversion* of the cross in the subjective sense of the cross' perversion of the world's theories of strength, economy, and violence; however, there is also the perversion *of* the cross in the objective sense of the church's perverting the cross by sacrificing it on the pagan altar of instrumentalism and by compromising its prophetic character in order to achieve political influence.

Caputo's *depravatio crucis* in the sense of the objective genitive connects him in a significant way to the peace church tradition and its negative interpretation of Constantinian ecclesiology. Caputo does not engage that tradition in any explicit manner; however, he is certainly not unaware of it. In point of fact, he actually references two of the more influential scholars in that tradition. First, when trying to position Derrida with reference to social theory, Caputo distinguishes him from the liberalism of John Rawls and the communitarianism of Stanley Hauerwas. Caputo criticizes the essentialism he finds in Hauerwas' emphasis on the "deep truths in the tradition upon which the individual draws as long as he remains tapped into its flow."[14] He assumes, perhaps erroneously, that Hauerwas holds too pious a position with reference to the authority and stability of the historical church community.

Second, and most recently, while examining the political and social implications of Jesus' poetics of the kingdom, Caputo declares that he avoids using the phrase "the politics of Jesus," primarily because of its ambiguity and the possibility of its being misused. He notes that such a phrase can be used by John Howard Yoder but also by George W. Bush—the latter sealing its fate for Caputo! Although he does not question Yoder's use of the nomenclature, he claims that he prefers to avoid it.[15] Consequently, since Caputo has at least mentioned, if not used, Hauerwas and Yoder, I propose here to examine his *depravatio crucis* and its critique of the Constantinian church with constant attention given to how it compares and contrasts to their positions. I contend that there is an interesting complementarity among their various interpretations, although significant distinctions cannot be dismissively glossed.

To comprehend Caputo's theopoetics of the kingdom and his postsecular *theologia crucis*, one must understand his underlying theology of the name of God and of the event. Caputo confesses that the name of God is a powerful and beautiful name, actually a hypernym, a name above every name, a name that names what we most desire. Accepting Augustine's claim of the *cor inquietum*, the "restless heart" that propels us toward God, he considers the name of God to be the name of that which we love most passionately.[16]

Remaining in an Augustinian mode, however, one also further influenced by Derrida's deconstructive perspective on the divine name, Caputo insists that we cannot avoid the following persistent question: "What do I love when I love my God?" The systemic uncertainty as to what the name of God names ensues from the endless translatability and substitutability of that name; that is, the name of God contains something uncontainable, which means that it cannot be domesticated and defined by the closure of referentiality. The name of God, like any other constructed cipher, may be constantly deconstructed, since its meaning can be disseminated across a broad nominal field. In other words, Caputo inquires as to whether what we call "God" might not also be called "love," "justice," "gift," or "truth." Indeed, he insists that theology may well be understood as the ongoing deconstruction and re-inscription of the plurivocal name of God, a twofold process of historical association and messianic, or deconstructive, dissociation.[17]

Yet, if the name of God contains something uncontainable, precisely what is that uncontainable and undeconstructible something? Caputo claims that it is an "event," the coming (*venire*) out (*e*) or breaking out (*e-venire*, e-vent) of the aleatoric, of the unprogrammable occurrence that shatters every horizon of expectation.[18] Events exemplify Derrida's notion of the "perhaps," not in the sense of what "may be," but in the sense of "what may happen"; events just happen beyond any foresight or foreconception of what is to come.[19] Actually, to be more precise, Caputo declares that events are not so much what happens, as with some historical occurrences, but what is stirring or active *within* what happens.[20]

This more subtle distinction of the event signifies that it betrays a messianic structure to experience. The event signals something that is always "to come," the invention (*in-venire*), the in-coming, or the advent (*ad-venire*), the coming-to, of an absolute future that will never be present.[21] This messianic structure of the event places a demand on every present, issues an unconditional summons or call to humility and openness; that is to say, the messianic prohibits premature closure or the dogmatism of a Cartesian certainty.[22] Since the future present, which can be anticipated and, therefore, somewhat controlled, defines the limits of the possible, the absolute future promised by the messianic is actually an expression of the impossible. Consequently, the lure of the messianic, the attraction of the "perhaps" that transcends human control and ingenuity, results in a passion for the impossible, a desire beyond desire, a love for something that is totally other and that lures us forward.[23]

Caputo asserts that theology as the hermeneutics of the "eventful" name of God is a "spectral hermeneutics," an interpretation of the "spirit" of the event that constantly haunts every divine name, not as some semantic fullness or ontological essence, but as that uncontainable, unprogrammable messianic summons toward which all names of God strive.[24] As a result, he centers his theological thought on God as event, God as a task or a deed, not as an entity or a metaphysical principle. God is the impossible, the divine event that shatters every human construction, that summons, demands, lures, and promises. The messianic event astir in the name of God convicts through its prophetic critique of every conditional and finite attempt to identify, define, or confine God within the conceptual constraints of human logic and language. Yet it also affirms with a gracious "yes" to existence, with the promise of transformation, rebirth, and hope.

Consequently, the event astir in the name of God is provocative and evocative, the impossibility of an unconditional promise that constantly actualizes the potentiality of that which eye has not seen nor ear heard. For Caputo, then, theology is always responsive, always an answer to the summons and demands coming from the event harbored in the name of God, always motivated by the transcendent other, the unknowable, the subversive and disruptive impossible possibility always to come.[25]

Notwithstanding both his insistence that the name of God is endlessly translatable and deconstructible, hence always demanding the
risk of non-knowing and knowing otherwise, and also that the event
can never be present in any definitive, exhaustive, and essentialist
sense, Caputo does not remain indecisive concerning valid ways of
confessing God as the messianic unconditional promise of hope.[26]
This "confessional" position is quite consistent with Caputo's basic
acceptance of undecidability, a Derridean idea that according to
those who adopt the "axiomatics of indignation" manifests the relativism and hermeneutical nihilism inherent in deconstructive
thought. They mistakenly synonymize undecidability with indeci-
siveness, the paralysis of never choosing an objective meaning or a
valid position.

Yet this misdefining is dialectically contrary to its genuine intent.
For Caputo and Derrida, undecidability references the unprogram-
mability of the event of meaning, acknowledges that a genuine decision, like a genuine experience, is something that shatters horizons of
expectations, that cannot be organically or logically inferred, but
comes as a surprise, as the impossible. That the event or meaning
cannot be projected or calculated is exactly what demands that a decision be made. Undecidability, therefore, does not preempt decision—it prescribes it, requires it, makes it unavoidable.[27]

In regard to theology and religion, undecidability establishes
faith as the proper response to the provocation of the divine unconditional promise. Faith cannot be collapsed into knowledge, if by
knowledge one means methodical computation and certainty. Caputo agrees with the Pauline expression of faith as "knowing in part,"
as seeing "through a mirror dimly." Faith is not knowing who we are,
where we are, or what is happening in any dogmatic or absolute
sense. It is, instead, to believe with hope and expectation, to make a
decision regarding what we love when we love our God with full
recognition of the risks involved. Faith is believing in the midst of
asking God to help our disbelief, to trust in God with fear and trembling amid undecidability.[28]

Caputo's emphases on event and undecidability position him
surprisingly close to aspects of Hauerwas' and Yoder's theology of
the kingdom. For example, Hauerwas constantly affirms the contingent and historical nature of Christian faith as the narrative of particular events instead of the universality of rational truths.[29] Corre-
spondingly, he concludes that "theology can never be finished . . . because the story we tell resists any premature closure."[30] Indeed, he
goes so far as to adopt the language of postmodernism and repudiate

metanarratives, the idea that one can develop a grand story that inculcates and governs all other smaller stories. He categorically denies that the gospel is such a metanarrative, that it "occupies an epistemological space that assumes a superiority over all other narratives." Instead, he avows that the gospel is a "particular story of Jesus, the Son of God, known through cross and resurrection."[31]

Similarly, Yoder himself does a fairly nice impression of Caputo's poetics of undecidability and the weak force of the event when he addresses the theme of the kerygma. He seizes on the etymology of its root, *keryx*, which means "to herald" or "to proclaim." The kerygma of the kingdom as proclaimed by the herald "is not permanent, timeless, logical insights but contingent, particular events," which never have to be accepted or believed. They are non-coercive for two reasons: first, the event itself is contingent and singular and second the herald of the event has no status or sovereignty with which to compel belief. One may always reject the event without fear of reprisals or violence.[32] Such positions would make Caputo proud to be an Anabaptist!

Given all of the above, one should not be surprised that Caputo's theology of the event and the name of God has "doctrinal" content, a specific meaning that he accepts as existentially valid and as appropriate "grounds" for a critique of alternative interpretations. He testifies that his devilish hermeneutics of the event discloses a God far different from the traditional deity of classical theism, from the metaphysical principle of Being, or the Ground of Being, or Self-Subsistent Being. The event astir in the name of God should not be considered as revelatory of a cosmic potentate micromanaging and manipulating reality, or as a transcendent warrior god casting lightening bolts like Zeus or killing babies in Jericho like Yahweh. Instead, the impossible God of love discovered in the event is a God who disrupts such grandiose theories of power, prestige, and brutality. The name of God harbors the power of a weak force, a force that does not plot but promises, that does not exploit but entices, that does not violate human freedom but vitiates destructive structures of power and oppression through the power of powerlessness and the seduction of divine suffering. In other words, Caputo professes that his theology of the event tracks St. Paul's shocking and even scandalous theology of "the weakness of God" expressed so powerfully in 1 Corinthians.[33] Caputo indicates that his hermeneutics of the name of God, his theology of the event, and his postsecular theopassionism find specific textual and historical particularity in the New Testament idea of the kingdom of God. The kingdom of God actually incarnates, embodies, or "[stretches] out in space and time" the name of God within a uniquely Christian context.[34]

He is particularly interested in Jesus' kerygmatics of the kingdom and how one might interpret Jesus' proclamation as a distinctive poetics of the kingdom of God—by which Caputo means a poetics of the impossible, since Jesus teaches that the kingdom of God is the kingdom of excess, of the unanticipated, and of what is always "to come." Caputo is explicitly interested in how Jesus' proclamation of the kingdom correlates so well with the notion of the event and with Derrida's idea of *différance*. For Derrida, *différance* references both the difference that characterizes any system of signs and also the deferral that leaves open the contingency of meaning. *Différance*, therefore, operates in tandem with the idea of undecidability to ensure that individuals never deceive themselves into thinking that they can achieve absolute certainty or absolute truth. *Différance* keeps language open, meaning unsettled, and knowledge forever mindful that there can be no dogmatic closure. Consequently, for Derrida, *différance* can have nothing to do with kingdom; there can be no kingdom of *différance*, since *différance* rejects any overarching principle, any sovereign criterion of meaning that can close the process of interpretation. But, of course, what *différance* rejects is analogous to what one finds in the socio-political idea of kingdom–the rule of some sovereign prince, the application of some definite hierarchy of control.[35]

Nevertheless, Caputo contends that if one understands the kingdom of God from the perspective of how Jesus interprets and embodies that kingdom, then there is a certain irony to the kingdom of God that does allow it to be connected to *différance*. He discovers in Jesus' poetics of the kingdom a certain perverse disruption of what kingdom means, an ironic reversal of the usual categories of sovereignty and prestige. Indeed, Jesus' prophetic logic of the kingdom establishes a disconnect between it and the world, a critical differentiation that calls the world into question, that contradicts the world by speaking a word of divine judgment against the world and its adherence to protocols of violence, greed, oppression, and alienation. Jesus claims that the kingdom of God is a reality in which individuals should love their enemies, in which the criterion for giving is the extravagance of "everything," in which the response to evil is not more evil but forgiveness, in which such forgiveness should be granted seventy times seven times, in which the insult of a slap should bring the response of the offer of another cheek, in which the first will be last, the rich cannot buy their redemption, and the innocence and weakness of a child most successfully symbolize the proper model for entry into the kingdom community.

If the kingdom of God is the divine rule of God in the lives and hearts of individuals, that rule is predicated upon *metanoia*, "repentance," but not so much repentance as pain felt again over an offense as upon the willingness to change one's mind (*meta*, "again" or "after, and *noia*, "to think") and one's heart to re-think time, politics, ethics, justice, love, giving, salvation, and even God Godself. One simply cannot continue to think as the world thinks. Only through *metanoia*, through a repentant attitude open to the new creation of divine rule, may one enter into the kingdom of God.[36]

If *différance* and event both result in keeping structures from hardening and closing down, if they continually disrupt, question, and deconstruct contingent traditions, interpretations, and calibrations of meaning, then Jesus most assuredly reveals a kingdom-less kingdom of divine *différance* and of the messianic event astir in the name of God. According to the sane and logical principles of the world, the kingdom of God is nothing more than an expression of madness, a paralogetic and dangerously impractical set of beliefs that can only be destructive of all that is beautiful, good, and true. To live according to the kingdom's directives would result in anarchy, or as Caiaphas explains so reasonably and realistically to the long-robed religious powers-that-be, those dedicated protectors of the *status quo*, it would result in lawlessness and the destruction of the community.

And Caputo agrees; well, at least with the world's verdict that the kingdom of God threatens madness and anarchy. It does do just that by intent. He certainly gets no quarrel from Hauerwas regarding the disruptive dynamics at work in the kingdom poetics. In point of fact, Hauerwas uses the same vocabulary of "anarchy" to address the disordering impact of the deconstructive reign of God in the world.[37] Yoder goes so far as to translate *euangelion*, "the good news" or "gospel," with the word *revolution*![38] All agree with Brian McLaren, who designates Jesus' revelation of the kingdom as coming in "primal, disruptive, inspiring, terrifying, shocking, hopeful words and ways of a revolutionary who seeks to overthrow the status quo in nearly every conceivable way."[39] Caputo is not alone, therefore, in claiming that Jesus' kerygma of grace, mercy, and love, his dining with sinners and visiting tax collectors, his healing of lepers and menstruating women, his privileging of the under-privileged, and certainly his impertinent criticism of empty religious ritualism and arrogant self-righteousness are all direct subversions and disruptions of the community's conservative values. Jesus decries those values for under-valuing and de-valuing the widows and the orphans, the hungry and the victimized, the sick, and the stranger.

The event astir in the name of God pronounced by Jesus contradicts the world, deconstructs its institutional arrogance, and articulates the divine "no" against its violence and its domination. Jesus reveals a "sacred anarchy" that prophetically protests the profane order of the "real" world.[40] For that world, everything turns on power, on brute strength and coercion. The world constantly calculates the future, performs its profit/loss equations to ensure success, celebrates the rule of the privileged, the wealthy, and the influential, constantly hoping for, or helping along, the extinction of the poor, the weak, and the different who simply cannot adapt to its social Darwinism.

According to the sacred anarchy of the ironic kingdom of God, survival of the fittest is not the standard for human relationships. The kingdom welcomes everyone, the same and the different, the lovable and the unlovable, the repentant and the unrepentant, and summons all who come to accept their obligation to embrace the different, love the unlovable, and forgive the unrepentant. But the world considers these directives to be foolishness and impossible to follow. But the kingdom *is* impossible; it is a passion *for* the impossible; and its citizens are impossible people who believe that with God all things *are* possible. They have faith that justice, love, forgiveness, and hospitality are always near, always "to come," that perhaps, in the sense of the messianic "perhaps," the transformative event of the rule of God will attenuate the world's injustice, its hatred, its vengeful spirit, and its inhospitable bigotry toward the "least of these."[41]

Caputo states that no one should be surprised at the world's response to Jesus' proclamation of the kingdom. Such an anarchical indictment of the world's values cannot be tolerated. The political rulers determine that Jesus must die; he must quite logically become the victim of the very violent order of reality that he so assiduously critiques in the name of God. Ironically, however, the religious rulers agree and consider such violence to be properly administered "in the name of God!" Jesus' revelation of the messianic event at work in the name of God, therefore, comes to unique expression in the "crucial event" of the cross, and through that expression, Jesus remains faithful to his kingdom kerygma that the world's values of coercion, revenge, and prestige have no place in the rule of God.[42] God's kingdom has no army; it owns no weapons cache; it does not seek to establish itself through force; it refuses to compromise and instrumentalize suffering and violence. On the contrary, at the cross of Christ,

God sides with the suffering of the innocent one victimized falsely as an outlaw by the powers-that-be. Through the *"perversity* and disorder of [Jesus'] death, *per passiones et crucem* . . . God reveals his power through weakness, his heights through lowliness, his wisdom through foolishness."[43]

Caputo's perspective on the revelatory power of the cross tracks rather well with René Girard's reinterpretation of the "triumphalism" of the crucifixion. Repudiating the triumph of the cross as some supernaturally militaristic and aggressive victory of God over the worldly powers, Girard recognizes it as the victimization by those powers of a God whose suffering love and forgiveness manifest the genuinely demonic and malicious nature of the profane order. As he states it, "The powers are not put on display because they are defeated, but they are defeated because they are put on display."[44] Girard, therefore, certainly seems to offer a functional substitute for Caputo's *depravatio crucis*.

Of course, Girard supplies only one of several paraphrases of the perversion of the cross. For example, Caputo also directly correlates with Yoder and Hauerwas, since the latter two join him in accentuating the centrality of the crucifixion. Indeed, Hauerwas goes so far as to assert that the cross functions not only as a symbol of God's kingdom but as in some respects the very coming of that kingdom itself.[45] The cross marks the spot where one most clearly sees Jesus "bringing the new order of God's rule."[46] What Jesus does through the cross performatively reveals the kingdom as a "community of the cross" whereby God's perspective on reality is taken more seriously than the politics of the world.[47]

Likewise, Yoder deciphers the cross as the sign of Jesus' obedience to God's rule as it subverts the structures of the world.[48] The cross event reveals the world's hatred of the divine milieu of forgiveness and love but clarifies the genuine meaning of *agape*, in that the "forgiving death of the innocent at the hands of the guilty" indicates that divine victory over the world comes through suffering and weakness and not through violent self-defense.[49] Yet, precisely with reference to this seditious nature of the cross event, Yoder insists on using the notion of the "politics of Jesus," given that the crucifixion was essentially political. Its display of "social nonconformity" and "moral clash with the powers ruling . . . society" in reality offers a "political alternative to both insurrection and quietism."[50]

One need only consider the broader context of the crucifixion to appreciate the above interpretations. When Peter responds in a worldly fashion to Jesus' arrest by drawing his sword and doing vio-

lence to one of the guards, Jesus has him sheathe it immediately and
heals the inflicted wound. He informs Peter that such violence is not
how things are done in God's kingdom. When Pilate, the personifica-
tion of Roman power and domination, inquires into Jesus' role as the
King of the Jews, Jesus informs him quickly that his kingdom is *not of
this world*; his kingdom does, however, threaten the not-so-peaceful
Pax Romana, not through open combat, but through the ignominy of
being its latest victim. Finally, even as the power of Rome, with the
blessing of the temple's defenders of the faith, drive the nails into his
body, Jesus' prayer is not to ask God for some heavenly battalion of
angels to strike or for some massive natural disaster to consume his
enemies; instead, he asks God for forgiveness, to pardon them because they are so blinded by the world's values and so indoctrinated
by the profane structures of the principalities and powers that they
do not truly know what they are doing.

Precisely here the true Spirit of God manifests itself as the divine
contradiction of the world—but a contradiction that desires to transform the world, to redeem it by calling it to change its heart and mind
and remain open to the passion for the impossible kingdom always
"to come." In other words, the cross of Christ is the event that perverts the world's sinful economy of violence and sovereignty in order
to convert it to the weak force of divine promise, to the gracious non-
economy of the gift, forgiveness, justice, and love.

Caputo argues, as does Hauerwas, that the majesty of the cross is
not a show of worldly power but of forgiveness, a prophetic "no" to
the suffering and injustice that marks the kingdoms of humanity and
an unconditional "yes" to the coming of peace and justice that marks
the kingdom of God.[51] Furthermore, this unconditional word of love
comes without sovereignty, without the manipulative and irresistible
force of some "omnipotent onto-theo-cosmo-logical power source"
ensuring that a predetermined divine plan will be actualized as intended and without obstacle.[52]

But how can the kingdom of God possibly be a kingdom without
sovereignty, the rule of a God without the necessary supernatural enforcement mechanisms required to ensure that the divine intent will
always be done on earth as it is heaven? After all, does God not hold
the power of creation and destruction, of salvation and damnation,
and of intervention within whatever natural and/or social contexts
God arbitrarily decides to affect? Does Scripture itself not talk of God
as a warrior, as an immovable deity whose plans cannot be thwarted
and whose ways cannot be understood? To conjecture that Jesus'
kerygma of the kingdom and his death on the cross may actually re-

veal a God of risk and uncertainty, a God who does not micro-manage reality, whose will may be thwarted by those who refuse to respond to God's call, and who may even be victimized by the coercive structures of the world can be nothing more than a rejection of the one true God, an idolatrous replacement of the Lord of the Universe with the projection of an anemic and feckless deity that makes no demands and exercises no influence on human affairs.

Caputo does acknowledge the unsettling nature of his theology of divine weakness. He confirms that theology has always been "intellectually bipolar," obsessed on the one hand with the idea of divine authority and power, with God as the omnipotent impassible Being Itself who can out-think, out-achieve, and out-last all of creation, while unable to dismiss on the other hand the significant biblical expressions of a suffering God who accepts the risks of love and who protests against the injustice and violence of human persecution.

Certainly if one centers theology on the revelation of God in Christ, then both Jesus' kerygma of the kingdom and his death on the cross compel a theopoetics of the weak force of God. The cross reveals a God whose redemptive prowess depends upon the power of powerlessness, the unconditional call of grace without sovereignty, without mandate and intimidation, the powerless potency of the name of a God who can be strong-armed by the aggression of the world, denied, ignored, and even murdered, yet who in that weakness displays the power of forgiveness, the power of what Anthony Bartlett terms "abyssal compassion," and the power of a tenacious summons to justice and reconciliation.[53] The cross mediates a *"non-coercive heteronomy,"* the promise, address, or invitation from God as the Wholly Other whom human beings have the power to ignore.[54] But, then, according to Girard, this "non-coercive heteronomy" is the only consistent response that a nonviolent deity can give. Such a God "can only signal his existence to mankind by having himself driven out by violence–by demonstrating that he is not able to establish himself in the kingdom of Violence."[55]

As Caputo claims, the revelation of the name of the promising and beckoning God on the cross is the perverse core of Christianity— that singular event where the weak force of the event, the uncertainty and impossibility of an undecidable faith in the transformative dynamic of the divine promise of peace perverts the world's profane specifications for power, sovereignty, and divine authority. That divine provocation of peace and pardon is unconditional, given excessively and unilaterally regardless of human response and even to the point of death; however, given that the call may be ignored, silenced, and distorted by human evil, it is an unconditional call without sovereignty, without the absolute warrant that God can compel and constrain human obedience.[56] Consequently, for Caputo, the weakness of God is the potency of the divine tenacity in relentlessly disrupting, soliciting, subverting, contradicting, and perverting the world's esteem for the economy of retribution, intolerance, and dominion. That is the weak force of the event astir in the name of God, the *différance* of a kingdomless kingdom of the irony and anarchy of grace.

Caputo considers St. Paul's gloss on the logic of the cross in 1 Corinthians 1 to be a provocative and stimulating synopsis of his "under-nourished" theology of the event.[57] As stated above, he explicitly coopts Paul's vocabulary about the "weakness of God" from this passage; however, the passage supplies not only semantics but theological substance as well. Caputo considers the Pauline interpretations of the weakness and foolishness of God to be a constructive translation of the deconstructive elements of his theopoetics of the kingdom. The unconditional rule of God without sovereignty appeals directly to those whom the world deems to be nobodies, the being-less non-beings that have no standing or rights in the profane configurations of social prestige, influence, or control. They are the *ta me onta*, the "things that are not," the despised who are *not* wise, or *not* noble, or *not* mighty according to the kingdom of the world (1 Cor. 1:28). Yet God chooses these mediocre non-entities through which to confound the world, to disrupt it, to pervert it, to shame it, and to turn its idolatrous and narcissistic pretense that it is the ground for everything into–*nothing*.[58]

The chapter also contributes something even more amazing to Caputo's postsecular theology of the weakness of God. He notes that one possible Latin translation of the Greek verb *appolumi*, "to destroy," in 1 Corinthians 1:19, which states that God "will *destroy* the wisdom of the wise," is *destruere*. This is the root for *destructio*, the word that Luther uses with reference to his criticism of medieval scholasticism and its *theologia gloriae*. Yet Martin Heidegger's term, *Destruktion*, which is the primary philosophical source for Derrida's *déconstruction*, may well come from Luther's text. Consequently, Caputo translates the verse into postmodern nomenclature as: "'I [God] will *deconstruct* the metaphysics of presence of the strong onto-theologians.'"[59] Caputo's Pauline, postmodern version of God, then, is of a God of subversion, a God who undermines the *status quo* and the Powers That Be, a God who is neither the Ground of Being nor infatuated with ontological prestige, but who is the invocative event, the weak messianic summons, that never allows injustice, violence, oppression, suffering, and dehumanization to exist unperturbed and unrestrained. The weak force of the event of God is in reality the Spirit of God as a messianic nuisance and a prophetic irritant constantly annoying the world. In other words, divine redemption ensues from divine deconstruction![60]

Caputo asserts quite strongly that his theology of the weakness of God should not be interpreted as a passive or indolent faith, one that may draw some attention in the academy as a quaint intellectual exercise in revisionist theology or philosophy of religion but that has no pragmatic import for social ethics or for politics. He declares that, on the contrary, the passion for the impossible, the messianic summons of the event at work in the kingdom of God, and the promissory logic of the theology of the cross demand a fervent, even obsessive, concern with a certain *imitatio Christi* by which those who follow Christ function as the salt of the earth and the light of the world.

Caputo rejects any "two-worlds" hypothesis that segregates the kingdom of God from the various kingdoms of the world, a position that Yoder labels "Neoplatonic," one that rejects the facticity of the political and social effects of God's work.[61] The Sermon on the Mount does not detail an idealistic lifestyle that will characterize some future millennium existence or some eschatological community existing post-historically in a timeless New Jerusalem. That sort of ersatz piety may well be one of the most egregious evasions imaginable of Jesus' call to discipleship. Although, as stated above, Caputo is wary of speaking of the "politics of Jesus," he is not timid in stipulating that one must move from the poetics of the kingdom to an ethics of compassion—what he years ago called an "ethics of the cross!"—to what could be termed a politics of the impossible.

In truth, Caputo simply affirms as indisputable that theology is always political and that politics always retains some trace of theology. Consequently, to interpret Jesus' kerygma of the kingdom as apolitical is a devastating reductionism that totally ignores its subversive and deconstructive intent. Furthermore, to deceive oneself into thinking that theoretical construals of divine sovereignty do not have residual implications for secular politics manifests a naiveté that can accept or promote oppressive and violent social structures. As Hauerwas observes, the very semantics of "kingdom" provides "a reminder that any Christian ethic that is not first of all a social ethic is less than Christian."[62] Those who respond to the invitation and promise of the non-sovereign God who confronts us in the event of the divine kingdom must remain vigilant and instantiate the politics of the cross in such as way as to give feet to the prayer that God's kingdom may come on earth as it is in heaven. And that is precisely how God's kingdom comes, according to Caputo, specifically as individuals accept the "responsibility to breathe with the spirit of Jesus, to implement, to invent, to convert this poetics [of the kingdom] into a praxis."[63]

Caputo argues vehemently that the kingdom does not pervert and convert the world through the magical intervention of some omnipotent deity who pushes aside hurricanes so as not to damage Pat Robertson's kingdom, or who intends to show in battle that he is a bigger god than Allah to make Lieutenant General Boykin look like a military genius, or who in an act of divine arbitrariness and favoritism heals one cancer patient while allowing hundreds of others to die.[64] On the contrary, for Caputo, God institutes the divine reign of grace and love through the faithful actions of people with a passion for the impossible, through the passion of impossible people who enter inner-city neighborhoods to tutor children; who travel to the Gulf to rebuild Katrina-damaged homes; who believe that "family values" have less to do with gay marriages and more to do with fighting poverty, illiteracy, and bigotry; and who do not confuse spreading faith, hope, and love with exporting democracy and capitalism.

Those who share a mimetic sympathy with Jesus, who desire what he desires, embody the kingdom's *politica negativa*, the negative politics of prophetic action, "the politics of mercy and compassion, uplifting the weakest and most defenseless people at home, a politics of welcoming the stranger and of loving one's enemies abroad."[65] Caputo considers this constant invention of God's kingdom, the socially relevant and transforming dynamic of the weak force of divine deconstruction, to be an example of Augustine's notion of *facere veritatem*, of "doing the truth." If Jesus is the way, the truth, and the life, then the only proper way for Christians—or anyone of like mind—to follow Jesus' example and obey his commandment of unconditional love is to establish the truth of God's non-sovereign sovereignty by being doers of the Word of the cross and not hearers only.

Caputo once again advocates a kingdom theology quite comparable to Girard's, who likewise stipulates the political relevance of the kingdom of God as a process of imitation. Girard decrees a total rejection of the mimetic rivalry that leads to competitive violence and to the very logic of scapegoating that one finds adopted by the world with reference to Christ. Instead, one should follow, that is, imitate, Christ's example and show compassion for the victim of oppression and coercion.[66] Jesus desires only to imitate the nonviolent God whom he calls "Father"; consequently, his kingdom kerygma centers on the invitation for everyone to imitate his imitation of God.[67] Were everyone to desire what Jesus desires, the sociopolitical implications would be: no violent act would demand vengeance, "no cheek would be struck," and no enemies would exist to be loved.[68] But, of course, Girard concedes, as does Caputo, that obedience to the principles of God's non-sovereign rule cannot be compelled.[69] Consequently, in the kingdom of God imitation follows invitation and not intimidation.

As mentioned earlier in this essay, Caputo is not as sanguine about the communitarian idealism that he thinks characterizes Hauerwas' admiration for the purifying energy of tradition. Of course, he agrees with Hauerwas that one cannot avoid the historical and linguistic contextualization of traditions, and he concedes that his theopolitical poetics of the kingdom as dependent on the religio-ethical actions of individuals require that faith cannot avoid confessional particularity and theologies cannot escape the conserving memories of cultures.[70] Still, he also recognizes the negative political and social potentialities inherent in any tradition's or confessional orthodoxy's deceiving itself into thinking that it has received the final revelation from God, that God has chosen a concrete community to be the favored few who possess absolute knowledge and truth. Whenever that occurs, whenever the finite considers itself capable of the infinite, then all manner of hell breaks loose, usually in the form of some variant of violence, whether emotional, spiritual, ethical, or even physical. Unless ecclesiastical traditions maintain a healthy "heretical imperative,"[71] what Derrida would term a "filial lack of piety,"[72] then the theology of the weakness of God, of the non-sovereign event astir in the name of God, becomes a strong theology of certainty and control. The church consolidates its power, demands uniformity, and easily rationalizes in the name of a holy and righteous God its oppression and exclusion of any heterogeneity.

Under such circumstances, all of Jesus' teachings about the first and the last, about who gets invited to the wedding, and about forgiveness, compassion, and servanthood get contaminated by conventions of command and control that remarkably resemble the worldly criteria that Jesus came to subvert. Instead of being the society through which the weak force of the cross perverts the violence and arrogance of the world, the church perverts the word of the cross through the spiritual adultery of its affair with the world.

Caputo laments not only the perversion of the cross that occurs when the church's internal politics mirror the very perspectives of the world that Jesus sought to indict and replace but also the perversion that occurs when the church allies itself with the profane and violent political philosophies of secular culture. He labels such an unholy alliance "Constantinianism" and warns that the Constantinian church loses its deconstructive, prophetic, and transformative dynamics when it becomes too intimate with the state. When the church enters into "lethal alliance with the power of some Constantine," the non-sovereign, provocative power in the blood of the lamb on the cross gets replaced with the sign of the cross as an ensign of military might and imperial homogeneity. Then blood can begin to flow in the name of a hierarchical and manipulative power of ecclesiastical sovereignty.[73]

Under these circumstances, Christian theology has symbolically painted up its lips and rolled and curled its tinted hair and joined the "city of man," prostituting itself to the world. Caputo here adopts Kierkegaard's image of "rouged theology," the result of the church's lust after social prestige, influence, and affirmation.[74] That lust deceives the church into rejecting the promise of the non-sovereign call of the weak event operative in the kingdom of God in order to compromise with the principalities and powers that reject the "new creation" offered by Christ. When the church embraces the world and its canons of domination, authority, and violence, then it perverts the cross by confusing patriotism with obedience, legislated morality with imitating Christ, the Pax Americana with the peace that passes all understanding, and preemptive war to spread democracy with the Model Prayer.

Predictably, Yoder and Hauerwas join Caputo in denouncing how Constantinianism perverts the kingdom of God proclaimed by Jesus. Hauerwas calls Constantinianism the temptation to feel safe and at home in the world through the use of an "alien power," that is, a power alien to the divine power of powerlessness in God's kingdom.[75] For example, he notes the liberal democratic statute of "freedom of religion" as a promise of shelter for the church; consequently, the church feels a political obligation to support that principle and to defend the social mechanisms necessary to shield it, even if it means employing violence. In other words, surrendering loyalty to God's kingdom of non-sovereignty seems quite justified in this context.[76] Hauerwas actually symbolizes the defilement of the church in viewing the world through "Constantinian cataracts" with Tolkien's ring of power, since whenever the church agrees to wear the insignia of the world's political criteria, "systemic forces of corruption dig deep into [its] soul."[77] As a matter of fact, he goes so far as to conclude that the Constantinian church's latest prostitution with the world's political and cultural powers-that-be signals a "new universal religion," a new symbiosis of empire and *ecclesia* under the guise of "the omnipotent state," what Derrida might term the sovereignty of the rogue state.[78]

Yoder brazenly indicts the Constantinian church for withdrawing from the "suffering line of the true prophets" and joining forces with Caesar to legitimize the status quo. He accuses the church of an unchristian mathematics–"the calculation of the lesser evil" as the proper role for Christian ethics.[79] He interprets the Protestant "ethic of vocation" as a particularly insidious variant of the unholy alliance between the church and the kingdom of the world. Instead of living according to the messianic and anarchic standards of God's kingdom, Christians today, especially those who hold positions of authority in the world, feel justified in "playing the game" according to the world's rules. Consequently, "what it means to do the proper thing in one's given social setting is determined by the inherent quasi-autonomous law of that setting, whose demands can be both known and fulfilled independently of any particular relation to the rootage of Christian faith."[80] He concludes that under these circumstances, the only way one can genuinely follow Jesus is by rejecting the Jesus associated with the "official, conformist, power-related religion of the West."[81] One must repudiate Constantinianism as "a structured denial of the gospel."[82]

In his critique of the Constantinian church, Caputo concentrates on its relationship with political and social violence. He takes that relationship as a synecdoche that indicates the demonic and idolatrous character of a Christendom cloned from the DNA of the world. Just war theory is a perfect example of perverting the cross to compromise with politics. Caputo claims that this oxymoron, "just" war, should "stick in the throat of any follower of Jesus."[83] He wonders just where such an idea can be inserted into the Sermon on the Mount! It does not seem to fit in the Beatitudes, where Jesus blesses the peacemakers; perhaps one could place it as a parenthetical idea after getting slapped on one cheek but before turning the other; or it might fit nicely either around Jesus' prohibition against returning evil for evil or his prescription that we should love our enemies and bless those that persecute us.

It is in this context that Caputo references Derrida's discussion of the sociologist Carl Schmitt, who develops his concept of friendship on the issue of sharing a common enemy, and who argues that such an idea is not necessarily inconsistent with Christianity, given that one may separate Christian ethics from politics. In other words, Caputo indicates that Schmitt sees no necessary disconnect between loving one's enemies and slitting their throats! For Schmitt, sovereignty is an issue of the exception, the real power that comes from making and/or accepting rules and then disregarding them on ad hoc occasions.[84] So Jesus may make the rules for the metanoetic life of the kingdom, but in the Realpolitik world of secular existence, the church can make exceptions in following Jesus and enter into a confederacy with worldly violence.

Unquestionably, Caputo has introduced what might be considered the Shibboleth for Yoder and Hauerwas with reference to discerning loyalty to the kingdom of God or to the kingdom of the World. For the two of them, there can be no more essential mark of the perversive and anarchic power of Jesus kingdom kerygma than its call for the refutation of the world's approval of violence, revenge, and dominance. Hauerwas isolates nonviolence as "the very heart of our understanding of God," while Yoder equates it specifically with Jesus' command to love one's enemies and insists that it is "nothing more than a logical unfolding of the meaning of the work of Jesus Christ himself."[85] Hauerwas correlates Jesus' call for nonviolence with his prophetic iconoclasm, his fundamental intent to neutralize the idolatry of power that worships violence and coercion as the way to peace. Only false gods of "Gentile" sovereignty have to be defended forcefully and visciously, whereas the true God of Christ "can take the risk of ruling by relying entirely on the power of humility and love."[86] Caputo would certainly agree with Hauerwas' contention that nonviolence is not an alternative form of power, an eccentric strategy for overcoming war by wearing down the principalities and powers through passivity and kindness. Instead, Hauerwas argues that Christians should be nonviolent for no other reason than to be faithful to Jesus' poetics of the kingdom.[87] In reality, Hauerwas takes his perspective to the extreme of reducing the population of those who may rightly understand the Sermon on the Mount only to pacifists![88]

Yoder distills the issue down to the distinction between the prophetic and the institutional. God's summons to live out the kingdom is a call to the prophetic vocation of remaining consistent with the weakness of God even when that requires the censuring and impeachment of the world's corrupting power. Divergently, the institutional call is always a call to conservativism, to maintaining and defending the existing state of affairs by any and all means.[89] Constantinianism inevitably leads the church to abrogate its prophetic function and augment the state in its institutional role as guardian of the status quo. This entails the church's subordinating the cross to the sword and consenting to the "moral obligation to support and participate in the states legal killing (death penalty, war), despite contrary duties which otherwise would seem to follow from Jesus' teaching or example."[90]

Of course, certain Christians may not consider the church's embrace of political violence to be an exception to the logic of the cross. In his sermon, "A Nation at War," his homiletical apologia for President Bush's Iraqi War, Charles Stanley concedes that "God is not excited about war. He does not enjoy bloodshed and vengeance." On the other hand, however, he asserts that "God is not against it"![91] Through certain readings of the Old Testament and the oft-misused Pauline passage in Romans 13, Rev. Stanley proclaims the "biblical" authority that should lead Christians to support the war. Indeed, he goes so far as to defend it in the face of Jesus' kingdom kerygma by taking the usual evasive maneuver of privatizing Jesus' Sermon on the Mount. Loving enemies, turning cheeks, and avoiding vengeance only apply to Christian individuals, not to Christian individuals as citizens of a nation. Had Saddam Hussein personally slapped you, you should turn the other cheek. But since, according to the Bush administration's simulacrum of reality, he apparently slapped America, we need to bomb the hell out of him! On the upside, I suppose, one should at least credit Stanley for omitting the usual just war argument from his sermon.

Or consider another fundamentalist pastor, one no longer with us, Rev. Jerry Falwell. In October 2004, in a somewhat artificial debate with Jesse Jackson, Falwell made the following statement: "You've got to kill the terrorists before the killing stops and I am for the President—chase them all over the world, if it takes ten years, blow them all away *in the name of the Lord.*"[92] Obviously, Falwell was referencing another name of God than the one Caputo translates by the poetics of the kingdom and the word of the cross. No weak force inviting, calling, and promising here; no messianic, prophetic passion for the impossible, contradicting and perverting the world's paradigms of power and vengeance here; no non-sovereign divine suffering love here. No, just another chorus of Praise the Lord and Pass the Ammunition. Were Falwell to rewrite Charles Sheldon's book *In His Steps,* WWJD, "What Would Jesus Do?" might well be modified to "Whom Would Jesus Destroy?"

Or consider Rev. Mark Driscoll, the pastor of Mars Hill Church in Seattle. He made it into the pages of *The Wittenburg Door* because of a message he gave at a Christian men's conference. He invited five guys on stage to hit him, to take their best shots as an indication that being a Christian was not a sissy or effeminate lifestyle. They refused, but Driscoll went ahead and engaged in a bit of self-flagellation to make his point. Driscoll claims that the book of Revelation reveals a Jesus "with a tattoo down His leg, a sword in His hand and the commitment to make someone bleed. That is a guy I can worship. I cannot worship the hippie, diaper, halo Christ because I cannot worship a guy I can beat up." Then he immediately states his conclusion: "I fear some are becoming more cultural than Christian...."[93] *Mirabile dictu*, Nathan the Prophet could have done no better job of inducing self-incrimination!

Driscoll's invitation to pugnacious Christian discipleship as taking right crosses would appear to Caputo as an invitation to the wrong cross. That Jesus was tattooed with the violent marks of Roman "justice" yet petitioned God to forgive his torturers seems to Caputo to reveal a Jesus far different from Driscoll's Rambo Christ. He might point out to Driscoll that early in Revelation, the Lion of Judah turns out to be a Lamb as if slain—or one might say, somewhat sheepishly, that Revelation teaches that only someone who had been beaten up was worthy to open the book! Caputo would waste no time in pointing out the astonishing irony of Driscoll's conclusion, that it is he, and Falwell, and Stanley, who are more cultural than Christian; it is they who have bowed before the throne of Constantine and confused the world's power, vengeance, and phallocentric domination with the grace and compassion of the crucified Christ.

Just more "rouged theology," theology of the strong force, "Gentile" theology that predicates power on lording it over others, asserting unchallenged authority, always being first, exercising the sovereignty of "kicking ass." In the genuine Gospel according to Mark (the Evangel, not Driscoll), the one that Caputo would prefer to read, Jesus makes it clear "it is not this way among you, but whoever wishes to become great among you shall be your servant; and whoever wishes to be first among you shall be slave of all. For even the Son of man did not come to be served, but to serve, and to give His life a ransom for many" (10:43-45). Not a bad translation of the theology of a suffering God; not a bad revelation of the weak force at work in the event harbored in the name of God as the one who lures and promises; not a bad poetic expression of the disruptive, contradictory, deconstructive, and metanoetic non-sovereignty of the kingdom; not a bad denunciation of the world through the perversion of the cross.

Caputo's *depravatio crucis*—the "perverse core of Christianity" that he holds fast in an approximation process of the most passionate inwardness–poetically reimagines God and existence from a Christocentric, anarchistic, and messianic theopassionism of the event. Depravatio cruci also prophetically admonishes those who pray for God's kingdom to come on earth not to succumb hypocritically to the "earthy" standards that pervert and profane the weak force of divine grace, mercy, and love.

Regarding the prophetic caution of his theopoetics of the perversion of the cross, Caputo grants what he terms the "most elemental fact of Christian political reflection," which is quite simply that the church has stereotypically violated the word of the cross and unequally yoked itself with the unbelieving world and its secular criteria of power, prestige, and retribution.[94] Furthermore, in a remarkably candid *mea culpa*, he admits his own guilt over the same sin. Caputo surrenders to a pragmatic situationalism and accepts the "sorry truth" that as long as we live east of Eden and west of any possibility of instantiating the impossible kingdom to come, resisting evil often demands more evil, that under certian circumstances it is politically foolish *not* to counter-punch, socially suicidal *not* to wield the sword, and hermeneutically fallacious *not* to distinguish Jesus' socio-political context from our own.[95] For this reason, he translates "just war" theory into what he calls the "lesser-evil" theory and rationalizes this enervated translation by discriminating our existence under a liberal democracy from Jesus' existence under the Roman Empire—a discrimination that Yoder lists as the third example of misinterpreting the social ethics of the kingdom![96]

Caputo does not want to attenuate the importance or the inviolability of Jesus' anarchic principles of love, forgiveness, and suffering; however, he remorsefully sanctions disregarding them under certain conditions. As Hauerwas somewhat satirically notes, such compromising is in essence to believe that "on the whole, we should be non-violent except when there is a real crisis."[97] In other words, although followers of the non-sovereign God must always consider absolute pacifism to be the ideal and must never confuse justified violence with justice, they must occasionally, albeit reluctantly, bow before Constantine's throne, embrace the very principalities and powers that violated Jesus and rejected the weak force of divine grace, and slit the throats of the enemies they profess to love!

That Caputo, himself, is hypocritically a Niebuhrian Realist may be added to the list of several criticisms that one can direct at his postsecular theology of the weakness of God.[98] Somewhat ironically, he

172 Peace Be with You

writes his prescriptions of the sacred anarchy of the kingdom and of the unconditional but non-sovereign event of God as a physician in need of healing himself! He does risk perverting the cross by joining with those addicted to the "Gentile" norm of sovereignty specified by Carl Schmitt. Constantinianism, Niebuhrian Realism, Self-Serving Pragmatism, and Caputoan "Lesser Evil" Occasionalism are all expressions of sovereignty as the exception. That is to say, these positions may affirm that Jesus does reveal an anarchic kingdom that appears mad and ineffectual to the world, a kingdom of the non-sovereignty of promise and invitation, one that suffers violence instead of imposing it, even to the crucial point of allowing the ungodly political power of the world to exterminate God's personified gift of forgiving love. They may also advocate the truth of the kingdom as *facere veritatem*, the "doing of the truth" as practical obedience to Jesus' kerygma of non-sovereignty, the passion for the impossible as the messianic applicability of the word of the cross to the profane structures of political and social reality. Nevertheless, the mimetic rivalry of the world seduces them with the forbidden fruit of instrumental reasoning, which baptizes the desire for justice in the stagnant waters of justified violence and coercion instead of in the pure rivers of righteousness and the living waters that flow from Jesus' pierced side.

Yoder, who coins the phrase "self-serving pragmatism," considers all of the above as just so much idolatry, as the exchange of the true God of peace and nonviolence with the graven image of human compromise.[99] He would explicitly categorize Caputo's compromise as an example of the lesser evil calculation mentioned above. Quite often, the confusion of instrumental violence with the gospel's mandate for justice simply deteriorates into collapsing the kingdom kerygma into the best interest of class, race, or nation.[100] Yoder goes so far as to label this corrupting toxin of means/ends reasoning the "crusader's thesis" and considers it to be a principal principle of Constantinianism.[101]

Hauerwas concurs with Yoder and Caputo that the demon of instrumentalism is a species of Constantinianism that easily possesses the church and perverts it. He calls it a "hard habit to break," an addiction to power and control justified by the laudable desire to achieve the kingdom of God on earth.[102] Yet this demon deceives by employing the false premise that the church's task is to ensure that "history come[s] out right."[103] Hauerwas espouses, to the contrary, that Jesus' kerygma calls the church to metanoetic living and to obedience to the Sermon on the Mount, and that the contemporary conflict in any given ecclesiastical era is whether the church will "remain loyal to God's kingdom" or "side with the world."[104]

Yet, compromising the promises of God, pretending only to use and not be abused by the pretentiousness of the world's economy of revenge, and prescribing violence and domination as acceptable analgesics that can cure the disease of injustice only results in the reflexivity of undermining the kerygma of the kingdom as unconditional without sovereignty.[105] Indeed, when the church adopts the world's definitions of power and success, it self-medicates with a potent *pharmakon* that ostensibly offers the curative of security and peace but infects with the poison of duplicity and disobedience, resulting in what Derrida would term an "autoimmunity" by which a perspective adopts the very tactics it is attacking and, consequently, ends up attacking itself in attacking the other.[106]

For instance, if the world calibrates sovereignty according to the principle of the exception—such as President Bush's exercise of executive power through his 157 signing statements challenging over 1,100 provisions in congressional acts he signed into law, seventy-eight percent of which were direct constitutional challenges—then Caputo's Lesser-Evil Occasionalism manifests the kingdom of the World, not the kingdom of God. It, along with every other ecclesiastical compromise and expression of rouged theology, makes an exception, asserts its right, its power, to make an exception. It acknowledges, with a note of contrition, that although Jesus teaches nonviolence and calls for a subversion and a prophetic rejection of "Gentile" methods, under certain conditions and in certain circumstances, citizens of the kingdom of God must assert their own sovereignty to pervert the cross and follow the norms of the kingdom of the world to approximate the sacred anarchy of the weakness of God in a godless environment.

Moreover, Caputo's remorseful accommodation to a strong theology destabilizes the second component in his theopoetics of the kingdom, its unconditionality. When the non-sovereignty of the kingdom deteriorates under the justified violence of political common sense, then, likewise, the unconditionality of the kingdom takes on a massive load of conditions. The church affirms the unconditionality of loving the other, except, of course, when social conditions require the more prudent approach of mistrusting the other as a potential enemy. This prudence leads, in turn, to the unconditionality of loving one's enemies being reconsidered under the conditions in which one's enemies really do intend to harm, at which time, judicious behavior would dictate a formidable defense or even a preemp-

tive strike. Were our enemies to harm us successfully, then the uncon-
ditionalty of divine forgiveness remains operative except under the
conditions in which we could possibly retaliate so as to ensure that
they never try it again.

Under all these conditions, the kingdom of God begins to look,
for all the world, like *all the world*, quite a conditional and sovereign
existence. One might say that it manifests a conditionality with sovereignty that perverts the perversion of the cross and results in the alleged "nobodies" called by the weak force of God impersonating the
prestigious, pragmatic, and powerful somebodies that make ex-
tremely patriotic inhabitants of Constantine's empire. In the end, the
final issue becomes quite Pauline: Who is Lord? Is it Caesar or Christ?
Is it the principalities and powers of this world or is it the God and Father of our Lord and Saviour Jesus Christ who deconstructs the vain
potentates of worldy power through the lure of the weak force of the
agapic event? A decision must be made, since when Jesus details the
principles of the kingdom of God, he issues no signing statements!

Of course in all fairness, I, too, must articulate a *mea culpa*. When
I join Caputo's self-criticism of his occasionalism, I pharisaically note
the speck in his eye while blinking back the log in mine! I join Hauerwas in his passion for pacifism but his recognition of how impossible
it is to live it out consistently. I agree with Yoder that we need no other
reason to obey Jesus' kerygma of the peaceable kingdom than the fact
that we should live according to God's suffering love. I celebrate Girard's re-interpretation of redemption as the rejection of the violence
of pragmatic scapegoating and the acceptance of the crucified Christ
as my mimetic exemplar. I embrace Caputo's poetics of divine non-
sovereignty and yearn to exist in the metanoetic context of unconditional *agape*. But, east of Eden and west of the absolute future of the
messianic to come, I find it impossible to walk in those steps.

Still, as Caputo counsels, we must maintain a passion for the impossible, hope against hope for the promised peace, remain in the undecidability of a faith in that which is to come, and believe that with
God all things are possible. We must trust that the lure of the weak
force of God will lead us to desire the *imitatio Christi*, to oppose the
Constantinianism of self-serving pragmatism, and be converted
from the perversion *of* the cross to the *perversion* of the cross.

NOTES

1. John D. Caputo, *Deconstruction in a Nutshell: A Conversation with Jacques
Derrida* (New York: Fordham University Press, 1997). Hereafter cited DN.

2. Søren Kierkegaard, *Attack Upon 'Christendom,'* trans. Walter Lowrie (Princeton: Princeton University Press, 1968).

3. Jacques Derrida, *Circumfession: Fifty-nine Periods and Paraphrases*, in Geoffrey Bennington and Jacques Derrida, *Jacques Derrida* (Chicago: University of Chicago Press, 1993), 156.

4. For an early explanation of what he means by "cold hermeneutics," see John D. Caputo, *Radical Hermeneutics: Repetition, Deconstruction, and the Hermeneutic Project* (Bloomington, Ind.: Indiana University Press, 1987), 187-206. See also his engagement with Jim Olthuis over just how cold-blooded or warm-hearted his radical hermeneutics really are: James Olthuis, "A Cold and Comfortless Hermeneutic or a Warm and Trembling Hermeneutic: A Conversation with John D. Caputo," *Christian Scholar's Review* 19 (1990): 345-62 and John D. Caputo, "Hermeneutics and Faith: A Reply to Prof. Olthuis," *Christian Scholar's Review* 20 (1990): 164-70.

5. Caputo uses this phrase to categorize those "irresponsible critics" who condemn Derrida for espousing a "kind of anarchistic relativism in which 'anything goes.'" Deconstruction stands indicted for denying the law of gravity, for rejecting reason, and even for Mormon polygamy by individuals who apparently have never read any Derrida–or, at least, who have read very little (DN, 36-44)!

6. John D. Caputo and Gianni Vattimo, *After the Death of God*, ed. Jeffrey W. Robbins (New York: Columbia University Press, 2007), 127. Hereafter cited AD.

7. John D. Caputo, *More Radical Hermeneutics: On Not Knowing Who We Are* (Bloomington: Indiana University Press, 2000), 193-219. Hereafter cited MRH.

8. John D. Caputo, "Beyond Sovereignty: Many Nations Under the Weakness of God" *Soundings* 89 (Spring/Summer 2006): 22.

9. AD, 73. Caputo insists that as Derrida rightly passes for an atheist, he rightly passes as a Christian (136).

10. John D. Caputo, *What Would Jesus Deconstruct? The Good News of Postmodernism for the Church* (Grand Rapids: Baker Academic, 2007), 32-35 (hereafter cited WWJD?); John D. Caputo, *The Weakness of God: A Theology of the Event* (Bloomington: Indiana University Press, 2006), 118 (hereafter cited WG); MRH, 240; AD, 130.

11. WG, 34.

12. Ibid., 42-43.

13. Ibid., 42-54.

14. DN, 109.

15. WWJD?, 94.

16. WG, 284-85; WWJD?, 38; AD, 58-59; John D. Caputo, *Philosophy and Theology* (Nashville: Abingdon Press, 2006), 72. Hereafter cited P&T.

17. John D. Caputo, *On Religion* (New York: Routledge, 2001), 127 (hereafter cited OR); WG, 2-7; Caputo, "Beyond Sovereignty," 22-23; John D. Caputo "What Do I Love When I Love My God? Deconstruction and Radical Orthodoxy", in *Questioning God*, eds. John D. Caputo, Mark Dooley, and Michael Scanlon (Bloomington: Indiana University Press, 2001), 304; "Temporal Transcendence: The Very Idea of *à venir* in Derrida," in *Transcendence and Beyond: A Postmodern Inquiry*, eds. John D. Caputo and Michael Scanlon

(Bloomington: Indiana University Press, 2007), 195.

18. DN, 117-18. See Jacques Derrida, *Rogues: Two Essays on Reason*, trans. Pascale-Anne Brault and Michael Naas (Stanford: Stanford University Press, 2005), 135; Jacques Derrida, "Psyche: Inventions of the Other," in *Reading de Man Reading*, eds. Lindsay Waters and Wlad Godzich (Minneapolis: University of Minnesota Press, 1989), 28.

19. WG, 12. Jacques Derrida, "As If It Were Possible, 'Within Such Limits' . . ." in *Negotiations: Interventions and Interviews, 1971-2001*, ed. and trans. Elizabeth Rottenberg (Stanford: Stanford University Press, 2002), 344.

20. AD, 47-48.

21. OR, 7-8.

22. Caputo, "Temporal Transcendence," 199.

23. OR, 13-14, 92; WG, 102-106; WWJD?, 78-79; MRH, 262-63; John D. Caputo, "The Experience of God and the Axiology of the Impossible," in *Religion After Metaphysics*, ed. Mark A. Wrathall (Cambridge: Cambridge University Press, 2003): 143; "Apostles of the Impossible: On God and the Gift in Derrida and Marion," in *God, the Gift, and Postmodernism*, ed. John D. Caputo and Michael Scanlon (Bloomington: Indiana University Press, 1999): 186; *The Prayers and Tears of Jacques Derrida: Religion Without Religion* (Bloomington: Indiana University Press, 1997), 49-51. Hereafter cited PT.

24. WG, 6; AD, 51.

25. John D. Caputo, "In Search of a Sacred Anarchy: An Experiment in Danish Deconstruction," in *Calvin O. Schrag and the Task of Philosophy After Postmodernity*, eds. Martin Beck Matuštík and William L. McBride (Evanston: Northwestern University Press, 2002), 235; WG, 6-7, 90.

26. Caputo insists that "deconstruction does not demolish authority" but functions in a salutary manner to prevent authorities, traditions, and doctrines from presuming to be absolute and inviolable truth (MRH, 199-200). Consequently, he sees no problem in avoiding the "bloodless abstraction" of refusing to acknowledge historical and cultural expressions of God, expressions that find validity within specific communities. He simply wants confessional creeds not to "close the circle of faith" and to still the restless heart that drives the passion for the impossible (OR, 34-36).

27. WWJD?, 67; DN, 137; PT, 338; "What Do I Love When I Love My God?," 296; John D. Caputo, "Instants, Secrets, and Singularities: Dealing Death in Kierkegaard and Derrida," eds. Martin Matuštík and Merold Westphal (Bloomington: Indiana University Press, 1995), 216; John D. Caputo, "Richard Kearney's Enthusiasm: A Philosophical Exploration on *The God Who May Be*" *Modern Theology* 18 (January 2002): 93.

28. Caputo "What Do I Love When I Love My God?, 314.

29. Stanley Hauerwas, *The Peaceable Kingdom: A Primer in Christian Ethics* (Notre Dame: University of Notre Dame Press, 1983), 14. See also Anthony Bartlett, *Cross Purposes: The Violent Grammar of Christian Atonement* (Harrisburg, Pa: Trinity Press International, 2001), 25.

30. Stanley Hauerwas, *Cross-Shattered Christ: Meditations on the Seven Last Words* (Grand Rapids: Brazos Press, 2004), 17.

31. Stanley Hauerwas and Romand Coles, *Christianity, Democracy, and the Radical Ordinary: Conversations Between a Radical Democrat and a Christian* (Eugene, Ore.: Cascade Books, 2008), 341-42. Bartlett considers the resurrection

to be the "bottomless affirmation of nonretaliation, or forgiveness, for all violence." Whereas violence traditionally leads to the lifeless corpse, the resurrection reveals the divine "glance of compassion and life begun over." It is, indeed, the sign of forgiveness as compassion for the enemy even as the enemy persists in his cruelty and, therefore, God's final attestation to the impossibility of retributive violence (154, 157).

32. John Howard Yoder, *The Royal Priesthood: Essays Ecclesiological and Ecumenical*, ed. Michael G. Cartwright (Grand Rapids, Mich.: Wm. B. Eerdmans, 1994), 256.

33. AD, 64; WG, 27.

34. WG, 13, 101.

35. Caputo, "In Search of a Sacred Anarchy," 226-29; PT, 124; WWJD?, 35; DN, 102; WG, 24-32. Brian McLaren agrees that the word *kingdom* may be problematic for contemporary readers of the New Testament. Quite often, the word conjures up images of domination, absolute control, and even phallocentrism; however, precisely for these reasons, Jesus' use of that term provokes an irony that may shock individuals into re-thinking the distinction between divine rule and human dominion (*A Generous Orthodoxy* [Grand Rapids: Zondervan Publishing House, 2004], 80-81).

36. PT, 223; WWJD?, 85; Caputo, "What Do I Love When I Love My God?, 306. For a broader critical engagement with Caputo's idea of *metanoia*, see my "Prayers of Confession and Tears of Contrition: A Radically 'Baptist' Hermeneutic of Repentance," in *Religion With/Out Religion: The Prayers and Tears of John D. Caputo*, ed. James Olthuis (New York: Routledge, 2002), 62-79.

37. Hauerwas, *The Peaceable Kingdom*, 142.

38. John Howard Yoder, *For the Nations: Essays Public & Evangelical* (Grand Rapids, Mich.: Wm. B. Eerdmans, 1997), 166-69.

39. Brian D. McLaren, *The Secret Message of Jesus: Uncovering the Truth that Could Change Everything* (Nashville, Tenn.: W Publishing Group, 2006), 31.

40. WG, 13-17; WWJD?, 86. "Violence" may be defined in several ways. J. Denny Weaver defines it specifically as some action that does harm or damage. The damage may be physical–torture or killing–psychological–diminishing a person's dignity or self-worth–and societal–racism, sexism, or economic policies that promote poverty (*The Nonviolent Atonement* [Grand Rapids, Mich.: Wm. B. Eerdmans, 2001], 8).

41. WG, 9, 109-11; OR, 92-93.

42. AD, 63.

43. John D. Caputo, "Toward a Postmodern Theology of the Cross: Augustine, Heidegger, Derrida," in *Postmodern Philosophy and Christian Thought*, ed. Merold Westphal (Bloomington: Indiana University Press, 1999), 213 (emphasis added).

44. René Girard, *I See Satan Fall Like Lightening*, trans. James G. Williams (Maryknoll: Orbis Books, 2002), 139-43.

45. Hauerwas, *The Peaceable Kingdom*, 87.

46. Stanley Hauerwas, *Against the Nations: War and Survival in a Liberal Society* (Minneapolis: Winston Press, 1985), 55.

47. Stanley Hauerwas and William H. Willimon, *Resident Aliens: Life in the Christian Colony* (Nashville: Abingdon, 1989), 47.

48. John Howard Yoder, *He Came Preaching Peace* (Eugene, Ore.: Wipf and

Stock Publishers, 1998), 18-19.

49. John Howard Yoder, *The Royal Priesthood: Essays Ecclesiological and Ecumenical*, ed. Michael G. Cartwright (Grand Rapids, Mich.: Wm. B. Eerdmans, 1994), 147.

50. John Howard Yoder, *The Politics of Jesus* (Grand Rapids, Mich.: Wm. B. Eerdmans, 1972), 43, 63, 97, 132. Bartlett insists that the subversive dynamic of the cross sustains its constant interrogation of Christianity. It must always function in the church as the source of "[p]erplexing questions" and never lose its "confounding, destabilizing, provocative [and] recreative" power (2).

51. WWJD?, 82; Hauerwas and Willimon, 47.

52. WG, 39.

53. By "abyss," Bartlett references "the depth of injustice, meaninglessness and horror [to which humanity] can sink." Christ's redemptive act of compassion occurs in the midst of this abyss, thereby granting that in spite of the horror, there is also forgiveness and love. Jesus' abyssal compassion, therefore, is "the active moment itself of the gospel" (18, 24, 39)

54. MRH, 186.

55. René Girard, *Things Hidden Since the Foundation of the World*, trans. Stephen Bann and Michael Metteer (Stanford, Calif.: Stanford University Press, 1978), 219. Ted Grimsrud emphasizes that biblical justice never plays the sycophant before retribution but always serves reconciliation, which demands that one must rule out "death-dealing acts as tools of justice, such as war and capital punishment." He counsels that the manner in which Christians repel injustice must be consistent with divine redemption and not with the oppressive methods of the world ("Healing Justice: The Prophet Amos and a 'New' Theology of Justice," in *Peace and Justice Shall Embrace: Power and Theopolitics in the Bible*, ed. Ted Grimsrud and Loren L. Johns [Telford, Pa: Pandora Press U.S., 1999], 77, 83).

56. WG, 17, 26; WWJD?, 82; "In Search of a Sacred Anarchy," 227-28; PT, 124.

57. WG, 7-8.

58. WG, 45; WWJD?, 14-35; MRH, 218; OR, 124. Caputo has long used this Pauline phrase *ta me onta*. Cf. *Against Ethics: Contributions to a Poetics of Obligation with Constant Reference to Deconstruction* (Bloomington: Indiana University Press, 1993), 55, 237; *Demythologizing Heidegger* (Bloomington: Indiana University Press, 1993), 7, 183; "In Search of a Sacred Anarchy," 239.

59. WG, 46.

60. Caputo, "In Search of a Sacred Anarchy," 241-42; WG, 34. Jim Wallis actually positions the prophetic tradition, which Caputo so dearly loves, as a preferable third between the extremes of secular humanism and religious fundamentalism (*The Soul of Politics: A Practical and Prophetic Vision for Change* [New York: The New Press, 1994], 33).

61. WG, 52; Yoder, *For the Nations*, 82-83. Weaver concurs that Jesus does not teach a "passive nonresistance" but that citizens of the kingdom of God must take the initiative "to expose and neutralize exploitative circumstances"; yet, this must always be done through active nonviolence (37).

62. Hauerwas, *Against the Nations*, 108.

63. WWJD?, 95. Richard Kearney agrees with Caputo that God's historical and social embodiment depends upon the response of human beings who

will answer the divine summons to live out God's kingdom in the world. Likewise, he contends that living out the kingdom means showing mercy to the "least of these" and imitating a God of "radical nonviolence" ("Thinking After Terror: An Interreligious Challenge," in *Religion and Violence in a Secular World: Toward a New Political Theology*, ed. Clayton Crockett [Charlottesville: University of Virginia Press, 2006], 219). Ray Gingerich argues that living out the kingdom incarnationally in society is the only way to communicate the gospel adequately. But he cautions against reducing this practical expression of the kingdom to "an elitist sectarian group"; it should "constitute the fabric of our institutions" ("Reimaging Power: Toward a Theology of Nonviolence," in Grimsrud and Johns, 215).

64. WG, 42-43; AD, 64-65; "The Experience of God and the Axiology of the Impossible," 139.

65. John D. Caputo and Catherine Keller, "Theopoetic/Theopolitic" *Cross-Currents* 56 (Winter 2007): 106; WWJD?, 87. Jim Wallis grants that, in a post-9-11 world, "blessed are the peacemakers" are troubling words to hear. Indeed, he considers "love your enemies" to be Jesus' most difficult saying for American Christians. He wonders how many sermons on these two kingdom sayings have been preached over the past several years (*God's Politics: Why the Right Gets It Wrong and the Left Doesn't Get It* [San Francisco: HarperCollins, 2005], 16).

66. René Girard and James G. Williams, "The Anthropology of the Cross: A Conversation with René Girard," in *The Girard Reader*, ed. James G. Williams (New York: Crossroad Publishing Company, 1996), 278-79.

67. Girard, *I See Satan Fall Like Lightening*, 13.

68. Girard, *Things Hidden Since the Foundation of the World*, 211.

69. Girard and Williams, 274.

70. P&T, 53; PT, 68, 181; AD, 156-57.

71. Peter Berger, *The Heretical Imperative: Contemporary Possibilities of Religious Affirmation* (Garden City, N.Y.: Anchor Press, 1979), 26-31. Berger uses this phrase to indicate the necessity of keeping traditions loose and open to plurality. Playing off of the etymology of "*hairesis*" as meaning "to choose," he suggests that traditions should never close themselves off to alternative interpretations, even if those interpretations introduce the crisis of decision within the community, that is, prohibit a monolithic homogeneity among adherents to a particular culture or heritage.

72. Jacques Derrida, *Points . . .Interviews, 1974-1994*, ed. Elisabeth Weber (Stanford: Stanford University Press, 1995), 130.

73. PT, 245. James Carroll points out that prior to Constantine, the cross was not utilized as a Christian symbol, given its association with the heinous Roman method of execution. Only after Constantine's "vision" prior to the Battle of Milvian Bridge, which Eusebius reports was of a spear-shaped cross and not the *chi rho*, did it become a primary ecclesiastical sign (*Constantine's Sword: The Church and the Jews* [Boston: Houghton Mifflin Company, 2001], 175). Caputo has been significantly influenced by the work of Catherine Keller who considers that the theological notion of omnipotence lies behind contemporary theories of preemptive war and American imperialism. She notes President Bush's use of evangelical language when referencing the American people's democratic idealism and how neoconservatives endorse a

Pax Americana that depends upon the idolatry of domination. The collusion between divine omnipotence and national imperialism is but the latest version of the "Constantinian conversion" of empire to Christianity ("Omnipotence and Preemption," in *The American Empire and the Commonwealth of God: A Political, Economic, Religious Statement*, eds. David Ray Griffin, John B. Cobb, Jr., Richard A. Falk, and Catherine Keller [Louisville: Westminster/John Knox Press, 2006], 126-34). See also Wallis, *God's Politics*, p. 142.

74. WG, 8, 42-43; Søren Kierkegaard, *Fear and Trembling/Repetition*, ed. Howard V. Hong and Edna H. Hong (Princeton: Princeton University Press, 1983), 32.

75. Stanley Hauerwas, *Performing the Faith: Bonhoeffer and the Practice of Nonviolence* (Grand Rapids, Mich.: Brazos Press, 2004), 238.

76. Stanley Hauerwas, *After Christendom? How the Church is to Behave if Freedom, Justice, and a Christian Nation are Bad Ideas* (Nashville: Abingdon Press, 1991), 71. See also Weaver, 84-85, 90.

77. Hauerwas and Coles, 7. The phrase "Constantinian cataract" comes from Lee C. Camp, *Mere Discipleship: Radical Christianity in a Rebellious World* (Grand Rapids: Brazos Press, 2003), 34.

78. Hauerwas and Willimon, 42. Derrida, *Rogues*, 96-97.

79. Yoder, *The Royal Priesthood*, 154.

80. John Howard Yoder, *The Priestly Kingdom: Social Ethics as Gospel* (Notre Dame: University of Notre Dame Press, 1984), 63, 82-83.

81. Yoder, *He Came Preaching Peace*, 53.

82. Yoder, *The Royal Priesthood*, 245. David Odell-Scott offers a fascinating example of the Constantinian hybridization of politics and the gospel in his close critical reading of the Chalcedonian Creed as Christological orthodoxy. Along with revealing the internal inconsistencies that mar the idea of "two natures in one person," he illustrates how that doctrine functions as a theo-political vindication of the nexus between empire and church. What better *apologia* can one have for maintaining the necessity of both political sovereignty resident in the emperor and ecclesiastical sovereignty resident in the clerical magisterium than the idea that Jesus was both divine *and* human. Furthermore, this "two nature" Christology and "two kingdom" church-state polity establish conformity on both social and doctrinal grounds. To be a good Christian is to be a good Roman and vice versa. Most egregiously, however, this cross-breeding of empire and *ecclesia* results in final authority resting in the empire. As Odell-Scott indicates constantly in his work, it was the emperor who summoned the bishops to council, and it was the *Pax Romana* that was passed off as the peace of Christ (*A Post-Patriarchal Christology* [Atlanta: Scholars Press, 1991], 74-90).

83. WWJD?, 98.

84. Caputo, "Beyond Sovereignty," 27; John D. Caputo, "Without Sovereignty, Without Being: Unconditionality, the Coming God, and Derrida's Democracy to Come," in Crockett, *Religion and Violence in a Secular World*, 141; MRH, 75-77.

85. Hauerwas, *The Peaceable Kingdom*, xvii; Yoder, *The Politics of Jesus*, 238.

86. Hauerwas, *The Peaceable Kingdom*, 79.

87. Hauerwas, *Performing the Faith*, 203. When referencing the "principalities and powers" in contemporary theology and biblical studies, one should

not avoid allusions to the magisterial study of Walter Wink, who has detailed in three volumes the socio-political implications of this Pauline phrase. Wink contends that the principalities and powers refer to the destructive and oppressive social, political, and economic structures of existence. He claims that they display both an inner and an outer aspect. The outer aspect is the concrete form they take through church, state, or specific organizations. The inner aspect concerns the "spirit" or ideological component that legitimates and empowers the concrete form (*Naming the Powers: The Language of Power in the New Testament* [Philadelphia: Fortress Press, 1984], 5). For example, the state can be an external demonstration of a certain spirit of nationalism that seduces citizens to a form of idolatry. Wink claims that nationalism can be so "pernicious, so death-dealing, so blasphemous" in its enticement to a patriotic idolatry that "whole generations are maimed [and] slaughtered" in service to it (*Unmasking the Powers: The Invisible Forces that Determine Human Existence* [Philadelphia: Fortress Press, 1986], 87). He refers to this idolatrous network as "the Domination System" and its animating spirit as "Satan" (*Engaging the Powers: Discernment and Resistance in a World of Domination* [Minneapolis: Fortress Press, 1992], 9). He argues that Jesus engaged this system overtly, denounced it, and sought to replace it with the nonviolence of the Kingdom of God (82, 189). Unfortunately, the church has not been faithful disciples of Jesus' kingdom kerygma, failing on so many occasions to unmask the powers and, under certain circumstances, actually entering into complicity with those powers (150-51, 264).

88. Stanley Hauerwas, *Unleashing the Scripture: Freeing the Bible from Captivity to America* (Nashville: Abingdon Press, 1993), 64.

89. Yoder, *The Politics of Jesus*, 107.

90. Ibid., 194.

91. http://www.basicchristian.com/warwithIraq.html This URL gives an annotated response to Dr. Stanley's sermon, which is, apparently, no longer available online. This response includes Stanley's text clearly differentiated from the text of the respondent.

92. http://transcripts.cnn.com/TRANSCRIPTS/0410/24/le.01.html (emphasis added).

93. http://www.relevantmagazine.com/god_article.php?id=7418

94. WWJD?, 100.

95. Ibid., 101.

96. Yoder, *The Politics of Jesus*, 17.

97. Hauerwas, *Unleashing the Scripture*, 48.

98. I have addressed a few of these other criticisms in "Poetically Negotiating the Love of God: An Examination of John D. Caputo's Recent Postsecular Theology" *Christian Scholar's Review* 37 (Summer 2008): 483-97 and "Risking Love and the Divine 'Perhaps': Postmodern Poetics of a Vulnerable God" *Perspectives in Religious Studies* 34 (Summer 2007): 193-214.

99. Yoder, *For the Nations*, 195.

100. Yoder, *He Came Preaching Peace*, 20-21. Caputo expresses a variant of Yoder's point when he warns that the "love of God" may be easily confused with "somebody's career, or somebody's ego, or somebody's gender, or somebody's politics . . . to which it is systematically sacrificed" (OR, 92-93).

101. Yoder, *The Royal Priesthood*, 157. Camp agrees with Yoder and con-

nects instrumental reasoning to the church's erroneous assumption that Jesus' kingdom kerygma is simply "not relevant" and cannot, or should not, be taken literally (34).

102. Hauerwas, *After Christendom?*, 18-19.

103. Hauerwas, *The Peaceable Kingdom*, 106. Camp agrees that Christians do not need to "run the world," especially if that means running it according to the world's criteria. Instead, the church should live out the fruit of the Spirit as something of a "whistleblower" pointing out to the world that "the way things are" is not the way God intends them to be (107-108).

104. Hauerwas, *Against the Nations*, 129.

105. WWJD?, 82; WG, 17, 38, 90; Caputo, "Without Sovereignty, Without Being," 137.

106. John D. Caputo, "Without Sovereignty, Without Being: Unconditionality, the Coming God, and Derrida's Democracy to Come," in Crockett, 148-49.

Chapter 9

A VIEW FROM THE PORCH: A CASE STUDY IN LIMINALITY AND LOCAL THEOLOGY

James F. S. Amstutz

INTRODUCTION

Churches in the United States exist in the milieu of a "functional Christendom."[1] While there is no legally established and funded state church, there is a long and storied history of church-state collaboration. Even in the postmodern context where the voice of the church has been deemed irrelevant and pushed to the margins, the remnants of the church's once prominent and central role in society remain. Congregations in my local community still have the American flag in their sanctuary; pastors are called upon to give the opening prayer at borough council meetings; and one congregation hosts the Fourth of July community fireworks display. As Alan Kreider asserts, "Wherever we live in the West, we will go on living in the shadow of Christendom."[2]

The central role churches once enjoyed in civil society began shifting as the forces of postmodernity took root. Blue laws were banished, the voice of the church became one among many, and people's lives became increasingly complex. Alan Roxburgh observes:

> The forces of fragmentation were shaping a different social reality from that of center and periphery. In the meantime, the

churches accommodated themselves to their new situation by adopting and accelerating the creation of this private center. They became the moral chaplains of culture, holding a religious monopoly over the private religious experience of the individual. This accommodation reached its zenith shortly after World War II and found its most expressive form in the emergence of the suburban congregation. [3]

Akron Mennonite Church (AMC) is an Anabaptist congregation in suburban northern Lancaster County, Pennsylvania. Standing in the stream of the Radical Reformation, Mennonites in North America assumed a position on the margins of civil society. Distinctive language, dress, and a self-sustaining rural existence led to the moniker "The Quiet in the Land." Their Historic Peace Church tradition and a deep memory of persecution reinforce this separateness. Akron Mennonite is a relatively new congregation (1959) often comprised of transplanted Mennonites from across the U.S. and Canada who are currently working (or have in the past) at one of the Mennonite agencies in Akron (Mennonite Central Committee, Ten Thousand Villages, and Mennonite Disaster Service).

Seen as one of the more "progressive" Mennonite congregations in the area, Akron finds itself in a peculiar position. On the one hand, it embraces the radical teachings of Jesus found in the Sermon on the Mount. That, by definition, puts us at odds with much of mainstream society and the plethora of conservative, evangelical churches in Lancaster County. On the other hand, Akron has always articulated a desire to be a "community church."[4] But therein lays the dilemma. Given the polarities of becoming a chaplain to society or withdrawing from the public realm, is there a viable third way someplace in the middle? This case study will attempt to speak to that journey of discovery and transformation.

GETTING ON THE PORCH

Porches by definition are liminal spaces. A porch is a transitional space *connected* to the house but not *inside* the house. Porches are open to the public but not fully public space either. The mail carrier or a person delivering a package is assumed to have access to the porch. We meet friends and neighbors but also strangers on the porch. The liminal nature of a porch serves as a powerful metaphor for a peace church in a Christendom world.

It was in fact a broken-down porch on Franklin Street in Ephrata that helped Akron Mennonite Church find its way in civil society with a new model of engagement. Through a relationship with one of our members, we became acquainted with Sharon Robinson. Sharon was a twice-divorced single woman who worked at one of the local super markets in the meat department. She was giving primary care to her eight-year-old grandson at the time, and it was his friendship with a boy from our church that helped Sharon meet Susan from our church.

In the course of informal conversation around play-dates, baseball games, and school activities, Sharon told Susan the story of her broken-down porch. Several previous offers to help her fix it went unfulfilled. Neither did she have the resources to have someone do the work. On faith, Susan said "Maybe my church can help." At the time, Susan was part of an experimental group at church called the "Listening Ministry Team (LMT). Fourteen individuals were committed to meeting weekly during Discipleship Hour (former Adult Christian Education) around three practices.

1) *Listening to Scripture*. Members were committed to dwelling daily on their own and collectively on Sundays with Luke 10:1-12. The story of the sending of the seventy into the towns and villages where Jesus himself intended to go was a formative text to re-learn how to enter our local community. The goal was to internalize the text in such a way that participants would see themselves as the "sent ones" in their particular context.

2) *Listening to the local community*. LMT members were asked to begin interviewing their neighbors and colleagues at work to simply learn their stories. Several in the group volunteered as tutors for at risk students at Akron Elementary School. One of the literacy coaches at the school was part of the LMT and became the bridge person for this connection. Two members worked at the local hospital and began listening differently to patients, especially those who had no family connections. The group began reading about poverty culture through accessible books such as *Nickel and Dimed: On Not Making it in America,* by Barbara Ehrenreich, and *What Every Church Member Should Know about Poverty,* by Bill Ehlig and Ruby K. Payne. Others were volunteering with Homes of Hope, a local transitional housing ministry for homeless persons, and Summit Quest, a local residential treatment facility for troubled boys.

3) *Listening to one another in the integration of gospel and culture*. Each Sunday gathering began with a half hour devoted to Luke 10. It was read aloud, and we gave ample space for reflection and shared insights. It wasn't long before the community stories and the biblical story began to intersect. People named the baggage they needed to

leave behind to reenter the community as bearers of good news. They began seeing how the kingdom of God had come near in a tutoring session or an unplanned encounter on the sidewalk or break room. Sharon's broken-down porch was one of the stories that surfaced in the group.

ASSESSMENT

An ad-hoc group was formed to explore the possibility of repairing Sharon's porch. A skilled carpenter and a professional painter from AMC teamed up with Susan and examined Sharon's porch. They estimated it would cost $3,000 to cover materials and labor. Now what? AMC has a long history of sending work groups (youth and/or adults) for short-term work projects through programs such as Mennonite Disaster Service (MDS) and SWAP (Sharing With Appalachian People), a program of Mennonite Central Committee. The summer before this porch project took shape, the church had sent it's large youth group and advisors to Kentucky for a week of home repair with the SWAP program. It was well funded and supported widely by the congregation.

When the idea of repairing Sharon's porch right here in the local community was raised, several in the congregation said, "Why should we fix her porch? We can't just go around fixing people's porches." Others asked "But what do *we* get out of it?"

When mission work is "out there" it is much easier to support and fund. We had a working model of sending youth and adults from the church to places of critical need, and this essay is not a critique of the good work accomplished through those initiatives. What was so fascinating was how ill-prepared we were to articulate a local theology that made sense to us across the street. Clemens Sedmak in his helpful work[5] says that

> Doing theology means listening to the voices of those without voice, seeing the power of those without power, honoring the life of those without life.
>
> Asking theological questions, questions of ultimate concern, is too important a task to be left to professionals.
>
> Actually, it is not so much the ability to talk but the abilities to listen and to observe that make a good theologian.
>
> Theology unites individuals in a common struggle, the struggle for the kingdom of God. Theology is a communal enterprise.

Akron Mennonite Church began to realize through the conundrum of what to do about Sharon's porch that *we* also needed to assess what was broken, rotted, and in need of repair in ourselves. While we could articulate why the youth group going to Kentucky for two weeks was an expression of our Anabaptist theology, we couldn't do the same for a potentially messy engagement on nearby Franklin Street. Perhaps our porch was broken as well.

DECONSTRUCTION

Deconstruction is defined as "A strategy of critical analysis of (esp. philosophical and literary) language and texts which emphasizes features exposing unquestioned assumptions and inconsistencies."[6] The master carpenter examined Sharon's porch from top to bottom. Some of the damage was obvious; rotted floor boards, a cracked foundation, holes in the roof. Other needs could only be known as the project got under way. Only as the floor boards were pulled up would the extent of the structural damage be known.

Congregations who have been schooled for decades in the "attractional" model[7] of ministry and program believe they are being community minded by advertizing their services in the local paper, making sure the sign out front is well lit with a catchy proverb on the marquee each week, and inviting their friends to church. All the focus is on the predetermined services and programs that happen *inside* the church building. By no means are these services and activities trivial or unnessary. Pastors ignore these "bread and butter" aspects of ministry at their peril. What is missing is any listening and learning "out there" in the community that is not already on the church's turf.

Churches living in the shadow of Christendom after World War II came to embrace the fact that no longer would civil society deliver their children back to them, let alone people in the community. They began marketing their religious goods and services to the local community.

Demographic numbers were gathered through census data or para-church agencies to identify target populations and perfect strategies to reach these groups. Rarely is this commodification of the people who make up the neighborhoods and community surrounding a given congregation ever questioned. The alternative is to "narrate the numbers." Patrick Keifert argues persuasively that

> The numbers gathered in demographic surveys become part of (1) the biblical narrative, (2) the narrative of the local church, (3)

the local church's role as public moral companion within civil society, and (4) the narratives of real, specific persons and households within the service area of the local church.[8]

It began to dawn on the Listening Ministry Team and others working on the Porch Project that the relationship developing with Sharon and her family was just as important as the physical work of fixing her porch. What was her life like in this community that we share? And how does her story intersect with the biblical narrative of Luke 10 and our desire as a church to be "salt, light, and a city on a hill?"

As the relationship and conversations deepened, so did the awareness of what members of Akron Mennonite Church had to deconstruct in our relationships with those outside our middle-class orbits. They included:

1) Money is what people in poverty need most.
2) We have the know-how to fix this problem.
3) We deserve something from this experience.
4) Our reality is normal.
5) God will bless our good intentions, regardless of the outcome.

Middle-class church members know how to "pray and pay" when it comes to charitable giving and worthy causes. Take note of the flurry of activity in any small town or suburb between Thanksgiving and Christmas. Toys, coats and mittens are collected. Food baskets are given to "needy families" and money is raised for an orphanage overseas. Again, all worthy causes. But as Shane Claiborne insightfully observes, "I believe that the great tragedy of the church is not that rich Christians do not care about the poor, but that they do not know the poor."[9]

As the messiness of literally *facing* the issue of poverty emerged, church members at Akron Mennonite began to encounter the reality of their own existence. If our social and employment orbits are all with other middle-class people, we will not come to appreciate the complexities and challenges of living below the poverty line. When it was "discovered" that one in four children at Akron Elementary School, just a half mile from the church, were receiving free and reduced lunches, members were shocked. That many poverty families at Akron Elementary? Who are these people? Where do they live? How did we miss this? Sharon's story began to inform and speak into our story as a congregation. We had much to confess in our ignorance of how little we really knew about our community.

What we needed to do was raise our "cultural intelligence."[10] We assume that when persons are sent overseas with a mission board or service agency they will be given adequate orientation to another culture. They will study the language, habits, cultural norms, foods, and deeply held assumptions of the society they will enter as a guest. How many churches see themselves as a guest in their host community?

This is precisely where Luke 10 can be most instructive. The disciples Jesus sent out two by two had to rely on the hospitality of their hosts who reciprocated the peace that was extended them. They were not to move about from house to house (presumably looking for better accommodations) but to stay in one place and earn their keep. We imagine these light-traveling missioners joining in the household economy; working the fields, tending the family flock, or helping in the shop. Imagine the conversations around the dinner table where Jesus tells them to "eat what is set before you." Might these Jewish "sent ones" be lodging and sharing table fellowship in the homes of Gentiles? These were localized, cross-cultural encounters.

Peace churches must not only generate an ecclesiology shaped around the nonviolent way of Jesus, they also need to integrate a proactive missiology that takes the *shalom* of the kingdom of God into the neighborhoods, streets, and porches of those who inhabit the same community.

One poignant moment during the demolition phase of the Porch Project was when Sharon and Susan brought coffee and doughnuts for break. Sharon's grandson Cameron also served cups of cold water for everyone. AMC volunteers and Cameron's father Tim all enjoyed this "porch communion." This glimpse into another economic and social reality around coffee, donuts, and conversation incarnated that "the kingdom of God had come near."

REBUILDING

A proposal was made to the church's Outreach Commission to grant half the cost of the porch project from the "Missional Challenge Fund." Over $30,000 is set aside each year in this fund to release the missional imagination among members at AMC and provide the necessary funds to empower passion and vision. Guidelines mandate that there be personal involvement, and that the project is in keeping with our Anabaptist-Mennonite core values and vision. The porch project met all of the criteria, and half the necessary amount was given.

Two AMC women met with Sharon to work out an affordable payment plan for her to cover ten percent of the total cost. She readily agreed, and envelopes with her $10 payments arrived in the church office weekly. Creative ways were found to raise the balance of the funds. A member of the church famous for her apple pies, put several up for a silent auction. Three junior high girls sold handcrafted jewelry during coffee/tea fellowship. Susan made sweets and accepted donations.

There were complaints about too many announcements being made about the porch project and that the foyer was being cluttered by all these sales. Interpretive leadership was needed at this juncture to put things into perspective. Was Susan too new a member to garner credibility? What if the porch project announcements had been made by a charter member? The youth group raises thousands of dollars each year for their mission trips and convention travel expenses. Why were we not complaining about these activities? In the end, all the necessary funds were raised, but it caused us once again to examine our implicit assumptions about what we do and why.

With the volunteer help of Sharon and Cameron's father Tim, the master carpenter finished the work. The professional painter and his partner helped Sharon paint the newly remodeled porch. It was beautiful, and Sharon was thrilled. Susan donated a bench to put on the newly painted porch as a welcoming gift and affirmation of Sharon's hospitality.

FINISH WORK

We live in a culture greatly shaped by an assumption of "economism."[11] So ingrained is the assumption of a cost-benefit expectation that even charitable acts of kindness are given with some implicit strings attached. If gratitude is expressed to the givers, then all is well. If valuable life lessons are learned on the part of youth encountering poverty culture, then the high cost of travel and accommodations are justified. But there is always that expectation that *something* will be gained in returned. The seventy were sent to "cure the sick, and say to them, 'The kingdom of God has come near to you'" (Luke 10:9). Even when their ministry of healing and proclamation is rejected, they are still to say "Yet know this: the kingdom of God has come near" (10:11).

Venturing into the local community as moral companion means that sometimes we are received and sometimes we are not. Either way, showing up is not contingent on how we are received. The proclamation and the responsibility to be there is the same. Susan's relationship with Sharon preceded the porch project and continued long after its completion. AMC had no expectations beyond that relationship. An invitation from Susan for Sharon to attend one of our fellowship meals was a painful reminder of the hidden barriers that still exist in our church when she canceled at the last minute. We assumed that she would feel safe and comfortable in our space. We still did not see the invisible barriers that Sharon saw clearly at Akron Mennonite Church. And yet, we did not know what seeds may have been planted through the porch project.

Some months later I received a call from the chaplain at Lancaster General Hospital. They said "Sharon Robinson is a patient here. She says she's not a member of your church, but that you know her. She said to tell you that she's the *porch lady*." I went immediately to find Sharon facing surgery for a malignant brain tumor. We sat and talked for some time, finding a number of new common interests. I prayed with her and met her two daughters on my way out. A few weeks later, after a very difficult time of post-surgery set-backs, Sharon died peacefully at the home of her sister.

Because Akron Mennonite Church was the only connection Sharon had to any church in the community, we were asked to host her memorial service. I met with her two daughters to plan the service in consultation with her sister. I helped them make connections with the local funeral home and contacted our hospitality committee.

As the day for Sharon's memorial service drew near, I began to realize that I would need to prepare a little differently for this service. The presumed points of reference, symbols, hymns, religious language, and Mennonite upbringing simply were not there for Sharon's family. How would I speak into Sharon's life and context? For the first time in my pastorate at Akron Mennonite Church, we had to come up with a makeshift ash tray for our porch. Would this be a formal or casual event? We began to recognize that our role was to be hospitable; to make room on our porch and in our sanctuary for these special guests who felt brave enough to enter our space.

The liminality of that experience for me as a pastor and for those members who had gotten to know Sharon through the porch project was telling. We still had a long way to go toward becoming church with an understanding of our own community. The service went well, and Susan and I both shared about our friendship with Sharon. Connections with one of Sharon's daughters remain. The ties that bound us together through the porch project, her illness and death, were indeed blessed.

SALT, LIGHT, CITY ON A HILL:
EXCURSIONS INTO MORAL COMPANIONSHIP

The porch project opened up new possibilities for the role of Akron Mennonite Church in the greater Akron-Ephrata area. A second discernment group met, this time centered around the adaptive challenge of how to engage actively in the local community while not sacrificing a core Anabaptist identity. A group of seven gathered weekly during Discipleship Hour to begin exploring this question with some intentionality. A passage from the Sermon on the Mount, Matthew 5:13-16, was chosen as the text for dwelling with Scripture. Here Jesus tells his followers that they are to be salt, light, and a city on a hill. We took time to go deeper into each of these metaphors to see how they might inform the question before us vis-à-vis being a peace church in a Christendom world. The group called itself the "Mission, Identity, and Community (MIC) focus group."

A case study was brought by one of the members about a sister Mennonite congregation that had dropped *Mennonite* from its name. The pastor had attended a seminar at Willow Creek Church on how to market the congregation to the local community. In keeping with this desire, the congregation went from from calling itself a Mennonite church to a *community* church. The pastor explained that they are still a Mennonite congregation. They just didn't want "Mennonite" to get in the way of reaching out to new people who didn't grow up in the church.[12]

As mentioned earlier, Akron Mennonite Church had a similar inclination in the early stages of their formation in 1959. In the Twenty-Fifth Anniversary Booklet we read:

> The group agreed that it wanted to be a community church. The feeling was expressed by some that the name *Mennonite* should be eliminated if we wanted to have our membership growth from both Mennonite and non-Mennonite individuals. Our final conclusion was that the name *Mennonite* should be included and that we still could be a community church.[13]

How ironic that this same discussion was now being revisited almost fifty years later! On the other hand, we also discovered that nothing was overtly included by the founding members about this desire of reaching the local community. Nothing in the mission statement or membership covenant articulated a theology that made community inclusion a core value and practice of the newly established Mennonite congregation in Akron.

Some of the key findings of the MIC group were centered on a more nuanced understanding of both salt and light. Salt, we discovered was used as a catalyst in earthen ovens in the first century, to help make the fire burn hotter. That definition seemed more evocative than the typical flavoring or preserving aspects of salt. What would it mean for Akron Mennonite Church to be a catalyst in our community? How could we help the fires of God's kingdom "on earth as it is in heaven" to burn hotter?

We let our imaginations explore alternative understandings of light beyond the proverbial lighthouse. We are several hours away from the nearest ocean, so that image held less appeal to us than others. What about runway lights at an airport? Or the courtesy lights in a darkened theater or concert hall? They help people find their footing or to land safely and to stay grounded. That seemed to fit the ethos of the congregation, as opposed to something with high visibility and "showy."

Then we discovered that the word *Akron* in Greek literally meant "city on a hill." It's the same root for the Greek *acropolis*. There was no getting around the fact that Akron Mennonite Church is a congregation with some inherent gifts to share beyond ourselves. We are on the hill and cannot be hid.

These conversations and discoveries made an impact on the MIC group, and they were shared with the congregation periodically in reports to Council and the monthly church newsletter. A "Vision Progress Report" later documented the initiatives taken by the congregation over the past six years to live into this renewed commitment.

Three experiences illustrate ways Akron Mennonite is trying to live into its identity as moral companion to civil society in our local context.

Salt

The first scenario involves a fellow employee of one of our members who was being summoned to district court for back rent on her house trailer lot. Donna met Lisa at the local hospital where they both work. Lisa always paid her house trailer lot rent, but not always by the deadline. She works three jobs and has a special needs child that requires her to make frequent trips the larger medical center in Hershey. Donna said "Maybe my church can help."

I met with Lisa and Donna and learned more of her story. We set up a visit with the school social worker since Lisa's child attended Akron Elementary School. The social worker helped Lisa to sort out all of her receipts and document the fact that she was not as far in arrears as the property management company claimed. I called a real estate agent friend who did some research on the group that owned the trailer court. The one near Akron was one of twelve across the state, and a sister company managed the specifics of the rentals, collections and evictions. Their offices were twenty miles away, and my phone calls and voice messages were not returned.

The social worker and I volunteered to attend Lisa's court appearance. We met her in the lobby of the district court building and waited until her number was called. We literally sat in her corner. Lisa shared how the last time this happened she never got to speak, and she was found guilty and had to pay all the costs. Today she spoke up. She told the judge she had documentation and receipts and that she had told the company about her special-needs child. In a matter of minutes her rather large debt plus penalties and fines were reduced down to below $200. The representative from the property management company was herself the mother of a special-needs child and worked a minimum wage job for this company. Both Lisa and this employee seemed caught up in a faceless system of volume-driven profit.

Light

Summit Quest Academy is located just down the hill between Akron and Ephrata, about a mile from Akron Mennonite Church. They are a non-secured residential treatment facility (for profit) for boys age eleven to eighteen who are either sex offenders, have been sexually abused, or both. A lay pastoral team member and I set up an initial visit to meet with two staff people and ask two questions: What is the day to day reality here at Summit Quest? And how might Akron Mennonite Church be helpful? The boys are in two age-based housing complexes with 24/7 supervision. They are either in school (run by the State Intermediate Unit), in treatment, or some sort of activity or recreation.

There are a few outside groups like the Lion's Club and a catholic Priest who bring in outside programs on a weekly basis. A father-son group from a local church organizes a recreation night in the Summit Quest gymnasium. "What we don't have is any music," said one staff member. Another said, "We could use some tutoring help as well. The boys are on their own since the school is all run by the I-U and Summit Quest has no control on the content or follow-through."

Making these needs known in the church led to a new attendee at AMC volunteering to teach guitar to the boys. He taught guitar at

one of the large suburban high schools, but his first teaching assign-
ment was at one of the inner-city elementary schools in Lancaster
where children from four different homeless shelters attended. He
said that everything he had been taught about music pedagogy in
college had to be set aside to connect musically with these kids. He
was also amid a masters program with an emphasis on teaching
music in poverty settings. Funds were made available from the junior high youth group annual Christmas gift auction and from the Listening Ministry Team to buy new guitars or refurbish those donated.
Each week for a year, music filled the air in the Summit Quest meeting room.

Two newly married young adults, both psychology majors and
employed by the nearby mental health hospital, volunteered to organize tutoring sessions. They met weekly with whatever boys the
staff felt needed the most support during a given week. Several others at church also did some tutoring, and despite some miscommuni-
cation and erratic follow-through on the part of Summit Quest staff,
this program too was successful.

While these initiatives were happening, we also set up several
tours of Summit Quest for AMC members. Ten to twelve people on
two separate occasions made the visit to Summit Quest. This helped
deepen the awareness and commitment to our initiatives of walking
along side the boys and staff there. We learned how difficult it is to
work at Summit Quest and that they typically have a very high staff
turnover rate. One staff person we interviewed shared her passion
for these boys and their difficult circumstances that separated them
from home and family. She said that if they failed at Summit Quest in
their treatment, they would be incarcerated.

Toward the end of this year of engagement with Summit Quest,
we learned of a town meeting that was held at the Akron borough
hall, called by one of the council members. The presenting issue was
the high number of "elopements" by the boys at Summit Quest and
the increased police calls this triggered. The concern was that the fre-
quency of these unauthorized escapes from the Summit Quest
grounds was costing a disproportionate amount of police time for
Ephrata and Akron borough police.

I was able to attend the second of three town meetings. I shared
the minutes of the first meeting with members of the Listening Ministry Team and those involved with volunteer work there. Representatives from state senators and representatives were there, along with
a high-level staff person from the Department of Public Welfare for
the state of Pennsylvania. Several citizens in the audience spoke

about their fear of these boys escaping, coming on to their property, and being a threat to other children in the community.

Summit Quest staff clarified that all of the boys are carefully screened before being placed here and that anyone with violent tendencies is not accepted. One man said, "If something isn't done, we could have a Virginia Tech situation here," referring to the tragic Virginia Tech shootings perpetrated by a former student. Here was a public dialogue about a troubled population in the local community. What voice would the church have in such a setting?

Thankfully, a number of people who had actually volunteered at Summit Quest and visited the campus spoke up. They shared about working firsthand with the boys, things they accomplished, and success stories they had witnessed. I shared about what our church was doing with music and tutoring. An older gentleman pointed out that at least these boys were getting the treatment they needed and that it just happened to be in our community. The alternative was for them to go untreated, which might harm more people in the long run.

City on a Hill

During December 2007 I received an e-mail from Nicole, the social worker at Akron Elementary School. She shared how so many families were in desperate need of rent assistance with children at the elementary school. They begin a downward spiral with a sense of hopelessness in their eyes. She said that the school social service fund can help some, but it wouldn't be enough. "What can be done? Are there churches that can help out with rent?"

The scenario is all too common, and any pastor knows that these requests are on the rise in almost every community. Churches can be very generous with above-budget funds, especially around the holidays. What might be different about responding to this request?

I shared parts of Nicole's e-mail right before the congregational prayer one Sunday morning in early December. I made the observation that AMC has a generous "Agape Fund" for benevolent needs within the congregation. "The Agape Fund is for us. What if we raised some funds to help out a family in the local community?" That was all that was said.

The chair of the stewardship committee was at my doorstep first thing Monday morning. He was understandably concerned that we still had not met our end-of-year giving, and now we were potentially siphoning away donations to an above-budget project. He was right. I said I hoped it would not have to be either/or but could be both/and. Could we raise these funds to help families directly *and* meet our budget commitments?

By the end of the year, over $8,000 donated to the Agape Fund had been earmarked for rent assistance. And, by the time the books were closed at the end of the year, we had met budget. I contacted Nicole and her colleague Ann, the other school social worker. Together we generated a list of families in need and drafted checks to cover one or two month's rent. The checks were made payable directly to the landlords and hand-delivered by the social workers to each of the families. What made this feasible was the high level of trust our church placed in the social workers. Nicole was invited to share during Discipleship Hour in January, and a large number of adults attended. She simply told stories, connected the dots, and spoke into the reality of these families with children in the same classrooms as many of our children at the church.

I also shared this story at the January ministerium breakfast, suggesting that next time other churches help support families in the school closest to their church. I know at least two congregations responded by contacting the social workers. I continued to stress to these pastors and to our own members that it is far easier to write a check than it is getting to know one of these families and entering into their reality as a friend. Could we become salt, light, and a city on a hill?

CONCLUSION

In a perfect world, life would be fair. People living in poverty learn quickly that life seems fairer for some than for others. A class society is one in which people do not get what they deserve by virtue of what they produce; the formula seems so simple, and yet it is so pervertible, for what does "deserving" mean?[14] The question of who is "deserving" continues to linger.

Akron Mennonite Church is making a pilgrim's progress on the missional journey. The beginnings of a local theology are slowly emerging. Learning to listen to those in the immediate context in which the church is located is taking root as an ongoing habit and practice. The church is beginning to hear the narratives of our community. Previously we were aware mainly of statistics prayed about but not fully understood. Now "the homeless" have names like Michele and Ryan. A free and reduced lunch recipient at Fulton Elementary School is named Cameron. A twice-divorced grandmother, working a minimum wage job and trying to raise her grandson is named Sharon. Never mind that her house is a wreck and her porch is literally falling to pieces; so is her life.

Akron Mennonite Church has learned that, despite our best efforts and good intentions, we cannot fix everything. We are learning the complexities, inconsistencies, and frustration of trying to serve the poor. The brokenness of people's lives sometimes leads to grief and shared pain. Incarnational theology is costly when thinking in economic terms, which is something we do most of the time. The experiments in the community and what continues to be learned among church members is that relationships make the difference. When we get to know one another, we begin to care for and love one another.

Middle-class church members are learning to leave behind their stereotypes and fears, the extra baggage for the missional journey. People on the margins in our community are also discovering that there really are compassionate people left in the world willing to listen and walk alongside.

Listening and dwelling with Scripture has become a transformative experience. The church is learning, if slowly, that reading the Bible for *formation* is a different experience than simply reading for knowledge. As a missionary document, the Scriptures tell us the story of God calling, gathering, teaching, and sending a worshiping community, a community with an alternative identity to "all the other nations." This community is sent to all the places that Jesus himself intends to go and where God has already been. By definition, that challenges the proscribed boundaries and orbits of our middle-class lives. We are learning to reclaim our memory through the biblical story.

We are reminded often that, as a pilgrim people, we must always remember where we came from. Slaves in Egypt had no vision of an alternative future, filled with hope and possibility, without God. With God, they did. Brueggemann calls this a *gifted existence*, and the only way to sustain such a life is to stay connected to the giver of that gift.[15] This happens in worship and discipleship training within the life of the church, which we generally know and do well.

What we are also learning is that it can happen in the community, out there, and *for the life of the world*.[16] As our missiology begins to meld with our ecclesiology, this once distinct line and demarcation becomes blurred, *as it should be*. No longer content with a silo existence as a church in the community, Akron Mennonite is learning what it means to be a community-minded church.

Much learning is still in front of us. Many members continue to express fear that, if we become a "community church," we will lose our Anabaptist-Mennonite identity. On the contrary, it is becoming clear through the careful reading of formative texts like Luke 10 and Matthew 5 that listening and entering into the life-world of those in the local community can actually help the church to focus and sharpen such an identity.

For too long, Mennonites in North America have grown comfortable with being identified as the quiet in the land. We are learning that perhaps being "called out" is more about differentiating from the dominant narratives and captivities of empire in a market-driven, consumerist society than it is about habits of distinctive dress and eschewing tobacco and alcohol.[17] Gradually, Akron Mennonite Church is becoming known as that church in the community that supports and helped start Homes of Hope, sends volunteers to Summit Quest Academy, and helps tutor students at Akron Elementary. We are becoming known as that church that holds seminars about poverty and affordable housing and knows school social workers by name.

The work in front of us is to reflect on what we are learning and where this may yet lead us. Can we learn to be the church outside of the physical building and our normal routine? That question continues to challenge us.

An environment has been created among the pastors and leaders at Akron Mennonite Church that embraces emergence, experimentation, and missional imagination. This atmosphere is starting to feel normal, and yet the church is still very much on the way, still wandering in the wilderness of liminality and discontinuous change. A new identity is in formation, but it remains somewhat fragile and negotiable. The reign of God is all around us, within us, and in our community. We are beginning to see Christ in the everyday and connect the dots between what we profess and what we practice.

Sharon's porch became a powerful metaphor, a meeting place and threshold space where two worlds intersected and sometimes collided. Akron Mennonite Church is learning that assessment, deconstruction, and rebuilding is time-consuming and messy, but it is the work that God is calling us to. With a view from the porch, we pray for eyes to see and ears to hear where God, and neighbors like Sharon, may be leading us next.

NOTES

1. Craig Van Gelder, "Missional Challenge: Understanding the Church in North America," in *Missional Church: A Vision for the Sending of the Church in North America*, ed. Darrell L. Guder (Grand Rapids, Mich.: Wm. B. Eerdmans, 1998), 50, 60.

2. Alan Kreider, *The Change in Conversion and the Origin of Christendom*

(Harrisburg, Pa.: Trinity Press, 1999), 99.

3. Alan Roxburgh, *The Missionary Congregation, Leadership and Liminality* (Harrisburg, Trinity Press, 1997), 10.

4. Ura Gingerich, *Akron Mennonite Church: 1959-1984* (Akron, Pa.: self-published, 1984), 4.

5. Clemens Sedmak, *Doing Local Theology: A Guide for Artisans of a New Humanity* (Maryknoll, N.Y.: Orbis, 2002), 10, 13, 15.

6. *The New Shorter Oxford English Dictionary*, vol.1 (New York: Oxford University Press, 1993), 611.

7. Roger Finke and Rodney Stark, *The Churching of America 1776-1990: Winners and Losers in Our Religious Economy* (New Brunswick, N.J.: Rutgers University Press, 1992), 17; and Guder, et al, *Missional Church*, 83-85.

8. Patrick Kiefert, *We Are Here Now: A New Missional Era* (Eagle, Idaho: Allelon Publishing, 2006), 79.

9. Shane Claiborne, "Downward Mobility in an Upscale World," *The Other Side* (November 1, 2000), 11.

10. David Livermore, *Serving With Eyes Wide Open: Doing Short-Term Missions with Cultural Intelligence* (Grand Rapids: Baker Books, 2006), 110. "Cultural Intelligence (CQ) is a matrix that consists of four different emphases, all of which are linked together . . . : (1) knowledge CQ, (2) interpretive CQ, (3) perseverance CQ, and (4) behavioral CQ."

11. Jane Collier and Rafael Esteban, *From Complicity To Encounter: The Church and the Culture of Economism* (Harrisburg, Pa.: Trinity Press, 1998), 10-11. "It is the economic aspect of our lives that more than any other shapes our understanding, our evaluations, and our aspirations, and hence conditions our actions. . . . Even our personal lives are shaped by calculations of value, of gain and cost, of sound investment and satisfaction of wants."

12. Francine Fulton, "Mennonite Church Changes Its Name To Sandy Hill Community Church," *The Penny Saver: Conestoga Valley and Pequea Valley* edition, April 26, 2006.

13. Gingerich, 4.

14. Richard Sennett and Jonathan Cobb, *The Hidden Injuries of Class* (New York: WW Morton and Co, 1972), 250.

15. Walter Brueggemann, *The Land: Place as Gift, Promise, and Challenge in Biblical Faith* (Norristown, Pa.: Fortress Press, 1977), 57.

16. Alexander Schmemann, *For the Life of the World: Sacraments and Orthodox* (Crestwood, N.Y.: St. Vladimir's Seminary, 1973).

17. Michael Budde, *The (Magic) Kingdom of God: Christianity and Global Culture Industries* (Boulder: Westview Press, 1997), 14-15.

Chapter 10

IS VOLUNTARY BAPTISM THE ANSWER TO THE CONSTANTINIAN QUESTION?

Anthony Siegrist

This essay was originally presented at a conference on being a peace church in a Constantinian world. The assumptions behind the theme of the conference and this subsequent volume of essays—the critique of Constantinian Christianity—lead me directly to the work of John Howard Yoder. Yoder's project is generally understood to suggest that a thoroughgoing anti-or non-Constantinian theology, Anabaptist or otherwise, is both profoundly christological and pacifist. However, what is not often recognized, even as theology done in a Yoderian tone gains currency, is how the practice of voluntary baptism regularly has an effect converse to its intention in that its voluntary nature supports the very Constantinian Christianity it would rather subvert. Our best anti-Constantinian intentions uphold *instead of undermine* the marriage of church and sword. A description of this phenomenon constitutes the initial move of this essay.

The second move, woven alongside the first, is a constructive attempt at offering an alternative understanding of voluntary baptism by means of re-emphasizing the objective qualities of this practice and by reconsidering the roles of the three agents involved—the triune God, the baptismal candidate, and most importantly the church itself. My methodology here will not be to simply recommend a return to the baptism of infants but rather, through insights from Karl Barth, Talal Asad, Charles Taylor, and others, to recover an awareness of the action of God who calls us to and initiates baptism. The action of the church as the community of God responds and takes the leading role in this practice. Such a renewed awareness is necessary and applicable for church communities both at the center and on the fringes of the Anabaptist or believers church traditions.

There are, however, a number of things I do not intend to do here: First, I do not intend to deal substantively with polemics between traditions regarding the appropriate age of baptismal candidates. Second, I do not intend to offer an apologetic for anti- or post- Constantinian theology or church life as such. Such work has been done by others on numerous occasions. Instead of being energized by historical polemics, my argument is driven by the reality that the practice of voluntary baptism is carrying the day among the emerging new mainline churches in English-speaking North America and by the fact that traditional apologetics for voluntary baptism on the basis of faithful discipleship simply break up against the fully dug in Constantinianism of a large portion of those communities that confess the importance of such baptismal practice. It is difficult to claim that voluntary baptism supports lives lived after the example of Jesus when many who have been baptized as adults show little hesitation in taking up arms on behalf of their nation state. In broad strokes what this argument becomes, then, is a reminder that being peace churches is nonsensical apart from a robust theology of a loving God that actively chooses to be implicated in the everyday practices of the church.

This essay is certainly not the first to make such an observation about the voluntary nature of joining the church, particularly as it is associated with Yoder's work.[1] Oliver O'Donovan in his book *The Desire of the Nations* criticizes Yoder's voluntarism.[2] His charge is supported, perhaps surprisingly, by Stanley Hauerwas and James Fodor in a footnote in their essay "Remaining in Babylon: Oliver O'Donovan's Defense of Christendom" in that they say O'Donovan is "on to something" when he criticizes Yoder's voluntarism.[3] Since O'Donovan's charge against Yoder has already been engaged by the very capable Alain Epp Weaver and Travis Kroeker I don't feel the need to take this up myself.[4] My intention in this essay is not to use Yoder as a foil but only as a starting point. I actually think that Yoder's short work *Body Politics* lends much to our conversation about how the baptism of adults might undercut instead of support Constantinianism.[5]

The rest of this essay, then, is an exploration of the many ways voluntary baptism supports Constantinianism despite its best intentions.[6] Although this presentation does lean heavily in the direction of theology proper I envision it most fundamentally to be a work of pastoral theology.

VOLUNTARY BAPTISM AND ETHICAL DISUNITY

We must begin our discussion in the area of ethics because this brings us into contact with how many churches that practice voluntary baptism read the Bible.[7] At the heart of most of these traditions lies the assumption that identifying oneself as a Christian is meaningless without attempting to live according to the life and teachings of Jesus of Nazareth. To begin with ethics is not to say that moral duty precedes grace or even worse, that sin is more fundamentally world-shaping than the love of God seen through Christ; rather, it is just to say that voluntary baptism is incomprehensible without an assumption that human intentionality is meaningful. To begin with concerns about ethics is to acknowledge that the aspect of the Christian life that is most available to others is not what one believes but how one acts. Baptism is about responding to the priority of God's grace, and it sets the pattern for the ethical field in the abstract and for the Christian life in the everyday world of work, decisions, discernment, and the innumerable other tasks that make up the Christian life.

Christians who practice voluntary baptism in North America are profoundly confused about the ethical implications of the commitment to Christ that they profess in their baptisms. This does not mean that individuals in these communities do not have strong convictions, but rather that the these communities are far from agreeing in even the most facile way what living the Christian life might look like. To make the point stronger, these Christians are often misled to assume that their admission into a community or polity such as the church has little or no bearing on how they then participate in other bodies. This is clearly demonstrated by the way in which we fail to present any sort of unified witness on ethical issues. We fail to agree among ourselves as to which issues even *are* ethical issues. This can be seen in the constant drama that unfolds in Christian communities and institutions along the split between the religious Right and Left over issues of poverty, abortion, homosexuality, war, capital punishment, environmentalism, etc.

What should be even more shocking is that neither side seems to think that such division is a problem, or that ethical unity among

Christians should be a matter of grave concern.[8] Far too often both sides are in such a hurry to make their agenda public that the whole process of moral discernment among Christians has been discarded as simply taking too long in a world that revolves around the twenty-four-hour news cycle. As a result these ethical divisions have become normalized and cease to scandalize Christians or to prompt repentance. It is now assumed that it is perfectly natural for the church to be deeply divided and even to fight with itself in public.

Not only does this mean that the ancient tradition of ecumenical councils, stemming from the resolution of the controversy regarding the acceptance of Gentiles, has now been reduced to exchanging sound bites via television or the web, but it also means that the witness to the good news of the resurrection of Jesus the Messiah has become incomprehensible to a world that has largely ceased paying attention. Now, variety on one level is to be expected and in many cases should even be appreciated. However, the case that I am trying to make here is that in the area of ethics these "differences" go virtually the whole way down and are quickly becoming unbridgeable, if indeed we even cared about bridging them. But, you might ask, what if anything does this indictment have to do with voluntary baptism or Constantinianism?

Since the Second Great Awakening and the advent of the Evangelical movement in the United States, voluntary baptism has been gaining steam in North America.[9] It now takes no special feat of imagination to think that the Evangelical movement spearheaded by the Baptists, given weight by megachurches, animated by charismatics, and given vision by the "emergent" church is the new mainline both in the U.S. and in Canada. It is also no secret that by and large these groups practice voluntary baptism and are, to the extent that the terms are still useful, opposed to the Constantinian synthesis.[10]

It is clear historically and theologically, if it is not so in the news, that conservative politics has no fundamental claim on evangelicals, much less the broader category of those churches that practice voluntary baptism. Likewise a stereotypically progressive agenda has no fundamental claim on these churches either. What does have an indisputable claim on those who practice voluntary baptism—evangelicals included—is a straightforward reading of the Gospels to the effect that Jesus' teaching holds normative sway in the search for a contemporary ethic; the theology that holds up voluntary baptism is senseless without this basic assumption. This claim holds not on the basis of a shared theory of ethics but on a shared approach to the position of Scripture in the church over and against a development in the Christian tradition that is assumed to have strayed from it—that is, infant baptism.

What this boils down to is an almost syllogistic claim: *if a given Christian community practices voluntary baptism that community should view the Christian life in much the same way as other communities that do so.* This is the case because voluntary baptism only makes sense within a certain way of reading Scripture.[11] That this ethical unity does not exist leads me to the logical conclusion—in the case that logic might be needed as a stand-in for personal experience—that baptism in these communities is far too often merely the fulfillment of a social expectation and is disconnected from discipleship.

PASTORAL MINISTRY AT THE RELIGIOUS BUFFET

The work of the sociologist Christian Smith presented in his book *Soul Searching* provides both an appropriate transition from the preceding discussion of ethics and useful perspective for the following exploration of pastoral concerns related to the contemporary practice of voluntary baptism in North America. Smith's research is intriguing in that it shows that religion as such among American youth is not waning as is often feared by their devout elders. However, Smith did not find that the faith of these young people retained the depth that might characterize their predecessors. Despite the fact that about seventy-five percent of American teens say their faith is somewhat or very similar to their parents, only a minority, according to Smith, are absorbing the substantive content and character of the religious tradition they claim to belong to.[12]

The language, and therefore experience, of Trinity, holiness, sin, grace, justification, sanctification, church, Eucharist, and heaven and hell appear, among most Christian teenagers in the United States at the very least, to be supplanted by the language of happiness, niceness, and an earned heavenly reward. It is not so much that U.S. Christianity is being secularized. Rather more subtly, Christianity is either degenerating into a pathetic version of itself or, more significantly, Christianity is actively being colonized and displaced by a quite different religious faith.[13]

There are some important parallels here to the study of Canadian teenagers done by Reginald Bibby and Donald C. Posterski in the 1980s.[14] What the work of all three of these scholars clearly shows is that candidates for baptism—especially young people—are in a profoundly vulnerable spot.

The philosopher Charles Taylor, in his landmark book *Sources of the Self*, sheds light on this phenomenon from a different angle. Taylor suggests that members of modern society generally agree on the importance of ideals such as justice and beneficence.[15] Or in Taylor's own words "We are meant to be concerned for the life and well-being of all humans on the face of the earth; we are called on to further global justice between peoples; we subscribe to universal declarations of rights" (515).

An example is the proliferation of the now-ubiquitous benefit rock concert. These events are held to raise awareness and money for causes that it is assumed everyone agrees should be remedied: starvation, poor farmers, HIV/AIDS, the wrongfully imprisoned, and so on. Taylor's insight is particularly germane to this current project when he argues that the high standards of modern morality demand "strong sources" (516). The question that arises then is "whether we are not living beyond our moral means in continuing allegiance to our standards of justice and benevolence" (517). The crux of the matter is simply that while high moral standards, if rather vague generalities, exist in the pervasive sense that Taylor suggests, then modern persons are particularly ill-positioned to respond to these standards. The challenge is that while justice and beneficence may be acknowledged as goods, thick descriptions of what these are and how such descriptions might be arrived at exist only as highly contested and divisive theories.

Modern candidates for voluntary baptism live in a society that places high moral demands on their lives. A the same time, many of them lack a deep grounding in a faith community that might enable them to live up to their own expectations. We are therefore forced to wonder whether or not the current practice of voluntary baptism or contemporary theologies of voluntary baptism can adequately take these realities into account. I suggest that inadequate catechesis allows many young people whom we baptize to assume that there is little difference between the "good" of the Christian faith and the "good" of modern liberalism. Since modern society simply assumes the primacy of the free choice of the individual and still expects us to be "good" people, to pursue justice and charity as in the benefit rock show and the green capitalism movement, this is easily synthesized with the demand to be "good" placed on us by churches that practice baptism upon the voluntary choice of the individual.

This synthesis is a tacit and hidden Constantinianism. This synthesis serves as the matchmaker between churches that practice voluntary baptism and modern culture, facilitating the birth of Christian communities that are superficially anti-Constantinian but readily support state-sponsored violence.

It may well be the perceived irreligiosity of teenagers that has influenced many communities to baptize *children* under the guise of voluntary baptism. In some churches the age at which new believers are baptized has dropped so low as to make the baptism of prepubescent persons commonplace. The limited data and anecdotal evidence show this to be the case.[16] This has been likely caused by sheer force of socialization in cahoots with a lack of any integrated theology of the place of children in the church. An important exception here is likely the Amish, among whom baptism is usually practiced in close conjunction with marriage and an adult decision to join the community.

The reality of baptizing children while professing voluntary adult or even believers baptism is highly problematic. The baptism of children becomes merely an exercise in unbroachable social expectations—a liturgical Pavlovian drill. This illuminates a deeper problem—namely, that in the baptism of prepubescent children neither the theology of grace and God's election emphasized by infant baptism nor the response of faith and discipleship emphasized by believers' baptism is fully recognized. In their place is a synthesis of false voluntarity and veiled civil religion.

This sort of easy baptismal reductionism may lend itself well to the phenomena Smith observes. These children join their respective church communities in only the most superficial of ways, acquiring membership in name but clearly not being in a position to plumb the deeper wells of doctrine nor able to grasp the radical nature of the call of Christ. For them joining the Christian community is a social rite of passage—a gate-keeping ceremony initiating them *not* into a life of discipleship but into the next developmental stage in communities where joining the church carries no penalties and demands no social distancing from the mainstream. Is this anything but Constantinianism?

This strange synthesis of false voluntarity and veiled civil religion is supported by an unaddressed fear of death and a mechanical understanding of God's grace. All churches have to account for the presence of children in their midst and answer the question of how these persons are incorporated into the body of Christ. Some churches shackle themselves with the extra burden of having to solve the upsetting conundrum of children who die before coming to a saving faith in the gracious work of Christ. In wanting to uphold the necessity of faith for salvation, these churches place themselves on the horns of a pastoral dilemma; in wanting to preserve human freedom they are bound to it and cast their children down at the mercy of their own decision.

To save God from the awkward position of having to condemn children to eternal conscious torment the notion of an "age of accountability" is dubiously affirmed. This doctrine cobbled together with obscure biblical references is designed to show that God would not condemn unbelievers who had never reached the developmental stage that might allow them to distinguish right from wrong.[17] While this doctrine does in some cases pacify worried parents, it creates not only theological problems but also pastoral dilemmas. At what age is one actually accountable before God?

And if this can not be answered uniformly, then surely there must be some developmental test that might tell parents and ecclesiastical authorities when each child had reached the stage of accountability before God, at which point the fires of hell would be warmed on their behalf. Such a test would prove difficult to contrive and would always be *contrived*. The simple result though is that parents and pastors alike encourage children to be baptized at the very first demonstration of religious curiosity, or if not *actual* curiosity then the first time they can pronounce the word *propitiation*. It is regrettable that parents have placed their faith in a programmed response of their child, but it is more regrettable that their children must have their growth in faith short-circuited by parent's lack of trust in God's goodness.

The correction for this mistake lies not only in redefining the age at which baptism is socially expected but also in a general reaffirmation of the doctrine of grace in such a way that it is deeply integrated with believers church theology, if believers' baptism is what we are hoping for. At first glance such a proposition might appear to be a pining after the assurances of Calvinism. However, while much might be gained from paying more attention to Calvin, modern Calvinism is no balm for the Constantinian itch.

It will always be true that commitments such as baptism (and marriage) are made without knowing the full extent of what will be required. This is inevitable and that is precisely what ought to make the decision a well-thought-out one. This however is not an excuse for willful ignorance—the willful ignorance shown by those who would be baptized without really knowing what is expected of them.

More importantly, it is no excuse for the church leaders' tacit misrepresentation of the Christian faith through inadequate catechesis. A key feature often lacking in catechetical teaching is the priesthood of all believers. One way of describing this is to call baptism the ordination of the laity. Now clearly if it is such an ordination, it is a fairly weak one, for most actual ordinations imply that the ordained will not kill others. Voluntary baptism rarely has this implication. Again the Amish tradition is a fruitful example here inasmuch as it makes clear that everyone, or all males in the Amish case, is agreeing in requesting baptism to serve the community as its minister should the lot ever fall on them.[18]

While it is true that the indiscriminate (or worse) baptisms performed from time to time in some traditions is a disturbing part of the church's history, it is also the case that simply limiting baptism to those who have made a profession of faith does not solve all our baptismal problems. The lack of rigorous catechesis among voluntary baptism practicing churches is a glaring manifestation of this. Here we can lay blame in part at the feet of American revivalism. Revivalism's preoccupation with crises conversions has stretched the link between baptism and church membership to the breaking point.[19] Few traditions have been immune to this influence. A baptism brought on by a crisis conversion in the revivalist tradition too often remains only a personal subjective matter and fails to properly involve the church. The revivalist tradition is not the only culprit here; its genealogical twin modern individualism must also be indicted.

In different ways the work of sociologists Robert Bellah, Reginald Bibby, and Robert Putnam describe the growing social fragmentation that exists in North American society as it moves into the twenty-first century. They describe a society in which the communal character of religion is disintegrating as the ongoing rush of consumerist and individualist waves pull faith communities apart.[20] Their work shows the uphill battle Christian communities face in allowing baptism to be an act of discipleship within a particular community—to be more than one more choice at the buffet of identity, community, spirituality, and meaning. In such an acidic cultural environment Christian communities are provided with an opportunity to reinvigorate the practice of baptism.

Although the current situation may look at first glance virtually identical to the situation of the early church in which that community was a minority in a largely pagan society, the current age is different in an import way. In twenty-first century North America Christian communities that practice voluntary baptism are not persecuted; they are not socially disadvantaged in any important way. What they are is one minority community among many—by all appearances just one more voluntary association.

VOLUNTARY BAPTISM AS A
CHALLENGE TO POLITICAL INTEGRITY

Baptism ought to be a political act. If this is true of baptism generally, then it is even more obviously true of voluntary baptism. While
modern assumptions have driven a wedge between the religious and
the political, it cannot be denied that a rite of initiation such as baptism ought to have at the very least a political *sense*. That voluntary
baptism has lost its political character is congruent with the loss of
Christianity's political character generally. Christianity is mostly
thought of as a religion in the modern sense, primarily individual
and private—a system of personal beliefs about the afterlife, metaphysics, and the role of a first-century Jewish carpenter in the unseen
spiritual realm. But *this criticism of contemporary Christianity is not new*;
in fact, we might even say this critique is rather tired and has become
more or less free-floating rhetoric detached from its theological
tether. In many cases this critique has sadly only advanced as far as
talk; it has not been extended to reform the very practices which
allow the language of faith as individual and private to make sense.
There is no more pressing location for this reform of praxis than in the
ordinance which initiates believers into the community.

There are significant exceptions to the sweeping generalizations
just made. There are churches that have recognized the indispensably
political nature of both the gospel and the community it gathers
through the Spirit of Christ. Yet even many of these churches fail to
recognize the depth to which they have imbibed the modern heresy
of privatized religion. This is seen in the fact that many churches that
have responded to the critique raised above have taken up activism
on the assumption that this is a way of being faithful to the political
nature of the gospel. What many of these churches have not recognized is that even in their activism they fail to properly reject the notion that the state is the arbitrator of justice and that the state is the
proper bearer of the mantle of history. Or to put it another way, the
goods which constitute the state remain the canon against which the
church's political agenda is measured, and they provide the gram-
matical frame into which the church's political speech is poured.

This is evident in the way that these churches have allowed
"rights" terminology to become commonplace in conversations
within the church itself. This is germane to our ongoing discussion in
that the salvation attested to in the act of baptism too easily becomes
a salvation of secondary importance. Since the politics of the state has
provided the necessary salvation for our communities and science is
in the process of saving our bodies, baptism easily becomes only a

matter of saving the soul. It becomes speculative, abstract, and invisible–only a sign of what has happened on a spiritual plane. Thus in traditional evangelical circles baptism has lost communal significance, but activist Christians are no better off since for them baptism is simply a public symbol constrained by the very terms of that public.[21] In both cases baptism is domesticated by a false soteriology.[22]

The interesting parallels in redemption mythology between Christianity and the modern political milieu have not only been observed by theologians. The anthropologist Talal Asad also makes note of this in his book *Formations of the Secular*. One of the arguments that Asad makes in this book is that although the projects of liberal modernity and the Christian New Testament give similar pride of place to redemption mythology, important differences between the two do exist.[23] A political danger here is that in the modern perspective there ceases to be any way to conceptualize the difference between suffering that might be redemptive from that which is not; all suffering is painted with the same brush and is to be avoided at any cost. Not only does this compromise the work of Christ, but it also makes problematic the witness of Christian martyrs and, not long after, the character the Christian witness itself, for it is only a short and very logical step from the way the presence of suffering energizes the projects of modern liberalism to a gospel of acquisitiveness—"health and wealth."

This riff on Asad's poignant observation shows that the roots of contemporary voluntary baptism in the breakdown of the old Christendom—the Protestant Reformation and its cousin the Enlightenment—make the practice particularly vulnerable to constant reinterpretation in the current political environment. The temptation for baptism to be reinvented in such an idolatrous mode can be called the challenge of voluntarism.

The politics of baptism has suffered inasmuch as its voluntary nature has been twisted by the forces of democracy, as has just been alluded to, and revivalism. The result is that many churches that practice voluntary baptism have been disfigured under the influence of voluntarism and have taken on a contractual polity mirroring the ideology of liberalism. We might put this slightly differently and say that the priesthood of all believers has been massaged into the voting right of all believers–polling has taken the place of discernment. The problem is not with the voluntary nature of the community—as opposed to a Constantinian alternative—but with the way this too easily becomes a sort of *voluntarism* in which all members choose and construct their own God and in which liturgical practice is fashioned after the mood of the day as determined by polling the audience. Not only does this undermine a strong theology of God's grace and revelation, but, to go a step further, it reduces God from acting subject to a constructed object and the inevitable result is always idolatry.

This individualism can and must be separated from the essential "voluntary" nature of the believers church. This voluntary nature reflects *the non-coercive quality of God's election*. It also embodies the love shown in the character of Jesus' earthly ministry and the way in which the ongoing invitation to would-be followers affirms the personhood of every hearer of the good news. Voluntarism on the other hand denies the reality of God's call and reduces the church from a community gathered around the risen Lord in love and trust to an interest group based on selfishness and fear.

Even worse, voluntarism, as I have already suggested, can go hand in hand with a turn to a new Constantinianism. Some North American Christians have turned modern voluntarism into a license for not committing to any particular church community; some have turned it into a license to acquiesce to civil religion.[24] It cuts both ways, and the lordship of Christ is denied in both.

CHALLENGES TO THEOLOGICAL INTEGRITY

We turn now to what might be considered theology proper and by doing so deal with some of the fundamental issues at hand. This has the effect of serving as a summary of what has been discussed thus far as well as to issue a firm diagnosis of the underlying problems that have manifest themselves within the ethical, pastoral, and political rubrics.

We must begin with incarnation itself. In this most surprising of actions, God reveals himself as one who searches, finds, and redeems those beings in creation made in the very image of God—the very creatures who have rejected fellowship with God through breaking the covenant.[25] God is clearly revealed as one who initiates and effects the salvation of the person, all the while preserving the integrity of the person inasmuch as God does not *violently force* himself upon humanity but reveals himself in love and vulnerability. Further, in the event of Pentecost God reveals himself as one who empowers human witness to God's activity and calls out a people to bear this cause and to live proleptically the affect of his redemption as a community gathered around the work of Jesus. God calls forth praise from this community and promises that even that which embodies separation from himself and rejection of God's saving acts will not prevail against this community drawn together and empowered by the very Spirit of God.[26]

If voluntary baptism fails to recognize the calling nature of God it fails to be Christian baptism. *Voluntary* baptism fails to be Christian baptism if it does not recognize that it is God who calls and humans who respond. Thus the baptism of believers must recognize the truth that the baptism of infants clearly proclaims, which is that this practice of the church is not self-generating—it happens not on the initiative of the individual—but is instead a response to God's initiatory action. The practice of voluntary baptism fails to recognize the completeness and sufficiency of God's saving act if it does not locate the faith of the individual in the prior graciousness of God.[27]

On the other hand, the very mode of God's revelation and saving action upholds the importance of the action of the individual as a genuine response to God's action. In this way baptism encapsulates the very nature of the Christian life as something neither passive in nature nor self-generating. Voluntary baptism fails to properly witness to God's empowering action if it is anything less than the individual's initiation into the community of believers that now according to the reconciling power of God knows no preference for worldly power nor separation along social lines previously thought uncrossable, whether they be lines of ethnicity, class, or gender. In like manner baptism fails to be more than a mechanistic initiation if it does not embody the gift of God's Spirit to the community and recognize that God has chosen to act through this body of believers.

Voluntary baptism also falls short if it fails to speak of the cosmic nature of baptism, that is, its eschatological character. The practice of voluntary baptism falls short if it is not the sign of a new birth properly embodied and pointing toward the future when the reign of God will be brought into full actuality.[28] Rebirth and the participation in Christ's resurrection must be embodied in baptism in such a way that the practical outworking of such regeneration is to be expected as intrinsic to the act itself. As the reader has likely anticipated, this means that baptism is more than a mere symbol of an event that has taken place in a spiritual realm. We might say that it is an *effectual* or *performative sign* pointing to the sufficient work of Christ and actualized by the power and authority of Christ's Spirit and Bride.[29]

On either side of the description of baptism just given lie the dangerous temptations of rationalism and spiritualism. Precedent for these two dangers lies near to the early Anabaptist movement itself, where much ink was used by Anabaptist leaders in an attempt to differentiate themselves from the radical spiritualists who placed more emphasis on the experience of the heart and less on the physical acts of the church. The difficulty here is found in that it is hard on a practical level, as it is historically, to parse between radical spiritualism and the important role of the Spirit. The controversial figure of Hans Denck may stand as an historical example. A sound doctrine and practice of believers' baptism needs a clearly recognized pneumatology.

On the other side of the path from the spiritualist danger lies the rationalist one. The stream of early Anabaptism that has survived as today's Mennonite communities and may have even influenced the early Baptists largely has walked in this ditch. In the rationalist way of thinking, baptism and communion are only symbols done in memory of a past event—they hold no effective or performative power. This essay has already critiqued this view in several ways, not least the way a memorialist theology of baptism enables a continued voluntarism and the disintegration of a unified ethical or political witness. Both spiritualism and rationalism fail to recognize the goodness of creation and the ability of God to make use of common elements and practices. In various ways they fail to give due recognition to the three agents involved in baptism—the triune God, the church, and the individual.

We have begun to note already how this discussion cannot be divorced from theological anthropology. This line of thought must now be pursued further. In Jesus' calling of the disciples and empowering of the church humans are revealed to be capable of bearing faithful witness to God. In God's grace humans are given worth as beings and caused to be capable of bearing the title "children of God." In the gathering and sending of the church Christian communities are given a uniting center and a common goal. Centered outside themselves in Christ believers are given the mandate of calling others to their center and subsequently into their midst. Empowered by the Spirit of God, humans are made capable of discernment and exercising redemptive discipline in communal matters.

Believers baptism denies itself then if it is not confident enough in its own ordering of "the good" to recognize itself as properly public—as a visible action consistent with the goals and values of the Christian *polis*.[30] The truth of God's action is denied if churches falter in their expectation that those baptized will bear witness to Christ. Such is also the case if an expectation of unity is given up or if discernment is discarded in favor of making decisions through either the opinion poll or a blind following of uncritiqued tradition. The transformative reality of being children of God is denied if baptism becomes either a matter of socialization or even worse a method of becoming part of the community at large—Constantinian civil religion. Theologically, then, we see that it is harmful to think of baptism as something initiated by the individual, as something that simply symbolizes a transaction between the one baptized and God, ignoring the role of the church community. Likewise it is harmful to think of baptism as purely a symbolic or memorialist gesture lacking Divine empowerment through the Spirit's presence in the church.

My conclusion in short is that voluntary baptism is certainly not the answer to the Constantinian problem. In fact it perpetuates a new incarnation of this ancient heresy! On the other hand believers' baptism or even better *disciple baptism* might go a long way in pursuing Christian faithfulness in times that are politically and economically uncertain but certainly are violent.

NOTES

1. In Yoder's work the issue of voluntarity shows up most clearly when he discusses the choice that individuals make to become part of a discipling community. In his book on Yoder, Mark Thiessen Nation observes that one of the distinctives of the Anabaptist vision Yoder noted in some of his early essays is that "Anabaptists believed membership in the church was voluntary." This was used to explain the redemptive but necessary practice of church discipline (*John Howard Yoder: Mennonite Patience, Evangelical Witness, Catholic Convictions* [Grand Rapids, Mich.: Wm. B. Eerdmans, 2006], 47). Yoder himself says, "From the perspective of individualism the communal quality of the radical Protestant moral witness seems to be tyrannical, if one fails to recognize that one's belonging to that community is free"(*The Priestly Kingdom: : Social Ethics as Gospel* [Notre Dame, Ind.: University of Notre Dame Press], 25).

2. Oliver O'Donovan, *The Desire of the Nations: Rediscovering the Roots of Political Theology* (Cambridge: Cambridge University Press, 1996), 223-224.

3. In Stanley Hauerwas's *Wilderness Wanderings: Probing Twentieth-Century Theology and Philosophy* (Boulder, Col.: Westview Press, 1997), 224, n15.

4. Alain Epp Weaver, "After Politics: John Howard Yoder, Body Politics, and the Witnessing Church," *The Review of Politics* 61.4 (Fall 1999): 637–674; "Why O'Donovan's Christendom is Not Constantinian and Yoder's Voluntareity is Not Hobbesian: A Debate in Theological Politics Redefined," *The Annual of the Society of Christian Ethics* 20 (2000): 41-64.

5. John Howard Yoder, *Body Politics: Five Practices of the Christian Community Before the Watching World* (Scottdale, Pa.: Herald Press, 1992, 2001), ch. 3; likewise, Yoder's description of various "neo-Constantinianisms" provides license, or at least creates elbow room, for my argument in this essay ("Christ the Hope of the World," in *The Royal Priesthood: Essays Ecclesiological and Ecumenical*, ed. Michael G. Cartwright [Scottdale, Pa.: Herald Press, 1998], 192-218) .

6. Since Constantinianism is a theme of this volume I don't feel the need to present a working definition of the term or to defend the historical analysis that underwrites it.

7. In beginning with ethics I follow the work of the b/Baptist theologian James McClendon; *Ethics: Systematic Theology*, vol. 1 (Nashville: Abingdon, 2002).

8. For a difficult but profound treatment of the phenomena of the reification and calcification of church division see Ephraim Radner, *The End of the Church: A Pneumatology of Christian Division in the West* (Grand Rapids, Mich.: Wm. B. Eerdmans, 1998). For more on why ethical unity should be a priority for Christians see John Howard Yoder, "The Nature of the Unity We Seek: A Historic Free Church View," in *The Royal Priesthood: Essays Ecclesiological and Ecumenical* (Scottdale, Pa.: Herald Press, 1998), 221-30.

9. For a description of the denominations empowered by the Second Great Awakening see Mark A. Noll, *A History of Christianity in the United States and Canada* (Grand Rapids, Mich.: Wm. B. Eerdmans, 1992), 163ff.

10. A quick survey of megachurches shows that with a few exceptions these churches practice voluntary baptism. To pursue this further see the work of the Hartford Institute For Religion Research, a institute of Hartford Seminary. On the web at http://hirr.hartsem.edu/megachurch/mega churches.html

11. This sort of a claim is similar to the way James McClendon articulates the "baptist vision" in *Doctrine: Systematic Theology, Vol. 2* (Nashville: Abingdon, 1994), 45.

12. Christian Smith, *Soul Searching: The Religious and Spiritual Lives of American Teenagers* (New York: Oxford University Press, 2005), 36,171.

13. Ibid., 171.

14. Reginald W. Bibby and Donald C. Posterski, *The Emerging Generation: An Inside Look and Canada's Teenagers* (Toronto: Irwin Publishing, 1985), 115-128.

15. Here I would like to highlight the level at which this agreement occurs at a general or superficial level. Taylor is obviously not unaware of the conflict over how these well-acknowledged generalities are applied. This general agreement, however, does not cool the mutual irritation among church communities who agree on the practice of baptism but disagree on ethical matters. *Sources of the Self: The Making of the Modern Identity* (Cambridge, Mass.: Harvard University Press, 1989), 515ff.

16. James Leo Garrett claims that this happens in some Baptist churches at an age as young as six. "Baptists Concerning Baptism: Review and Preview," *Southwestern Journal of Theology* 43.2 (Spring 2001): 65. Also see and Timothy George, "The Southern Baptists," in *Baptism and Church: A Believers' Church Vision*, ed. Merle D. Strege (Grand Rapids, Mich.: Sagamore Books, 1986), 47. According a 2006 survey by the sociologists Donald Kraybill, Conrad Kanagy, Ronald Burwell, and Carl Bowman the average age of baptism for members of Mennonite Church USA is 13.92. In the Brethren in Christ denomination the average for members is 19.3. However, this average age is deceptive. In fact, in the BIC denomination more than 65 percent were baptized before the age of 16 (with about 11 percent appearing to have been baptized as infants in other denominations). This would seem to indicate that in a de-

nomination where the average age of baptism was over nineteen, over half of its members had been baptized by that community itself before they turned 16. Data provided in private correspondence by Conrad Kanagy and Ronald Burwell, June-July, 2008.

17. 2 Sam. 12:23 is often cited to show that infants will not be condemned.

18. John H. Hostetler, *Amish Society*, 4th. ed. (Baltimore: Johns Hopkins University Press, 1993), 78. This practice could surely be adapted for use by communities who include women in all roles of church leadership.

19. Marlin E. Miller, "The Mennonites," in *Baptism and Church: A Believers' Church Vision*, ed. Merle D. Strege (Grand Rapids, Mich.: Sagamore Books, 1986), 23.

20. Robert D. Putnam, *Bowling Alone* (New York: Simon & Schuster, 2000). Reginald Bibby, *Mosaic Madness* (Toronto: Stoddart, 1990); Robert N. Bellah, et.al., *Habits of the Heart* (New York: Harper & Row, 1985).

21. For more on how the church might itself be a public see Reinhard Hütter, *Suffering Divine Things: Theology as Church Practice* (Grand Rapids, Mich.: Wm. B. Eerdmans, 2000), 158–70.

22. To further explore this line of thought see William T. Cavanaugh, *Theopolitical Imagination: Discovering the Liturgy as a Political Act in an Age of Global Consumerism* (New York: T & T Clark, 2002).

23. Talal Asad, *Formations of the Secular: Christianity, Islam, Modernity* (Stanford: Stanford University Press, 2003), 61.

24. Bibby makes something of the same observation in *Mosaic Madness*, 93-94.

25. This series of ideas relies heavily on Karl Barth, *Church Dogmatics: The Doctrine of Reconciliation*, IV.1, trans. G. W. Bromiley (Edinburgh: T & T Clark, 1956).

26. Barth, *The Teaching of the Church Regarding Baptism*, trans. E. A. Payne (London: SCM Press, 1948), 16ff.

27. Here we follow Barth in his revision of Zwingli, *The Teaching of the Church Regarding Baptism*, 20.

28. This inasmuch as we can say that the reign of God is currently *real* but not fully *actualized*.

29. Clearly a fuller project would have to flesh out the notion of an effectual or performative sign. Here however I will simply point to the work already begun by James McClendon in "Baptism as a Performative Sign" in *Theology Today* 23.3 (October 1966): 403-416; and *Doctrine*, 386-406.

30. Cf. Arne Rasmusson, *The Church as Polis* (Notre Dame, Ind.: University of Notre Dame Press, 1995), 174–374.

Chapter 11

USING GIRARD TO ADDRESS FACTIONS IN A CHRISTIAN COMMUNITY

Jean F. Risley

René Girard describes a process whereby scapegoating and ritual sacrifice can be used to alleviate the conflict caused by factions in a community. For Girard, the work of Jesus on the cross brought an end to the use of sacrifice as a way to deal with our potential for violence in our conflicts. But the question remains: what do we do instead? How do we live with each other in the shadow of the cross knowing that scapegoating and sacrifice are no longer an option for us? The answer lies in reversing those factors present in scapegoating sacrifice, the factors that enable it to work, and to substitute other attitudes and behaviors based on the teaching and model of Jesus.

In order for scapegoating to be effective in addressing the problem of factionalization within a community, three factors must be present:

- secrecy and lack of conscious awareness of the process;
- lack of empathy with potential victims;
- negative emotional reactions to those perceived to be different.

The absence of any of these factors can disrupt the scapegoating process, but addressing and reversing all of these factors is necessary for an alternative to the scapegoating process to become normative.

If we are to appropriate what we learn from Girard, we need to engage the work of Christ in reversing these three factors in ordinary daily life. We need to establish alternative practices and habits of interaction which, by incorporating the teaching and behavioral model we receive in Jesus, enable us to approach our potential differences in ways that do not lead to conflict or require violent resolutions.

ENABLING A SCAPEGOATING PROCESS

In his book *Saved from Sacrifice*,[1] Mark Heim describes Girard's understanding of scapegoating sacrifice and the conditions which must be present for a scapegoating resolution to conflict to be effective. The ideas in this section are based on that material. The following sections will present principles and techniques for reversing the factors which permit those conditions as well as experience in using these techniques to address conflict in a particular community.

How scapegoating helps

Scapegoating and the sacrifice of a scapegoat are behavior patterns that are manifest when the level of internal conflict in a community becomes so intense that it threatens the dissolution of the community. The cause or causes of conflict may be internal or external, but it is the fact of the conflict, not its content, that leads to the need for a scapegoat. The intensity of conflict in the community feeds on the anxiety and stress of the people:

> Everyone becomes a model for everyone else, and everyone models the same thing: defensive fear, preemptive attack. Sacrificial rituals or mob persecution won't stop germs or invading armies, but they can address the effects of both on the internal life of a community. (50)

The accusations used in scapegoating behavior are not directly related to the actual causes of the crisis in a community. But attacking the scapegoat does in fact "solve" the problem of conflict in the community, whether or not it has any effect on the actual cause(s) of the crisis facing the community. The communal action against the victim restores the community to its sense of solidarity.

> This sudden war of all against one delivers [the community] from the war of each against all. The sacrifice of one person as a scapegoat discharges the pending acts of retribution between members of the group. It "clears the air." The contagion of reciprocal violence is suspended. A circuit breaker has been

thrown. The collective violence is reconciling because it reestab-
lishes peace. (43)

Although we may believe that ritual sacrifice and scapegoating are
obsolete, the problem that they address is still with us. We still experience the intense anxiety and stress caused by the conflicts in our
midst. Even in this time,

> the problem sacrifice addresses is very real. Yet the traditional
> ways of applying a sacrificial solution are in fact in bad repair.
> To suppose that we have replaced them or that their enfeeble-
> ment poses no threat to us is naïve. (61)

We need to be aware of the factors which make scapegoating possible
and find alternative ways of addressing the factionalization among
us without the need for a sacrificial victim.

The role of secrecy

For a scapegoating process to work effectively, the participants
must not be consciously aware of what they are doing or why they are
doing it.

> Classically, when religion or politics has been all about the prac-
> tice of scapegoating, it has been silent about any direct account
> of it. So long as we are immersed in it, we can conceive of what
> we are doing only in other terms. (65)

The people of a community overwhelmed by conflict and crisis do not
stop to think rationally about the causes of the crisis to prepare a plan
to address them. The crisis is too pressing and emotionally charged to
allow the space for reflection, and the community is too polarized for
the give and take of cooperative problem solving. When a scapegoating solution appears, it seems to have occurred spontaneously and
with almost miraculous clarity to the whole community at once, without any particular person or group responsible for initiating it. Members of the community are unaware of any "source" for the solution to
their problem.

When a scapegoat is found, the community suddenly and unanimously identifies that person or persons as the immediate cause of
the crisis it is facing. The "cause" is stated in simple and simplistic
terms, a clear and focused sound bite that the community can easily
hold on to, despite the emotional turmoil which is making it so hard
to think clearly. The simplistic explanation of how the victim caused
the crisis becomes the primary line of conversation throughout the

community, crowding out any attempt to deal with the crisis in other terms. The explanation usually involves violation of deeply held values of the community, some form of behavior so bad that it is immediately obvious to all that it would lead to a disaster for the whole community. This engagement of deeply felt values allows members of the community to be convinced of the victim's guilt and responsibility on an emotional level, without the risk and uncertainty of rational consideration of actual cause and effect.

It is a key point for Girard that effectiveness of the sacrifice of a scapegoat depends on obscurity surrounding the way the process works.

> If it were obvious to all that sacrifice was a ploy in the ordinary round of rivalry and violence, it would be much less effective. The questions would inevitably turn back upon the act itself. Without a canopy of sacred awe and the conviction of unspeakable crimes, suspicions might arise about whether the victim was chosen arbitrarily, about the interests of those who picked the victim, about the possibility that we too could become victims. In virtually all traditions it is not considered safe or auspicious to pry too much into the sacred mysteries, for fear that this will derail their success. (51)

Secrecy about and lack of awareness of the process are critical for a scapegoating solution to conflict to be applied effectively.

The role of lack of empathy

To maintain the emotional distance from a potential scapegoat that makes him or her a good candidate for sacrifice, it is critical that members of the community not see that person as "just like" themselves. A potential victim must be seen as a person of extraordinary power, either in ability to do harm or in ability to protect the community from harm. Anything that forces the community to see the victim as an ordinary human being among others breaks the mystique of power and calls into question the efficacy of the sacrificial solution.

It is also critical that no one in the community be able to sympathize with, and thus be likely to defend, the potential victim.

> Sacrifice is successful when no one takes the side of the suffering one, no one thinks that person is innocent, no one withholds participation in the collective violence against that person, no one considers his or her death a murder, no one remembers the victim as such after the victim is gone. (65)

The action of the community must be unanimous to be effective, and any sympathy with the victim will interrupt the sacrificial dynamic.

The role of negative emotional reactions to difference

How does one become the one who is suddenly and unanimously selected to be the scapegoat? While selection does not depend on reasoning about the cause of the crisis, there are characteristics which will make a person a more likely choice to serve as a scapegoat.

> As to *who* is guilty of the crisis-causing act, the accusation will name someone who has committed incest, or witchcraft, or blasphemy, or some other crime that upsets order and offends the divine. The one named will likely prove to have qualities unrelated to the accusation, qualities that make him or her liable to marginalization or isolation. Whether one person or a few, they will start with few natural defenders and end up with none. . . . being too different makes you a prime candidate to become a scapegoat blamed for the crisis. (51)

Members of a community typically have an unconscious sense of those who are different in their midst. People naturally feel more comfortable with those who are predictably like themselves, those whose feelings and motivations they share and who function with similar behavior patterns. Conversely, those who are in some way different are less predictable, less resonant and reassuring, and in a sense seem less safe. When tensions are high in a crisis, relationships with those who are different are typically invested with an increasingly heightened level of anxiety.

Just as folk seem to know who to go to for advice, or comfort, or a good time, they also know who to step back from and avoid when things get tense.

> Scapegoating sacrifice is a shape-shifting dynamic. There is no permanent class of victims, no permanent members of the unanimous mob. This by no means denies that, for instance, racism, economic exploitation, and gender discrimination are realities. These are forms of oppression with their own logic, and ones easily co-opted to sacrificial ends. In crisis, scapegoats are likely to be chosen from those already marginal and isolated according to one of these factors. (62)

REVERSING THE FACTORS

It is clear that we will continue to experience conflict among ourselves, caused and intensified by mimetic rivalry. We know that ritual sacrifice is not an acceptable solution to our problems with conflict, but what do we do about it?

> [It is not] sufficient simply to instruct us about our situation, for we are all too fully enclosed in the scapegoating process to be able to break the spell. It is historically hard to see this process for what it is. And it is much more difficult for us to recognize our own actions as scapegoating. (196)

Our challenge is to create a positive and self-reinforcing cycle within our relationships that favors a new pattern of behavior.

What should this new pattern of behavior be? What is the result that we want to see in ourselves when we have left our old practices behind?

> The New Testament writers do not tire of emphasizing that the key mark of the new community is the way it brings together what one would ordinarily presume to be conflicting parties, and does so by peaceful means, not by sacrifice. Christ has broken down barriers, and in this body of believers there is neither Jew nor Greek, slave nor free, male nor female. (229)

The early church was very clear about the source of the power to make this kind of a change:

> The miraculous effect of the risen Christ through the spirit is the reconciliation of the sharpest and strongest differences, resolution of conflicts that could and would, normally, tear a community apart. (229)

So, then, how do we engage the risen Christ in ending the threat that conflict poses to our communities? How do we appropriate the teaching, example, and death of Jesus to address our own pressing needs? What we need to do is to engage the model that Jesus gives us, the demonstration of the character and person of God as expressed in a human life:

> A model who is a real human being, and with whom one is actually in relationship, is by far the most transformative reality. And this is who Christ is in the lives of Christians. The availability of this model is a divine act of grace. Its presence does not violate the character of natural human life, but it also cannot be

explained or expected as an extrapolation of that life alone. The death of Jesus cuts to the heart of what has gone wrong with our mimetic nature, and the living presence of Jesus is a model for healing it. (243-244)

This model is available to us through our understanding of the person we know through Scripture and by participation in a living relationship with the risen Christ in faith through the power of the Holy Spirit.

Jesus explained in his teaching and demonstrated by his example the reversal of each of the factors that make the use of scapegoating sacrifice effective. His truth telling, openness to loving all others, and acceptance of those who are different are seen throughout the Gospels. To change our behavior patterns it is necessary not just to stop but to reverse each of the factors, using this model that we see in Jesus.

In the following sections we will look at specific ways to engage this model of Jesus to reverse the three factors, through the experiences of a particular church. This church, a small, two-hundred-year-old congregation in the Hudson River valley north of New York City, was deeply divided and arguing about the arrangements for worship during the summer. When fall came and a new pastor arrived, both factions seemed ready to walk out opposite doors of the church. The people were stressed and hurt by the conflict, and the community which had nurtured them for many years seemed ready to fracture and fall apart.

By the grace of God, it was possible to address and reverse each of the factors which might have led to a sacrificial solution to the situation and to rebuild a healthy, mutually supportive community. As each of the factors was addressed, a mix of teaching and practice was used, so that people could be aware of the theological issues involved as they gained experience in a more Christ-like approach to each other. Talking about conflict, developing empathy for each other, and changing reactions to the experience of difference were each addressed through this combination of teaching and direct practice.

Bringing what is concealed to light

Jesus said, "I am the way, and the truth, and the life" (John 14:6), and he consistently spoke the truth with those he met. From the Samaritan woman at the well to the rich young ruler, he kindly spoke the unvarnished truth to all levels of society. As at dinner with Simon the Pharisee, he was upfront and explicit about the processes and feelings that were hidden behind the facade of polite behavior. Jesus made it a practice to bring what was hidden, particularly what was hidden in the human heart, to light. For us to follow this model Jesus gives, we need to be able to tell the truth about ourselves, our feelings and the movements in our relationships with each other.

Keeping conflict unmentionable makes it invisible and unapproachable but at the same time highly emotionally charged. In order for folks to be able to relax and talk about what is happening in their midst, one or more leaders—pastors or respected lay people—must introduce and model truth-telling about the reality that the community is experiencing.

This truth-telling needs to incorporate certain characteristics which we see modeled in the teaching of Jesus. It must be gentle and compassionate, as opposed to judgmental, so that others feel welcome to join in the conversation without prejudice. It must be clear and specific, so that the content is not subject to misinterpretation or lost in word games. Its main points should be captured in meaningful sound bites, so that the ideas can be easily held in mind, recalled, reconsidered, and brought to mind to address specific situations. It should have a light touch, using humor which is affectionate, respectful, and inclusive, to break through the level of tension and hypersensitivity that usually surrounds conversation about a difficult topic.

The following are excerpts from the first sermon given by the newly arrived pastor, coming into a church electric with conflicting factions. The initial goal is to bring the reality of conflict into the open as a topic of conversation:

> I am the new kid on the block in this congregation, but over the summer even I heard rumors that we were not all of the same mind. We are one church, one people of God in this place, but I understand that there has been considerable conflict over one thing or another. In fact, some of the people who shared with me about the areas of conflict were not sure about whether to tell me about it or not.

Conflict is embarrassing, and no one wants to admit it exists. However, since no one can address it until they can feel comfortable about admitting it is there, the pastor needs to set the tone for the conversation. Conflict is real and unpleasant, but it is not the end of the world as we know it.

> As it turns out, my reaction to the news was quite different. For me, conflict is a normal part of our learning to live together as the family of Christ. A church is a family, and we all know that

you can chose your friends but you can't choose your relatives. We are each unique individuals, with our own different perspectives. . . . In fact if there is no conflict, no differences that we are working through with each other, there are two possibilities: either the church is dead, and no one cares strongly about anything any more; or Christ has come again and we have all been transformed into angels in heaven.

Conflict is about our different callings, hopes, and priorities. It is to be expected even when we are on our best behavior, working to do what we believe to be God's work. It is a result of our caring, of our trying to do our best, and it shows that we *do* care and we *are* trying to do our best.

So on the subject of the summer worship schedule, I have some good news and some bad news. The good news is that summer is over, and that particular conflict is behind us. The bad news is that there will always be something to disagree about. . . .

Conflict is and will continue to be a part of our lives, so we need to get over the conviction that once we get through today's particular issue, we will all be in agreement tomorrow. That is just not going to happen. The reality is that there is a purpose in our conflict, if we use it to grow in love for each other.

Every disagreement is a chance to practice being loving brothers and sisters in the family of Jesus Christ. Every disagreement is a chance to show how we can be loving to our neighbors even if we happen to be mad at them at the moment.

Since conflict is going to be part of our life together for the foreseeable future, we do not need to be upset about the prospect. We simply need to live and grow through it.

The result of this material, although shocking at first, was to make conflict an acceptable topic of conversation. The emotional intensity in talking and thinking about specific events was reduced, and people were able to express both their feelings about treatment they had received as well as the feelings which led to their own behavior. Emotional tension was reduced when people could say how much they had been hurt, rather than simply reliving, one more time, the incidents which had hurt them. Once this hypersensitivity was reduced, people were better able to see their own behavior more objectively and talk about it honestly with each other.

Engaging openness and empathy

Jesus expected all of those who followed him to love each other. He said, "By this everyone will know that you are my disciples, if you have love for one another" (John 13:35). He was clear that this love was for all and not just for particular friends. He said, "If you do good to those who do good to you, what credit is that to you? For even sinners do the same" (Luke 6:33). For Jesus, being part of his family meant being able to empathize with, sympathize with, and care about every other part—openly, freely, and generously—as he did. To live up to his model, we need to find a way to open our hearts to each other and live in active love.

Developing an appreciation for each other as human beings, engaging each other openly and feeling empathy for each other, is not easy, especially when the other is an enemy, an opponent, or a potential victim. When we are polarized against specific people, we do not see the underlying common humanity we share. Their strengths, their values, and the struggles they have come through to reach the positions they hold are invisible to us. We are unable to see these others as whole persons; as a result we do not empathize with their feelings or have the ability to anticipate and share their pain.

One way to break this isolating distance from a particularly difficult other is to invite an interested third party into the relationship between us—God. If we can approach the other with an awareness of God's perspective, we can see that person from God's point of view, as a beloved but far-from-perfect person with unique preferences, abilities, faults, hopes, and blind spots.

We can engage our hearts in caring for another by accepting and praying for the other's needs and desires, by bringing that person before God in prayer. This needs to be a prayer purely for the benefit of the other, looking at the other through God's own perspective and not from our own. This prayer is not "God, please straighten them out and fix their attitude," but "bless them and help them achieve what they care about so deeply." When we bring a person before God to pray for the real concerns of the heart, it is impossible to withdraw to a depersonalized view of that person afterwards.

When we pray for another freely out of God's love, speaking the words out loud, a miraculous thing happens. The Holy Spirit joins in our prayer, strengthening us and transforming our hearts as we pray. We engage with God in our good wishes and best intentions for the other, and we are changed in the process. Strangely, a similar transformation also happens in the recipient of the prayer. Hearing a sincere expression of good will and appeal to God on our behalf by someone we thought of as an enemy is intensely powerful. How can we not feel gratitude and even the possibility of affection for one who has been willing to step out and support us in our struggles?

There are many materials available to help this kind of prayer experience. Most are categorized as Christian education resources on the topic of intercessory prayer, which combine teaching about prayer with specific exercises and practices. The material used in this particular church was a program called *Prayer Ministry Training*,[2] which included video presentations with an accompanying discussion guide created by Rev. Sandy Millar of Holy Trinity Brompton Church in London, the church in which the Alpha program originated.

The group of people who gathered for this program on prayer included church leaders who were part of each of the factions in the church. Twelve to fifteen people attended the sessions, including most of those who had the strongest feelings in the conflicts. It is likely that the attendance of opposing leaders was motivated in part by mistrust—a concern about what their opponents might be up to if left alone. Whatever their original reason for coming, all of the participants became engaged with the material presented and were willing to engage in the exercises freely.

This particular material included some specific guidelines for prayer practices which turned out to be very helpful. In each exercise, a team of two people would pray for one person, and the groups in prayer would contain either men or women but not both. The result of this dynamic was that each person had the opportunity to pray for and be prayed for by members of the opposing faction. Those offering prayer learned to ask the recipient about needs and concerns, and they learned to listen carefully and check to make sure they understood what was wanted. The program lasted for six meetings, each with prayer opportunities, and it ended with a session of prayer for filling with the Holy Spirit.

The program and practice of prayer was deeply moving and transformative for all the participants. There were tears as "tough guys" who had been in opposition for years heard the loving care in each other's voices. There were times of hard work, as folks stretched to reach into God's perspective despite a long history of wrongs on both sides. In the end participants were able to see and relate to each other as complex and complete human beings and no longer through the lens of the divisive issues. Participants had a chance to experience the good will of each of the others, allies and opponents, and they could no longer fit either into one-dimensional stereotypes.

Building positive appreciation for differences

Jesus also set the example in openness and care for those who are different—and not just in good or unimportant ways. He ate and drank with social outcasts, treating them with respect and friendship. He did not shy away from those whose disease symptoms made them repulsive. He was open to listening to all those who came to him or called out to him for help, and he was open to receiving them as they were. If we are to follow his example, we must learn not to avoid those who are distasteful, irritating, or pig-headed. We must learn to accept their idiosyncrasies, treat them with sincere respect, and be open to appreciating the best that they have to offer in their own way.

The goal is to change our reactions, our habits of mind, from our negative feelings—distrust, dislike, irritability—to positive ones like hope, energy, and enthusiasm. It is fashionable to agree, these days, that diversity is good, or at least that the kind of comfortable diversity that does not challenge our preferences and values is good. We observe that genetic diversity is good for many kinds of populations, from plants to animals and human communities. The challenge for us is to move our intellectual conviction of the value of diversity to the level of our feelings and our automatic reactions. We need to believe, deep down, that living and cooperating with others leads to better results in our common efforts and more fun along the way. If the various parties within a community expect this to be true, if it reflects their experience with each other, they will make it so going forward. To reach this conviction, members of the community need to see and experience the value of differences in action.

The first experience to move the community in this direction is engagement in a dramatized attempt of stereotypical opposites to work together. This simple skit is called "The Special Event Hospitality Committee." Two characters, Oliver Organized and Sally Spontaneous, try to talk about the dinner they are putting on together, and they drive each other crazy. Then the dialogue is played again, with each character sharing thoughts at the same time. The difference is quite a shock, as the audience can hear how hard both are trying to make a successful event, each in his or her own way.

Exposure to this simple exercise of hearing the thoughts behind the "normal" dialogue can be amazingly effective in waking up folks to the possible perspectives behind the unsurprising words. Spontaneous folks suddenly get a glimpse of how hard the more organized one is trying to make things work. People on the organized side suddenly get a picture of the unexpected richness and fun a spontaneous

one can bring into the event. All are surprised to see how the best intentions of each side drove the other side further and further away.
All the right ingredients are present, but the mix goes terribly wrong.
The questions about how things could be done differently becomes
practical and urgent, because the listeners can see how easily we all
fall into the same kind of traps.

The second experience brings home and internalizes the learning
from the first. It happens over time, by intentionally building learning experiences into actually doing the work of the church. It involves
creating teams to work together on specific activities which consist of
two polar opposites—those with different talents, those with different personalities and styles, or those who have been on opposite sides
in conflict.

The activities are chosen to reflect an area that the two participants have in common, for example a concert event for those who
love music, a building project for two craftsmen, a children's program for two teachers. A third participant in each team acts as observer and facilitator, mostly listening, providing the safety of a neu-
tral observer and keeping the others conscious of engaging their differences in a positive way.

In practice, these activity assignments can work out very well.
The initial conversations between team members can be uncomfortable as participants are unsure of their welcome with each other. The
presence of the third party sets a standard of courtesy, and things
seem to smooth out once the work itself becomes the common focus
of attention. With a third party present, both tend to try to live up to
their own best behavior. Watching a shared success grow out of the
contributions of both makes the appreciation of the other's value a reality. Each begins to build an inventory of positive memories from the
shared experience that can be passed on to others. Occasionally a
strong minded person may need to experience more than one of this
kind of joint project experience to get the point, but, as the local culture changes to "this is the way we do things around here," there are
additional models and even peer pressure to demonstrate the bene-
fits of working together.

LIVING WITH THE FACTORS REVERSED

How does it feel to live together after the three factors have been
reversed? We are still sinful people, and we do step on each other's
toes from time to time. We are still different from each other, and we
still compete for time, attention, and resources to do what we believe

is important. What is changed is the way we approach each other, sympathize with each other, and deal with our conflicts.

Our interactions are different, less emotionally charged, less subject to misunderstanding, and more trusting of our processes and of each other. When one church leader was asked how she could stand to work with a former opponent, she said, "He's changed. He acts different now." He understood his position slightly differently. He said, "I haven't really changed. I still think the same things. They just don't upset me so much any more." The reality is that neither had changed in character, convictions, or point of view, but both had changed in the way their perspectives were expressed and in their tolerance for and willingness to work with each other.

As the community gets used to a new way of relating, the expectation in an interaction between people on opposing sides of an issue is that conversation will be characterized by safety, trust, hope, and patience. It is no mistake that the fruits of the Spirit are "love, joy, peace, patience, kindness, generosity, faithfulness, gentleness, and self-control" (Gal. 5:22-23). In practice, brothers and sisters in Christ can expect to experience these traits from their opponents as well as from their supporters on any particular issue.

There is a confidence in members of the group, as they approach a controversial issue, that the outcome will probably be good, even if it is not exactly the result each had advocated at first. There is an expectation that the process may take longer than it should, and that there will be weird moments and unexpected insights along the way. There will often be an undercurrent of humor and laughter at our own and each other's foibles as we go. There may also be occasional intense moments of surprising closeness and unexpected support as we share and respond to each other's deepest values and concerns. There is a sense that, even if the resolution is not "my" solution, it is "our" best shot at a solution in an imperfect world, with fallible human beings, and within the limitations of our situation.

Rewarding visible results of transformation

How do we encourage and reinforce our new behavior patterns? Once we can talk openly about conflict, we can also talk openly about change. We can appreciate and acknowledge change when it has happened, and we can honestly notice when it has not happened. Folks in leadership can explicitly consider the evidence of transformation in those around them, can create experiences to encourage learning for those who need it, and can reward and welcome back those who cross into the new behavior patterns.

The results of transformation are clear and easy to see. People clearly demonstrate that their feelings have changed by getting along together. A period of "doing time" or "paying dues," in which combatants have the opportunity to work with those who used to drive them crazy, is one way to demonstrate that change has actually happened. Some will get the point quickly, and some may need more than one chance to work with an opponent, perhaps with a coach or mentor, to understand what makes the difference.

Because we can talk about conflict and change, we can also talk about improvement. We can appreciate and celebrate the progress we see in each other. Simple feedback, from "you did good" after a tense moment to "you handled that beautifully" after a serious crisis, helps reinforce our new behaviors and remind us that we are all together on the side of Christ.

Letting go of expectations and revenge

We need to be reminded, as an ongoing process, of our need to forgive and to be forgiven. This is an important part of our worship, and it is a part that is often taken for granted or gotten through mechanically. It is critical that we take confession, forgiveness, and the need to forgive others seriously; that we pay attention to it; and that we engage in it regularly. As the opportunity for confession is offered in the context of worship, it must be made real, practical, and personal to our own lives and behaviors. One member of a congregation said, "When you get ready for the prayer of confession, you should give us some examples of things we need to confess, so that we can think about it. It's hard to remember the real things we've done wrong." Real awareness of the ways we have hurt others is critical to appreciating our own forgiveness and passing it on to those who have hurt us.

It is important to stay conscious of the link between being forgiven and forgiving others who have harmed us. The Lord's Prayer reminds us by asking that we would be forgiven as we forgive. It is possible, for example, as people greet each other with peace in worship, to remind them that it is a good time to forgive those they greet for anything that has left a residue of resentment or desire for revenge. It can be a time to remember to forgive those not present, even those who have died, not just for small slights but for major intentional sins that have caused great grief.

The importance of conscious appropriation of forgiveness to let go of the cycle of vengeful violence can not be overestimated. One highly disciplined Sunday school teacher who had trouble with another with a casual, laidback style, said "I kept listening to how you said we had to forgive other people. I decided I just had to forgive her. Now she doesn't bother me so much any more." The two went from hardly being able to work in the same room to actively and warmly supporting each other in complementary aspects of their work. What might have been a continuing feud and constant irritation became, by following the teaching and example of Jesus, the core of a loving and supportive partnership, visible for the whole community to see. It was a transformation worthy of imitation, and led to comments like, "If they can get along like that, then maybe I can do it too."

CONCLUSION

There are a wide variety of ways to reverse each of the factors which enable scapegoating sacrifice. It is up to the leaders and activists in each community to find or develop the ones that will work for their people. The activities described here are examples of one set of patterns which have been effective in a single community. The challenge to each of us as we grow in Christ is to engage the model and teachings of Jesus as they best relate to our own context. The resulting transformation of people and processes is always worth the effort as we grow more and more into the image of Christ.

NOTES

1. S. Mark Heim, *Saved from Sacrifice: A Theology of the Cross* (Grand Rapids, Mich.: Wm. B. Eerdmans, 2006).
2. Available from Alpha USA.

Chapter 12

GOD IN THE HANDS OF ANGRY SINNERS: THE MISDIAGNOSIS OF WRATH AND EPHESIANS 2

David B. Miller

> The God that holds you over the pit of hell, much as one holds a spider, or some loathsome insect, over the fire, abhors you, and is dreadfully provoked; his wrath toward you burns like fire; he looks upon you as worthy of nothing else, but to be cast into the fire; he is of purer eyes than to bear to have you in his sight; you are ten thousand times so abominable in his eyes as the most hateful venomous serpent is in ours.[1]

It was early spring of 1973, in Mrs. Wharton's junior English class, that I first encountered the wrathful fury of God as mediated by Jonathan Edwards' sermon, *Sinners in the Hands of an Angry God.* Long included in the anthologies of American literature, Edwards' sermon has had wide reading in the high school and college classrooms of the United States. This popular reading, in contexts commonly nervous and usually less than nuanced in their conversations about God, has likely done much to shape popular notions of the wrath of God. These notions, often deeply rooted before reading of the biblical text, too easily serve as a lens through which the biblical text is interpreted.

This paper, modest in its scope, attends to a biblical text that has suffered much misreading related to popular notions of the wrath of God. The following paragraphs are an exploration of the charge of misreading and a proposal for an alternate reading that coheres with the internal logic of the text. This alternate reading adds to the growing body of work that is rethinking our understanding of the atonement and the necessity of Christ's death on the cross. The text is from the opening lines of Ephesians 2:

> You were dead through the trespasses and sins in which you once lived, following the course of this world, following the ruler of the power of the air, the spirit that is now at work among those who are disobedient. All of us once lived among them in the passions of our flesh, following the desires of flesh and senses, and we were by nature children of wrath, like everyone else. (Eph. 2:1-3)

My interest in this text—and suspicion of popular commentary on the text—first emerged out of a pastoral encounter with survivors of abuse. These persons had heard this text expounded in tones that echoed Edwards' imagery of the loathsome spider. From pulpits and Sunday school classes they heard of a God whose own violence had seemed to fund and encourage their abuse. They challenged me as a pastor to read the text through their eyes and answer their agony.

I was and remain aware that coming to the text with the provocative and disturbing questions which had been raised by this group of survivors can result in an exercise in eisegesis rather than exegesis. However, it is equally possible that the dominant and enduring reading of a text may be buttressed by eisegetical habits that have long been hidden under the authority of tradition.

The following pages pay particular attention to the phrase "children of wrath" (*tekna phusei orges*) in Ephesians 2:3 and its relationship to the understanding of the atonement in this epistle. This includes a survey of interpretive choices by commentators and translators as well as a proposal for an alternate reading of this phrase. The significance of the concept of *he orge tou theou* is well established in the text and thought of the New Testament writers.[2] However, the central place of this concept in Western substitutionary theories of the atonement[3] may have served to unduly narrow the possible semantic range surrounding *orge*, predisposing interpreters to limit the meaning of the term as found in our text.

A brief survey of contemporary English renderings of Ephesians 2:3 reveals that many modern interpreters have agreed with C. F. D.

Moule's conclusion that the adjectival genitive construction of *tekna phusei orge* is a Semitic idiom, best rendered "people worthy of [wrath].[4] This same position was earlier taken by S. D. F. Salmond, who, however, noted the text's ambiguity as to who is the subject expressing wrath:

> But is it man's wrath or God's? The word is certainly used of the passion of wrath in us (Eph. iv.31; Col. iii.8; Jas. i.19; etc), and so the whole phrase is understood by some to mean nothing more than that those referred to were given to violent anger or ungovernable impulse. But this would add little or nothing to what was said of the lusts of the flesh and thoughts, and would strip the whole statement of its point, its solemnity, and its universality. It is the Divine wrath that is in view here. . . .[5]

The translators of the Jerusalem Bible and the New English Bible attempted to remove this ambiguity by explicitly inserting God as the source of wrath under which humans now stand. The New International Version, while resisting the impulse to supply God (absent in the Greek manuscript), identifies humans as "objects of wrath," thereby locating the source and problem of wrath outside of themselves. Together these translations make wrath a problem external to human beings and locate it either expressly or by implication in God. The New Revised Standard and New American Standard in more wooden fashion maintain the ambiguous phrase "children of wrath" and make no attempt to resolve the difficulty by introducing God into the formula.

Among more recent commentators, the basic approach taken by the former three translations is followed. F. F. Bruce[6] draws a parallel between this construction and the declaration of David in response to the prophet Nathan (2 Sam. 12:5), "the man who has done this is a 'son of death' (Hebrew: *ben mawet*), that is, he deserves to die." For Bruce, the human problem is defined in this passage as existence under the judgment of God. Marcus Barth[7] supplies "God" as the source of wrath in his own translation of the text. Concerned with anti-Semitic overtones in the text, he looks to the prophets (Amos, Hosea, Jeremiah, and Ezekiel) to find examples of "good" Jews speaking so harsh a critique against fellow Jews. He locates Paul in this company—granting permission to Jews to be self-critical. The net emphasis of his discussion is to locate wrath with God.

Leslie Mitton suggests two options as possible readings. One option, in line with those we have noted, is "people worthy of God's wrath."[8] His second option hints at the possibility of an alternate reading, seeing a parallel in the phrase "sons of disobedience" found in verse 2. He writes:

> Children of wrath is another instance of a Hebraic idiom like "sons of disobedience." "Sons of disobedience" means people whose lives are marked by disobedience. So children of wrath means people in whose lives you can see the effect of wrath, that is the punishment that follows sin, the evil consequences of sin. (86-87)

Mitton hints at but hedges away from a different reading that would change the diagnosis of the human problem. Wrath remains external to humanity, a consequence of sin. This reading still requires that wrath be resolved outside of humanity rather than within humanity.

More recently, Tom Yoder Neufeld has provided a far more careful analysis of this passage. His introduction into the discussion of the role of the powers and Miroslav Volf's concept of being colonized by evil is an important contribution and moves toward a change in diagnosis. This introduction of the role of the powers speaks of the need for human deliverance from evil (rather than from God!). However, Yoder Neufeld maintains, in the end, that *children of wrath* "refers not to their own anger, but to God's wrath or judgment."[9]

The above combine to provide a fairly unified though nuanced reading of Ephesians 2:3. However, do the readings and the reasoning do justice to the text of Ephesians? A number of the interpretations build their arguments on intertextual parallels—to the neglect of the intratextual data of Ephesians. This is evident also in Kittel's discussion of *orge*,[10] where the understanding of orge in Ephesians is regulated by Romans 9:22ff. In a similar way, Bruce[11] finds in Romans 5:12 a window through which to understand the meaning of Ephesians 2:3.

The danger in such intertextual search for meaning while not adequately dealing with the internal evidence is that any unique contribution of the Ephesian epistle may be lost under the regulative authority assigned to the epistle to the Romans. Is it possible that orge in Ephesians 2:3 is speaking about a problem significantly different from the use of the term found in Romans or Galatians?

It is noteworthy that among the mentioned commentators, Mitton is the most careful to explore intratextual parallels before turning to other sources to find corollary texts which may illuminate the meaning of Ephesians 2. The result is his recognition of a second interpretive option. However, he does not follow through on the logic of the argument begins. If *uios ths apeitheias* does stand as a parallel to *tekna phusei orge* and Mitton recognizes that the former means "people whose lives are marked by disobedience,"[12] why not continue the logic to identify the latter as those whose lives are marked by (their own) wrath—rather than as "people in whose lives you can see the effect of wrath, that is the punishment that follows sin" (86)? Wrath, rather than being viewed as the punishment of God, is understood as the human problem—a wrath that emerges from within human beings and who give expression to this wrath in violence and hostility.

To be children of wrath, then, rather than carrying a notion of being under judgment, would be understood to be "wrath-filled children." This is consistent with both the structure and concepts Mitton identified in verse 2. Wrath, in this understanding, like disobedience, is a problem resident in humans which needs to be remedied—not a problem in God which needs to be satisfied!

The disobedience (v. 2) is the result of obedience to a foreign (fallen) power.[13] In similar fashion, this wrath (v. 3) is the result of misplaced obedience to *ta thelemata tes sarkos kai ton dianoion* (the desires of the flesh and senses). It is possible that Mitton's not completing the logic of the argument which he began is due to the dominant place that the conceptual framework of a satisfactionary view of the atonement with its emphasis on the themes of wrath and mercy have played in Western thought since the time of Anselm (if not Augustine). The predominant place that this one view has held in the West has tended to blind us to the multiple images of the atonement[14] present in the New Testament and created a setting in which we may well tend to force the texts to conform to our prior theories.

Barth proposes that a similar dominance (hegemony?) has been held by certain works in the Pauline corpus to set normative meanings for the entire collection. However, once the voice of Ephesians is allowed to speak freely a new picture emerges:

> Unlike Rom 1:16; 3:21, in Ephesians the gospel is not explicitly called the revelation of God's righteousness. It is named the "gospel of peace," and Jesus Christ himself is the bringer of the good news, even of peace (2:14, 17; 6:15). Therefore God's' work is not identified with salvation of this or that sinful man who may later join the ranks of those individually justified and sanctified, but with the union of formerly separated and opposed persons—this is their salvation, their life and new being. [15]

Barth goes on to assert that this dominance of Romans and Corinthians in setting the interpretive parameters for the work of

Paul (including those designated deutero-Pauline) has gone on "from Augustine to Luther and Bultmann" (44).

The reading of Ephesians 2:3 proposed above is consistent with the remedy for the human condition as interpreted by the author of this epistle. At this point, the writer introduces a dramatic turn in his argument. In sharp contrast to the parallel assessments of humanity as *sons of disobedience* and *children of wrath,* the writer declares, "But God who is rich in mercy" (2:4). Reminiscent of the prophet Isaiah's declaration, "for my thoughts are not your thoughts, neither are your ways my ways, says the Lord" (Isa. 55:8), Christ's work on the cross is not "becoming sin" (contra 2 Cor. 5:21), but coming among the disobedient, the wrath-filled, the alienated and estranged, and preaching peace (v. 17).

This preaching was not limited to the verbal proclamation of Jesus, but in the logic of this epistle, the cross itself became proclamation. The cross stands as testimony to God's response to human wrath. Christ, on the cross, takes our violence upon himself and, rather than retaliating, bears it. "That he might create in himself one new person in place of the two, so making peace, and might reconcile us both to God in one body through the cross, thereby bringing the hostility to an end" (3:15b-16). Here there is no need for a legal fiction to describe the cross. The remedy matches the need. In this line of argument, wrath is our problem, not God's. It is our alienation and hostility which must be overcome, rather than God's holiness which must be answered. For God has already, always been "rich in mercy" (3:4).

This is only the beginning. Such a remedy means that human relations—especially within the church—can never be merely tangential to salvation. The remedy produces a new person, not a new individual, but a new body with a corporate personality that is given to mirror and make manifest the one it calls its head. Barth again notes that the gospel of this epistle reaches new heights:

> [T]he emphasis placed in Ephesians upon the social character of God's work stands in contrast to the individualism of the alleged existentialist Paul. According to this epistle, God's dealings are with Israel and the nations, with the church and the powers of the world, in short with the whole creation. Instead of going out to save souls, God establishes his rule and kingship over heaven and earth. . . . The much praised peace of the soul looks like a ridiculous mini-achievement beside the peace and order brought to the world. (45)

These are vital and powerful assertions. Church history, at least since the church's change in social location under Constantine, repeatedly demonstrates how easily and often the vision of the universal reign of Christ established through the offering up of Christ's life has been and is twisted into a call to arms to extend the kingdom. This comes in stark contrast to the further logic and declaration of the author of this epistle that the church's struggle is "not against flesh and blood" (6:12). The ways of the kings and nations of the earth are projected upon God and then sacralized as the will of God.

It is precisely in the face of such dangers that the cross as an act of peacemaking, as God's means of going to war with the enemies of God through disarmament, must be studied and embraced. It will not work if the church abandons an ethical framework and vision of what this new person (body) created by the cross looks like in favor of some disembodied notion of salvation and an invisible church.

There is one further word from this epistle which must be considered in connection with this re-reading of Ephesians 2:3. We have explored wrath as the human problem, the cross as God's remedy to that wrath, for what purpose is all of this done? What is the place of the church in light of this?

I have already noted that the human problem was defined both in terms of wrath and obedience to alien (fallen) powers. Thus far we have only considered the former of these definitions. The latter view is highly significant in the world-view of the writer of the epistle to the Ephesians. The epistle opens with a celebration of the work of Christ—the purpose of God in Christ to "unite all things" (1:10) and the realization of that purpose in putting "all things under his feet" (1:22). The effect of Christ's death was not only to unite what had been estranged but also to subdue the alien powers, those cosmic forces aligned in opposition to God. For the writer, this victory is already complete at the cosmic level and in the process of being realized on earth. Those who follow Christ need to have "the eyes of their hearts enlightened" (1:18) to perceive this and live toward and for this reality.

The redemptive work of Christ, which has broken the domination of both the disobedience and the wrath, is not intended to be beneficial only for those who are followers of Christ. The writer offers us a far larger vision—this new body that has been created by Christ's act is to be a witness to "the powers and principalities in the heavenly places" (3:10). The shared life in this new body is to make apparent the manifold wisdom of God. For this act of Christ was able to accomplish what no other power could do, neither the law nor the *Pax*

Romana, to bring together those that were alienated into one body. It is because of this function of the body in witness that the means and methods of being a community cannot be considered secondary matters of what it means to be the people of God.

The chapter began with an eye toward two contexts to which I will now return. The first is the captivity of popular religious imagination to Jonathan Edwards-like depictions of the human condition before God. Edwards' locating of the problem of wrath in God rather than in humanity allows for the easy separation of Christian ethics from soteriology. One may in this model easily claim to have been reconciled to God (i.e., freed from God's wrath), while simultaneously dismissing the commandments of Jesus to love one's enemies. One can claim to be saved by the blood of the lamb while training and preparing to shed the blood of one's fellow human beings. If, however, the cross stands as remedy not to God's wrath but our own, then such separation is untenable. To deny Christ's remedy to our wrath is to deny the saving power of the cross.

The second context that stimulated this rereading of Ephesians 2 began with the questions of survivors for whom the models of the atonement promoted by the church had become meaningless. These models appeared to place God in the corner with the perpetrators of abuse. What happened when we reread the text?

We began to engage in what Stephen Fowl and Gregory Jones[16] have called "reading in communion." It was an exercise in which the church needed to take seriously the voices of those who are outsiders in our midst (113-16). As survivors loaned us their eyes, we more than occasionally gasped in horror at what we now saw. But in seeing anew, together, the cross ceased to be a symbol that funded silence in the face of abuse and instead became a sign of shelter and solidarity and authorization for truth-telling. Much of this healing and increased trust came in narrative form as stories were told, silence was broken, and traditional readings of texts were revised. The God encountered in these readings ceased to be the source of the wrath of the perpetrator and stood instead as the one ready to remedy human wrath.

NOTES

1. Jonathan Edwards [1739], *Sermons and Discourses, 1739-1742* (WJE Online Vol. 22) , ed. Harry S. Stout.

2. Stahlin, *orge* in *Theological Dictionary of the New Testament*, Gerhard Kittel and Gerhard Friedrich, trans. Geoffrey Bromiley (Grand Rapids, Mich.:Wm.

B. Eerdmans, 1968), 435.

3. John Driver, *Understanding the Atonement for the Mission of the Church* (Scottdale, Pa.: Herald Press, 1986), 50ff.

4. C. F. Moule, *An Idiom Book of New Testament Greek,* 2nd. ed. (New York: Cambridge University Press, 1958), 174.

5. S. D. F. Salmond, "The Epistle to the Ephesians" in *The Expositer's Greek New Testament,* trans. Roberstson Nicoll (Grand Rapids, Mich.: Wm. B. Eerdmans, 1967), 286.

6. F. F. Bruce, *The New International Commentary on the New Testament: Epistles to Colossoians, Philemon and Ephesians* (Grand Rapids, Mich.: Wm. B. Eerdmans, 1984), 284.

7. Marcus Barth, *Ephesians 1-3, The Anchor Bible Commentary,* vol. 34, ed. William Foxwell Albright and David N. Freedman (Garden City, N.Y.: Doubleday, 1974), 216.

8. Leslie Mitton, *The New Century Bible Commentary: Ephesians* (Grand Rapids, Mich.: Wm. B. Eerdmans, 1981), 86-87.

9. Thomas R. Yoder Neufeld, *Ephesians, Believers Church Commentary Series* (Scottdale, Pa.: Herald Press, 2001), 94.

10. Stahlin, 425/435.

11. F. F. Bruce, 284-285.

12. Mitton, 86.

13. Note Yoder Neufeld's excellent discussion of the control of an evil power, 92ff.

14. Driver, 244.

15. Barth , 44-45.

16. Fowl, Stephen E. and L. Gregory Jones, *Reading in Communion: Scripture and Ethics in Christian Life* (Grand Rapids, Mich.: Wm. B. Eerdmans, 1991), 19-21.

Chapter 13

MATTHEW'S POSTWAR LAMENT: "WE MADE THE WRONG CHOICE"

Reta Halteman Finger

Enter through the narrow gate; for the gate is wide and the road is easy that leads to destruction, and there are many who take it. For the gate is narrow and the road is hard that leads to life, and there are few who find it.
—Matthew 7:13-14

Between the life of Jesus in the 30s of the first century and the recording of that life in the 70s and 80s lies the Jewish/Roman War of 66-70 CE. Although I'd known that for a long time, it was not until more recently that I realized the impact that war must have had on the telling of Jesus' story.

At an Annual Meeting of the Society of Biblical Literature, I heard Thomas Boomershine and Philip Ruge-Jones perform the trial of Jesus in John in light of that devastating war.[1] It hit me like a bolt out of the blue. Why had I never before seen the Gospels through the lens of that war? This was the war that laid waste the land of Israel, destroyed the religio-political party of the Zealots as well as those of the Essenes and Sadducees, turned Jerusalem into a pit of starving cannibals under Roman siege, and left the sacred temple with not one stone on top of another.[2]

From the Jewish perspective, this war did not work. The Zealot belief that Yahweh God would fight with the Jews against Rome was crushed. If these people were still "the Chosen," God had not chosen to fight for them. Indeed, God had not done so for a very long time.[3] The glorious "wide gate and easy road" of war had led to destruction. Out of the ashes and bitter suffering of this time, both the Jesus-Jews and the other remaining Jews agreed that war and violence was apparently not what God had in mind. Each group, in its own way, began or continued the task of seeking the narrow gate and the hard road that leads to life.[4]

What I'd like to do here is use the insight from this war-that-did-not-work to highlight a few things from the Gospels that show us how the authors portray Jesus as a Messiah with a political and theological agenda *counter* to that of violence, war, and conquest.

Although we could examine any of the Gospels through this lens of the Jewish-Roman War, I'll be mostly focusing on Matthew with a few references from John. I chose Matthew for a couple reasons. First, it is generally agreed that Matthew is the most Jewish of all the Gospels and directed toward a Jewish Christian audience living in or near Palestine.

Second, unlike Luke, who chronologically separates the story of Jesus from the story of the early church, Matthew combines them. Matthew is often anachronistic, as when Jesus uses the word *ekklesia*, or "church," before the actual church existed. Matthew often references the Hebrew Bible out of context to highlight how Jesus fulfills Scripture. In this way, Matthew merges three different historical levels. As we become aware of these tensions or rough edges, it is easier to see ways in which the later church, through the Spirit and their terrible experience of war, gained insights into the life and teachings of Jesus that may not have been as obvious during his lifetime.

A UBIQUITOUS EMPIRE

But first we need to understand something of the political and cultural setting of first-century Palestine. This setting is not merely a backdrop. Just as present-day Iraqis cannot escape the ubiquitous presence of American occupation, so Palestinian Jews were kept under the thumb of Roman occupation. Empire was everywhere:

- from the wealth of Caesarea with its temples and huge theater;
- to toll booths where you had to pay each time you used the road to carry your produce to market;
- to a tax on every fish you caught in the Lake of Galilee;
- to the towers overlooking the sacred temple mount;

- to the olive trees that lined the roads and all too often held crucified insurgents nailed to their crossbars as an advertisement of Rome's power—and a warning to submit to it.

As the greatest empire the world had ever seen, Rome's gods were more powerful than any others. Rome's first emperor had been hailed as the Savior of the world, the great Benefactor of all peoples, the one who brings peace to the world. This mythology continued for centuries.

Rome was usually content to rule through client-kings and through the elite classes of a city or region it had taken over. Herod the Great was one such client-king, maintaining his status by building great Roman cities like Caesarea and naming it after Caesar. In first-century Palestine there was a delicate balancing act between the Roman governer (Pilate during the 30s), a Herodian king or tetrarch, and the upper-class chief priests who ran the temple system.

With no middle class as we understand it today, that left over ninety percent of the people living pretty much at or below subsistence level. It was in the interests of the Romans, the client-kings, and the priestly caste to tax the people so they could just barely get by on what was left of grain and olives, grapes, and fish after they handed over the bulk of it to the owners of the estates they worked. By this time, most of the arable land was in the hands of one to three percent of the upper classes, so most had become sharecroppers on land that had been their ancestral heritage. Taxes must be paid regardless of poor harvest years, so hunger and malnutrition stalked the peasants and made them more susceptible to plagues and many other illnesses that came along.

This brief summary of political and social realities is probably familiar to many. In the last thirty or forty years, huge advances have been made in understanding the cultural context of Jesus and the early church through the use of sociology, anthropology, economics, archeology, political analysis, historiography, and so on.[5] But few laypeople in our churches know that, and even fewer know how to integrate this material into their biblical interpretation and theology.

With no wars on our soil, most church people hold to a personal and individual faith separate from politics except for those on the Religious Right or Christian Zionists who mix religion and politics in quite a different way. For most of the rest, and for many of my students, Jesus was a peaceful, gentle shepherd who died on the cross because God wanted Jesus to thus save everyone who believes in him from their sins and from hell (an exaggeration, but holding some truth).

JESUS' ALTERNATIVE VISION

We now turn to Matthew's Gospel. The cultural situation I've explained above is usually only obliquely referred to in the narrative simply because Matthew's audience understood the context. They were living it. *How does this writer portray a Jesus who sets forth an alternative political vision to that of Rome's? What kind of empire* (basilaea *in Greek) does Jesus announce?*

We will look at selected passages briefly, but I hope it will whet your appetite to use this political lens and dig further into the wealth of texts that show how integral peacemaking and nonviolence are to the gospel of Jesus.

> An account of the genealogy of Jesus the Messiah, the son of David, the son of Abraham. Abraham was the father of Isaac, and Isaac the father of Jacob, and Jacob the father of Judah and his brothers, and Judah the father of Perez and Zerah by Tamar. . . .
>
> Obed the father of Jesse, and Jesse the father of King David. And David was the father of Solomon by the wife of Uriah, and Solomon the father of Rehoboam, and Rehoboam the father of Abijah. . . .
>
> So all the generations from Abraham to David are fourteen generations; and from David to the deportation to Babylon, fourteen generations; and from the deportation to Babylon to the Messiah, fourteen generations. (Matt. 1:1-3, 5-7, 17)

Matthew begins his narrative with a genealogy of the Messiah that in capsule form tells much of Israel's story. From the first sentence, Matthew announces that God's will and purpose pass through Israel, not Rome. Rome is not even mentioned.[6] Rather, this king will be from the royal line of David. Perhaps Israel's fortunes are changing.

> An angel of the Lord appeared to Joseph in a dream and said, " . . . do not be afraid to take Mary as your wife, for the child conceived in her is from the Holy Spirit. She will bear a son, and you are to name him Jesus, for he will save his people from their sins." All this took place to fulfill what had been spoken by the Lord through the prophet: "Look, the virgin shall conceive and bear a son, and they shall name him 'Emmanuel,' which means, 'God is with us.'" (Matt. 1:20-23)

The angel brings good news to Joseph that his betrothed, Mary, will bear a son whose name will be Emmanuel, "God with us." Perhaps at last God has sent someone to deliver them from Rome and

Rome's client-king Herod. He shall also be named Jesus, which means "God saves," for "he will save his people from their sins" (1:21).

In his book *Matthew and Empire*, Warren Carter asks, what sins are we talking about? Rather than the personal, individual sins we usually assume, Carter says, look at the context.[7] The genealogy is loaded with wicked kings and the sins of fathers handed on to sons. To look only at the heroes of Abraham, David, and Solomon, we find deception, racism, adultery, oppression, and murder. Name any of the ten commandments and all of them are flouted many times throughout this list. The man to be named "God saves" will save his people from their sins. Here salvation is corporate, not just individual.

> In the time of King Herod, after Jesus was born in Bethlehem of Judea, astrologers from the East came to Jerusalem, asking, "Where is the child who has been born king of the Jews? For we observed his star at its rising, and have come to pay him homage." . . .
>
> . . . . And having been warned in a dream not to return to Herod, they left for their own country by another road. (Matt. 2:1-2, 12)

By the second chapter, we meet naïve astrologers (some call them *wise* men!) who play directly into the hands of King Herod the Great. "We've come to honor the child born king of the Jews." But already the might of Rome's client-king comes down hard on any threat to his throne. The infant king escapes, but all the rest of the babies in his town are murdered.

> Joseph got up, took the child and his mother by night, and went to Egypt, and remained there until the death of Herod. . . .
>
> When Herod saw that he had been tricked by the wise men, he was infuriated, and he sent and killed all the children in and around Bethlehem who were two years old or under. . . . (Matt. 2:14-15a, 16)
>
> When Herod died, an angel of the Lord suddenly appeared in a dream to Joseph in Egypt and said, "Get up, take the child and his mother, and go to the land of Israel, for those who were seeking the child's life are dead." Then Joseph got up, took the child and his mother, and went to the land of Israel. But when he heard that Archelaus was ruling over Judea in place of his father Herod, he was afraid to go there. And after being warned in a dream, he went away to the district of Galilee. There he made his home in a town called Nazareth. . . . (Matt. 2:19-23)

After Herod dies, perhaps it is now safe to return to Judea. But Herod's son Archelaus rules in his place, so Joseph takes his family and moves to Galilee. The text does not tell us when or how Jesus found out about the massacre of the children in Bethlehem for his sake,[8] but it surely must have aroused a deep hatred, perhaps guilt, and a desire for revenge against such wanton cruelty.

> In those days John the Baptist appeared in the wilderness of Judea, proclaiming, "Repent, for the kingdom of heaven has come near." This is the one of whom the prophet Isaiah spoke. . . .
>
> "I baptize you with water for repentance, but one who is more powerful than I is coming after me. . . . He will baptize you with the Holy Spirit and fire. His winnowing-fork is in his hand, and he will clear his threshing-floor and will gather his wheat into the granary; but the chaff he will burn with unquenchable fire." (Matt. 3:1-3a, 11-12)

In chapter 3, John the Baptist next arrives on the scene, present-ing another threat to those holding political power. He looks all too much like the ancient prophets of centuries past who meddled so an-noyingly into political leadership. "Repent!" he shouts. "The end of this age and of your power has come. Someone greater than I is just around the corner—and boy, is he going to screw you!"

> Then Jesus came from Galilee to John at the Jordan, to be bap-tized by him. John would have prevented him, saying, "I need to be baptized by you, and do you come to me?" But Jesus an-swered him, "Let it be so now; for it is proper for us in this way to fulfill all righteousness." Then he consented.
>
> And when Jesus had been baptized, just as he came up from the water, suddenly the heavens were opened to him and he saw the Spirit of God descending like a dove and alighting on him. And a voice from heaven said, "This is my Son, the Beloved, with whom I am well pleased." (Matt. 3:13-17)

But when Jesus does show up, he surprises John by asking to be baptized, even though John's baptism is one of repentance. Never-theless, at that moment the Spirit descends on him and a voice tells him he is God's son. Did Jesus wonder what that meant? What kind of son of God would he be? Caesar is called a son of God; will he chal-lenge Caesar himself, or just the Herod dynasty?

> Then Jesus was led up by the Spirit into the wilderness to be tempted by the devil. He fasted for forty days and forty nights,

and afterwards he was famished. The tempter came and said to him, "If you are the Son of God, command these stones to become loaves of bread." (Matt. 4:1-3)

It doesn't take more than forty days in the desert with no food to figure out a few things. We often look at the three temptations as sort of an initiation ritual, some hoops Jesus has to jump through to make sure he can quote Scripture before he gets started preaching it to others.

But nothing could be farther from the truth. These are real temptations, and all three of them deal with political power. The devil knows how to catch him: "*If* you are the son of God, do this and this and this." As king, will you be able to feed your people? How will you demonstrate your superior power over the temple priests who regulate Israel's religious/economic system?

Again, the devil took him to a very high mountain and showed him all the kingdoms of the world and their splendor; and he said to him, "All these I will give you, if you will fall down and worship me."

Jesus said to him, "Away with you, Satan! for it is written, 'Worship the Lord your God, and serve only him.'" (Matt. 4:8-10)

But it's the temptation that Matthew puts in the third and climactic place that shows us most clearly Jesus' choice to renounce violence. The devil offers Jesus all the kingdoms of the world. "You can be the new emperor! You can challenge and conquer Rome and Rome's emperor! You just have to do it my way."

But Jesus understands that this deal with the devil implies violent conquest. You do not become emperor of the world without crushing any who would challenge you. "Yet perhaps the end would justify the means. Think of the good I could do once I got to the top. . . ."

Jesus cannot help but think of Judas Maccabeus leading a successful revolt against the Syrian prince 200 years earlier. Judas secured independence for his people which lasted a hundred years! Surely Jesus Emmanuel can do better than that! This could be really exciting!

We do not know how long Jesus struggled with the temptation of the myth of redemptive violence. Perhaps it was the story of the slaughter of the infants that so revolted him he renounced all violence. But in the end he realizes that the devil can make this offer only because all the kingdoms of the world belong to him. None of them survive and conquer without deception and cruelty and rape and torture and murder that come from the Evil One. Jesus now knows enough about the nature of God that to worship him is to serve him without violence.

POLITICS WITHOUT VIOLENCE?

But this hardly means Jesus is renouncing politics. Far from it! He could not escape if he tried. The next sentence is politically loaded: "Now when Jesus heard that John had been arrested, he withdrew to Galilee" (Matt. 4:12).

John has been arrested. "You stick out your neck; you speak truth to power; you act like a prophet—and there goes your freedom." One of the Herods is at it again, and of course we will find out later that John will lose his head for his outspoken tongue. No wonder Jesus clears out of Judea and heads for the safer region of Galilee. "He left Nazareth and made his home in Capernaum by the lake.... From that time Jesus began to proclaim, 'Repent, for the kingdom of heaven has come near'"[9] (Matt. 4:13, 17).

And it is here, in a little fishing village called Capernaum, that he introduces a different agenda: "God's empire is at hand. And you gotta repent because it's so radically different, it won't fit into your old way of life."

How is it different? Well, first Jesus has to do what any king would do—start raising a militia.

> As he walked by the Sea of Galilee, he saw two brothers, Simon, who is called Peter, and Andrew his brother, casting a net into the lake—for they were fishermen. And he said to them, "Follow me, and I will make you fish for people."
>
> Immediately they left their nets and followed him. As he went from there, he saw two other brothers, James son of Zebedee and his brother John, in the boat with their father Zebedee, mending their nets, and he called them. Immediately they left the boat and their father, and followed him. (Matt. 4:18-22)

So he goes down to the lake (rather than the caves of upper Galilee where the revolutionaries hang out), finds a few fishermen, and promises them a better career if they help him fish for people! So far, not much of an army . . . we'll see what happens in boot camp!

Later, in 10:1-4, Jesus will name twelve of them to symbolize the restoration of the twelve tribes of Israel. This is a deliberate political act of resistance against Rome, as well as a challenge to the Jerusalem elites who reject Samaritans as pagans and tax-collectors as impure traitors, and who treat Galilean peasants as country hicks.

> These are the names of the twelve apostles: first, Simon, also known as Peter, and his brother Andrew; James son of Zebedee, and his brother John; Philip and Bartholomew; Thomas and Matthew the tax-collector; James son of Alphaeus, and Thaddaeus; Simon the Cananaean, and Judas Iscariot, the one who betrayed him.

The next political act of Jesus is one to which we can well relate in our own American Empire. Jesus addresses the terrible health problems of the people, much of it brought on by the oppression of loss of land and high taxes.

> Jesus went throughout Galilee, teaching in their synagogues and proclaiming the good news of the kingdom and curing every disease and every sickness among the people. So his fame spread throughout all Syria, and they brought to him all the sick, those who were afflicted with various diseases and pains, demoniacs, epileptics, and paralytics, and he cured them. And great crowds followed him from Galilee, the Decapolis, Jerusalem, Judea, and from beyond the Jordan. (Luke 4:23-25)

Instead, with a single payer health insurance plan, Jesus "cures every disease and every sickness among the people, so that his fame spreads even throughout Syria."

> That evening they brought to him many who were possessed by demons; and he cast out the spirits with a word, and cured all who were sick. This was to fulfill what had been spoken through the prophet Isaiah, "He took our infirmities and bore our diseases."

The theme of physical healing is one we see throughout this Gospel, so that Matthew in 8:16-17 can identify Jesus with the Servant of Isaiah 53 who "took our infirmities and bore our diseases." In this way Jesus also undercuts the control of the temple system where priests alone were allowed to declare people well or sick, pure or impure, and thus who could enter the sacred temple for the forgiveness of sins.

What follows is the Sermon on the Mount, which can just as well be called the political platform of the One announcing the coming of God's empire. Among other exceedingly high standards of integrity and justice, Jesus includes non-retaliation of evil doers and loving one's enemies.

> "You have heard that it was said, 'An eye for an eye and a tooth for a tooth.' But I say to you, Do not resist an evildoer. But if anyone strikes you on the right cheek, turn the other also. . . .
>
> "You have heard that it was said, "You shall love your neighbor and hate your enemy." But I say to you, Love your enemies and pray for those who persecute you, so that you may be children of your Father in heaven. (Matt. 5:38-39, 43-45)

Let me now bring in a bit of literary analysis. The structure of this Gospel is one of alternating and interlocking sections of narrative material with speeches all the way through.

Narrative-Speech-N-S-N-S-N-S-N-S-N—with interlocking themes:
Speech 1—the words of Jesus—Matthew 5-7
Narrative 2—the works of Jesus—Matthew 8-9

This first speech section of the words of Jesus is followed by stories of the works of Jesus. How does he live out what he preaches? Chapters 8 and 9 are packed with the mighty deeds of Jesus for the sake of poor, downtrodden peasants, but I was especially struck by the second story in 8:5-13:

> When he entered Capernaum, a centurion came to him, appealing to him and saying, "Lord, my servant is lying at home paralyzed, in terrible distress." And he said to him, "I will come and cure him." . . .
>
> And to the centurion Jesus said, "Go; let it be done for you according to your faith." And the servant was healed in that hour.

Here Jesus heals the servant of a Roman centurion, a representative of the despised occupying enemy. Jesus puts into practice his own command to love the enemy. And because this Roman soldier lowered himself to ask one of the natives for help, Jesus even compliments him for his faith!

In chapter 10, the second speech section, the disciples are sent out on a mission:

> These twelve Jesus sent out with the following instructions: "Go . . . to the lost sheep of the house of Israel. As you go, proclaim the good news, 'The kingdom of heaven has come near.' Cure the sick, raise the dead, cleanse the lepers, cast out demons. . . . Take no gold, or silver, or copper in your belts, no bag for your journey, or two tunics, or sandals, or a staff; for la-

borers deserve their food. Whatever town or village you enter, find out who in it is worthy, and stay there until you leave. . . . See, I am sending you out like sheep into the midst of wolves; so be wise as serpents and innocent as doves." (Matt. 10:5-11,16)

This is not exactly the surge swarming over Baghdad and knocking down doors to search houses in the middle of the night. Nor is it a secret operation of the Marine Special Forces or the CIA. Instead, these people have been in Jesus' "boot camp" long enough to observe what he's been doing, and now they are supposed to do the same things: heal people and exorcize demons. Compared to the seventy-pound packs a Roman soldier carried in that day, or a contemporary one in ours, Jesus' "army" wears no shoes and carries nothing, not even a change of clothing or a copper penny. But even so, by their very solidarity with the people to whom they are sent, they are a threat to the powerful. They are going out as "sheep amid wolves."

Before we move to the end of Jesus' life, I will briefly call attention to only a few other ways that God's empire introduced by Jesus contrasts with Rome's Empire. A pericope included in all four Gospels is the feeding of over five thousand people.

> When it was evening, the disciples came to him and said, "This is a deserted place, and the hour is now late; send the crowds away so that they may go into the villages and buy food for themselves."
>
> Jesus said to them, "They need not go away; you give them something to eat." They replied, "We have nothing here but five loaves and two fish." He said, "Bring them here to me." Then he ordered the crowds to sit down on the grass.
>
> Taking the five loaves and the two fish, he looked up to heaven, and blessed and broke the loaves, and gave them to the disciples, and the disciples gave them to the crowds.
>
> And all ate and were filled; and they took up what was left over of the broken pieces, twelve baskets full. And those who ate were about five thousand men, besides women and children. (Matt. 14:13-21)

The political implications are enormous. If a king can feed his people in a world where there is perpetual uncertainty about harvests and never enough food, they will submit to no other sovereign. John's account makes this especially clear in 6:15:

> So they gathered them up, and from the fragments of the five barley loaves, left by those who had eaten, they filled twelve baskets. When the people saw the sign that he had done, they

began to say, "This is indeed the prophet who is to come into the
world."

When Jesus realized that they were about to come and take
him by force to make him king, he withdrew again to the mountain by himself.

Here again Jesus confronts Satan's first temptation, to turn stones
into bread for political power and fame. But John makes clear that
Jesus renounces that by withdrawing from the crowds. This reticent
behavior is quite consistent with Jesus' response to his disciples in
Matthew 20:20-28 who hope for honor and power in Jesus' empire.
But it will be very different from Rome's.

Jesus called them to him and said, "You know that the rulers of
the Gentiles lord it over them, and their great ones are tyrants
over them. It will not be so among you; but whoever wishes to
be great among you must be your servant, and whoever wishes
to be first among you must be your slave; just as the Son of man
came not to be served but to serve."

In God's empire, to be great is to be a servant; to be first you must
be a slave. Tyrants need not apply.

SNATCHING DEFEAT
FROM THE JAWS OF VICTORY

As we come to the last week of Jesus' life in Jerusalem, let's take
stock of several main character groups who drive this plot to its
penultimate conclusion. In addition to Rome's military occupation in
league with puppet rulers and elite temple priests, we have Jesus'
disciples and the crowds that follow him constantly.

"The crowds" are the lower classes, those living at or below subsistence, who see their only hope in what this new compassionate
"lord" has to offer. Jesus has not appealed to the upper classes and to
the Roman overlords. There is no record that he has even entered the
Galilean Roman cities of Caesarea, Tiberias, or Sepphoris. Instead, he
has promoted solidarity and community, healing and hope, among
the villages of the poor.

By and large, these people—the disciples and the many huge
crowds—are presented sympathetically in the narrative. Without
doubt, they are the characters with whom Matthew's audience identifies as they listen to the reading of this Gospel. They are the characters who have made Jesus enormously popular in Galilee. Now it is
Passover time, and the people come along with Jesus up to Jerusalem.

The disciples went and did as Jesus had directed them; they brought the donkey and the colt, and put their cloaks on them, and he sat on them.

A very large crowd spread their cloaks on the road, and others cut branches from the trees and spread them on the road. The crowds that went ahead of him and that followed were shouting, "Hosanna to the Son of David! Blessed is the one who comes in the name of the Lord!"

When he entered Jerusalem, the whole city was in turmoil, asking, "Who is this?" (Matt. 21:6-10)

Here the plot thickens, as the crowds are large and bold enough to copy the Roman pattern of a victory march of an emperor coming into his capital city to wild acclaim. As a group, they hail Jesus as the son of David who comes in the name of Yahweh! This creates an uproar in Jerusalem, only further exacerbated by Jesus' outrageous behavior in the temple (21:12-14). The synoptic Gospels see these symbolic actions as the catalysts which bring about Jesus' execution. Today we might call it nonviolent resistance.

Then Jesus entered the temple and drove out all who were selling and buying in the temple, and he overturned the tables of the money-changers and the seats of those who sold doves. He said to them, "It is written, 'My house shall be called a house of prayer'; but you are making it a den of robbers."

The blind and the lame came to him in the temple, and he cured them.

As we know, the empire and its regional puppet rulers will not put up with a threat to their power, so Jesus will be arrested, tried, and crucified. In Matthew 26:36-46, we find the most agonizing struggle in Gethsemane of all the Synoptics.

Then Jesus went with them to a place called Gethsemane. . . . He took with him Peter and the two sons of Zebedee, and began to be grieved and agitated. Then he said to them, "I am deeply grieved, even to death; remain here, and stay awake with me."

And going a little farther, he threw himself on the ground and prayed, "My Father, if it is possible, let this cup pass from me. . . ." [This happens three times.]

Jesus is clearly reliving his third temptation to be the world's emperor. But by the time he is arrested, he must have once again renounced violence, for he tells his audience to put away their swords.

Suddenly, one of those with Jesus put his hand on his sword, drew it, and struck the slave of the high priest, cutting off his ear. Then Jesus said to him, "Put your sword back into its place; for all who take the sword will perish by the sword. Do you think that I cannot appeal to my Father, and he will at once send me more than twelve legions of angels?" (Matt. 26:51-53)

It's not that he couldn't fight back. He has the option of instant mobilization of twelve legions of angels—"legion" being a Roman word referring to a cohort of 6000 soldiers. Seventy-two thousand angels is quite an impressive way to begin taking over the world. But in the long run it would have been a deal with the devil, since horrendous violence would have been used to justify the ends. The use of swords leads to death by the sword (26:52). Jesus rejects that approach, and in the short run he becomes the victim rather than the victor.

SWITCHING SIDES AT JESUS' TRIAL

Now I want to spend more time on the trial of Jesus as it is recorded in Matthew 27:1-2 and 15-26. The trial is set in motion through a conspiracy among the chief priests and elders—Jewish elites who condemn Jesus and *hand him over* to Pilate—and it ends with Pilate flogging Jesus and *handing him over* to be crucified.

When morning came, all the chief priests and the elders of the people conferred together against Jesus to bring about his death. They bound him, led him away, and handed him over to Pilate the governor. (Matt. 27:1-2)

and

After flogging Jesus, [Pilate] handed him over to be crucified. (Matt. 27:26)

Besides the prisoner Jesus, we have three sets of actors in this text, all of which have been part of Matthew's narrative throughout. Looming over everything that happens in Palestine is Rome, here represented by the governor Pilate and his support staff. Pilate's main concern is to maintain Roman hegemony and peace by squelching any political resistance or mob riots.

We also have the temple system, the wealthy elites through whom Rome exercises much control over the ordinary people. These elites are hypocrites par excellence, because as religious leaders their role is to represent God to the people and the people to God. Instead, their first allegiance is to Rome. This is nakedly demonstrated in John 18:15 when at the end of the trial, they reassure Pilate, "We have no king but the emperor"!

Matthew clarifies in 27:18 that their interest in handing Jesus over to Roman justice is jealousy of Jesus' charismatic leadership among the people. Pilate knows this and is not afraid to manipulate it for his own interests.

The third character in this drama is "the crowd"—the non-elite, lower-class people whose only political strength is in their numbers. Throughout the narrative, the crowds have been on Jesus' side. They have made him immensely popular. And he has inspired in them the hope of a better life, with adequate food and health care. To them, Jesus has literally become Emmanuel.

> Now Jesus stood before the governor; and the governor asked him, "Are you the King of the Jews?" Jesus said, "You say so." But when he was accused by the chief priests and elders, he did not answer. Then Pilate said to him, "Do you not hear how many accusations they make against you?" But he gave him no answer, not even to a single charge, so that the governor was greatly amazed. (Matt. 27:11-14)

Pilate begins by interrogating the prisoner to find out whether he sees himself as a populist liberator—a king trying to compete against the client-kings Rome has permitted. But Jesus won't cooperate, so he tries another tactic. Appealing to a custom of releasing a prisoner at Passover, Pilate gives the crowd a choice between releasing "Jesus Barrabas or Jesus who is called the Messiah" (15-17).

> Now at the festival the governor was accustomed to release a prisoner for the crowd, anyone whom they wanted. At that time they had a notorious prisoner, called Jesus Barabbas. So after they had gathered, Pilate said to them, "Whom do you want me to release for you, Jesus Barabbas or Jesus who is called the Messiah?" (Matt 27:15-17)

Both are political prisoners perceived as a threat to Rome's hegemony. Matthew calls Barabbas "notorious," which is the same word Josephus uses to describe the violent Zealot John of Gischala.[10]

In the Fourth Gospel Barabbas is called a *lestes* (Greek, 18:40), a term Josephus uses as a code name for the Zealots.[11] This warrior assumes that God wants Jews to violently resist Rome's occupation of their holy land. The names of both prisoners mean "God saves."

Barabbas literally means "son of the father," and the other Jesus has been named "son of God" at his baptism. Whom will the people choose?

Because they need public support, the chief priests and elders then do a massive con job on the crowd. Verse 20: They "persuade the crowds to ask for Barabbas and to have Jesus killed." With more time, we might reflect on how they managed to do that without attack commercials on TV and the Internet. Nevertheless, when you have the role of mediating God and God's forgiveness to religious people through the sacrificial and legal system which you control, you've got a heck of a lot of power. Just as many ordinary people in our country today vote against their own interests through clever advertising, so this crowd capitulates as well.

> The governor again said to them, "Which of the two do you want me to release for you?" And they said, "Barabbas." Pilate said to them, "Then what should I do with Jesus who is called the Messiah?" All of them said, "Let him be crucified!" Then he asked, "Why, what evil has he done?" But they shouted all the more, "Let him be crucified!"

Pilate eggs them on in verses 21–23, not because he wants to protect Jesus, but because he wants to gauge the level of popular support for him. If the support evaporates, Pilate can execute Jesus with impunity, whether or not he is guilty of insurrection. Verse 23: "they shouted all the more, 'Let him be crucified!'" It is clear to Pilate that Jesus has been publicly rejected.

Though Matthew implicates both the crowd and their leaders, the Roman governor does not come off any better.

> While [Pilate] was sitting on the judgment seat, his wife sent word to him, "Have nothing to do with that righteous man, for today I have suffered a great deal because of a dream about him." (v. 19)
>> So when Pilate saw that he could do nothing, but rather that a riot was beginning, he took some water and washed his hands before the crowd, saying, "I am innocent of this man's blood; see to it yourselves." (Matthew 27:24)

In verse 19, Pilate's wife pleads with him to have nothing to do with this righteous man. Perhaps in deference to her, in verse 24 Pilate publicly washes his hands and declares he is innocent of this man's blood. But that is an utter sham and hypocrisy, for in verse 26 he flogs Jesus and hands him over to be crucified.

Philip Ruge-Jones argues that, by the standards of integrity and honesty and transparency promoted in this Gospel, Pilate royally flunks. His hypocrisy matches that of the religious leaders. Ruge-Jones asserts:

> Pilate pays attention to incidentals and neglects justice.
> He washes his outside appearance but inside is filthy.
> He presents himself as seeking peace while holding to destruction.
> He says one thing and does the opposite.[12]

The conclusion drawn by all four Gospel authors who narrate the story of Jesus through their postwar lens is that all three actors in this drama made choices for violence—and all were wrong. Both the crowds and their leaders made the wrong choice of calling for the release of the violent insurrectionist—the terrorist, if you will—and the execution of the nonviolent prisoner.

By showing the behavior of the crowd, Matthew includes himself and his audience in a lament. "We were wrong; we are all implicated. We chose the wide gate and the easy road, and it has led to destruction. War does not work. Those who take up the sword die by the sword. Now we understand in a way we could not before, what Jesus was teaching and living out in our midst."

Then all four evangelists proceed to tell, as I have briefly shown in Matthew's Gospel, how Jesus as Son of God and Messiah renounces violence and demonstrates a radically alternative lifestyle. Through Jesus, God is showing us that never again will God fight violently on the side of any people or state. Instead, the risen Jesus' last words in this Gospel tell his disciples to make more disciples of all nations. Do not force them; do not kill them. Baptize them and teach them to obey what Jesus has taught and lived—the alternative, embracing, nonviolent ethic of God's empire.

PREACHING PEACE TODAY

I will conclude with several hermeneutical observations and suggestions for "preaching peace" in churches today. First, I believe that laypeople are more able to understand historical and cultural contexts of biblical texts than they are given credit for. We have lived so long with an individualist, personalist reading of texts that we need a new paradigm for preaching them in their original contexts. Plus, so much more is known today about ancient Greco-Roman culture than was known even one or two generations ago. This needs to trickle—rather, flow!—down to the pew.

This includes placing New Testament texts in their political settings within the imperial, hierarchical Roman Empire, as I have tried to show here. Many of these writings are documents of resistance against the values of the empire. Although the "Preaching Peace" website cautions preachers not to bring politics directly into sermons, it seems to me that if we can portray the political situation in Jesus' life, we can make careful parallels to current events.

For example, governments do not usually rush to war without the support of the majority of the people. The first Gulf War, the rapid attack on Afghanistan after 9-11, and the preemptive attack on Iraq were supported by the majority of polled Americans in highly charged emotional and political atmospheres. The crowds' response to the trial of Jesus could be a very appropriate text to use at such a time.

Other examples are imitating Jesus' methods of mobilizing people: sharing food together, accepting "unchurch-y" people into one's home and social life, working for more comprehensive health care. Jesus' sending out of his disciples to do what he was doing and to depend on householders for their support has parallels to community organizing efforts today—which is also political just as Jesus' program was. It was working "from below" rather than using a top-down approach.

Second, I believe that laypeople are more able to understand the literary contexts of biblical texts than they are given credit for. Because we often use the lectionary, with its snippets of texts taken from different genres in the Bible, we rarely see how these documents work as wholes. Here, I have tried to show how Matthew in particular shapes his entire narrative to present Jesus teaching and living nonviolence in the face of the often-brutal military occupation of the Roman imperium. Each Gospel has its own plot, which carries that author's theological emphasis. We overlook that entire theology when we don't see the Gospels as whole narratives.

Instead, what I hear from students who defend Jesus as a warrior are texts like Matthew 10:34, which even in its immediate literary context cannot support war, and the two-swords text in Luke 22:35-38.

> "Do not think that I have come to bring peace to the earth; I have not come to bring peace, but a sword. For I have come to set a man against his father, and a daughter against her mother, and a daughter-in-law against her mother-in-law and one's foes will be members of one's own household." (Matt. 10:34-36)

"... the one who has no sword must sell his cloak and buy one. For I tell you, this Scripture must be fulfilled in me, 'And he was counted among the lawless'; and indeed what is written about me is being fulfilled." They said, "Lord, look, here are two swords." He replied, "It is enough." (Luke 22:36-38)

In addition, because a few Roman centurions of the occupation are sympathetic to the Jews (as in Matt. 8 and Cornelius in Acts 10), some students presume Jesus approves of the Roman occupation as helpful and benign rather than representing the enemy one is called to love. These misconceptions must be dealt with in church and academy.

Even among the Historic Peace Churches today, our continuing cultural assimilation is leading to a lessening of commitment to nonviolence. In 2006 Conrad Kanagy, working from the Young Center in Elizabethtown College, surveyed Mennonite Church USA to find not only that the denomination is losing membership but also that members are more open to national security protected by violence.[13] In 1972, 81 percent of Mennonite said that, faced with a military draft, they would choose alternate service as a conscientious objector; by 2006 that number had dropped to 65 percent. Over half (56 percent) believe "it is all right for Christians to be in noncombatant services in the armed forces." It may say something about our schizophrenia to note that, although 93 percent believe that "peacemaking is a central theme of the gospel," 48 percent believe America is a Christian nation, and 25 percent support the war in Iraq (or did in 2006). Forty-two percent believe that "'the war on terror' is a religious battle"—in other words, a righteous struggle against evil.

Many parallels can be drawn between the ancient Roman Empire and our American Empire today. Though the devil will never realistically offer any of us the opportunity to become emperor of the whole world, the temptation to give our full allegiance to the United States of America as God's instrument for bringing righteousness and peace to the world is a lie we must resist. If God did not fight for his "chosen people" in the first century, God will not fight for America against those we perceive to be our enemies. There is a narrow gate which we must enter to find the alternative reign of God as exemplified in Jesus' life. The road is hard, but it is the only one that leads to life. We should be grateful to Christians and organizations committed to doing something about our confused thinking and contradictory values by inviting us through the narrow gate and onto the hard road.

NOTES

1. "Barabbas or Jesus: The Pilate Trial in the Aftermath of the Jewish War," by Philip Ruge-Jones and Thomas Boomershine. Annual Meeting of the Society of Biblical Literature, November 17-20, 2007, San Diego, California.

2. Flavius Josephus, *The Wars of the Jews,* especially Books 5 and 6. *The Works of Josephus,* trans. William Whiston, new updated ed. (Peabody, Mass.: Hendrickson 1987), pp. 696-750. For a brief contemporary tell-and-show, see the last 10-15 minutes of Part II of the videotape "From Jesus to Christ: The First Christians."

3. Jerusalem had been conquered by the Babylonians in 589 BCE and made "desolate." Josephus notes that Jerusalem had been taken five times before, yet neither its "great antiquity, nor its vast riches, . . . nor the greatness of the veneration paid to it on a religious account, been sufficient to preserve it from being destroyed" (Josephus, *Wars,* 6.10.1).

4. In the Talmud (Yoma 9b) the rabbis state that the second temple was destroyed in the year 70 C.E. because of "baseless hatred" among the Jews. So the Jewish War was a punishment from God because of the Jews' shameful behavior towards each other. Orthodox Jews remember this tragedy each year on the date of Tisha B'Av (the ninth day of the month of Av, which usually comes in August). Tisha B'Av is a day of fasting and mourning.

5. Some of these scholars are Warren Carter, Dominic Crossan, Richard Horsley, Bruce Malina, Jerome Neyrey, Douglas Oakman, John Pilch, Jonathan Reed, and others.

6. Warren Carter, *Matthew and Empire: Initial Explorations* (Harrisburg, Pa.: Trinity Press 2001), 76.

7. Ibid., 79.

8. Ann Rice, *Christ the Lord, Out of Egypt* (New York: Knopf, 2005), is a fictional, imaginative account of Jesus' early life and his curiosity about why his family went to Egypt and why no one will tell him the answer. When he finds out from elders in the temple, he collapses from the horror of it.

9. *Heaven* is a Jewish circumlocution for the name of God.

10. Gischala was a small town in Galilee in the first century. This "notorious" John resisted the Roman general Titus's offer of surrender, then fled in the night to Jerusalem where he pretended to be on the side of the elites but instead betrayed them to the Zealots. See Josephus, *Wars,* Book 4, chapters 2-3.

11. In Walter Bauer's Greek-English lexicon, *lestes* can mean either bandit or insurrectionist/revolutionary. In the highly political Jewish-Roman context of occupation and resistance, the latter meaning is obvious.

12. This quote and some of the observations about Jesus' trial before Pilate were drawn from the presentation at the Society of Biblical Literature by Philip Ruge-Jones and Thomas Boomershine in "Barabbas or Jesus: The Pilate Trial in the Aftermath of the Jewish War."

13. Conrad L. Kanagy, *Road Signs for the Journey: A Profile of Mennonite Church USA* (Scottdale, Pa.: Herald Press 2007), 127-128.

Chapter 14

MUST THERE BE SHUNNING? TRADITION, MIMESIS, AND RESACRALIZATION IN HISTORIC PEACE CHURCH ORTHOPRAXY

Jonathan Sauder

INTRODUCTION

How can the Historic Peace Churches, those denominations historically rooted in the Anabaptist tradition, along with the Quakers or the Religious Society of Friends with their English roots, claim to be "peace churches" if from the first generation of their existence particularly the Anabaptist groups in focus here have solved their disagreements by schism and staked their existence on the shunning and shaming of those whose sins became visible? Contemporaries of the early Dutch Anabaptists, for instance, described the high degree of churchly infighting they witnessed among Mennonites as "the war of the lambs." They were pointing out an obvious disjunction between making peace with distant military enemies and failing to be reconciled to neighboring brethren because of slightly differing convictions on how to express their shared faith in a shared practice.

We cannot be fair to the courageously prophetic and gospel-inspired witness of the first Anabaptists without favorably contrasting their polity with that of Christendom. So before we examine the limitations of the Historic Peace Churches, we must acknowledge the strides they made beyond the violent Christendom that had persecuted them into a separate existence.

First we will touch on the hermeneutic and theology that support Christendom's commitment to "the myth of redemptive violence."[1] Next we will look at how Jesus and Paul desacralized violence precisely by using the cross to reveal its mythic hold on our consciences.

We will see that in many ways Anabaptists succeed in desacralizing state church violence simply by following the nonviolent ethic of Jesus. Then we will inquire into how Mennodom[2]—"establishment Anabaptism" as distinct from Anabaptism as an emergent, sacramentarian critique of violent Christendom—so quickly began to resacralize many components of "nonconformity to the world" and came to rely on the ban and shunning of the impure as a means of generating and preserving its own cultural order. I will argue that this attenuated form of human sacrifice, consigning the morally incompetent to banishment, is a direct parallel to Christendom's long use of capital punishment.

Not only is it structurally parallel, but more importantly for our learning today, in an era when both the death penalty and shunning have fallen into misuse throughout much of the West, we must ask why we are still hermeneutically reliant on many of the deep assumptions of Christendom. We who claim to be churches of peace have yet to repent of this hermeneutical congruence with our former persecutors and must begin at once to Christianize the theology, soteriology, ecclesiology, and proselyte-making evangelism that have justified both Christendom and its mirror Mennodom for so long.

As a means to showing that there was and is an alternative understanding of Christian community, we will end with a brief look at the undeveloped legacy of Pilgram Marpeck's critique of Swiss Anabaptists.

CHRISTENDOM'S SACRED VIOLENCE

Since the era of Augustine, European Christianity had understood itself as the ark of safety from the lethal wrath of an Almighty God. "Almighty" meant that God was beyond good and evil and thus capable of doing anything. Paul Johnson cites and interprets Augustine thus:

His justice was as inscrutable as any other aspect of his nature. Human ideas of equity were like "dew in the desert." Human suffering, deserved or not, occurred because God was angry. "His life, for mortals, is the wrath of God. The world is a small-scale Hell." "This is the Catholic view: a view that can show a just God in so many pains and in such agonies of tiny babies." Man must simply learn to accept suffering and injustice. There was nothing he could do about either.[3]

On this view, it is easy to view sin as a problem for humankind primarily because of its magnetic effect on the deadly anger of a God too emotionally fragile to love a person while hating his sin. Thus the deadliness of sin comes to be seen as deriving more directly from its effect on the mood of a two-natured God than on its power to destroy a human by disintegrating her constitutional reliance on the love of God and neighbor. Of course the fact that sin will cause a person to *self*-destruct was never lost to view in Augustine's thought or in later Christendom. But the solution to sin quickly came to be seen primarily in terms of placating and reconciling God to humans. This was a fundamental reversal of the New Testament revelation of God through Jesus on the cross.

GOSPEL DESACRALIZATION

Nowhere does the New Testament speak of the need to reconcile God to humanity. Instead, God was in Christ reconciling the world to God's self. It was our deadly violence, our wrathful nature that was irreversibly revealed on the cross. It was God's bottomless forgiveness and unconditional love that was irreversibly revealed on the cross. And when he vindicated Jesus by resurrecting him and placing him at his right hand, he revealed that what the most religiously and politically conscientious men of Occupied Palestine had called the preservation of cultural order was really humanity's victimization of God.

Jesus did not come to save us from God's reaction to our sins. God came in Jesus to save us from our sins by absorbing and absolving them. Jesus revealed the righteousness of God's unconditioned forgiveness of our sins, not God's inability to forgive without first being appeased and reconciled.

But with the change in theology represented by Augustine (certainly not originated solely by him), the Christian faith in the "Jesus-ness" of God was lost and the "Godness" of Jesus was redefined in concepts that owed more to pre-Christian (and sub-Christian!) classical theism than to the foolishness of the cross. Theological courage was replaced by apologetic accommodation and Jesus' self-giving love was seen as an incalculably valuable but only partial revelation of a morally opaque God.

Thus it made perfect sense for Augustine to become the "theorist of persecution."[4] Love of sinners meant compelling them against their wills to conform to the doctrines and rituals that would appease God on their behalf. Torture as a means of saving them from God's wrath seemed self-evidently superior to a tolerance that would leave them outside of the ark of safety, the sacred precincts of the institutional church. Kindness to heretics in the name of Jesus would be a false and ineffective love in that it would misrepresent God as capable of "fore-giving," of loving outside the bounds of his fragile purity and thus compromising his very ability to exist.[5]

CANONICAL CONCEPTIONS OF SACRED VIOLENCE AND THE CONVERSION OF SAUL

In the Law of Moses, particularly in Leviticus, we see holiness defined as ritual purity and separation from the profane. The sacred, in this conception, was the realm of safety from the impulsive deadliness of God, a realm bounded by taboos and preserved by the expulsion or stoning of anyone who violated them. Thus a sinner had to be either shamed into conforming or sacrificed for the purity of the group. God was a being to be survived as much as to be trusted. Worship was made up of a mixture of paralyzing dread and confident petition. And a large degree of that confidence derived from conformity to the demands of ritual purity.

In the life of Saul of Tarsus, zeal for the law was the very thing that set him in direct opposition to the subversive direction of the kingdom of God on earth. He could not imagine, much less respect or worship, a God who would choose to be victimized by the very principalities and powers of which he had heretofore been seen as the sole sponsor. Saul's conversion took place when he saw that the judicial murder of Jesus spelled the end of the law's claim to be able to reconcile God and humanity.[6]

In the gospel of Paul, the law was one of the powers that, although meant by God for good, had enslaved humanity in enmity against God and thus rendered them incapable of believing that his ability to save was not limited to the boundaries of their culture. Paul was always grateful for the tradition that had cultured him, but he no

longer had the toxic gratefulness of the Pharisee in the parable of
Jesus who was thankful that he was a better person than others. Paul
did introduce himself as a Pharisee very late in his career and never
called on Jews to renounce their customs. But his gospel desacralized
the entire Jewish culture, all the way back to circumcision. That is,
there was no longer any need for ritual protection from a fundamentally human-hating God.[7] Would not God, who had freely given us
his treasured son, not give us all things?

In line with Paul's gospel, early orthodox worship of Jesus as
Lord and God provided Christians with critical distance from the
principalities and powers that were still in rebellion against God.
Those religious and imperial powers had conspired to preserve their
hegemony by condemning the creator's son to die the death of a common terrorist. And now they continued to deny that their rebellion
had been exposed. They still went on demanding a level of allegiance
that justified violence against anyone who didn't worship them. Orthodoxy, the "right praise" of Jesus, was not a ritual manipulation of
the polarization of love and deadliness in the heart of God but rather
a way of keeping one's moral consciousness, or conscience, free of
reenslavement to idolatry—the logic of sacrificing others for the sake
of a "cause," often for the sake of the will to purity.[8]

JESUS' DESACRALIZING GOSPEL

Jesus challenged the kind of holiness that maintained itself by
sacralizing, making sacred, certain rituals and symbols. His primary
symbolic action would be the (so-called) cleansing of the temple. Accompanying this was sharing table fellowship with those whose im-
purity would have been considered by most of his peers to be sure to
cross-contaminate his own holiness. Jesus championed those marginalized by the religious rigor, the family solidarity, the economic
predation, and the political oppression of his day. Unlike the Zealots,
he refused to sacralize the use of rebellious violence against structural violence. But it is possible that his slogan "take up your cross"[9]
was at that time a "standard phrase of Zealot recruiting."[10] Either
Jesus was holy and the religious and political powers were misrepre-
senting the nature of the sacred, or Jesus was a sinner and guilty of
compromising the holiness of God.

Jesus desacralized the principalities and powers, showing that in
their claim to preserve the moral order of the universe they were actually guilty of murdering God's prophets. When he died on their
gallows, he condemned their mode of preserving the many by scape-

goating the few, and when he rose again in forgiveness instead of vengeance, he inaugurated nothing less than a new creation. The former world order was organized around the law of retaliation. Not even God, the religious worshippers of violent transcendence believed, was allowed to break that law for long. When the "just one," the only one who can righteously retaliate against all of humankind, chose instead to forgive, what happened was nothing less than the unfounding of the world.

From then on, men and women made in the image of God have been called to become children of the most high, the one who loves without moral discrimination (Matt. 5:45) and whose transcendent perfection appears as mercy (Matt. 5:48; Luke 6:36), not annihilation. People scandalized by Christlike disavowal of violence confuse the Order of this World, which is passing away, with the very existence of the world.[11] Early Christians were accused of turning the world upside down and were considered by many patriotic Romans to be the enemies of the human race.

The prince and principle of this world is *satan*, the accuser. He works by bringing peace—violent, sacred peace—into human groups who learn to make peace by scapegoating or expelling one or more of their members whenever their sense of unity is threatened. The fallen powers organize the many against the few. They claim to preserve God's world by sacrificing the morally, culturally, or economically poor.

But since the first Pentecost after the ascension of Jesus, another spirit has been intervening and interfering with the violent order of this world. Jesus called his promised spirit the Paraclete, the advocate for the defense. The cross shows us with full clarity that God was lynched by our ways of maintaining our purity and security, our "justice," our "law and order."

The work of the Holy Spirit (John 16:8-11) is to 1) reprove the world of the sin of not believing that God is like Jesus; 2) reprove the world for its wrong understanding of righteousness by showing that Jesus, who appeared to us like a threat to our sacred order and thus as unrighteous, is in fact righteous because he is seated beside God; and 3) reprove the world for its way of judging people because the one who stabilizes this fallen world by means of arranging people in stances of mutual accusation and occasional mobilization for purposes of stoning or shunning somebody is finally judged himself.

CHRISTENDOM CULTURE
RESACRALIZES CHRISTIANITY

But Christendom soon resacralized the very symbols that had subverted a false sense of sacredness. Jesus had turned the Passover from a symbol of the use of another's blood to escape God's destroying angel into a symbol of how to participate with God in self-sacrifice to the point of laying down one's own life—not to protect impure sinners from a God of death but to reconcile them to the God of life. Christendom soon made the supper a sacrament, a sacrifice to reconcile an alienated God; a weekly journey into the terror-filled, deadly-to-humans sacred space of God's throne.

New Testament baptism for the remission of sins was admittance into the company of the forgiven, those who were not scandalized by God's choice of judging us by forgiving us rather than by destroying us. This forgiveness could be forfeited by the failure to extend it to others, specifically to others who didn't deserve it. (When it is deserved, it is reward, not forgiveness.) But it was hard to believe that God is allowed to be as forgiving as Jesus told Peter to be,[12] and in a very short time the churches were debating the possibility of restoring a member who had sinned after his baptism. The conditionality of salvation shifted from one's extension of the forgiveness of a world-loving God to those who haven't been able to experience or believe that forgiveness yet, to the ancient and much easier belief that a person's survival of God's deadly purity is contingent upon one's moral competency, one's ability to maintain the fragile status of holiness in face of the temptation to share table fellowship with publicans and sinners.

Orthodoxy, "right praise," originally used as leverage to set Jesus' followers free of bondage to the principalities and powers, now became itself an oppressive institutional power and was used as a lever to force all and sundry to conform to the allegedly sacred order. This conception of a violently constituted and divinely sanctioned cultural order was really a collapse into the very theology and soteriology from which the apostle Paul had been converted.

ANABAPTIST COUNTERCULTURE
DESACRALIZES TRADITIONAL CHRISTENDOM

Just as Jesus had desacralized the institutions and practices, such as temple and Sabbath, that were oppressing people instead of shepherding them in his day, the Anabaptists of the sixteenth century desacralized the sacraments of Christendom. The supper became a symbol of willingness to suffer with Christ at the hands of the principalities and powers who had been murderously trying to put the old world order back together again ever since the resurrection. Baptism moved from being a ritual of the insulation of infants from the lethal frown of God on sin to the commitment to participate in God's forgiveness of enemies rather than in their annihilation.

Just as Jesus had championed the victims of the principalities and powers in his day, Anabaptists desacralized Christendom by refusing to fight its enemies, the Muslim invaders. This all required tremendous theological, spiritual, and physical courage. (Nothing here should be understood as belittling this courage in the least. I am fairly certain, given my personal track record of complicit silence in the face of the rhetoric claiming divine sponsorship of American empire, that had I lived in the sixteenth century I would have been a *Halbtaufer*, a half-baptist who mentally followed the logic of the movement but didn't dare to go to the stake for it.)

How is it that just as the Jesus movement of the first century soon froze into Christendom, another sacred order structured around dread of God and the allegedly benevolent expulsion of dissidents, the Anabaptist movement of the 1500's, eventually froze into its own fortress? This one has been called "Mennodom," a similar fortress mentality also characterized by its tendency to preserve itself by means of excluding the morally weak to maintain its status before almighty God.

ANABAPTIST-MENNONITE TRADITIONALISM RESACRALIZES A SUBCULTURE

To be traditional is to be human. The tradition of the church provides the framework by means of which we can negotiate new experience in terms of prior commitments rather than having to spend all our energy in rethinking our assumptions on a daily basis. In *that* sense we must a-critically "indwell" our traditions to lead our everyday lives. Leslie Newbigin's appropriation of Michael Polanyi's epistemology for purposes of rethinking Christian traditioning is invaluable for anyone who wants to recover from static traditionalism but doesn't want to abandon or sell out her "birthright" in the tradition in which she worships God.[13]

Many people who've grown up oppressed under the corpse of a tradition develop a reactionary allergy to any sort of cultural patterning among Christians. These "liberals" thus prevent the recovery of a living, dynamic tradition. Tradition includes the tacit communication of values that are often inarticulable. Modern, "liberal" refusal of tacit solidarity within a local community of faith is as dehumanizing as "conservative" resistance to a tradition's self-criticism.

Christian tradition is indispensable to faithfulness. But it becomes an obstacle to faithfulness when it overvalues its current position, denies the temporal nature of human reality and of divine revelation, and stops the process of self-critique. As Jaroslav Pelikan has observed in a quote often cited, "Tradition is the living faith of the dead; traditionalism is the dead faith of the living."

Hans Urs von Balthasar says that God's "unforeseeable interventions," his "recurrent abrogation of the continuity of secular history," are themselves a key part of "the essential *content* of Israel's tradition, and consequently could not be lacking in the *form* in which Jesus received that tradition and incorporated it in his life. The history of Revelation shows the repeated suspension of tradition as being of the essence of tradition itself." In line with this argument of Balthasar's, I hope that the Holy Spirit will enable a recovery of Historic Peace Church traditions even if their adherents view the "suspension" involved in the recovery as a threat to the tradition rather than as a corrective of it.[14]

After discussing the question of "Jesus' continuity and discontinuity with the various forms of Judaism of his day," Stanley Hauerwas quotes Sean Freyne's comment that Jesus "was clearly striking at the very reason for existence of each of the groups and their philosophies. To do so in the name of God's final and irrevocable promises to his people was intolerable."[15]

A living tradition is dynamic. To be true to the tradition of the gospel is to allow the Paraclete to show each new generation the ways in which it is wrong about what sin is, what righteousness is, and what true judgment looks like (John 16: 8-11).

Protestants and Catholics were maintaining their sacral, nonpluralist societies by persecuting Anabaptists and other dissidents while at the same time refusing to disciple or discipline their own members. Anabaptists pointed out this inconsistency and determined to overcome it. I propose that one of many ways of understanding the nature of Anabaptism is to see it as a mirror of that inconsistency.

Instead of going all the way back to the theological scandal of the cross and the redefinition of salvation available in the resurrected and forgiving son of God, they seem to have substituted the nonlethal shunning for the tactic of execution and the nonmilitary congregational schism for the tactic of making war on the infidels.

Whereas the Pauline letters insist on the inseparability of reconciliation with God and union with fellow Christians, Mennodom was soon tempted to measure its fidelity by its willingness to discontinue table fellowship with those whose practices differed.

Orthodoxy had originally freed people from the service of false gods and oppressive powers but soon turned into a new set of shibboleths in service of a new spiritual-economic-cultural hegemony. *Orthodoxy mutated from evangelical counterculture to dominant culture.* Anabaptists were more concerned about orthopraxy, simple obedience to Christ's clear commands, than they were about systematic theologies that by their day had largely become apologies for disobedience to Jesus. Orthopraxy was originally freedom in obedience, freedom from the false "musts" of an unbelieving world that identified Christian empire with the kingdom of God. But within a century or so, much of Anabaptist *orthopraxy mutated from evangelical counterculture to quietist subculture.*

I believe that orthopraxy is both more basic to Christian faithfulness and more capable of cross-cultural translation than is orthodoxy. I am grateful for my upbringing within the traditions of a Historic Peace Church that values the incarnation of practical obedience to God over abstract articulation of soteriological theory. I am glad that the sort of thought experiment that this essay represents is not the kind of activity on which the people of God must rely to stay in touch with him. Neither do I expect my past years of self-interrogation on the largely autobiographical issues of this paper to be as capable of producing fruit in the kingdom of God as the simplest act of love for the needy by the simplest admirer of Jesus.

But I write this essay to encourage awareness that it is easy to misidentify the oppressive order of this world (Luke 22:25) as the holiness of God, especially when we are being materially benefited by it at the expense of those it is oppressing. It is easy to prefer corporate uniformity of practice and cultural boundary-line maintenance, funded by a dread of God's will to kill the deviant, to the kind of boundary-defying love of the impure sinner that characterized the life of Jesus.

Today's era of globalization and renewed cultural imperialism is exactly the wrong moment in world history to suggest that anyone, but especially Christians, attempt to live without tradition. The tradition of either the church or the world will provide the framework by means of which we grasp and place new experiences. In that sense we cannot help but dwell in a tradition. It is part of being human. Animals have only instincts. Humans are able to pass on to the next generation hard-won but often inarticulate portions of wisdom by training their children to obey Christ's simple commands first and not to insist on understanding the rationale behind them. Precepts are more durable, life giving, and understandable than concepts.

I have no faith in liberalism, the belief in the ability of human reason to map reality and route a better path for the future than what the Jesus *tradition*—the incarnation of the Way of Jesus—has laid out. This is why I am so concerned about the overvaluation of even our best traditions. I don't want us to have to discard them because we've misused them.

It is impossible to place too much value on the traditions by which we have been enabled to hear the gospel. But it is both possible and very easy to put the wrong sort of value on them. By the time of Jesus, many of the Jews had forgotten the words of the prophets of the Diaspora calling on them to recover their original identity as a priestly people who mediate the love of God to all peoples. The Pharisees of Jesus' day courageously resisted the cultural imperialism of Hellenism but failed in practice to subordinate and relativize all their boundary maintenance tactics to the love of the morally, spiritually, and financially poor. It is my thesis that the Historic Peace Churches similarly long maintained the sort of ethnic and cultural nonconformity to the dominant culture that enables mental "critical distance" from the assumptions of the violently ordered world around them but tended to rely on their exclusion of the unworthy and impure to keep them in good standing with God.

In both cases, as in the days of Moses and Augustine, the faithful tended to identify God as the one who would save them from himself[16] if they followed his prescriptions. Thus their principal mode of spreading their faith was by propagating a monocultural umbrella of protection from God, rather than by merely leavening each group they contacted with the subversive leaven of trust in God. Such trust in God in defiance of the mores of the oppressive power structures frees converts from the dictatorship of self-preservation, the worldly peace which is always bought at great cost to one's enemies and to the poor.

One of the results of the resacralization of Mennonite subculture is that new adherents are usually proselytes[17] and not converts. New Testament conversion is conversion to the perspective of the cross— the unmasking of all human and spiritual principalities and powers as the persecutors of Jesus rather than as his allies. But proselytes don't go through a *metanoia* into a different picture of God. They still view God as the enemy of the impure. They merely adopt a new set of

purity codes, whether that involves a doctrinal system or lifestyle re-
strictions. Proselytes try to secure themselves by adopting the prejudices and scapegoats of their new hosts, much as Peter, as yet uncon-
verted to Jesus' faith in his nonviolent father, tried to save his life
while warming his hands at the fire during Jesus' trial.

> In the great scene where Peter and the disciples display a false
> eagerness for the Passion, the Gospels suggest a satire of a cer-
> tain religious fervor which must be recognized as specifically
> "Christian." . . . They [the disciples] renounce the ideology of
> happiness and success but create a very similar ideology of suf-
> fering and failure, a new social and mimetic mechanism that
> functions exactly like the former exultation. The new manners
> of the disciples are reminiscent of the triumphant anti-exulta-
> tion of certain current Christian movements, their very clerical
> anticlericalism.[18]

I have never heard a better description of triumphalist sectarian-
ism than that passage from the writings of René Girard. It helps to
make visible the link between being persecuted and emphasizing the
use of shunning. When the persecuted are prosecuted[19] for defiling
the civil religion of a sacral society,[20] it is much easier for them to re-
constitute themselves as an expulsionary sect than as an inclusionary
open society. The former requires no metanoia, merely countercultural antagonism.

Historian John Ruth says of one Swiss Anabaptist congregation
in the early 1600s that the ban was "one of the main reasons for the existence of their fellowship."[21] Paton Yoder quotes North American
Amish in the 1800s as asserting that without banning and shunning
"the church of God cannot stand," and that shunning is "as important
as water baptism."[22]

Claus-Peter Clasen records that many people joined the Anabaptists not because of doctrine but because of strict discipline. Anabaptists repeatedly told Lutheran pastors that they would return to the
state church if it adopted the ban. Clasen then says that if the Anabaptists had ever become a majority in a region, there would have
quickly been "a social distinction between saints and sinners: quite
conceivably, indeed, to the dictatorship of the saints over the mass of
unregenerate sinners."[23] Menno Simons' "celestial flesh" Christology, coupled with the wider Anabaptist recovery of the doctrine of
the church as the socially visible body of Christ, predisposed him to
advocate a very strict practice of the shunning of sinners.

I think it is clear that similar to the standards of all other religiously serious people, the Anabaptist cultural order, the *Ordnung*, quickly began to change from being a tradition of freedom from the powers, a way of getting leverage against the lies built into Christendom culture, and became a power unto itself. And instead of opening out of Christendom into the reemerging Jesus movement of that day, it tended to turn into a closed loop pathway into Mennodom, a place of safety both from God and from true spiritual freedom.[24]

Anabaptist simple living and the use of peasant clothing was originally a witness against conspicuous consumption that mocks the poor. But it changed within a few decades in some communities to a form of social control, a shift from evangelical "nonconformity" vis-à-vis the imperial world order[25] to a sectarian uniformity that coerced assent to the norms of a sacred subculture.

Rudy Wiebe's Canadian Mennonite novel *Peace Shall Destroy Many* is a classic portrayal of a community in which this shift has been made permanent.[26] Sara Stambaugh's novel *I Hear The Reaper's Song* portrays Lancaster Conference's ethos shifting in the late nineteenth century from nonconformity coupled with a doctrine of hope in God's mercy to legislated uniformity and stricter dress codes directly triggered by a new sort of hellfire preaching.[27]

Donald Kraybill uses the common phrase "loss of face" when referring to a change in Ordnung.[28] He refers to "rites of surrender" to the Ordnung as "sacrifices" for the ordering and unifying of the community (33). He says that for most Amish the Ordnung "is a sacred order that unites members and separates them from the world" (98). He attributes to the shunning "potent power as a social control device" and says it has a "cardinal role in Amish identity and polity" (274 n23). The direct and ominous parallels between such language and the Pauline perspective on the law outlined above are too obvious to require belaboring. Jesus put the Powers to an open shame. Ordnung can easily become a Power that functions to "save face."

It must immediately be said, though, that Kraybill and I share a tremendous respect for the way in which the Amish care for the physically and economically weak members of their communities and that despite their authoritarian ways, they are a living witness against the toxic individualism that is rapidly disintegrating Western community. We will get nowhere by pointing out the faults of traditionalists and then mirroring them in reverse by trying to live out the perverse modern fiction of the "self-made man."

Miroslav Volf sees the logic of Serbian ethnic cleansing as a "will to purity." After cautioning against tracing all sins to any one principle, he says that "an advantage of conceiving sin as the practice of exclusion is that it names as sin what often passes as virtue, especially in religious circles." Volf describes the lethal logic of cultural purity as an attempt to repristinate one's heritage: "The origins must be pure: we must go back to the pristine purity of our linguistic, religious, or cultural past. . . ."[29]

This logic of cultural purity may not be exactly lethal throughout the five hundred years of Mennonite history, but it is still powerful. Witness, for example, the religious use of the German language for sacred worship among Mennonites in the Ukraine and the Americas centuries after they had begun to do secular business with their neighbors in the local vernacular.[30]

Culture is not an evil. But when humans are given to evil, their culture houses and propagates that evil. To be cultural is to be human. Animals have no culture, only instincts. The adolescent frustration with "cultural baggage" is a frequent component of humanity's periodic worship of its various animal instincts. According to Romans 1, the heathen worship of the creature and its appetites is idolatry. According to Romans 2 and 1 Corinthians, a culture structured around the condemnation of the idolatries of pagans is merely a refined and more egregious alternative idolatry. Religiously moral idolaters model their consciences around a lethally jealous god who requires propitiation of his dark side, and they are thus nearly impervious to God's cruciform propitiation (Rom. 3:21–26) of their sin of self-justification. All religious condemnation of people is a condemnation of Jesus.

> As Saul in his persecution of the disciples struck at Jesus himself, in a similar way every sin is targeted against him. Condemnation is always leveled against the one who was fundamentally against condemnation, and the persecution of fellow humans strikes that victim [Jesus] who has identified himself with all the victims of every persecution. The universality of the *expulsion* and thus the *exclusive nature of the substitution* are based on the *act of universal inclusion* of the one who stood for all by making himself one of them.[31]

How can one live faithfully within the cultural legacy, or even, in the case of a few readers, perhaps, within the current jurisdiction of such powers of Ordnung? I suggest that we practice the same "revolutionary subordination" within Christendom or Mennodom that John Howard Yoder recommended we use with relation to all earthly "Powers." Walter Wink says it quite succinctly:

By acknowledging that the Powers are good, bad, and salvageable—all at once—we are freed from the temptation to demonize those who do evil. We can love our enemies or nation or church or school, not blindly, but critically, calling them back time and again to their own highest self-professed ideals and identities. We can challenge institutions to live up to the vocation that is theirs from the moment theywere created. We can oppose their actions while honoring their necessity.[32]

DO THE PEACE CHURCHES IMITATE JESUS, OR GOD, OR BOTH?

Article four of the 1527 Schleitheim Confession renounces the sword as diabolical. Article six says that God ordains the sword outside of the perfection of Christ. This theological ambiguity still inheres in Historic Peace Churches today.

Anabaptist obedience to Christ's command not to kill is assimilable by a people committed to living a command ethic. But for most Anabaptist traditions the *imitatio Christi*, the imitation of Christ, is not conflated (as per Jesus' own logic in Matt. 5:45, 48), with the *imitatio Dei*, the imitation of God. Because Anabaptist theology has never become as thoroughly christological as Anabaptist ethics, the peace churches came to rely on a threat-based ethic and shunning-enforced obedience ethos. This sort of Ordnung sustained nonresistant praxis long after it had lost any truly *theo*logical credibility in the minds of its privileged adherents.

As soon as Anabaptists in Europe, the Ukraine, the Americas or elsewhere signaled that they were ready to accept a privilege—a "private law"—of exemption from military conscription in exchange for the refusal to challenge the theo-logic of Christendom, they were tolerated and their witness to a "simple life" was suddenly admired instead of vilified. Mennodom began to view itself as a subsidiary to Christendom rather than as an irreconcilable alternative. Mennodom and Christendom came to a tacit agreement that the Way of Christ and the Way of God were morally distinguishable. Radical discipleship was tolerated for as long as it didn't generate a radical theology, for such would again "turn the world upside down."

Soon there was no functional difference between Luther's two kingdoms of God and Mennonite two-kingdom theory. In line with the canonically justified self-contradiction of the Schleitheim Confession, Mennonites continued to speak of the kingdom of God and the kingdom of Satan but to live as though the latter were really a less than perfect, but nonetheless divine and sacred order. Persecution of Anabaptists ended when their witness became a witness to moral perfection and no longer a witness against reverence for and worship of transcendental violence.[33]

In the ministry of Jesus the "kingdom of heaven," what we might today term the "culture of God," was indistinguishable from the Way of Jesus. Historic Peace Church conscientious objection to war changed from following he Way of the kingdom of heaven, the culture of the father as indistinguishable from the Way of the son, to following a purity code to escape hell. This meant having faith *in* Jesus to save us from God's violent eschatological behavior rather than sharing the faith *of* Jesus—faith in God's Way of exceptionless love of enemy.

So of course many Historic Peace Church parishioners lost their "nonresistance" soon after losing their taboo-based cultural identity. This is not because cultural insularity is a precondition for obeying Jesus' love command but because they had for centuries been obeying the love command for the same reason they had been maintaining ethnic distinctives: the desire to escape God's wrath, not to imitate him. When their "distinctives" were seen to be arbitrary and nonbinding, their peace position, which had been just another component of sacred separatism, was also discarded.

Today the Historic Peace Churches have two options for continuing our peace witness: 1) more ecclesial legislation enforced by the fear of violating a taboo of the Sermon on the Mount and by the threat of shunning or; 2) continue the Anabaptist theological project that was discontinued in the sixteenth century and only recently recommenced in fits and starts in the late twentieth.

The first option has felt mandatory because the second option has not been taken. Historic Peace Churches have for several centuries been nonresistant *because of* their tradition and *despite their theology.* It is for this reason that as soon as they lost their religious taboos against pursuit of the arts or higher learning or even variegated dress patterns, they tended to lose their young men to the military. The Way of Jesus had been equated with a subculture and lost its theological warrant. Conscientious objection status as an expression of legalist conformity to a culturally anomalous holiness sect is really not "conscientious" at all if the CO has convictions against disruptively witnessing against the warmaking nature of Christendom. When a church stops enforcing its ethno-religious boundary markers and ceases cultural self-marginalization, it stands to lose any peace position that had derived its meaning from the imitation of Jesus but not of his Father. When the merciful holiness of Christ is viewed as an exception to a prior and more basic holiness of a Father God of redemptive violence, Christians will come to see nonresistance as anomalous and will "responsibly" imitate God.

Of course I recommend pursuing the second option. And I think a great place to start would be to revisit, strengthen, and extend two largely neglected trajectories outlined in an courageous essay by Harry Huebner two decades ago: 1) a critique of "canonical syncretism" in our theology, by which Jesus' witness to the nonviolent character of God is muted by our exegetical allegiance to a "strong biblicism" that requires us to "speak of God in terms of the aggregate of all past divine acts";[34] 2) a call to recover the "divine-human-moral-continuity-pacifism" hinted at by Menno Simons and Hans Denck, and to renounce the "divine-human-moral-discontinuity-pacifism" that has enabled Mennodom to live in non-prophetic symbiosis with Christendom for so long (256-259).

But I must hasten to say that this second option of recovering our theological courage (and a counter-imperial exegesis of the New Testament) will not be sustainable without being housed in a tradition. Conservatives tend to valorize cultural markers and mores as guarantors of the "holiness without which no man shall see the Lord" (Heb. 12:14 KJV). But liberals tend to abjure the cultural accrual of corporate identity (which harmlessly evolves along with any sustained community life) without which no community shall see tomorrow.[35] Both of us need to be less fearful and more vulnerable in different ways. Only God can build his church.

LISTENING TO MARPECK

The Swiss Brethren thought that their Dutch brother Menno Simons was too strict on his use of the ban, but even they themselves were not recognized by the south German Anabaptist leader Pilgram Marpeck as a true fellowship of Jesus Christ because of their attempt to do preventive ruling and judging about potential sin which Marpeck said "makes sin where there is none."[36]

> We are unable to participate with you in the fellowship of the body and blood of Christ . . . when it is done in impure fear and ignorant zeal—as indeed you have not participated with us, and still may not do so, because of a seared conscience. False, unjust judgments and verdicts follow from such impure fear, and Christ the Lord denies to His own the rights to these judgments and verdicts. (365)

My first reading of passages like this in Marpeck's correspondence with the Swiss Brethren, my spiritual forbears, was like the experience of finding a gold mine! It meant that the misuse of pious fear for purposes of generating cultural order is not something that only a "modern" takes exception to. It was contested and rejected as soon as Anabaptists began it.

Notice that Marpeck warns against an undifferentiated fear of God, a dread of God that demonstrates a failure to believe that God loves us as generously as the cross of Christ indicates. And he uses the term *seared conscience* to refer to the conscientious, religious refusal to believe the scandalous grace of God, rather than as a term of dismissal used to write off the heathen who resist being proselytized.

At another place he says, "For flesh and blood always fight against the law of grace, and so they must serve the law of sin, that is, fear of the wrath and the future punishment of God" (321). This is an amazing exception to the normal tendency of adherents of both orthodoxy and orthopraxy to interpret quivering fear of a lethal divinity as evidence of successful "conversion" instead of as a fallback into the "law of sin."

And on his previous page there is a faint echo of the original New Testament vision of a God who has always been for us but wasn't revealed as such until Jesus propitiated our wrath on the cross. He says with regard to the sacrifice Jesus made on the cross, "We have been paid" (320).

But what do we make of the fact that there are Mennonites and Swiss Brethren groups around today but no Marpeckites? Is that not evidence that God did not favor their nonjudgmental way of corporately representing the body of Christ? Longevity of institutional existence is one thing. It is fairly common and simple, almost self-propelled. Institutions take on a personality of their own and demand a loyalty that takes precedence over our forgiveness of the genuinely repentant. The reputation of the angel or principality that the "church" has become seems more important than patience with the weak ones.

On a Marpeckian analysis, both Pharisees and the Amish have a blessed moral tradition but tend to use it to establish their own righteousness instead of accepting the scandalous, boundary-obliterating forgiveness of God. All humans (except for little children, who for this very reason are already in the kingdom) are naturally terrified by the threat of Christ's new creation unfounding the old certainties, the old fears, the old sacred boundaries. And we recoil at the threat of the true moral and spiritual freedom into which we will be thrown if we

believe that Jesus of Nazareth is the plenary revelation of God himself. "If the son sets you free, you will be free indeed" (John 8:36 NIV).

We only learned who God really is in the moment when we expelled and killed him for disturbing the public divine order. The
preaching of the cross as the only way to know "the true God and
eternal life" (1 John 5:20 KJV) is still as much of a scandal in Christendom as it ever was in Rome. His disciples have no other way of representing him to his still terror-bound children today than by associ-
ating with the impure ones by whose expulsion the group has defined and defended its unevangelical purity and its honest worship
of the only kind of god it can respect.

So, back to the question of the short-lived Marpeckian tradition.
Longevity of the type referred to in "my words shall never pass
away" is a very different type of longevity from that of an institution.
This longevity of the subversive message of Jesus about God and us
is very real but is as untraceable with the tools of the "human sciences" as is any other work of the Spirit. It is untraceable precisely because it is benevolently subversive of any oppression of God's
human children by fallen powers. Fallen powers are those that had
originally served the purpose of shielding unregenerate people from
chaos but have now imposed a new order and false sacred zone of
their own.

Malevolent subversion, of course, is very traceable. It merely dis-
places one form of oppression or *junta* of oppressors with another.
The liberation theology of the zealots of Jesus' day was of this type.
Jesus borrowed enough of their rhetoric and shared enough of their
concerns to convince the conservative functionaries of the temple
system that he needed to be eliminated. But he was not one of them.

The message of Jesus has had an undeniable longevity without
resorting to resacralizing our institutional power over each other and
using it to guarantee self-perpetuation. But like the Marpeckian
movement, Jesus' true followers emerge and reemerge through the
centuries, fading out whenever traditionalist zeal embalms the living
forms and practices of one generation and thus misrepresents the nature of God to the next.

CONCLUSION

If the church were to reconceive of the nature of sin as endemic in
all, "saved" and "unsaved" alike, excommunication would be for refusing to forgive as often as it would be for refusing to renounce one
of the more visible vices. We would lose our deep belief in the re-

deeming power of shaming and convert to a belief in the redeeming power of mercy.[37]

If the church were actively seeking to rehabilitate and restore to human society those deemed morally irredeemable by the larger society, the church would again be persecuted for the reason Jesus was—taking the love of God "too far" and redefining holiness.

We need to follow the advice of Paul Keim and interrogate ourselves along these lines:

> What and whom are we willing to sacrifice to keep our consciences pristine? Our communities stable? Our worldview intact?
>
> Is it possible that we as peacemakers have simply exchanged one set of sacrificial mechanisms for others, . . . all the more intense and lethal among us since they cannot be expressed physically? Our victims bear marks, not on their bodies so much as on their psyches.
>
> [Learning from Girard] may help move us as peacemakers from the virtue of not killing others and the washing-the-hands mentality which *may* characterize sectarian and holiness communities, to active engagement in the defenseless unmasking of the scapegoat mechanism in our own midst.[38]

Proponents of shunning usually echo Augustine's logic of coercion. The motive justifies the means.

But if a dubiously "kind" expulsion and ban has been the bedrock of Historic Peace Churches' denominational differentiation for so many centuries, how can we survive if we discontinue it? Must there be shunning? The title of this paper is a variation on an important book by Raymund Schwager on *Must There Be Scapegoats? Violence and Redemption in the Bible*.[39] Schwager helps to link Jesus with the canonical trajectory of the Old Testament prophets and their critique of sacrificially constituted communities. Jesus' civil disobedience in the temple and his quotation from the prophets Jeremiah and Isaiah on that occasion was a confrontational way of alleging a link between a sacrificial, violent theology and an idolatrous and supremely selfish zealous nationalism. This paper has tried to tie into the same canonical trajectory of critique and alleges a link between an implicitly violent theology and a profoundly selfish zeal for ecclesially isolating the "saved" from the "unsaved."[40]

Jesus did not come to destroy the law or even to scapegoat it. But his way of "fulfilling" it was to radically redefine holiness as mercy. The most culturally and politically conscientious men of his day, both separatists and assimilationists in a rare show of solidarity, cooperated in condemning him. This essay does not advocate destroying Anabaptism or scapegoating our egregious mistakes. However, I expect that the ongoing work of the Paraclete in our subcultures will trigger the same kind of crisis in Historic Peace Churches that Jesus triggered in *eretz Israel* and Paul triggered in Diaspora Judaism.

We trust the Spirit to help us recover 1) countercultural, dynamic tradition; 2) the positive mimesis of discipleship;[41] 3) a nonviolent theology; and 4) the ongoing desacralization of the human-spiritual power structures that are being unmasked and disarmed by the gospel of Jesus, the crucified victim of our violent cultural human order, the logos of this world. Only the spirit can usher us into the forgiving culture of God and his logos. This will mean that for the first time in its history (unless we count Marpeckites and other similarly noncoercive groups), the church must commit to living in a constant state of autodesacralization.[42]

We must listen to the Spirit, not try to analyze our way home. For me to offer a programmatic, "Reformational" humanly achievable "solution" to the problems outlined in this essay would be a repetition of the historic failure of Christian pneumatology. Jesus gave us no plan for reform.[43] He did tell us to take up the instruments of our execution at the hands of whatever oppressive "powers that be."

Let us not assume that cross bearing was literal in first and sixteenth centuries and only figurative since then. Let us not nostalgically sacralize past witness (martyrdom) and fail to desacralize our own culture's worship of the bomb and the dollar.

> The concept of suffering runs deep in Mennonite identity. The martyrdom of thousands of early Anabaptists, the spiritual and cultural forbears of many modern Mennonites, is sacred history. . . . Kept rare and unusual, martyrdom is a matter of pride. Kept distantly past, it is uncontroversial and nearly incapable of challenge or disrespect.[44]

Jesus did not outline a plan for reform. That is the work of the Spirit. But he did give us a plan for life: death. He did give us a plan for showing the true nature of God to those who misrepresent him: Take up your shunning sentence and forgive and forgive. "Rejoice and be exceeding glad" (Matt 5:11-12 KJV).

But of course after all these centuries of the subversive work of the Holy Spirit, the leaven of the gospel has severely corroded the psychosocial machinery of shunning and the belief in the redeeming power of shaming. Even many of the most conservative churches in

Mennodom no longer can be counted on to expel a person for quietly believing that Jesus served a different spirit than that which energized Elisha when the two she bears killed children or Elijah when he torched fifty men at a time.

We must not fall into the temptation of self-immolation. Many early Christians, and perhaps some Anabaptists, were more excited about giving their bodies to be burned than about hoping all things, believing all things, enduring all things. Expulsion is no more profitable than is "membership in good standing" if we "have not charity" (1Cor. 13:3-7).

No prophet, principle, theory, or ecclesial "New Testament pattern" can maintain the continuous conversion from violence that the New Testament calls "faith." But the Spirit of Truth has come to lead us into all truth. And the Spirit has given us this understanding: we are in the true God in whom is no dark side at all (1 John 1:5, 5:20-21).

We don't need another reformation based on a dialectical, mimetic opposition to the sins of our fathers. We need Holy Spirit generated conversion from a god who sponsors violence. Little children, keep yourselves from idols.

NOTES

1. This is a concept that Walter Wink (*Engaging the Powers*, Minneapolis: Fortress, 1994) has shown to be very helpful in understanding why religion is often incapable of seeing its own violence. Together with him, I owe the main outline of the concept to the work of the French anthropologist René Girard. This paper will take for granted the heuristic value of Girard's important Mimetic Theory. He helps us to detect how our trust in the efficacy of expulsion for purposes of redeeming a sacred institution is symbiotically linked to our failure to develop a theology and hermeneutic worthy of the gospel of Jesus. I will not take the space to summarize or defend Mimetic Theory here and want to be clear that I believe that making heuristic use of a theory is possible without subscribing entirely to the theory as a whole. In this case that means that while I have found Girard's ideas immensely helpful in unmasking humanity's constitutional denial of its own violence and simultaneous projection of that violence onto its god/s I do not feel obliged to endorse every component of his systematic ethology.

2. I owe the concept of Mennodom to John Howard Yoder, the detective of neo-Constantinianism, and the neologism itself to Javan Lapp.

3. Paul Johnson, *A History of Christianity* (New York: Simon and Schuster, 1976), 121.

4. Paul Johnson, *A History of Christianity*, 116. Johnson immediately follows this phrase by saying that Augustine's "defenses were later to be those on which all defenses of the Inquisition rested."

5. Evil cannot long survive sustained exposure to the love of God. A man

who will not give up his evil can only experience God by way of fear and mistrust. But some holiness theories presume that God is too fragile to survive contact with sin – as though evil were more powerful than good.

6. Paul was raised within a moral culture. He was not a convert from an immoral lifestyle to an allegiance to moral standards. That sort of "conversion" is laudable but should not be confused with the *metanoia* that restructures the mind and will around the image of the crucified God, the one who forgives us not only when we're impure, but even when we've made him suffer unjustly for our sins. Any conversion that falls short of that will prepare a person to rate others by their purity and preserve oneself by excluding them. This sense of the fragility of one's purity and the immorality of the unconditional forgiveness of a sinful neighbor coheres with the image of God portrayed in much of the Torah. Paul's conversion was to a God of a love and mercy so large, so far out of the bounds of Torah observance, that his righteousness was visible only to the eye of faith (Romans 1:17a).

7. Read Exodus 4:24-26, noting its context of Moses' real obedience to and vulnerable, "Abrahamic" trust in God. Here circumcision is portrayed as satiating a bloodthirsty God who, *without reference to the fact that Moses is currently on God's own errand,* finds it necessary to kill him because of a breach of ritual. Only a determined bibliolatry, a refusal to acknowledge the theological dissonances and controversies inherent within and between the canonical testaments, can insulate a Bible reader from this evidence that Paul's theology itself, and not merely his "denominational" "membership" was changed by his years of reflection on the implications of the incident on the road to Damascus. Asserting that circumcision was no longer binding on all God's people made Paul a heretic according to the theological model which he had lived for when his name was Saul.

8. The figure of Phineas in Numbers 25 perfectly represents just the sort of "zealot" for purity that Saul of Tarsus had once been. In Psalm 106:30-31 Phineas' murder is counted unto him for righteousness and God is quoted in Numbers 25:10-13 as being satiated by human blood and reconciled to his people by means of Phineas' lethal religiosity. Priesthood pleasing to God is represented in these verses as the courage to offer human sacrifice in order to preserve the realm of the sacred and the people within it from the Final Solution of Almighty God to the Human Problem—utter annihilation. On this juxtaposition of violence, zeal, and holiness see John J. Collins, "The Zeal of Phineas: The Bible and the Legitimation of Violence," *JBL* 122 (Spring 2003): 3-21.

9. Today's equivalent might be "take up your electric chair," or "die the death of an insurgent."

10. John Howard Yoder, *The Politics of Jesus*, 2nd. ed. (Grand Rapids, Mich.: Wm. B. Eerdmans, 1972), 38 n28.

11. The "better dead than red" slogan of the Cold War era is not commonly heard anymore, but many culturally conservative Christians still maintain implicit bomb worship and would sooner destroy the world rather than convert out of the ancient, savage, and culturally primitive "New World Order" of the New American Century.

12. Matthew 18:22.

13. "I do not look at my eyes but indwell them, and so also with the lenses

of my spectacles. When I talk I do not look at my language as an outsider; I in-dwell it. It is part of me, and it is the means through which I try to understand the world." . . . "We turn our attention *from* them *to* the matter at hand." Leslie Newbigin, *Truth to Tell: The Gospel as Public Truth* (Grand Rapids, Mich.:Wm. B. Eerdmans, 1991), 46.

14. Hans Urs von Balthasar, *A Theology of History* (San Francisco, Calif.: Ignatius Press, 1994), 59 – 60.

15. Sean Freyne *The World of the New Testament* (Wilmington, Del.: Michael Glazier, 1980), 140. Quoted in Stanley Hauerwas, *The Peacable Kingdom: A Primer in Christian Ethics* (Notre Dame, Ind.: University of Notre Dame Press, 1983), 165.

16. This gendered designation for God is intentionally retained here to evoke the image, appropriate to the theo-logic of both Moses and Augustine, of a patriarchal insistence on maintaining personal or family "honor" by means of "honor killings" meant to recover the purity of a tribe or the reputation of its god.

17. I define the proselytizing that Jesus and Paul condemned as self-aggrandizing cross-cultural kidnapping.

18. René Girard, *The Scapegoat* (Baltimore: Johns Hopkins University Press, 1986), 159.

19. Both the preaching of the cross and the keeping of martyrologies remind us that "persecution" and "prosecution," which share the same Latin etymology (*persequor*), are not so easy to differentiate as their perpetrators allege.

20. Note Leonard Verduin's (non-Girardian) use of the concept of a "sacral society" as a designation for all pre-Christian societies as well as for Christendom in both its Catholic and Protestant forms. He asserts that it was the refusal on the part of the Protestant reformers to recognize that the New Testament revelation superseded such a conception that "caused the exodus of the Stepchildren," such as the Anabaptists. Leonard Verduin, *The Reformers and Their Stepchildren*, (Grand Rapids, Mich.: Wm. B. Eerdmans, 1964), 22-23.

21. John Landis Ruth, *The Earth Is The Lord's: A Narrative History of the Lancaster Mennonite Conference* (Scottdale, Pa.: Herald Press, 2001), 63.

22. Paton Yoder, *Tradition and Transition: Amish Mennonites and Old Order Amish 1800–1900* (Scottdale, Pa.: Herald Press, 1991), 108.

23. Claus-Peter Clasen, *Anabaptism: A Social History, 1525 – 1618* (Ithaca, N.Y.: Cornell University Press, 1972), 109-110.

24. Compare Jesus' comment about Pharisees closing the door of direct contact with the kingdom of God against those proselytes whom they were introducing into their tradition.

25. Romans 12:2, the historic Mennonite proof text for nonconformity, only warrants a cultural pattern based on the new mindset provided by the preaching of the cross. It does not legitimate mere separatism for separation's sake.

26. Ruby Wiebe, *Peace Shall Destroy Many* (Grand Rapids, Mich.: Wm. B. Eerdmans, 1962).

27. Sara Stambaugh, *I Hear the Reaper's Song* (Intercourse, Pa.: Good Books, 1984).

28. Donald B. Kraybill, *The Riddle of Amish Culture* (Baltimore: Johns Hop-

kins University Press, 1989), 97.

29. Miroslav Volf, *Exclusion and Embrace: A Theological Exploration of Identity, Otherness, and Reconciliation* (Nashville, Tenn.: Abingdon Press, 1996), 72, 74.

30. Geoffrey Dipple's *Just As In the Time of the Apostles: Uses of History in the Radical Reformation* (Kitchener, Ont.: Pandora Press, 2005) is an important corrective to the one-size-fits-all restitutionist theory of Anabaptist origins promulgated by Franklin H. Littell. But the *subsequent* generations of Hutterites, Mennonites, and Amish certainly have tried to repristinate the church with reference to a unified theory of the "Evangelical" or "Proper" sixteenth-century Anabaptists. This has often meant making language, dress, or other cultural forms a guarantee of ecclesial continuity with the New Testament and its alleged duplication in the sixteenth century sect of one's choice.

31. Raymund Schwager, *Jesus in the Drama of Salvation: Toward a Biblical Doctrine of Redemption* (New York: Crossroad Publishing, 1999), 192, emphasis in original. In a crucial passage on page 197 of the same book, Schwager insists that there is theological significance to the fact that after Jesus' crucifixion, his father did not follow the pattern of behavior modeled by the absentee landlord in the parable of the wicked vine-growers. According to Jesus, God the judge will discard the unrighteous. But Jesus was discarded. He went to hell. And to their shame theologians have not let that qualify their exegesis of Jesus' gehenna sayings. One of the most embarrassing lacunae in all of Christian theology is our failure to appropriate the faith *of* Jesus Christ in a God who is not the source of death but of life. (The promises of God in Jesus are not bait and threat, yes and no, but yes and amen.) According to Paul Jesus had faith. In place of sharing in Jesus' faith in his Abba, we have substituted instead a faith *about* Jesus (and sometimes about atonement theory), a Gnostic faith that is sometimes called a "saving knowledge of Jesus Christ." And by this means we reinstitute the very religious social discrimination that Jesus died to abolish.

32. Walter Wink, *Powers That Be: Theology for a New Millennium* (New York: Doubleday, 1998), 34.

33. "By 1558 there finally was relief for the 'Mennonites.' Their rigorous application of the 'sacred ban' had cleared them in the eyes of many thousands of honorable, reasonable persons from any suspicion of being Munsterites." Helmut Isaak, *Menno Simons and the New Jerusalem* (Kitchener, Ont.: Pandora Press, 2006), 56. Elsewhere in the book Isaak suggests, similarly to Claus-Peter Clasen, quoted above, that because Menno saw the church and the kingdom of God as coterminous and called on magistrates to depose false teachers, non-Mennonites would have fared poorly in any Mennonite-controlled region. He even suggests a close analogy to Calvin's Geneva.

34. Harry Huebner, "Christian Pacifism and the Character of God," in *The Church As Theological Community: Essays In Honor of David Schroeder*, ed. Harry Huebner (Winnipeg, Manitoba: CMBC Publications, 1990), 255.

35. Without which any cross-generational nurturing, or more literally, "culturing" of children is impossible.

36. Pilgram Marpeck, *The Writings of Pilgram Marpeck*, trans. and ed. William Klassen and Walter Klaassen (Scottdale, Pa.: Herald Press, 1978), 355.

37. Readers uncomfortable with Paul's apparent use of the satan as a re-

demptive agent of God in the common rendering of 1 Corinthians 5 will want to observe Dizdar Drasko's recovery of the ambiguity of the original Greek, and of Paul's use of rhetorical irony in his "With a Rod or in the Spirit of Love and Gentleness? Paul and the Rhetoric of Expulsion in 1 Corinthians 5" in *Contagion* 11 (Spring 2004): 161-180.

38. Paul Keim, "Reading Ancient Near Eastern Literature from the Perspective of Girard's Scapegoat Theory," 157-177, in *Violence Renounced: René Girard, Biblical Studies, and Peacemaking*, ed. Willard M. Swartley (Telford, Pa.: Pandora Press U.S., 2000), 172-174.

39. Raymund Schwager, *Must There Be Scapegoats? Violence and Redemption in the Bible* (San Francisco: Harper & Row, 1987)

40. My understanding of the historical Jesus has been profoundly shaped by N. T. Wright's reading of his gospel as a critique of zealous nationalism. My thanks to Michael Hardin for making explicit, in a recent conversation, this parallel between Jewish nationalism and the segregation of "the saved."

41. This is in contrast to the negative mimesis whereby proselytes find solidarity with a new sect by joining in its condemnation of the group from which it originally withdrew. The adoption of new taboos and mimetic rivalries with other sects claiming to be more "pure," "holy" or faithful to "the New Testament pattern" is a counterfeit discipleship. This false construal of the "straight and narrow way" is the logical result of the counterfeit evangelism that produces proselytes to a culture instead of converts to a new logos/logic of God and his forgiveness-based community.

42. Thanks to Brian McLaren for proposing this last item in a conversation after I presented an early form of this paper at the conference that generated this book. I hope my awkward new compound word doesn't misrepresent his insight.

43. Thus it is very important that we resist the urge to scapegoat scapegoaters or to shun shunners or to accuse accusers. We must not "found" a community on the claim that unlike our fathers we would never shun the prophets even while nostalgically decorating their graves.

44. Melissa Miller and Phil M. Shenk, *The Path of Most Resistance: Stories of Mennonite Conscientious Objectors Who Did Not Cooperate with the Vietnam War Draft* (Scottdale, Pa.: Herald Press, 1982), 221.

45. The author of 1 John closes his letter with a warning against idolatry. He does not have merely heathen idolatry in mind here. Throughout his preceding arguments it is clear that he is warning against an allegedly Christian theology in which God has a light and a dark side, a theology in which love and lethality are seen as morally compatible. According to this New Testament author, any theology not thoroughly restructured around the earthly Jesus is not about the "true God" and is thus equivalent to idol-making.

THE INDEX

A

Abelard, Peter: 63, 67, 75
agape: 159, 174
Agape Fund: 196-197
America:12, 18, 20, 46, 49-50, 83,
    90, 103-104, 106, 108, 111,
    139-141, 144, 146, 169, 184,
    199, 202-205, 209, 212, 234,
    244, 251, 260-261, 270, 276-
    277
  African-American: 10, 89
  Native American: 24
South America: 116
Amish: 207, 209, 274-275, 280
Anabaptist(s): 11, 70, 92, 187, 189,
    192, 199, 201-202, 213,263-
    264, 269-272-275, 279-280,
    283-284
anarchy: 157, 158, 162, 172-173
Aquinas, Thomas: 37, 66, 102
Arendt, Hannah: 65
Aristotle, Aristotelian: 37, 101-
    102, 104-106, 111, 150
Asad, Talal: 202, 211
Augustine: 31-33, 41, 45, 49, 52,
    121, 145, 152, 164, 239, 264-
    266, 273, 282

B

baptism: 9, 11, 201-215, 248, 258,
    269-270, 274
Barabbas: 257-258
Barth, Karl: 35, 202
Barth, Marcus: 236, 238-239
Bartlett, Anthony: 161
Battle Hymn of the Republic: 139-
    140

Beatitudes: 142-143, 167
Beck, Ulrich: 80
Being: 23, 155, 161-162
Bellah, Robert: 209
Berkhof, Hendrikus: 126
Bibby, Reginald: 205, 209
Blair, Tony: 80
Bonilla-Silva, Eduardo: 106-109
Brethren: 279-280
Bruce, F. F.: 236-237
Brueggemann, Walter: 142, 198
Bush, George W.: 13, 46, 152, 169,
    173

C

Caesar: 132-134, 167, 174, 245, 248
Calvinism: 208
Capitalism: 9, 30-31, 33-35, 42, 49-
    51, 164, 206
Caputo, John: 10, 19, 67, 148, 174
Catholic, Catholicism: 19, 20, 24,
    27, 29-30, 34, 64, 101-102,
    139, 194, 265, 271
Christendom: 28, 30, 32-33, 36, 44,
    70-71, 102, 149, 167, 183-
    184, 187, 192, 202, 264-265,
    269-270, 275-279
Christianity: 14, 28-31, 33, 36-37,
    39-44, 46, 50, 70, 103, 121,
    125, 144, 149-150, 161, 167,
    171, 201, 205, 210-211, 264
church: 10-13, 28, 30-36, 45-51, 55-
    57, 60, 70-73, 84, 93, 95, 101,
    103, 106-107, 109, 130, 145,
    151, 165-173, 183, 191, 194,
    196-204, 207, 209-210, 213-
    215, 223, 226, 230, 239-241,

244, 261, 264, 266, 269-274,
281-283
citizenship: 46, 101, 104
city-state: 105
civilization: 30, 50, 70, 93, 100, 103-
104
    Eastern civilization: 44
    Western civilization: 102, 51-52
community: 11, 18, 73, 93, 102,
    109, 122, 124-125, 130, 132,
    134, 151, 157, 159, 163, 165,
    187, 198, 202, 205-207, 209-
    213, 218-224, 264
    community policing: 82, 86-91,
    94
Constantine: 120-121, 140, 144,
    170-171, 174, 240
Constantinian: 9, 10-11, 13, 28-30,
    46, 71, 93-95, 102-109, 120-
    123, 150-52, 166-167, 172,
    174, 201-207, 211-212, 215
Cortright, David: 81
cross, crucifixion: 10, 43, 46-47, 59-
    60, 128, 134, 140, 49-151,
    155, 158-167, 169-174, 218,
    235, 239-241, 245, 264-268,
    271, 273, 280-281, 283
Crossan, John Dominic: 63, 142
culture: 10-12, 28-30, 33, 36, 42, 46-
    47, 52, 100, 146, 166, 185,
    190, 206, 259, 267, 272-273,
    275-276, 278, 283

D
Day, Dorothy: 19-20
death: 41-42, 46-47, 60-62, 65, 69,
    71, 123, 128, 143, 149, 159-
    161, 207, 223-224, 235-236,
    240, 256, 267, 269, 283
    death penalty: 61, 82, 169, 264
deconstruction: 75, 152, 163, 187
democracy, democracies: 33-35, 39,
    41, 46, 105, 164, 166, 171, 211
Derrida, Jacques: 149, 151-152,
    154, 156, 162, 165, 167, 173,

Descartes, Rene: 43
desire: 9, 36, 41-43, 45-51, 153, 160,
    172
Didbin, Michael: 145
différance: 156-157, 162
discipleship: 10-11, 110, 163, 170,
    202, 205, 207, 209, 283
domination: 13, 21-25, 52, 73, 82,
    94-95, 123, 131, 135, 150,
    158, 160, 166, 170, 173
Driscoll, Mark: 169-170

E
Eden: 56-57, 171, 174
Edwards, Jonathan: 234-235, 241
Einstein, Albert: 138
Emerson, Michael: 107-108
Empire: 9, 10-12, 17, 35, 46, 70, 100,
    121, 129, 134-135, 167, 199,
    244-247, 250-255, 259, 261
    Roman Empire: 30-31, 45, 50,
    70-71, 120, 123, 131, 133,
    141-145, 171, 260-261
Enlightenment: 30, 35, 41
ethics: 11, 32, 34, 38, 101-105, 108,
    122-126, 131, 163, 167-168,
    171, 203-205, 241
Europe, European: 18, 29-30, 49-
    50, 83-84, 104-105, 110, 264,
    277
evangelical(ism): 34, 49, 139, 204,
    211, 272, 275, 281
event: 20, 63, 66, 139, 148, 152-163,
    165-166, 170-174, 212-214,
    260
evil: 10, 19, 23-24, 30, 32, 41, 49-50,
    59, 64, 69, 92-93, 134-135,
    142-144, 156, 162, 167, 171-
    173, 237, 261, 276

F
faith: 12, 40, 43, 46-47, 67, 104, 109,
    139-140, 144, 149, 154, 161-
    165, 205-210, 213, 252, 265,
    271-274, 278, 284

Fodor, James: 202
forgiveness: 59-67, 71, 141, 156,
    160-161, 174, 232, 251, 258,
    265, 268-280
freedom: 9, 23, 34-40, 43-47, 51-52,
    128-129, 134, 140, 155, 208,
    272, 275, 280
Friesen, Duane: 86, 92
Freud, Sigmund: 42

G

genocide: 20, 24, 91
Ghiberti, Lorenzo: 56
Gilroy, Paul: 101, 105, 110
Girard, Renè: 10-11, 87-88, 159,
    161, 164-165, 218-219, 221,
    274, 282
Groarke, Louis: 36-39
God: 10, 12-14, 18, 20-27, 31-37,
    41-52, 55-73, 93, 120-128,
    131-135, 139-146, 148-174,
    186, 189-190, 193, 198-199,
    201-203, 207-208, 211-215,
    223, 226-228, 234-241, 243-
    251, 253-254, 257-284
Goldberg, David Theo: 104
Good News: 18, 52, 59, 67, 69, 122,
    143, 157, 186, 204, 212, 238,
    251-252
Gospel: 10-11, 17, 20, 25, 44-49,
    52, 58, 60. 68, 70, 101, 121-
    124, 129, 131-134, 140, 143,
    146, 148, 150, 155, 157, 167,
    170, 172, 185, 204, 210-211,
    224, 238-239, 243-246, 251-
    261, 264-267, 271, 271-274,
    283
Greco-Roman: 259
Guantanamo: 91

H

Hauerwas, Stanley: 10, 28, 49,
    102-109, 151-152, 154, 157-
    160, 163, 165-166, 168, 171-
    172, 202

Haustafeln: 129-130
Heidegger, Martin: 162
Hendricks, Osayande Obery: 111
hermeneutics: 10, 148-149, 153-
    155
Herod: 245, 247-250
Holocaust: 50
Holy Spirit: 25, 227-228, 246, 248,
    268, 271, 283-284
humanism: 42, 44, 80, 95
Huntington, Samuel: 126-129,
    131-134, 138, 145-146, 161-
    162, 167-168, 172

I

idol, idolatry: 31-32, 40, 45-46,
    211-212, 267, 276, 282, 284
Islam: 29

J

Jesus: 9-10, 13-14, 17-27, 29, 39, 40,
    43-44, 46-47, 49, 51, 56-73,
    121-136, 140-145, 148-151,
    156-161, 163-174, 184-185,
    189, 192, 198, 202-204, 212,
    214, 218-219, 223-227, 229,
    233, 238, 241, 243-261, 264-
    284
Johnson, Paul: 264
judgment: 10, 48, 51, 101, 131, 156,
    225, 236-238, 258, 271, 279
just war: 9, 19, 81-82, 91, 145, 169,
    171
justice: 9, 13, 19, 21-25, 32, 39, 41,
    50, 58-73, 86, 105, 123-124,
    152, 157-162, 170-173, 206,
    210, 252, 257, 259, 265
justification: 103, 124-125, 129-
    130, 145, 205

K

Kallenberg, Brad: 102-103, 106,
    110
Kant, Immanuel: 43
Kenya: 17-18

Kerygma: 150-151, 155-164, 168-169, 172-173,

King, Martin Luther Jr.: 93

Kingdom of God: 14, 18, 20-22, 25, 32-33, 45-47, 55-62, 69-73, 141-143-151, 155-158, 160, 163-168, 172-174, 186, 189-190, 266, 272, 277

Heaven: 59, 142, 248, 250, 252, 278

World: 71, 162, 173

Koontz, Ted: 92-94

Kraybill, Donald: 275

L

language: 24, 56, 85, 101, 108, 110, 125-126, 153-154, 156, 187, 189, 205, 210, 275-276

Leach, Pamela: 92

Lewis, C. S.: 48

liberalism: 9, 23, 30, 33-41, 43-46, 48, 102, 105-106, 111, 151, 206, 211, 273

Lipscomb, David: 146

love: 9-10, 13, 21-22, 31, 58-73, 92-93, 111, 122, 127-128, 130-134, 141, 143-145, 150-161, 164, 168-174, 203, 212, 226-227, 231, 252, 261, 265-267, 272-273, 277-278, 282

Luther, Martin: 121, 250, 162, 239, 277

M

MacIntyre, Alasdair: 101-102, 105-106

Marion, Jean-Luc: 64

Marpeck, Pilgram: 264, 279-283

Marx (ism): 29-31, 33-35, 38, 45, 49-50

McLaren, Brian: 9, 14, 157

Mennonite(s): 10, 92-93, 120, 184, 186-194, 197-199, 214, 261, 263, 273, 275-277, 280, 283

Mennonite Central Committee (MCC): 184, 186

mercy: 24, 59, 61, 63, 68, 125, 128, 131-134, 142, 150, 157, 164, 171, 238-239, 268, 275, 282

metanoia: 65-66, 157, 273-274

Michelangelo: 56

Middle Ages: 32, 50, 83

militarization: 86-87

military: 18, 34, 50, 80-83, 87, 92-93, 120, 139-140, 164, 166, 254, 260-261, 263, 277

modernity: 29-30, 32-33, 36-37, 42-45, 48-49, 51, 101-105, 211

Muslim: 18, 139, 270

N

Nationalism: 23, 104, 282

neighbor: 58-59, 83, 92-94, 125, 130-134, 226, 252, 265, 276

New Testament: 59, 68, 121, 124, 129, 141-143, 149, 155, 211, 223, 235, 238, 260, 265, 269, 284

Nietzsche: 38, 40

nonviolence: 9, 19, 70, 73, 82, 94-95, 102-105, 111, 142-144, 168, 172, 246, 260

O

Old Testament: 50, 59, 61, 68, 169, 282

Ordnung: 275-277

Other, The: 101, 227

P

pacifism: 80-82, 120, 134-135, 171, 174, 279

Palestine: 244-245, 256, 265

Paradise: 56-57, 60, 70

Paul (apostle): 58-60, 67, 69, 121-136, 143, 150-155, 162, 169, 174, 236, 238-239, 264-269, 272, 275, 283

Pax Romana: 136, 180
peace: 9, 13-14, 17-18, 21-22, 25, 30, 32, 41, 46, 48, 51, 55, 60, 62, 68-73, 80-81, 86, 91, 93-94, 107, 134-135, 138, 140-142, 145-146, 160-161, 168, 172, 174, 220, 238-239, 245, 256, 259-261, 278
Peace church(es): 51, 56, 91-94, 111, 121, 135, 149, 151, 184, 189, 192, 201-202, 261, 263-264, 271-273, 277-278, 282-283
peacemaking: 9, 17, 20, 26, 92, 107, 142-145, 240, 246, 261
Pelagius: 41
Percy, Walker: 20
Perkinson, James: 105, 109, 111
Peter (apostle): 56-57, 70, 159-160, 250-251, 255, 269, 274
Pharisees: 21, 25, 224, 267, 280
Philo: 58
pluralism: 38, 101
police: 81-94, 195
polis: 82, 214
politics: 12, 33-35, 38, 80-81, 102-105, 108-109, 122, 128, 136, 151, 157, 159, 163-165-168, 204, 210-211, 220, 245, 250, 260
Politics of Jesus, The: 121, 123, 135
(post)colonial: 9, 101, 103-110, 112
Postmodernity, postmodern: 63, 100, 148, 154, 162, 183
power: 22-23, 38, 40-41, 47, 49, 66, 84, 93, 101, 109, 120, 122, 125, 129-130, 141-142, 150, 155, 159-161, 165-174, 186, 213, 221, 240-241, 248-249, 254-255, 269, 273, 275, 281-282
powerlessness: 155, 166
powers, the: 10, 40, 92, 123, 125-129, 133-134, 136, 159, 237, 275, 277

propitiation: 208, 276
Protestant (ism): 30, 37, 47, 139-140, 167, 211, 271
punishment: 10, 61, 63-66, 69, 71, 237-238, 264, 280
Putnam, Robert: 209
Putt, B. Keith: 8, 10, 14, 19, 65

Q
Quakers: 263

R
race: 17, 34, 58, 84, 101, 109, 172
Rawls, John: 37, 151
Reagan, Ronald: 34, 42
recapitulation: 57
reconciliation: 14, 22, 27, 60-73, 81, 107, 124, 129, 161, 223
Reimer, James: 92
religion: 22-23, 29-30, 33-40, 46-47, 103, 138, 144, 154, 163, 166-167, 205, 207, 209-210, 212, 220, 245, 274
repent, repentance: 14, 18, 21, 26, 47, 60, 65-66, 148, 157-158, 248, 250, 264, 280
retribution: 59-68, 70-73, 123, 162, 171, 219
Rome, Roman: 30-31, 45, 50, 70-71, 82-83, 120, 123, 125, 128, 130-134, 136, 140-145, 160, 170-171, 243-261, 281
Rossing, Barbara: 142
Rwanda: 17-18, 24

S
Sacks, Jonathan: 138
sacrifice: 29, 46, 62, 70, 182, 218-224, 233, 264, 266, 269, 275, 280, 282
salvation: 12, 57-58, 60, 93, 129, 132, 157, 160, 207, 210, 212, 238-240, 247, 269, 271
Satan: 249, 254, 268, 277

scapegoat: 21, 25, 82, 87-89, 94, 164, 174, 218-224, 233, 268, 274, 282-283

Schindler, David C.: 40-41

Schlabach, Gerald: 9, 81-82, 86-87, 92

Scripture(s): 9, 46, 52, 57, 61, 122, 149, 160, 185, 192, 198, 204-205, 224, 244, 249, 261

secular: 28-29, 31-37, 45, 150, 163, 166, 168, 171, 205, 271

shame, shaming: 23, 162, 263, 266, 275, 282-283

Sheldon, Charles:169

shun, shunning: 11, 82, 263-264, 268, 271, 274-278, 282-283

Smith, Christian:107-108, 140, 205, 207

spirit: 24-25, 60, 63- 64, 67-69, 73, 92, 122, 126, 129, 134, 158, 160, 163-164, 210, 213-215, 223, 231, 235, 244, 248, 268, 281, 283-284

sovereignty: 81, 104, 127, 132, 155-156, 160-164, 168, 170, 172-174

Stanley, Charles: 169-170

Stout, Jeffrey: 102, 106

T

Tansey, Mark: 56

Taylor, Charles: 202, 206

temptation: 166, 211, 213, 249, 254-255, 261, 269, 277, 284

theology: 35, 37, 45, 49, 51, 92-93, 102, 108, 121-124, 129-130, 134, 149-155, 161-166, 170-173, 186-187, 192, 197-198, 201-204, 207-208, 212, 214, 245, 260, 264-265, 269, 277-283

theology of the cross: 150, 163

theopoetics: 148, 150, 152, 161-162, 171, 173

Tilly, Charles: 83-84

tradition: 12, 14, 24, 29, 36, 49, 81, 93, 101-102, 105, 109, 123-126, 131, 146, 149-151, 155, 157, 165, 184, 202-205, 209, 214, 221, 235, 263, 266, 270-283

traditionalism: 102-104, 106, 270-271

transformation: 22, 63, 67, 69, 121-123, 127, 129, 153, 184, 232-233

Tutu, Desmond: 67

U

undecidability:148, 154-156

United States: 12-13, 34, 84, 103, 139-141, 146, 183, 204-205, 234, 261

V

vengeance: 63, 68, 133-134, 141, 144, 165, 169-170, 268

victim(s): 11, 21-22, 24-25. 64-65, 69, 82, 150, 158-161, 164, 218-222, 227, 256, 265-266, 270, 276, 282-283

violence: 9, 13-14, 17-19, 23-25, 30, 34, 47, 62, 65, 69-73, 81-95, 103-110, 120, 128, 131, 134-135, 139-141, 143, 151, 156, 158, 160-174, 207, 219-221, 232, 235, 238-239, 244, 249-250, 255-256, 259, 261, 264-268, 278-279, 284

Volf, Miroslav: 59, 237, 275-276

voluntarism: 202, 211-212

W

war, warfare: 9, 12-13, 19-20, 37, 43, 47-50, 55-56, 80-82, 86, 91-92, 94, 100, 139-142, 145-146, 166-169, 171, 219, 240, 243-245, 259-263, 271, 278

West, Western: 28-30, 33-36, 48-49,

51-52, 68, 80, 82, 101-102,
167, 183, 235, 238, 264, 275
Willimon, William: 28
Wink, Walter: 19, 70, 276
World: 10, 12-14, 18, 25-35, 40-41,
44-50, 55-59, 67-73, 80, 91-
94, 106-109, 121-122, 127-
131, 134, 138, 141-145, 150-
151, 156-174, 184, 192, 198-
204, 213, 231, 235, 239, 245,
249, 253-256, 261, 264-265,
268-277, 283
wrath: 10, 71, 234, 236-241, 264,
280
of God: 10, 61, 144, 234, 236,
241, 265-266, 278, 280
children of: 10, 235-236-239

Y

Yoder, John Howard: 9-10, 82, 93,
102, 106, 108, 120-132, 135,
152, 154, 157, 159, 163, 166-
168, 171-174, 201-202, 276

Z

Zealot(s): 21, 129, 131, 243, 257,
267, 281
Zehr, Howard: 61
Zizek, Slavoj: 111, 150-151

THE CONTRIBUTORS

Andy Alexis-Baker is a Ph.D. student at Marquette University in Systematic Theology and Theological Ethics. He has published articles on Mennonites and policing in *Conrad Grebel Review* and a chapter, "Unbinding Yoder from Just Policing," in *Power and Practices: Engaging the Work of John Howard Yoder* (Herald Press, 2009). He is the co-editor, with Ted Koontz, of John Howard Yoder's *Christian Attitudes to War, Peace, and Revolution* (Brazos Press, 2009). Andy has also previously taught in Goshen College's peace and justice department.

Jim S. Amstutz, D.Min., is Pastor of Akron Mennonite Church, Akron, Pennsylvania (2001-present) and previously served as Senior Pastor, West Swamp Mennonite Church, Quakertown, Pennsylvania. He was Campus Pastor at Bluffton University (1986-1991) and served with Mennonite Central Committee (US Peace Section 1980-84; Akron Voluntary Service Unit 1991-1994). He currently serves as Chair of Homes of Hope-Ephrata (providing transitional housing for homeless persons), and is the Missional Church Development Coordinator for the Atlantic Coast Conference (MC USA). Jim is a graduate of Bluffton University (B.A.), Associated Mennonite Biblical Seminary (M.Div.), and Fuller Theological Seminary (DMin). He is the author of *Threatened with Resurrection: Self-Preservation and Christ's Way of Peace* (Herald Press, 2002) and editor of *Diary of a Kidnapped Colombian Governor: A Journey Toward Nonviolent Transformation* (forthcoming from Cascadia). Jim is married to Lorraine Stutzman Amstutz and together they parent three young adult children.

Sharon L. Baker is assistant Professor of Theology and Religion at Messiah College in Grantham, Pennsylvania. She works mainly in the areas of atonement theory, peace and justice issues, and comparative theology, and inter-faith issues. She authored the book *Razing Hell* (Westminster John Knox), along with a number of other essays published in academic journals and edited books.

Craig Carter is Professor of Religious Studies and Chair of the Division of Religious Studies and Christian Ministries at Tyndale University College in Toronto, Ontario, Canada, where he teaches courses in Systematic Theology and Christianity and Culture. He also serves as Theologian-in-Residence at Westney Heights Baptist Church, where he preaches regularly and teaches adult Sunday school courses. He did his Ph.D. on John Howard Yoder at the Toronto School of Theology under Dr. John Webster and has authored two books: *The Politics of the cross: The Theology and Social Ethics of John Howard Yoder* and *Rethinking Christ and Culture: A Post-Christendom Perspective* (both published by Brazos Press). He is currently writing a book on classical trinitarianism and human personhood for InterVarsity Press and is researching the thought of John Paul II on marriage. He lives in Toronto with his wife, Bonnie, and has three children and two grandchildren. Craig enjoys family gatherings, camping and canoeing, and reading mystery novels,

Reta Halteman Finger teaches New Testament in the Department of Biblical and Religious Studies at Messiah College, Grantham, Pennsylvania.

Ted Grimsrud, Professor of Theology and Ethics at Eastern Mennonite University in Harrisonburg, Virginia, is the author of several books, including *Theology As If Jesus Matters: An Introduction To Christianity's Main Convictions* (Cascadia, 2009) and *Embodying The Way Of Jesus: Anabaptist Convictions for the Twenty-First Century* (Wipf & Stock, 2007).

David B. Miller is Associate Professor of Missional Leadership Development at the Associated Mennonite Biblical Seminary in Elkhart, Indiana. He has taught at Hesston (Kan.) College and served as pastor of congregations in Pennsylvania and Indiana. In each of these settings he has been active in interfaith dialogue, supporting conscientious objectors, and deepening the church's commitment to following Christ in the way of peace.

Michael Hardin is the Executive Director of Preaching Peace. He graduated from North Park Seminary, Chicago. Michael is the author of *The Jesus Driven Life and* co-editor of *Stricken by God? Nonviolent Identification and the Victory of Christ* (Eerdmans 2007) and *Compassionate Eschatology* (Wipf & Stock, 2010). He is a long-time member of the Colloquium on Violence and Religion and has published numerous articles on the mimetic theory, Christian theology, and spirituality in *The Scottish Journal of Theology, St. Vladimir's Theological Quarterly, Brethren Life and Thought, The Covenant Quarterly, The Journal for Ministry in Addiction and Recovery* as well as *Violence Renounced* (Pan-

dora Press U.S., 2000) and *Essays in Friendship and Truth* (Univ. of
Michigan Press 2009). Michael is a singer/songwriter and with his
wife Lorri takes wilderness awareness and survival courses at The
Tracker School

Richard T. Hughes is Distinguished Professor of Religion and
Senior Fellow in the Ernest L. Boyer Center at Messiah College,
where he provides leadership for projects that focus on racial and in-
ternational reconciliation in various educational contexts. His seven-
teen books include *Illusions of Innocence: Protestant Primitivism in
America, 1630-1875* (Univ. of Chicago Press, 1988); *Myths America
Lives By* (Univ. of Illinois Press, 2003); *How Christian Faith Can Sustain
The Life of the Mind* (Eerdmans, 2001); *Proclaim Peace: Christian Pacifism
from Unexpected Quarters* (with Theron Schlabach, Univ. of Illinois
Press, 1999); and most recently, *Christian America and the Kingdom of
God* (Univ. of Illinois Press, 2009).

Brian D. McLaren is an author, speaker, pastor, and networker
among innovative Christian leaders, thinkers, and activists. Born in
1956, he graduated from University of Maryland with degrees in
English (B.A., summa cum laude, 1978; M.A., 1981). In 2004, he was
awarded a Doctor of Divinity Degree (honoris causa) from Carey
Theological Seminary in Vancouver, British Columbia, Canada. From
1978 to 1986, McLaren taught college English, and in 1982 he helped
form Cedar Ridge Community Church (www.crcc.org), where he
served as a pastor until 2006. His books include *The Church on the
Other Side: Doing Ministry in the Postmodern Matrix,* (Zondervan, 1998,
rev. ed. 2000), *Finding Faith* (Zondervan, 1999), *A New Kind of Christian*
(Jossey-Bass, 2001), *More Ready Than You Realize* (Zondervan, 2002),
The Story We Find Ourselves In (Jossey-Bass, 2003), *A Generous Orthodoxy* (Zondervan), *The Last Word and the Word After That* (Jossey-Bass),
The Secret Message of Jesus (Thomas Nelson, April 2006), *Everything
Must Change* (Thomas Nelson, 2007), *Finding Our Way Again* (Thomas
Nelson, 2008). Brian is married to Grace, and they have four young
adult children. For more information see www.brianmclaren.net

B. Keith Putt (Ph.D. Rice University) is Professor of Philosophy
at Samford University in Birmingham, Alabama. His research concentrates primarily on John Caputo's radical hermeneutics, Conti-
nental philosophy of religion, and postmodern philosophies of language. Among his recent publications are *Gazing Through a Prism
Darkly: Reflections on Merold Westphal's Hermeneutical Epistemology,*
ed. (Fordham University Press, 2009); "Reconciling Pure Forgiveness
and Reconciliation: Bringing John Caputo Into the kingdom of God,"
CrossCurrents 59 (Winter 2009); "Poetically Negotiating the Love of

God: An Examination of John D. Caputo's Recent Postsecular Theology," *Christian Scholars Review* 37 (Summer 2008); and "A Love That B(l)inds: Reflections on an Agapic Agnosticism," in *Transforming Philosophy and Religion: Love's Wisdom,* ed. Bruce Ellis Benson and Norman Wirzba (Indiana University Press, 2008).

Jean Risley is an ordained Presbyterian pastor (PCUSA) and currently a candidate for Doctor of Ministry at Andover Newton Theological School. She came to ministry after a professional career in artificial intelligence and technical management. These ideas and her book *A Place Where Everybody Matters: Life and Ministry in the Small Church* (2010) grew out of her five years as the pastor of Scotchtown Presbyterian Church in Middletown, New York. Her interests include the role of conflict in the church, the challenge of living faithfully in contemporary culture, the relationship between religion and science, and the implications of the Jewish backgrounds of Jesus and Paul. Her website at www.JeanRisley.com provides a forum for discussing these issues.

Jonathan Sauder is an independent scholar in Neo-Anabaptist thought and peace theology. He taught for eight years at Faith Mennonite High School, in Kinzers, Pennsylvania. He and his wife, Brenda, live near Lancaster, raising three children and operating a tree service. He was raised in a fundamentalist and sectarian branch of the Anabaptist tradition but is now attending Community Mennonite Church of Lancaster.

Anthony G. Siegrist is Assistant Professor of Bible and Theology at Prairie College in Three Hills, Alberta, Canada. He holds an M.A. from Eastern Mennonite Seminary and is a Th.D. candidate in systematic theology at Wycliffe College, Toronto School of Theology. Anthony has written and done editorial work at both the scholarly and popular level. He is currently writing his dissertation on believers baptism.

Derek Alan Woodard-Lehman is a doctoral fellow at Princeton Seminary. His work focuses on bringing the politics of nonviolence into conversation with the analyses of power provided by liberation theology, critical theory, cultural studies, and feminist-womanist theology. His work appears in journals such as *The Bible and Critical Theory, Studies in Christian Ethics, Cultural Encounters, The International Journal of Zizek Studies*, and *Journal of Religious Ethics.*

Breinigsville, PA USA
10 May 2010
237607BV00007B/5/P